D0049199

Stravinsky Inside Out

Stravinsky
Inside

Out

Charles M. Joseph

Yale University Press   New Haven and London

Title page photograph: Igor Stravinsky in 1934 (Photograph by
George Hoyningen-Huene; courtesy of the Harvard Theatre Collection)

Designed by James J. Johnson and set in Fairfield Medium type
by The Composing Room of Michigan, Inc.
Printed in the United States of America by R. R. Donnelly & Sons.

Library of Congress Cataloging-in-Publication Data

Joseph, Charles M.
Stravinsky inside out / Charles M. Joseph
p.   cm.
Includes bibliographical references and index.
ISBN 0-300-07537-5 (alk. paper)

1. Stravinsky, Igor, 1882–1971.   2. Composers—Biography.   I. Title.
ML410.S932 J68   2001
780'.92—dc21   2001000913

A catalog record for this book is available from the British Library.

The paper in this book meets the guidelines for permanence and durability of the
Committee on Production Guidelines for Book Longevity of the Council on
Library Resources.

10   9   8   7   6   5   4   3   2   1

For Lucy

Contents

Preface

Every age produces individuals destined to shape the cultural history of their times. Igor Stravinsky (1882–1971) was such a person. The mere mention of his name, like the name Beethoven, immediately triggers a flood of images—some accurate, others not. His presence defined many of the fundamental concerns, ideas, and attitudes not only of twentieth-century composers but of twentieth-century art. He captured the imagination of the age in a way that only Picasso and a few other contemporaries were able to do. The proliferation of superlatives that music history attaches to Stravinsky, however, consists of truths and fictions mingled so freely that distinguishing between the two presents a formidable challenge. Was he the century's greatest composer? Should he be considered a genius, an intellectual, an ideologue, an iconoclast, or just a hardworking artisan? How did he become such a powerful figure—an enigmatic icon, for some—capable of commanding the artistic world's attention over a large span of the century? In trying to answer these questions, we must first separate the public and the private man, for at times Stravinsky appears to have been two very different people.

Mythmaking is a calculated art, rooted in our need to create images and heroes. The forces that contributed to the mythologizing of Stravinsky are complex. How much did the composer, and those around him, consciously create the kind of protective blanket that often cloaks the real person? More broadly, what might this say about the changing cultural role of artists in our time? Was it the strength of Stravinsky's unquestioned musical achievements alone that elevated him to the status of an icon; or did the promotion of his image help to lift him to such a plateau? As art historian Alessandra Comini writes in *The Changing Image of Beethoven*: "Why Beethoven . . . became the paradigm of Germanic musical genius for nineteenth-century Europe has as much to do, and perhaps even more so, with posterity's perception of his life and character as it does with an appreciation of his musical achievements, towering as they were." Like Beethoven, and Picasso too, Stravinsky did little to resist the perception of his reputation as a courageous artist ready to defy precedent in the face of criticism.

The composer's life was shaped by an unusually swift succession of epoch-making events in a century characterized by constant dynamic change. His personal life was also marked by one upheaval after another, demanding the need for adaptability if he was to survive. Eventually the many pathways in his career led to the United States, where his Americanization dramatically influenced his actions and decisions, both personally and musically. To ignore the politics of the age, to disregard the century's many technological explosions, to underestimate the social context in which he participated as a very public figure, only crystallizes the many half-truths that swirl around his image. Stravinsky did not work in isolation, churning out one masterpiece after another, insulated from the rapidly evolving world in which he lived. To operate on such a naive assumption is to insult the inquisitive, rational, impassioned, pragmatic, and very human person that he was.

I have come to think about these issues only recently, for this is not the book I originally set out to write. Years ago I prepared a monograph on the composer's piano music, but without the benefit of his then unavailable sketches and drafts. Following Stravinsky's death, I awaited the settlement of his estate, hoping to study the manuscript sources. During the interim, and as a happy consequence of moving to Saratoga Springs—a city with a rich dance tradition—a new interest emerged. With a growing affection for dance sparked by my daughter Jennifer's love of ballet, I began exploring the Stravinsky and Balanchine partnership (about which I shall have more to say in a forthcoming book). When the Stravinsky archives in Basel, Switzerland, were opened to scholars in the 1980s, I began traveling regularly to the Paul Sacher Stiftung, where quite unexpectedly I stumbled across aspects of Stravinsky's life about which I either knew nothing or had entirely misperceived, particularly given what presumably reliable studies of the composer had related.

During several residencies in Basel, I sorted through thousands of unpublished documents. I read hundreds of unpublished letters, viewed hours of unreleased film clips, perused Stravinsky's library, and examined his informative annotations and marginalia. Each archival file brought new questions about the composer's interactions with others, his habits, his agenda, and often his privately expressed thoughts, some of which have been judiciously suppressed from the public record. Was this the same Stravinsky whose music I first encountered as a teenager, the same colossus of the twentieth century whose eminence is affirmed in virtually every music history text? Not only did I begin to sense that the composer's private life was at odds with his public image, but I quickly came to understand that the cultural context into which history so blithely drops him is too narrow, too pat, and consequently often skewed.

It was Stravinsky's music, of course, that first attracted me—dazzling pieces like *The Firebird* and the other early Russian ballets so familiar to musicians and nonmusicians alike. It was the energy of his rhythms, his punctuating silences, the kaleidoscopic colors of his orchestration, and the overall boldness of his musical language that enthralled me. It still enthralls me, both emotionally and intellectually. I confess this now, for in the pages that follow I do not address Stravinsky's music in any substantive manner. This is not a book intended primarily for musicians, whose grasp of musical syntax naturally shapes discussions of the composer's works in instructive but, necessarily, exclusionary ways. There are no musical examples, no compositional analyses to decode. Nor do I pretend to offer a musicological overview of the composer. Rather, I wish to revisit selected aspects of the composer's historicized image—a bequeathed image that continues to reverberate with almost scriptural authority. Mark Twain once quipped, "It's not what we don't know that hurts us; rather, what gets us into trouble is what we are absolutely certain of that just ain't so." Much that is written about Stravinsky distorts as much as it clarifies.

Proceeding in loose chronological order, the chapters that follow provide different viewpoints about selected passages in the composer's long, diverse, and astonishingly productive career. The first essay takes up some of those Twainian certainties in presenting a broad overview of the many purported truths and fictions characterizing our current image of the composer. The next two chapters offer perspectives on the evolution of, respectively, a specific work and a specific familial relationship. The first explores the context of one of Stravinsky's initial compositional ventures in America during the 1920s—and one of his most important ballets. In the second, I offer a personal remembrance about the composer's relationship with Soulima Stravinsky, his son and my former teacher. This complex father-son bond was especially close during the 1930s, just before the elder Stravinsky came to America. I make no pretense of objectivity in this essay, and my feelings about Soulima are, admittedly, complicated. Chapters 4, 5, and 6 trace the composer's encounters with the image-obsessed media of cinema and television during the 1940s, '50s, and '60s—encounters too often dismissed by musicians as peripheral. The final two chapters address Stravinsky's associations with and unfiltered views of others (writers, conductors, academics, performers, and so on), especially his close relationship with Robert Craft—a critical one that extended through the early 1970s and which Craft has continued to write about ever since.

At times my views are personal, and some might even consider them incendiary. Yet in addition to Stravinsky's many humane qualities, his perspicacious manner, his acerbic wit, his bottomless thirst for learning, he was quite capable of vindictiveness, duplicity, and contemptible behavior, even in his treatment of friends. Should such personal traits be discounted? Oscar Wilde's contention that only the artist's art really matters, while everything else should remain concealed, might seem reasonable at first blush, but it also invites a convenient preemption, denying reality and evading the legitimate pursuit of historical inquiry. Certainly creative lives are almost always marked by seductively diverting side roads frequently leading nowhere. The Stravinskyan landscape, too, is dotted with intriguing detours all along the way. But how does one know where a road leads until it is taken? In his *Life of Alexander*, Plutarch insisted that one distinguishes a person's character not so much from "the great sieges or the most important battles" but from the most unlikely "action of small note." The idea of placing art in the context of a life has become a volatile issue among scholars. Positivists consider it irrelevant, pitting "coldly formalist" analyses against the "warm and fuzzy" meanderings of the so-called new musicology (to invoke some of the sloganizing that inflames a divisive, tiresome, and ultimately brittle distinction). Shouldn't we at least consider the possibility that the causal relationships driving the composer's actions were often entangled, sometimes at deeply embedded levels? And only after considering those relationships, as Roger Shattuck has observed, can Stravinsky's music "ascend to the ineffable."

In our post-Watergate world, the words of the Wagnerian zealot Hans Pfitzner resonate: "Beethoven should have burned his sketchbooks. Now hordes of incompetent musicologists are snooping among these intimate notes that are none of their damn business." Like Beethoven, Stravinsky retained most of his compositional sketches; but like Samuel Johnson, the composer often reviewed and then destroyed many of his personal letters and files with the intent of concealing what posterity might construe as evidence. For the humanist, fortunately, Stravinsky didn't destroy nearly enough. Moreover, a reconsideration of his life comes at a propitious time in the life of inquiry: attributable to everything from feminist criticism to a comprehensive challenging of the canon, recent years have seen a rethinking of many preconceptions, as in profiles of Josephine Baker, Napoléon Bonaparte, Edgar Degas, Charles Ives, Thomas Jefferson, Clare Boothe Luce, Douglas MacArthur, Sylvia Plath, Eleanor Roosevelt, and many others. The explicitness of such accounts has created discomfort over intimacies revealed and indiscretions unmasked. If some of these issues initially seem tangential, it may be that we've come to accept a "don't ask, don't tell" approach as a glib way of holding the truth at bay.

Inquiry can be disquieting, sometimes divulging truths we don't really want to know. Why then submit Stravinsky to what some may consider mere grave trampling? Of course it is not so tidy as that; nor should clear-cut linear connections between creator and creation be understood as the real litmus test of the value of historical inquiry—inquiry that not only allows but obligates humanists to interpret the facts. That said, the goal here certainly isn't to indict the composer (or others) on the grounds of any sanctimoniously declared mores. Stravinsky's personal papers, it is true, do occasionally disclose inexpiable opinions, but these documents should not be indiscriminately construed as a smoking gun. History simply deserves to judge for itself how a demythologized portrait of the composer may sharpen our understanding of his life as an important cultural figure.

"The moment you cheat for the sake of beauty, you know you are an artist," wrote the poet Max Jacob in his 1922 Art poétique. Stravinsky was the most wonderful cheater there ever was—much to music's and history's betterment. He knew exactly when and how to exceed existing musical conventions and boundaries in a cogent and convincing way. Yet I wonder how many within the humanistic community, let alone beyond, recognize how the seeds of Stravinsky's marvelous aptitude for "cheating" are reflected within the constitution of the man himself. Moreover, the composer would surely have endorsed Joseph Esherick's claim that in music, as in architecture, "Beauty is a consequential thing, a product of solving problems correctly." To assume that Stravinsky solved these problems in a vacuum, immune to the forces that surrounded him—forces to which he was always keenly attuned—leads us away from rather than toward a deeper understanding of the man and his music.

Image is inextricably linked to packaging. The historiography that envelops our image of Stravinsky has at times become the product of a revisionism aimed at marketing him. For all the efforts to project the image of a stoic, rational, unemotional composer whose music expressed nothing beyond its own internal logic, Stravinsky was a man of enormous passion. Consequently, he enjoyed and endured the joys and sufferings that passion leaves in its wake. As the journalist Janet Flanner observed, he was not only inventive but also contradictory, prickly, insatiably curious, constantly agitated, and "always at the boiling point of gaiety or despair." In a 1937 interview with *Musical America,* Stravinsky recalled a physician telling him that humans completely regenerate themselves every fifteen years: "Every fibre, every nerve, every muscle is entirely new; in fact each most *minuscule* cell is not itself, but another. How then am I the same man I was fifteen years ago?" the composer asked. It was one of many public pleas beckoning others to permit him and his music to regenerate also. How much our own view of Stravinsky is allowed to change, and how different history's view evolves now that nearly twenty years have elapsed since his papers were released, are questions that we are only beginning to answer. The following pages are offered to invite some reconsiderations, and even some doubts—doubts that entreat us to keep such questions alive, and to recognize just how wondrously complex and human this creative master really was.

Acknowledgments

The research for and publication of this study would not have been possible without the help of numerous scholars, institutions, grant agencies, and close friends. First and foremost, I owe a special debt of gratitude to the Paul Sacher Stiftung in Basel, Switzerland, one of the most marvelous, efficiently run research institutes in which I have had the privilege of working. A grant from the Sacher Foundation allowed me to spend the entire 1991–92 academic year studying the Stravinsky collection of primary source materials. The many archivists (even then still busily unpacking, sorting, and cataloging the enormous treasury of materials from the Stravinsky estate) interrupted their own important work to provide constant assistance in retrieving materials and answering my endless questions. A word of thanks to Hans Jans, André Baltensperger, and Ulrich Mosch, who successively supervised the Stravinsky collection during my studies in Basel over several years. Herr Mosch's patience and willingness to help me in every way is especially appreciated. Thanks also to Ingrid Westen, whose encyclopedic knowledge of the Stravinsky archives saved countless hours by steering me in the right direction on so many occasions. In the many citations of the Basel archives I have made in this study, Frau Westen's help in identifying source materials should be assumed.

Without the continuing support of my own academic institution, Skidmore College, the completion of this project would have been unlikely. Dean of the Faculty Phyllis Roth was steadfastly helpful in allowing me to move forward. The two Department of Music chairs who witnessed the growth of this project, Thomas Denny and Gordon Thompson, as well as the college's Faculty Development Committee, consistently invested their trust in my work.

Likewise, I wish to thank the William R. Kenan Jr. Charitable Trust for its endowment of a chair at Skidmore, providing me with needed time to complete the actual writing. Travel grants from the National Endowment for the Humanities underwrote several trips to Switzerland to examine the Stravinsky source materials, the cornerstone of my research. Thanks to the Howard D. Rothschild Fellowship in Dance, awarded by the Houghton Library of Harvard University, I was able to complete research in the Harvard University Archives, and especially in the Harvard Theatre Collection, where Fredric Woodbridge Wilson and Annette Fern were of enormous help.

In addition to the Sacher repository, I also found valuable unpublished sources in the music division of the Library of Congress and in the School of Music Library and the Beinecke Rare Book and Manuscript Library of Yale University. In New Haven, both Kendall Crilly and Suzanne M. Eggleston were very helpful in preparing materials before my arrival, thus saving me considerable time. My appreciation to Dorothy J. Farnan for permitting me to reprint a previously unpublished letter to Stravinsky from Chester Kallman (copyright by the Estate of Chester Kallman).

Others from beyond Saratoga Springs were enormously generous in various ways: allowing permission to quote, responding to constant inquiries, clarifying issues, proofreading sections of early drafts. These include Jeff Ankrom, Cyrilla Barr, Malcolm Brown, Gina Dries of Schott Musik International, Joan Evans, Allen Forte, Paul Griffiths, Carolyn Kalett of Boosey & Hawkes, the late Charles Kuralt, Kevin LaVine, Brigitta Lieberson, Edward Mendelson, David Oppenheim, Tony Palmer, the late Jerome Robbins, Wayne Shirley, Richard Taruskin, Stephen Walsh, and from Moscow, Victor Varuntz, who kindly translated several of Stravinsky's early Russian letters. I owe a word of thanks to Professor Claudio Spies of Princeton University, who was good enough to read the initial draft of this study. His corrections and suggestions impelled me to rethink certain issues in constructing what I hope is now a more balanced portrait. Many of my most cherished friends were consistently supportive in guiding and encouraging my work: Maureen Carr, Mina Miller, Douglas Moore, and especially Richard Parks.

Numerous colleagues at Skidmore beyond my own academic discipline provided inestimable help as well, especially given the interdisciplinary nature of this study. These include Isabel Brown, Hunt Conard, Terry Diggory, Jane Graves, Jay Rogoff, Deborah Rohr, Jan Vinci, Eric Weller, and Joanna Zangrando. A very special word of thanks to my dearest colleague and friend, Isabelle Williams, who was kind enough to read the entire manuscript and offer valuable and substantive last-minute suggestions. Her exacting attention added immeasurably to bringing my task to fruition. Some of my students enrolled in a Stravinsky seminar brought refreshingly new ideas to my thinking. They are too numerous to include here, although I would like to mention specifically Carey Forman for both his technical expertise and careful proofreading of some initial drafts.

One could not find a more supportive, efficient, and knowledgeable editor than Harry Haskell. His perceptive suggestions, gentle nudging, guidance in matters of both text and iconography, and his considerably broad understanding of the humanities provided direction at every point. He also displayed boundless tolerance in enduring a barrage of questions at each step of the book's development. As the book's manuscript editor, Phillip King brought a much appreciated clarity to the final text. Yale University Press has been a wonderful partner throughout the publication process.

How does one thank one's immediate family for being immersed—whether they liked it or not—in Stravinskyana for a period extending over too many years to remember? My daughters, Amy and Jennifer, grew up humming the composer's music, while enduring repeatedly the same Stravinskyan anecdotes their father inflicted upon them. My wife, Lucy, not only read the text and offered suggestions but also helped in researching the Plaut and Lieberson collections at Yale. Just as important, she suffered my daily emotional swings, ranging from irascibility at one end of the spectrum to irascibility at the other. In between, I fear, the variation was negligible.

Books are seldom written in complete isolation. The company that witnessed the evolution of this one is very much appreciated. It was a long journey but a good one, accompanied by many friends and colleagues to whom a simple but sincere acknowledgment seems quite insufficient. To one and all, "Thank you, my dear," as Stravinsky himself would have said.

A Note on Sources

I have chosen not to include a formal bibliography for two reasons. First, the Stravinsky materials to which I refer throughout the text are fully documented in the endnotes listed for each chapter. Readers unfamiliar with the vast Stravinsky literature, but still interested in pursuing these references further, will be able to do so from the information I provide there. In those instances where certain sources are particularly useful, I have elaborated this in the note itself. Second, the majority of sources upon which I depend are unpublished documents from Basel and elsewhere and do not lend themselves to any useful bibliographic citation. Until the Sacher Stiftung is able to publish a comprehensive catalog of its holdings, providing specific dates of letters, the contents of the composer's library, and so on, tracing these unreleased sources is nearly impossible unless one visits the Stiftung itself. Even the citing of microfilm numbers would not be particularly useful since the Sacher Stiftung, understandably, cannot duplicate any materials for circulation. The Stiftung does provide a listing of the composer's manuscripts and sketch materials, as well as an annual booklet, *Mitteilungen der Paul Sacher Stiftung,* in which new acquisitions and summaries of current Stravinsky research are published.

It is virtually impossible to discuss Stravinsky's life without relying on the writings of the composer's longtime associate, Robert Craft. Some of the so-called conversation books by Stravinsky and Craft were published in two editions: one in Great Britain and one in the United States. Citations herein refer to the easily obtainable U.S. paperback publications by the University of California Press, as indicated in the notes themselves. Other important sources were released after the composer's death by Vera Stravinsky and

Robert Craft. A particularly valuable one is Craft's diary, first released in 1972 but significantly updated and expanded in 1994, titled *Stravinsky: Chronicle of a Friendship* (the more recent edition is used here). Two additional secondary sources have been especially useful: Vera Stravinsky and Robert Craft's *Stravinsky in Pictures and Documents,* and *Stravinsky: Selected Correspondence,* in three volumes, edited by Craft.

Craft responded to several questions that I posed during the early 1990s while researching unpublished primary sources in the Basel archives, and over the next few years he generously shared his thoughts about these illuminating documents. In the end, however, he took exception to my discussion of several issues and withdrew his support for the book. Because it is still unclear who controls the rights to certain unpublished materials in the Stravinsky estate, I have regretfully had to restrict myself to summarizing some letters and typescripts rather than quoting from them as originally planned.

A word on the use of compositional titles: there are many variants, and little standardization. Sometimes the polyglot composer titled his works variously in Russian, French, Italian, and English—often freely interchanging them. He also abbreviated the titles when speaking or writing about his compositions. Thus, the Concerto for Piano and Winds was often referred to simply as the Piano Concerto, and I have followed this practice. And in discussing the ballets, for example, I use the more familiar English title, *The Firebird,* for *L'Oiseau de feu,* while for *The Rite of Spring* the French title, *Le Sacre du printemps,* is employed. There is no set standard in these matters, and I have aimed only for internal consistency regarding each piece.

Stravinsky Inside Out

C·h·a·p·t·e·r ·1·

Truths and Illusions:
Rethinking What We Know

> Of all living composers, none has provoked so many studies, commentaries and discussions as Igor Stravinsky. . . . The eminent place occupied in contemporary art by the composer might partly explain this flowering of criticism. But he is not the only one up on the heights, and yet, nearly always, Stravinsky is the center of our discussions of music. Despite all previous explanations, we realize as time goes on that the problem continues to present itself under new aspects. There is, therefore, a Stravinsky "enigma."
> —Boris de Schloezer, *Modern Music,* 1932

It is little wonder that more has been written about Igor Stravinsky than any other composer of the twentieth century. His "psychic geography," as Leonard Bernstein once described it, was an enormously complex landscape. He relished confounding society's paradigm of what a classical composer ought to be. He wanted, perhaps even needed, to be seen as the "other." And like so many cultural icons, it was his nonconformity that best captured the essence of his widely recognized, and some would even say peculiar, image. One often didn't know where the composer stood on an issue, or when and for what reasons he was apt to change his mind—sometimes quite suddenly and apparently without cause. Anticipating Stravinsky's next move was always a futile chase. He was an agglomeration of inconsistencies, an enigma, as Schloezer observed—or so it initially seems. Ultimately, it was all part of a carefully cultivated image. This is not to suggest that the composer's actions were disingenuous or contrived: promoting any kind of anomaly seemed perfectly natural to Stravinsky. He simply wore his eccentricity as a badge for all to see. It helped to define his center.

It is not only—perhaps not even primarily—the remarkable achievement of his music that elevates Stravinsky to a level of recognition few classical composers attain; rather, it is the bundle of perceptions that has grown up around him. At times this imago has swelled to almost mythical proportions, making him easily one of the most identifiable figures in all of music history. Perhaps that is what Aaron Copland meant when he remarked, "It is just because the secret cannot be extracted that the fascination of Stravinsky's *personality* continues to hold us." Or as Nadia Boulanger, who knew the composer well, observed: "Stravinsky's personality is so peremptory that when he picks up something, you don't see the object so much as the hand holding it."

How Stravinsky projected his "hand" is not such a mystery. He worked at it constantly. He was more than willing to indulge in self-promotion. He eagerly seized whatever new technological marvel was available (perforated rolls for the pianola, commercially released recordings, films, television, air travel enabling transcontinental junkets from concert to concert), and he possessed a rare facility for toggling smoothly between the worlds of high and pop culture in a way that no composer before him could. His name is found not only in every standard music history text but often as the correct "question" on television's *Jeopardy*. His face is on stamps issued by the post office, and he even turns up in Clint Eastwood's movie *Bird* (1988), a biography of jazz legend Charlie Parker (wherein Parker asks to study with Stravinsky, as did others, including George Gershwin and Cole Porter).

Cultural Literacy, E. D. Hirsch's controversial inventory of the five thousand concepts, dates, names, and expressions that "every American needs to know," is a highly restrictive document: one had to be quite distinguished to join the fraternity of Hirsch's scroll. Copland didn't make the list, nor did other important twentieth-century composers, including Béla Bartók, Claude Debussy, Dimitri Shostakovich, and Charles Ives; certainly not Arnold Schoenberg, despite his vastly important compositional achievements. Stravinsky's longtime collaborator George Balanchine is missing, as are Martha Graham, Agnes de Mille, Josephine Baker, and Isadora Duncan. And where are such legendary American jazz musicians as Parker, Duke Ellington, Billie Holiday, and Art Tatum? Yet Stravinsky *is* there, sandwiched between the Strategic Arms Limitation Treaty and "Take Me Out to the Ball Game." Even more bizarre, *Time* conducted a poll in 1999 to choose the one hundred most influential people of the twentieth century. In the category of Artists and Entertainers ("twenty pioneers of human expression who enlightened and enlivened us"), Stravinsky joins a list that includes Picasso, Le Corbusier, T. S. Eliot, and Charlie Chaplin as well as Frank Sinatra, Bob Dylan, Oprah Winfrey, and Bart Simpson.

Would such barometers, slick as they are, have impressed Stravinsky?

Without question. The composer made it his business to collect and peruse various encyclopedias and "Who's Who" registers. Herbert Spencer Robinson's *Dictionary of Biography* (1966), for example, was carefully combed by the composer. Stravinsky listed on the inside back cover the names of people that in his estimation should have been included—Boulez, Stockhausen, Eugene Berman, Paul Horgan, Gerald Heard, while disputing the inclusion of others ("Schütz!?" he exclaims). Perhaps even more telling, he would always check to be sure he was included. If not, he would sulk in the margin, "Why am I not mentioned?"

Stravinsky wanted to be sure that others recognized him. His memory was elephantine when it came to remembering people who offered what he interpreted as invective, even those he publicly praised but privately berated. In the front of his copy of Minna Lederman's 1947 *Stravinsky in the Theatre* (given to him by the author "in remembrance of a most pleasurable undertaking"), Stravinsky pasted a review of the book by Virgil Thomson in the *New York Herald-Tribune* of 29 February 1948. The "symposium is frankly a plug for the great White Russian," wrote Thomson, "rather than a discussion of his works in disinterested terms. The opposition is nowhere represented." And even though Thomson's analysis was quite right—the book is strictly a collection of highly flattering essays—Stravinsky didn't want any opposition. It was *he* who always declared himself on the opposite side of issues, relishing his antipodal role. Thomson's commentary annoyed the composer, not because it was inaccurate, but probably because it hit a little too close to the truth.

People generally prefer their artists walled off from the world, reclusively engaged in a tortuous struggle with their souls while praying for some type of divine intervention. The stereotype is comfortable, for it conveniently relegates creative minds to a mysterious place where we needn't go, let alone compete. Such parochialism implies that artistic endeavors are immune to a host of cultural influences that constantly shape the human condition. But artists too, maybe even especially, are the carriers of cultural history—and none more so than Stravinsky, who relied so deeply on indigenous models to guide him and his music throughout his life. The romantic archetype of the monastic composer working in seclusion was as foreign to Stravinsky as one could imagine. Stravinsky had to survive by his own wits. After all, if he was to make a living without having to resort to teaching like most composers, he would have to be visible—or, more crassly put, marketable—beyond the small circle of classical music enthusiasts.

Charles Dickens's admonition that "People should not be shocked by artists wanting to make money" was a favorite Stravinskyan line. While Dickens made a living through his writing, his fame enabled him to prosper all the more through lucrative speaking engagements in America. But Stravinsky's willingness to step beyond what the public wanted to believe was the cloistered life of any truly serious classical composer easily outdistanced that of Dickens. There was a distinctly Barnum-like side to the composer, a mercantile réclame that walked hand in hand with his creative spirit. Certainly Stravinsky was not the first classical composer to market his own works, but the extent to which he did smacks of a populism more often associated with a completely different musical world. Stravinsky's materialistic consciousness is difficult to separate from his compositional achievements, so pervasive and aggressive were his attempts to keep his music before the public by carefully sculpting his own image. Of the voluminous archival documents surviving, an astonishingly large proportion deals exclusively with business matters, especially self-promotion. Much of it reflects mere squabbling, hucksterism, and pure gamesmanship. Nonetheless, it bespeaks who he was, even if musicians prefer to dismiss this aspect of his nature and focus only on his compositions. Stravinsky needed to be public, to be accepted, even to be popular. And he was.

More than any other composer of art music in this century, Stravinsky was able to make the leap from a rarefied intellectual world to the status of pop hero, an icon, in much the same way Albert Einstein did. The composer was widely respected by a public that understood his music about as much as they understood Einstein's special theory of relativity. Howard Gardner, in *Creating Minds,* suggests that Einstein's broad notoriety arose not so much from what he did but how he presented what he did. "Even when quite old," Gardner writes, Einstein "never lost the carefree manner of the child, who would not permit society's conventions or the elders' frowns to dictate his behavior." And like the ill-tempered child who will do whatever is necessary to be heard, Stravinsky simply had to win every fight, probably accounting in part for his need to carp over the smallest matters. Like Einstein, there was an impish side to Stravinsky, even into his eighties. His friend the writer Stephen Spender described a meeting in 1962 as the octogenarian composer prepared to leave for Africa. "He was excited," recalled Spender, "and showed me Alan Moorhead's books, especially a photo of a rhino. 'I want to see that animal,' he said. 'It's like this . . .' suddenly he was on all fours, his stick with hook turned up like a horn, his eyes glazed—a rhinoceros."[1]

Stravinsky was remarkably childlike in other ways as well: at one moment carefree and innocent, at another overwhelmed by the tragedy of existence.

Igor Stravinsky, early 1960s
(The Fred and Rose Plaut Archives, courtesy of the Yale University Music Library)

He worried about how he fit into the grand scheme of things. In fact, it was this Cartesian need to understand his place in the grandly designed hierarchy that explains many of the composer's actions, especially his need to be famous and, more to the point, to be admired. In his introduction to Leo Tolstoy's *Anna Karenina,* Malcolm Cowley speaks of the author's insecurity, beginning with the loss of his mother when he was two and shaping his life thereafter: "This need for love—and also for admiration—gave him a lover's clairvoyance, and he was never indifferent to people: everyone was charged for him with positive or negative electricity. I think this continual watchfulness helps to explain his fictional talent. . . . It gave a feeling of centrality to his work, a sense of its existing close to the seats of power."[2] Certainly there was no indifference in Stravinsky's life, no middle ground. He felt strongly about everything. He resisted those who disagreed with him, and he continually sought reassurance of his own position. Like his contemporary Sigmund Freud, Stravinsky embraced his fame vengefully, as a highly visible means of winning some measure of retribution against those who had failed to recognize his abilities, especially during his formative years.

The composer commented on every biography and magazine article written about him, sometimes ranting over the most trifling errors. An article by Winthrop Sargeant, for example, in a March 1953 issue of *Life* was marked extensively ("alas, it proved a very poor article with many mistakes in it," Stravinsky wrote on the envelope in which it was sent to him), even though it was essentially a harmless piece. The most superficial articles, including one in the May 1947 issue of *Junior Bazaar,* did not go unnoticed, as the many mistakes Stravinsky circled in his copy disclose. Throughout his library, the margins of journals and books spill over with his bristling: "This is entirely wrong," "All lies," "What an idiot," "I never said that," "Who cares," "How can this person be so dense?"

Those who risked writing biographies of Stravinsky suffered his special wrath, as he would studiously read and comment on most every issue an author might raise. The marginalia in his copy of Frank Onnen's 1948 monograph, retained in the Sacher Stiftung, is typical of the composer's running commentary: "Why to write such useless books? Yes, useless and full of mistakes and wrong information." He meticulously corrected spellings, transliterations, and dates in red and blue pencil. When Onnen mentioned Stravinsky's "Serenade in A Major," the composer answered, "Never!—just in A." Any instance of sentimentalizing a work meets with protest as well. Of the *Ebony Concerto,* written for Woody Herman in 1945, Onnen said, "It is a deeply moving piece over which lies the sadness and the melancholy of the blues, the old laments of a race that was from generation to generation oppressed and downtrodden." In response, the composer underlined the passage in red and added one of his favorite markings, "!?!"

Yet nowhere is Stravinsky's outcry huffier than in a firestorm of criticism aimed at Eric Walter White, for many years considered the composer's most reliable and comprehensive biographer. When a friend of Stravinsky's praised White in 1947 as an "ardent admirer" and his work as generally complimentary, the composer retorted:

> I am in possession of Eric Walter White's book. Sorry not to share your reaction to your description of this musicography [*sic*] as "a most ardent Stravinskyite." Not his previous book, *Stravinsky's Sacrifice to Apollo,* nor his present work on me do advocate his understanding of my entire creative output. I won-

der reading his two books on me, why write at all when exhibit such consistent restraint and an absolute absence of genuine enthusiasm, nothing to say of his utter lack of discrimination of facts. . . . Side by side with correct information he uses excerpts from writings of rather biased and dubious sources, such as Mme. B. Nijinska's legends and S. Lifar's impudent revelations of late Diaghilev's jealousies. A "most ardent" admirer would undoubtedly find other means to express his appreciation—Beware![3]

The "present work" to which the composer referred was *Stravinsky: A Critical Survey,* a monograph that especially irked him. He retained a copy of the book (now held by the Sacher Stiftung), fuming in the margins over virtually every point White raised. The biographer criticized the *Duo Concertant* (for piano and violin), remarking, "Indeed the quality of much of the music is below par." Stravinsky responded by writing, as he so often did, a question mark in the margin. When White described the "Jig" as "boring," the composer wrote "?Why?" And when White claimed that "in all these works [Stravinsky's violin and piano pieces, Samuel] Dushkin collaborated with Stravinsky in writing the violin part," Stravinsky circled the statement and added in the margin, "absolutely wrong"—though as the sketches in the Stiftung clearly reveal, Dushkin played a far greater role in assisting him than history has claimed, or Stravinsky was ever willing to admit.[4]

Sensitive to Stravinsky's notoriously short fuse, especially when it came to anyone audacious enough to claim to understand him, White made every effort to present a fair and accurate biographical account. Often he asked the composer for suggestions, sending him prepublication typescripts and inviting him to offer revisions, especially in the process of writing his important and still often used (though obviously dated) 1966 biography. White patiently endured Stravinsky's sententious harangues in return.[5] The composer's exchanges with White are characteristic of his inclination to vent his frustrations, though often his condemnations were deflected to others and not shared with White directly. In an article in the summer 1948 issue of *Tempo,* "Stravinsky as a Writer," White concluded that the composer disliked Beethoven, citing as evidence a statement by C.-F. Ramuz, author of the text for *L'Histoire du soldat (The Soldier's Tale),* that "Stravinsky was violently anti-Beethoven during the First World War." Stravinsky sent his reaction to Robert Craft—a harbinger of his trust in the young man he had met only a few months earlier (although they had corresponded since 1944). The missive lists a string of refutations pointing to both White's faulty views about Ramuz as well as his misinterpretations of Stravinsky's position on Beethoven.

Nor did it matter whether his unsuspecting foil was a reputable biographer or an unknown college student. In a letter of 16 November 1953, a young woman from Emory University, speaking for several students studying the opera *The Rake's Progress,* confessed that she was "mystified over the reception your work received with so many of the New York critics," and asked for the composer's reaction to the "hostile attitudes" of such detractors. The student certainly didn't need to ask twice (probably didn't need to ask once), and the composer immediately answered:

> I never understand what exactly are the critics complaining about when criticizing my music. Is there not in my music craft or art enough (for only these things should be the object of serious criticism), or do the critics merely not recognize them for lack of competence? The critics, if sincere, are usually disappointed at not finding in my music what they are looking for. Some time they deplore it, more frequently they attack me and almost always they become resentful. But where is the guarantee that their judgment, or opinion, is a professional one. And, after all, are they so important in the history of musical creation. P.S.—A quotation from Verdi's letters: "fortunate is the artist whom the press hates."

Stravinsky's ubiquity earned him the label "the world's greatest living composer," and it was an appellation he did nothing to dispel.[6] Not only Picasso but also American cartoonists caricatured him, finding him recognizable enough among the general public to ring a bell whenever "long-haired" contemporary composers were being lampooned. Stravinsky relished the notoriety, as the newspaper cartoons saved in his archives demonstrate. He was a media star, and he played the role splendidly in radio and magazine interviews, before television cameras, and wherever a crowd would gather. He needed the spotlight.

Broadway offered such glittering exposure as to be irresistible. When Billy Rose invited the composer to contribute some ballet music to a show, Stravinsky accepted, even though some thought his decision ill advised. His private papers disclose that he turned down several commissions, including one for a cello concerto (although the composer never especially liked the instrument anyway), so he could do Rose's show at the Ziegfeld Theater. The chance to mix, even indirectly, with the likes of Bert Lahr, Teddy Wilson, and Benny Goodman—"show business"—was appealing. It gave him an instantaneous American celebrity status.

Sometimes he threatened to steal the spotlight—or at least baited others into thinking that he might. A 1918 letter from Ramuz to René Auberjonois

Picasso's caricature for the cover to the sheet music of the composer's 1919 *Ragtime*

confirms that Stravinsky seriously entertained the idea of participating himself in the premiere of the original stage production of *L'Histoire du soldat*, as one of the actors. "Stravinsky told me last night his intention to dance the last scene," wrote an excited Ramuz. "This would be perfect; encourage him." This dance was the closing one, the rhythmically intricate "Marche triomphale du diable," and Ramuz cajoled Stravinsky to do it, although ultimately the composer declined. Often through his words and actions he would teasingly throw out such tantalizing prospects, though as he neared commitment to his overly zealous suggestions he rethought the potential consequences. Whether it was dancing the part of the devil, agreeing to interviews, implying he would accept a compositional commission or consider writing an article or a book, a discrete behavioral pattern emerges. Those who were involved in such exchanges seemed destined to ride a wave of anticipation and frustration. Seldom did Stravinsky flatly promise to do something and then renege, but there is a sense that he rather enjoyed seeing others scurry for his attention. Such conduct, consciously or otherwise, provided a no-lose situation for the composer. He remained in total control.

As Stravinsky's archives reveal, he freely mingled his own blend of insecurity, rage, obsession, anguish, depression, cynicism. Yet his resilience and irrepressible joy for living, especially as it bursts forth in the athletic vitality of his music, could weather any emotional storm. Still, he felt that cultural history frequently swindled its artists (including him, of course) in discounting their creative efforts as mere baubles. Consequently, he felt victimized, not held in the same esteem as history's more acclaimed scientists and thinkers. In this regard, one senses an empathy with Gustave Flaubert, whose biography and voluminous letters Stravinsky knew well. His copy of Flaubert's writings was presented to him by Francis Steegmuller—a translator of Flaubert and a writer for whom Stravinsky had unusual respect—and is copiously marked.[7] Flaubert's ill health, his constant warring with critics, his realist penchant for objectivity, his repulsion of the conventional (the *idées reçues*), his precision in finding the mot juste—all surely resonated with the composer. Tchaikovsky also annotated and underlined sentences in his edition of Flaubert's correspondence, writing that the novelist was both a hero and a martyr—surely descriptions with which Stravinsky identified.

Dozens of passages marked in Stravinsky's copy might just as easily have been written by the composer himself: "You know that beautiful things cannot stand description," "Criticism occupies the lowest place in the literary hierarchy: as regards form, almost always: and as regards moral value, incontestably," "I maintain (and in my opinion this should be a rule of conduct for an artist) that one's existence should be in two parts: one should live like a bourgeois, and think like a demigod." And what could better capture Stravinsky's own Apollonian view of musical expression than Flaubert's pronouncement to his mistress, Louise Colet: "I refuse to consider Art a drain." "Some day much of contemporary literature will be regarded as puerile and a little silly, because of its sentimentality. Sentiment, sentiment everywhere! Such gushing and weeping! Never before have people been so softhearted. We must put blood into our language, not lymph, and when I say blood I mean heart's blood; it must pulsate, throb, excite." Even Flaubert's exchanges with his editor, sniping over some suggested revisions in *Madame Bovary*, are strikingly similar to Stravinsky's constant bickering with his own publishers and agents. In a passage underlined in Stravinsky's copy, Flaubert wrote: "I will do *nothing*. I will not make a correction, not a cut; I will not suppress a comma; nothing, nothing! But if you consider that I am embarrassing you, if you are afraid, the simple thing to do is to stop publication of *Madame Bovary*. This would not disturb me in the slightest." Such all-or-nothing threats, as will become evident, were standard for Stravinsky.

Flaubert's indignation is mirrored in Stravinsky's petulance and defiance. While the composer claimed "it was wrong to have considered me a revolutionary," he enjoyed the iconoclastic role into which history, rightly or wrongly, thrust him. He saw himself as one of history's significant "shakers," a free-spirited renegade who jostled the cultural world to which he contributed for over half a century. History often likens him to the insurgent Beethoven, pausing at the gateway of nineteenth-century Romanticism, then rebelliously striding through its front door waving his inalienable artistic rights. From 1913 onward, Stravinsky was similarly typecast. He was forever the bellicose little Russian who wielded his own brand of swashbuckling panache, cutting his own swath—a swath that some insist ushered in the rapidly changing tide of twentieth-century modernism. For many, his landmark ballet, *Le Sacre du printemps (The Rite of Spring)*, served as modernism's flagship—its "birth certificate," as Pierre Boulez dubbed it. Even on the eve of the millennium, readers polled in the *BBC Music Magazine*'s December 1999 issue overwhelmingly named the earth-shattering ballet the most well-known, popular, influential composition of the twentieth century. T. S. Eliot first heard the score in 1922 and compared its importance to that of Joyce's *Ulysses*, which Eliot was then reading (and a copy of which Stravinsky owned). Like Joyce's novel, according to Eliot, *Le Sacre* was emblematic of both complexity and simplicity in contemporary life. It was a simple work, Eliot observed, yet frightening in its primordial artistic vision. Eliot was hardly the only "man of letters" who recognized the importance of Stravinsky's sweeping achievements. The English poet and critic Sir Herbert Read observed that, although it might seem odd to some of his colleagues, it was neither a poet nor a painter who stood as the most representative artist of the century, "but a musician—Igor Stravinsky."

Spender once asserted that the fundamental aim of modernism was the confrontation of the past with the present. It is as accurate a description of Stravinsky's music as any. The past, full of memories and fictions, was very much an integral part of Stravinsky's being. As Roger Sessions once claimed, "the past which Stravinsky often consciously evokes is not either a real past . . . but a very much frozen image of a past which itself never existed except as a kind of elegant fiction. The artificiality is entirely conscious." Still, in some ways Stravinsky cannot rightly be touted as modernism's most notable proponent. "For the committed modernist, the audience doesn't exist," writes Suzi Gablik in *Has Modernism Failed?* And as for the century's other great in-novator, Arnold Schoenberg, modernism was inextricably bound up with (to use his own expression) "the morality of art" in a world gone amoral. But for Stravinsky, the audience *did* matter, though he would consistently deny it; and sometimes, it seems, the morality of art was invoked only when it served his purpose. No matter: it is not Beethoven's or Schoenberg's or Stravinsky's helmsmanship of any artistic movement or ideology that is important; rather, it is their individualism that transcends whatever pigeonhole into which his-tory wishes to squeeze them.[8]

Successes and hierarchies were decidedly important to Stravinsky. While certainly *his* accolades were always deserved, the success of others accorded equal praise often appeared inexplicable. He would have concurred with Jean Cocteau's sardonicism: "I believe in luck. How else can you explain the suc-cess of those you don't like." Even when Stravinsky expressed regard for his collaborators, a recognition of his personal assistance was always demanded. He clipped and saved a 1927 article appearing shortly after the premiere of his and Cocteau's *Oedipus Rex*. The review began, "*Oedipus Rex* opera-orato-rio by Cocteau set to music by Stravinsky." The composer was offended, un-derlining the sentence, circling Cocteau's name, and writing a question mark next to it, implying that Cocteau had been accorded far too much credit. Even as his health failed in the late 1960s, Stravinsky still patrolled newspapers and journals for perceived injustices. His last major composition, *Requiem Can-ticles,* was choreographed by George Balanchine as a memorial to Martin Luther King, Jr. The composer saved the review from the *New York Times* of 3 May 1968, underlining the description, "Balanchine's *Requiem Canticles* to the Stravinsky score of the same name," insinuating that Balanchine, like Cocteau, didn't deserve so much press.[9] As his cryptic grumbling in hundreds of such articles and reviews retained in his papers attests, Stravinsky kept care-ful score of such matters.

The freewheeling composer's cognizance of his position, and the license and leverage to which he felt it entitled him, remained virtually uncurbed. His ego could be quite robust, and touched with a pungent sense of humor. A 1963 letter from the editor in chief of *Musical America* informed Stravinsky that "our annual poll of critics voted almost unanimously for Igor Stravinsky as 'Musician of the Year.' Would you send me an autographed photo. It will hang in my office for all New York critics to contemplate." Stravinsky underlined the word *almost* in red, and then the word *contemplate,* adding at this point, "except those who didn't vote for me of course."

A few years earlier, in 1961, when he was invited to join the editorial board of a prestigious new music periodical, the composer hesitated. It was duly explained to him that the editorial board would include some of the most distinguished composers and theorists of the day—Elliott Carter, Aaron Copland, Lukas Foss, Walter Piston, Roger Sessions, and others. Stravinsky responded that he would conditionally "consent" to serve, but only if certain already approved appointees would now be immediately dismissed. "I know you well enough to know that you will understand me," he confided to the editor. To which the editor replied, "I know that your wishes will serve the best interests of the journal," and accordingly the board was, to use the eager editor's euphemism, quickly "reconfigured."

So sure of himself was he that Stravinsky assumed his clout extended beyond the arts. And why not, he thought, since he knew that others with similar reputations were parlaying their names and positions to whatever advantage might be gained. As more unpublished letters reveal, in 1947 Stravinsky wished to have his son-in-law enter the United States from postwar France. Anticipating difficulty with immigration authorities, the composer contacted Edward R. Murrow through the Columbia Broadcasting System (with which Stravinsky was then associated through a recording contract), hoping the eminent broadcaster would intercede. Such requests had to be handled tactfully so as not to offend the easily insulted composer. The supervisor of music at CBS responded that Murrow felt the situation would need to be handled discreetly, since any pressure by CBS might cause the officials to review the case with "unusually careful scrutiny." But "Mr. Murrow suggests," this letter of 30 January 1947 continued, if the composer's son-in-law "encounters difficulties at Ellis Island that he let me know immediately. Mr. Murrow will then take all possible steps to facilitate his entry through the influence of this organization."

At times, Stravinsky would have others intercede for him seeking favors, or at least investigating possibilities best kept quiet. The composer's friend Goddard Lieberson, with whom he worked on so many audio recordings for Columbia Masterworks, was sometimes enlisted to explore what the future might hold. Stravinsky was living in Los Angeles in the 1950s, for example, and according to all that we have been told was happily ensconced with no thought of moving yet again (he had lived in Russia, Switzerland, and France

before moving to the West Coast in 1940). By 1957 he was, for many musicians, an American hero, and works like his highly successful ballet *Agon*, created with Balanchine and first staged by his New York City Ballet on 1 December of that year, took the dance world by storm. The composer proudly
claimed America as his home, and his triumphs in both Los Angeles and New
York bespoke the continental expanse of his fame.

Yet an unpublished letter discloses that he may not have been all that content with his adopted homeland. Only ten days before *Agon*'s stunning first
performance, Lieberson wrote to shipping magnate Aristotle Onassis in
Monte Carlo "on behalf of my friend, a very distinguished man, Igor Stravinsky." He informed Onassis, in confidence, that the composer now probably
wanted to return to Europe and settle there. Monte Carlo was at the top of his
list, given the composer's "pleasant days in the Diaghilev period." He suggested to Onassis that Stravinsky would of course be "an artistic asset of some
value" in the reconstruction of the Monte Carlo Ballet—a project to which
Onassis was then devoted. Moreover, Lieberson was obviously empowered to
negotiate some type of business swap, adding that if Onassis would furnish a
home for the composer in Monaco, Stravinsky, in return, might consider providing the music for "a commissioned ballet or something of the sort."[10]

That Stravinsky was in a position to even contemplate bartering with global
industrialists such as Onassis indicates what an outsize image he had by mid-
century. History usually traces his first real international visibility to 1913 and
the cataclysmic *Sacre*, a genuine sea change whose widening ripples em-
anated from Paris, throughout Europe, to America, eventually leaving much
of the art world shaken. So extraordinary was its impact that nearly three
decades after its premiere even Walt Disney capitalized on its commercial potential by including portions of it in his cinematically innovative *Fantasia* of
1941 (as discussed in Chapter 4). Excerpts from *Le Sacre* continue to be used
in film scores whenever the darker side of human nature needs to be punctu-
ated by "barbarian and primitive music—Zulu music," as the critics first con-
demned the score. The murderous, blood-drenched scene in the atrocious
1995 B-movie thriller *Jade* serves as one recent example. With an abundance
of aspiring young film composers around, the choice of Stravinsky's still sav-
agely evocative ninety-year-old score attests to the music's longevity.

Stravinsky's fame carried with it all the demonstrable trappings of social
success, even if at times such success was accompanied by the ludicrous
tabloid excesses of what we now quickly dismiss as the ravings of paparazzi.
While he was on tour in America in 1937, a Cleveland newspaper carried the

Stravinsky appeared frequently on the covers of American magazines,
as on this one from July 1948

banner headline "Igor Stravinsky—Small Body but a Giant Brain," with the
equally witless subtitle "Composer Abhors Communism, Likes Poker, Wine."
His portrait appeared on the covers of *Time* in 1948 and *Newsweek* in 1962.
His name was as likely to pop up in the pages of the *Saturday Review, Vanity
Fair, Life,* and the *Atlantic* as it was in professional music journals. Sometimes the information included was correct, other times not. In a 1935 issue
of *Time,* for example, *Le Sacre* is feared as "a threat against the foundations
of our total institutions [standing for] all the unnameable horrors of revolu-
tions, murder and rapine." Both the infamous ballet and its composer had
become significant emblems in American society.

More recently the 1913 masterwork has become no less than an inter-
galactic "emissary of Earth," as it is called in Carl Sagan's *Murmurs of Earth.*
Stravinsky's Columbia Symphony Orchestra recording of the "Sacrificial
Dance" from *Le Sacre du printemps* is aboard the *Voyager* spacecraft, launched
in 1977 and intended to explore the outer solar system in search of extrater-
restrial civilization. As the starship's only twentieth-century example of
"earthly" Western art music, the ballet was meant to represent "a raid by a keen

The Stravinskys at the White House, as reported in an Italian newspaper,
January 1962

intellect upon a zone of imagination that developed when our ancestors lived
in societies resembling those we now elect to call primitive."[11]

His notoriety extended everywhere, including to the White House, where
the Stravinskys dined in "Camelot" with JFK and Jackie. The composer originally declined the invitation, saying he was "touched and honored" but just
too busy with concert engagements. After Arthur Schlesinger, Jr., Kennedy's
special assistant, exerted a little pressure, Stravinsky was gently nudged until
he changed his mind.

Moreover, if there is any lingering doubt about the composer's celebrity,
his archives reveal that being invited to 1600 Pennsylvania Avenue was hardly
the only engagement on his calendar. A 1963 telegram confirmed the octogenarian's arrival among America's beautiful people: "I would like the pleasure
of your company at a party in honor of Jerry Lewis and Mort Sahl, in my home
friday night/saturday morning, July 12/13, 1963 beginning at 1:00 a.m. until
(?). Signed, Hugh Hefner." From the 1913 scandal of *Le Sacre du printemps*
in the Théâtre des Champs-Elysées of Paris to a 1963 bash at the Playboy man-
sion—now there's a fifty-year odyssey few ships have sailed. Stravinsky seriously considered joining other crossovers to the pop world, initially consent-
ing to be interviewed for Hefner's magazine. Acting as a go-between, the editor
for *High Fidelity* cautioned Stravinsky about being seen alongside *Playboy*'s
centerfold nudes. But in a letter dated 22 October 1964, Stravinsky remarked,

"I like very much the idea of *Playboy* photographs as accompanying scenery to an interview," although he did not have time at the moment, "but a postponement is not a refusal."

Being interviewed by *Playboy* surely appealed to the composer because other celebrities had done likewise, and the magazine's circulation of three million was further evidence of his ability to straddle the pop and serious cultural worlds. Moreover, the risqué humor of the magazine would not have gone unappreciated by a man whose archives include several instances of crude comments, as well as his own hand-drawn, unflattering caricatures of women. *Playboy* submitted eighteen proposed questions addressing the composer's "need" to make others enjoy his music, but the questions were so ludicrous that Stravinsky ultimately declined the interview.

The composer's image was further defined by his friendships—or more correctly, his casual acquaintances—with a galaxy of movie stars and film directors, especially during the 1940s. Privately, he muttered about the empty-headed Hollywood "scene" and the "intolerably boring" parties he attended regularly. Yet attend them he did. A quick glance at Vera Stravinsky's diary from the period reveals that hardly a day passed without a luncheon, dinner, or some social evening spent with such celebrities as Elizabeth Arden, Charles Boyer, Maurice Chevalier, Joseph Cotten, Ronald Colman, Bing Crosby, Bette Davis, Melvyn Douglas, Joan Fontaine, Greta Garbo, Greer Garson, Benny Goodman, Alfred Hitchcock, John Houseman, Harpo Marx, Mary Pickford, Vincent Price, Basil Rathbone, Ginger Rogers, Frank Sinatra, Gene Tierney, Orson Welles—and the list goes on. He would join them for a movie, at a celebrity golf tournament benefit, for an evening at home, and countless soirées. Some became close friends, such as Edward G. Robinson, who stood for Stravinsky when the composer completed his citizenship papers. While such a star-studded list might at first seem peripheral, the ostentation of such a world certainly helped push Stravinsky toward the film industry around the same time. Even in the early 1960s, long after his cinematic flirtations had ended, he still enjoyed the company of entertainers, including Jerry Lewis, who often attended recording sessions, and Danny Kaye, who would sometimes accompany Stravinsky to rehearsals, carrying his scores.

His carefully tweaked public persona provided access not only to Disney but to David O. Selznick, not only to Kennedy but to Nikita S. Khrushchev as well. Even two years after Stravinsky's unprecedented return to Russia in 1962 during the Soviet Union's prethaw days, a letter from Anatoly Dobrynin thanked him for sending a congratulatory note to Khrushchev on his seventi-

Stravinsky with Edward G. Robinson, one of several celebrity friends,
in Hollywood, 1935

eth birthday. The composer could be as political or apolitical as the occasion
warranted, as evidenced in his files by, for example, correspondence with officials of the Third Reich and with Mussolini—whom, it must be said, he knew
and admired.[12]

The entry of the United States into the war frightened him terribly, and he
feared he would again be forced to find sanctuary in another country. During
the early 1940s he became an American "patriot," to use his own term. From
his California home he tracked the movement of American troops on a map;
he made quite an issue of participating in mandatory gasoline rationing; he
even rearranged (illegally) "The Star-Spangled Banner" as a symbolic contribution to the war effort. How far had Stravinsky, the "cultural Bolshevik," as
he was called in 1933, come in separating himself from his past? When a 1948
article in the *San Francisco Examiner* reprinted communist charges that
Shostakovich was writing "rotten bourgeois music," Stravinsky felt compelled
to respond the very next day and to disassociate himself from the Soviet
regime. "I am not a Russian composer, anyhow. I am happy to be an American

citizen. It is like Germany with Hitler, for thinking they have rules with no exceptions. I am pleased to be free to create things which are always an exception." The response, intended to be supportive of a fellow composer, fell far short of defending Shostakovich; rather, it simply called attention to himself, and somewhat self-righteously at that. "I am Stravinsky and that is enough," he once responded to a reporter when asked to compare himself with his contemporaries. In Stravinsky's appraisal, there were no comparisons worth making.

He also retained a file marked "Olin Downes/Shostakovich 1949." The documents within retrace the pressure brought to bear by some members of the American press for Stravinsky to welcome Shostakovich, who traveled to America to attend the Cultural and Scientific Conference for World Peace in New York. Yet because the conference sponsors were charged with acting as a "Communist front" by the House Un-American Activities Committee, Stravinsky wished to remain uninvolved. Shostakovich made several anti-Stravinsky and anticapitalist statements, some of them before a very public audience in Madison Square Garden. Stravinsky also kept a note from the leader of the Communist Party USA stating that "American communists

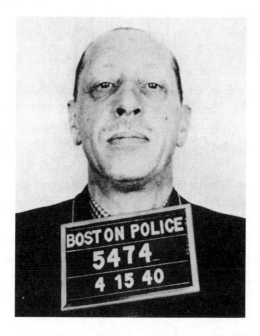

Arrested in Boston, April 1940, for illegally arranging "The Star-Spangled Banner"

would support Russia in the event of a war." He underlined the statement and wrote in the margin, "the U.S. needs more *Patriots* like Stravinsky." Clearly a public confrontation was brewing and Stravinsky wanted nothing to do with it. To curb the potentially volatile situation quickly, the composer instructed his attorney on 31 March to respond to United Press International: "It is Stravinsky's conclusion that public controversy is not his field; and that he should refrain from the unnecessary continuation of such controversies." Such an advancing-to-the-rear strategy was indicative of his first priority—to protect his own image.[13]

And protect it he did in every conceivable way. Many radio interviews, presented so as to appear that the composer's comments were tossed off the top of his head, were in fact carefully scripted. Drafts were submitted to the composer and corrections made with an eye toward casting him in the most favorable light. Certainly such cosmetic changes in language seemed reasonable: Stravinsky was a perfectionist who insisted on controlling as much as he could. Yet the ruse of spontaneity is another matter, showing how far he was willing to go in creating the image he wanted. Nor is this to suggest that Stravinsky wasn't very fast on his feet. To the contrary, he could extemporize with extraordinary alacrity, and often did so, especially when an opportunity worth seizing materialized unexpectedly.

In a 1945 interview in Montreal over Radio-Canada, the composer was asked about his *Circus Polka* for elephants, written a few years earlier: "I was commissioned to write this polka by the Barnum and Bailey Circus. George Balanchine got the idea of a mixed ballet for ballerinas and elephants." An accurate description, but when the interviewer inquired, "Did you not follow there the tradition of the great French painters such as Toulouse-Lautrec in his *scene de cirque*," Stravinsky responded, "Precisely . . . it is a musical equivalent of a painting by Toulouse-Lautrec, a satire on a familiar subject. Just as Toulouse-Lautrec depicted a Montmartre scene in terms of visual objects, so this *Circus Polka* suggests a typical circus scene in terms of sound." A commendable answer, but as his unpublished notes reveal, doubtlessly fabricated. There is absolutely nothing to suggest that Stravinsky had such a model in mind, and in all probability, as the archives also reveal, it was Balanchine who may have had a hand in suggesting the model Stravinsky adopted, including the famous Schubertian paraphrase that ends the piece.

The *Circus Polka* was a "gig," an easy commission to be tossed off effortlessly (though as with everything he undertook, the composer completed the project with careful thought, as the Basel sketches reveal). Stravinsky's clever

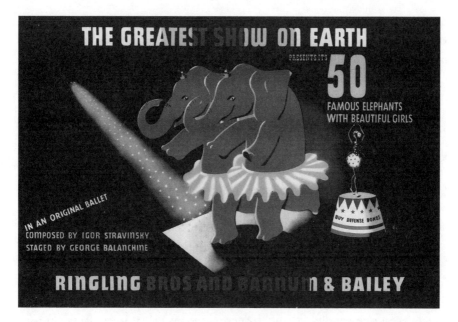

Circus Polka advertisement, by the New York illustrator and painter E. McKnight
Kauffer, best known for his poster designs for American war relief agencies during
the 1940s (Courtesy of the Harvard Theatre Collection)

on-the-spot rationalizing on Radio-Canada was typical posturing, intended to
lend a sheen of credibility to the many populist and what some considered
shallow works written in the early '40s, including a tango, the refurbishing of
the national anthem, Rose's Broadway show, and the frivolous big band swing
style of the *Scherzo à la russe*. These were frothy works that seemed out of
character for the composer the public knew and wanted—and Stravinsky was
harshly rebuked for them by critics who sensed that he was floundering.

The composer strongly felt he could further enhance his image by pro-
jecting himself as a wise and broadly humanistic philosopher of the arts. When
Nijinsky's daughter Kyra proclaims in Tony Palmer's important documentary
film of 1982, *Aspects of Stravinsky* (discussed in Chapter 6), that unlike her
instinctively driven father, Stravinsky was a great intellectual, she reinforces
another common fiction—a mirage the composer skillfully devised. The confusion arises from Stravinsky's genuine and intense interest in most everything, his need to examine things in a way many artists ordinarily do not. Once
again, the composer does so in a childlike and marvelously wide-eyed way. An-

dré Gide's observation that "the wonderful thing in Goethe's *Erlkönig* . . . is that the child is not so much terrified as charmed, that he surrenders to the mysterious blandishments the father does not see," is in fact a fair depiction of Stravinsky's own modus.[14] He needed to experience things firsthand, to see for himself. He was a tactile man whose senses guided him as he went, literally "feeling" his way, especially at the keyboard, for new ideas.

That included his interest in American jazz, which for Stravinsky meant *la musique nègre.* Josephine Baker's tumultuous impact and success in Paris in the mid-1920s did not go unnoticed by him, nor by F. Scott Fitzgerald, Cocteau, or Janet Flanner, who wrote so perceptively of the composer. Picasso painted Baker. Hemingway befriended her (and was a fan of Stravinsky's music as well, especially since Stravinsky read his novels soon after he learned English). Of course Stravinsky was familiar with rag music from earlier years, but it was not until he arrived in America that he had a chance to see and hear for himself live jazz by African-American musicians.

Ever since his first trip to America in the mid-1920s, Stravinsky eagerly sought every opportunity to hear jazz performed live. He was captivated by its freedom, its expressive qualities. When he returned to New York in 1940, having by then settled in the United States, he continued to listen to what he considered the only authentic style of American music. The *New York World-Telegram* reported that the composer visited the Savoy Ballroom in Harlem, where he was particularly impressed by the improvisational talents of the musicians. These were quickly to become shaping sources that provided powerful models from which Stravinsky continually learned. Nor can there be any question that these influential lessons were appropriated and directly incorporated into his "jazzy" music, especially during the 1940s.

Stravinsky's sense of musical inquiry really cannot be accurately described as a goal-oriented, linear learning process in the artisanlike way such a label is often narrowly applied to artists. Certainly he believed in a "learn as you go" approach, but his desire to encounter unfamiliar music was not motivated by an urge to acquire or refine compositional tools, although in fact this was a natural consequence. Rather, Stravinsky constantly sought sounds that were foreign to him, largely *because* they were foreign to him. Ignorance in any form bothered him. As soon as a new book or recording was given to him, he had to consume it. He simply could not stand not to know something, and whatever the nature of that something was made little difference.

He regularly became sidetracked in the same way that any intelligent individual awed by the cosmography of being sometimes feels temporarily overwhelmed by the vastness of one's own ignorance, but soon recovers from and moves on. Yet often Stravinsky didn't move on, at least immediately. He felt compelled to stop and have a look around. His senses were, to use William James's description, "tuned receivers," always on the lookout for incoming signals. Still, there was not always a need to get to the absolute bottom of a matter. He was a browser, not a scholar. His curiosity was more guileless. Like the child with a new toy who simply has to take it apart and see what makes it work, the composer couldn't keep his hands off anything. But once the mechanism is understood, the fascination quickly vanishes, and there is now the next toy to disassemble and make sense of. He seems to have become bored easily, and there is almost an urgency to get on with things, rather than lingering on causal relationships or "deep grammatical levels."

Stravinsky's panorama was wide, but not always particularly deep or focused. He read a lot of Freud, for example, but did not especially understand the intricacies of the psychologist's theories. Nor should this be misperceived; for it is not an indictment of any superficiality, though his detractors certainly would argue that it is, but rather a recognition that his purpose in examining a specific matter was satisfactorily met at whatever point *he* deemed it satisfactorily met. He learned only what he wanted and needed to learn, and he was honest and perceptive enough to know when those needs were fulfilled. All those neoclassical reworkings of ragtime, jazz, Bach, Pergolesi, and other preassembled models during the 1920s, or his assimilation of Schoenberg's serial techniques during the 1950s, stand as evidence of a composer who absorbed ideas with an astonishing grasp.

Yet this was not enough. Stravinsky wanted, even needed, to be viewed as a deeply informed scholar, a skilled sophist both wise and clever enough to discern the sometimes nuanced differences of recondite discourse. Nowhere was his quest for intellectual respectability more shrewdly advanced than in his accepting the Norton Chair of Poetics at Harvard—the very cradle of American academic intellectualism as Stravinsky saw it—for the 1939–40 academic year. Not only did the ivy-covered post provide a legitimate excuse to leave France before the inevitable Nazi occupation, which Stravinsky fully anticipated, but it allowed him to don the clothes of a polemicist and refute the widespread opinion that he was musically and intellectually no more than a lightweight thinker—a "little Modernsky," as Schoenberg once cruelly satirized him in a composition of his own.

How much of those now famous Harvard allocutions known as the *Poetics of Music* flowed from Stravinsky's own carefully thought out meditations no longer remains much of a riddle for historians. Many of his thoughts were significantly shaped by others. The last years in France were especially painful for Stravinsky, full of personal depression and dwindling public success. He wrote to his friend Pierre Suvchinsky that he had reached "a dead end." Suvchinsky provided the composer with reading materials to stimulate his thinking. In Sancellemoz, he introduced him to *La Nausée* (1938), Jean-Paul Sartre's first major novel. And though by 1952 Stravinsky would write to his son Theodore that he had "absolutely no sympathy" for Sartre's existential notions, in the late 1930s, while he was formulating his thoughts for the Norton lectures, there is little doubt that the young philosopher's views exerted considerable influence among the circle of intellectuals who surrounded the composer.[15] Freud's theory of the subconscious was also a favorite topic, as was the Renaissance philosopher Nicholas of Cusa's linking of mathematics and art as an expression of universal order. In a fine biography of Nadia Boulanger, Léonie Rosenstiel suggests that Paul Valéry suspected Boulanger of serving as a medium wherein Valéry's own *Poetics,* written years earlier, was transformed into Stravinsky's *Poetics.* Moreover, Valéry regarded "Stravinsky's latest work as nothing less than philosophical plagiarism," Rosenstiel contends. Obliquely or otherwise, Valéry's hand is certainly evident. Still, the French musicologist Roland-Manuel (Alexis-Manuel Levy, 1891–1966) was the principal ghostwriter for the Harvard lectures, regularly sending drafts to Stravinsky, who (as the archival copies in Basel show) would then make relatively minor revisions.[16]

Nor, as many scholars have pointed out, can the strong influence of Suvchinsky be missed. In 1939, the same year as the Norton lectures, Suvchinsky's article "La Notion de temps et la musique," in *Le Revue musicale* (May–June), employed parallel terminology in addressing several of the temporal aspects of music that Stravinsky dwells on in his Harvard lectures. The composer even points directly to the article and its explanation of *chronos,* admitting that Suvchinsky's "thinking is so closely akin to mine that I can do no better than to summarize his thesis here." Yet the sources for Stravinsky's thinking, as expounded by Roland-Manuel, are multiple. Aquinas, Darwin, Freud, Maritain, Montaigne, Pascal, and Valéry are all invoked throughout the lectures as a collective *vox Dei.* Nicholas of Cusa is not mentioned by name, although Stravinsky's frequent allusions to Renaissance theology, modernism, and academicism cut directly to several fundamental tenets argued by him in such theses as *De concordantia catholica* (1433) and *De docta ignorantia* (1440), in which Cusa declared that any truly learned individual is aware of his own ignorance. Much of this thinking was in the air and certainly very familiar to scholars of the period.[17]

The French astronomer and philosopher Jules-Henri Poincaré (most remembered by mathematicians for his work with Fuchsian functions, and well known to French intellectuals of the 1930s), for example, spoke eloquently of correlations between the subconscious and ordering in mathematical discovery. And there is no doubt that Stravinsky believed in the powers of the subconscious as a reliable guide. The pages of Poincaré's *Foundations of Science* (published in 1913, the same year as *Le Sacre*) are filled with thoughts that could easily be substituted for Stravinsky's Norton text. Even though there is nothing to confirm that Stravinsky knew Poincaré's work thoroughly, the composer's emphasis in his second and third lectures on ordering and the creative process resound in Poincaré's essay "Mathematical Creation," with its insistence that "a mathematical demonstration is not a simple juxtaposition of syllogisms [but] rather it is syllogisms placed in a certain order, and the order in which these elements are placed is much more important than the elements themselves."[18]

In many ways, then, the *Poetics* is a contemporary reflection of a general school of ontological thinking, rather than the unique ideas of a single composer. That Stravinsky borrowed, modified, or in some cases virtually stole ideas from his contemporaries is not so unusual. That he felt perfectly comfortable doing so was just one more indication of how important he considered himself. He felt entitled to appropriate ideas, as long as they were good ideas, as he once said, since those were the only ones worth the effort of stealing.

Three years after his residency in Cambridge, Harvard sent Stravinsky the only copy of the English translation. Maximizing every opportunity, Stravinsky knew there was still considerable mileage for them available on the lecture circuit and in radio interviews, magazine articles, and such. His transcript is meticulously marked throughout with phonetic inflections designed to ensure his smooth delivery in the still unfamiliar English language (the lectures at Harvard were given in French). But the remarks themselves are largely the same as Roland-Manuel's original ideas. Now renamed "Composing, Performing, Listening," he delivered passages from the *Poetics* as part of the Moody Foundation lectures at the University of Chicago in 1944. Jacques Maritain, the neo-Thomist philosopher who had become a guru for Stravinsky in earlier years, was teaching there and actually attended the presentation. Thereafter, Stravinsky repeated his remarks at Englewood College in Wisconsin (with Boulanger in attendance), again a few months later at Mills College in California, and in Philadelphia on a program of the Arts Alliance. In each case, the lecture was mainly a rephrasing or reordering of the original.

When Harvard University Press agreed to publish the English-language version of the original *Poetics of Music* in 1947, the composer and friend of Stravinsky Nicolas Nabokov was initially asked to prepare the translation. Since he was unavailable, the task fell principally to Ingolf Dahl, one of the composer's close American associates. Years after the publication appeared, Paul Henry Lang launched a critical salvo in the *New York Herald-Tribune*— an attack that did not escape Stravinsky's attention: "Stravinsky explained his esthetic creed in [his] *Musical Poetics*. It is a very bad book, a sort of inverted ostentation, insolent and enigmatic, and as evidence of his beliefs he offers not logic but new dogma: the new hedonism of the composer 'in quest of his pleasure.' Pleasure here means a sovereign ability to play with music. And he carries this attitude out in his music. The soul is banished and although the ingenuity and spirit applied [is] endless and inexhaustible, one is perilously close to feeling the same elation one experiences when watching a juggler work."[19]

Stravinsky retained the article, writing in the margin, "Why should a learned musician be so deaf to contemporary music?" But Professor Auld Lang Syne, as the composer dubbed him, was merely saying what many detractors had long thought about the *Poetics,* and for that matter about the music. In fact, the origins of the book tell much about the content of its ideas. The composer seems to have exerted almost as much energy haggling over the specifics of the original Harvard contract with Edward Forbes and the payment of ghostwriting fees to Roland-Manuel as he did formulating his own philosophical position. In a letter from Forbes in June 1939, Stravinsky was encouraged to live in one of the student houses and, if he was to do so, was instructed to use the piano only between one o'clock and ten. The salary ($9,000) and travel fees ($1,000) had to be negotiated. The number of lectures was at issue; Stravinsky agreed to no more than six, although eight was customary. Harvard had hoped that he would spend much more time with the students than the two hours a week to which he agreed. (Among the twelve or so students with whom he worked were Jan LaRue, William Austin, William Denny, and Vladimir Ussachevsky.) The list of contractual particulars is endless, and throughout the summer, in letter after letter, Stravinsky tenaciously negotiated every one.

Of course, the foundational ideas expressed in Roland-Manuel's drafts obviously were approved by Stravinsky, but to a sizable extent the *Poetics* lectures served more as a public demonstration that the composer resourcefully employed to impress the "Harvard and Radcliffe esthetes" (as Frederick Jacobi described them), whose approbation was more important to the composer than he was willing to admit. Those who point to the *Poetics* as evidence of his deeply felt intellectual predilections are pointing in the wrong direction. At the time, the lectures were useful to Stravinsky, like so many crucibles in his life, but in later years he openly admitted that they were merely part of the past, and should be read as such.

Stravinsky understood, as his friend Aldous Huxley wrote in *The Doors of Perception* (1954)—a book also retained in Stravinsky's library, as were so many of Huxley's—that "highly educated people find it all but impossible to pay serious attention to anything but words and notions. The arts, relegated to the less important non-verbal sphere of knowledge, are almost completely ignored." Ironically, Huxley's statement was a call for drug experimentation and the virtues of mescaline as a way of cutting through the clutter of words and explanations that too often, in his estimate, squelch pure beauty. Stravinsky saw it quite differently. If he was to win his slice of posterity, he felt, he had to compete with such "words and notions." He would have to beat the intellectuals at their own game.[20]

Yet how could Stravinsky have been an intellectual? He was the least sedentary, most edgy creature imaginable. "I wait like an insect waits," he said, conjuring up a vision of a spider motionlessly stalking its prey; but his analogy, though charming, could not have been farther off the mark. The notion of the fidgety composer patiently waiting for a musical or intellectual idea simply to wander into his web approaches absurdity. He was generally an impatient man who demanded that both simple needs and complex issues be resolved quickly and clearly. He expected people to be as decisive as he usually was, and not to waste his time. Closure was much more to his taste than tolerance. Intellectual inquiry moves at a pace that was unacceptably glacial for Stravinsky's frenetic metabolism. And though he possessed neither the temperament nor the time to be an intellectual, there was a part of him that wanted to be thought of as such.

Although the composer sometimes eagerly served up apologias that betrayed more sciolism than careful thinking, at other times the very idea of intellectual discourse was curtly dismissed as nothing more than mummified babble. ("I have no time for such meaningless philosophical discussions," he would often reply to inquiries.) It was useless, he contended, to turn something vibrant into an inanimate "object of philosophical speculation." His correspondence is again revealing, for, in a complete turnabout, he would on occasion reply to such questions, frequently taking the time to explain his viewpoint painstakingly, even invoking Schopenhauer and company in the process of arguing a lengthy elucidation of his point.

In April 1958 a senior at Simmons College wrote to Stravinsky, stating that she was writing "a book called Stravinsky's Ballets" and asking about what became his most notorious statement, "Music is by its very nature, essentially powerless to *express* anything at all." "This is a very radical statement," the student wondered, "since your ballets express so much. Would you be kind enough to enlighten me as to your present views on this statement?" And a few weeks later, Stravinsky actually took the time to respond: "My statement that music does not express anything but itself is not contradictory to the fact that music connected with a spectacle, a show, a dance may produce a different and even better impression than that when it is put to its own shifts. Music is nothing but an art of organization of sounds, and a faculty to express things outside of itself can not be considered as a criterion of its value. As Schopenhauer pointed out, music is an independent and self-contained universe in which the human mind has created the material and reduced them to order. That is all I have to say about the expression and/or in music."

Stravinsky was constantly asked to justify his seemingly paradoxical pronouncement on music and expression—a conundrum doubtless calculated to chafe those who wished to relegate music to nothing more than "sentimental twaddle," as he put it. Almost ten years earlier, he explained his position to the writer Merle Armitage by once more summoning the memory of Schopenhauer's words, thereby implying that great thinkers think the same thoughts. But the archives demonstrate that, rather than having any particular interest in the German philosopher's broader message, Stravinsky virtually hit upon Schopenhauer's views adventitiously. Certainly he would have at least been acquainted with Schopenhauer by way of Tolstoy (who may have stimulated his interest in all things Greek as well), but it is doubtful that his interest was on the same enraptured level as Tolstoy's "endless ecstasy over Schopenhauer," experienced during the summer of 1869, after writing *War and Peace*.

It was the abridged Schopenhauer that Stravinsky was primarily interested in. Correspondence discloses that friends would actually send him neatly quotable passages of Schopenhauer that could easily be called up to corroborate his own views. There were other cribbed sources too. Stravinsky's library contains a book from 1948 titled *Music and Literature,* by Calvin S. Brown. Though the book itself is unmarked, the composer pasted inside the front cover a book review by *Los Angeles Times* critic Albert Goldberg from 30 October 1949. When Goldberg referred to Brown's quoting of Schopenhauer ("musical sounds inhabit and form a universe of their own"), Stravinsky underlined the section in red. Two months after the Goldberg review, Stravinsky's December reply to Armitage began: "When I said that 'music is by its very nature . . .' many people felt very unhappy about it. Now I see that Schopenhauer, 100 years ago in the crest of the 'Romantic' period, expressed the same thought in different words: 'Music is not a reproduction of the external universe, but is rather an independent and self-contained universe in which the human mind has created the materials and reduced them to order.' Fortunately, then, I am not entirely alone in thinking this way."[21]

None of this is to say, however, that Stravinsky wasn't a voraciously inquisitive man by nature. His extant library alone displays an amazingly catholic variety of books, on everything from yoga to psychocybernetics. His musical interests were perhaps more capacious than those of any other composer in this century. He seems to have come by his curiosity naturally and early on, rather than developing it gradually through any planned curriculum. Of course there were teachers and lessons, but this was far too prescriptive a path for his free-spirited sense of discovery to follow. He drew no arbitrary boundaries, either chronological or stylistic, as he listened to, played, and studied whatever there was to be heard. Even as a student, his curiosity ranged freely—too freely, in fact, for Nikolay Rimsky-Korsakov, his sometimes rigid mentor, who evidently advised the youth to avoid listening to Debussy lest he end up liking him. But Stravinsky did listen to Debussy, and Wagner, and virtually any composer he could, all the while gathering information to be retrieved, assimilated, or discarded as his needs and tastes dictated.

He welcomed the attention of the intellectual community, but like Rimsky, who openly deprecated the ivory towerism of academicians, Stravinsky kept a safe distance from any long-term institutional affiliation. He taught a little in Paris at the Ecole Normale de Musique, and at Fontainebleau for Boulanger. He was invited to do some master classes in the early 1940s at Tanglewood, and appeared at the University of Illinois in 1949 and 1950 in support of his son Soulima. He conducted a few master classes at the University of Texas, the Eastman School, and Princeton in the late '50s and early '60s. Still, he made it clear that teaching sapped creativity and that, unlike his counterpart Schoenberg, he didn't need to teach to survive. Indeed, that he could prosper as a working composer while Schoenberg had to teach was a considerable source of satisfaction to him.

The composer refused most honorary doctorates. Such declinations were empowering, enabling him to demonstrate just how meaningless these vacuous tributes were in validating his importance—he wanted people to know that such academic pretensions were beneath him. But frequently, in predicatory letters to those offering the honors, he could not resist sermonizing. To a 1950 Harvard invitation offering an honorary doctorate, the composer responded: "It is impossible for me to accept this flattering bestowal because the idea of possessing any honorary title has always been and still is strongly against my principles." Yet in a subsequent letter to Harvard he more fully explained those "principles" in another typical peroration: "In science the title of 'doctor' is conferred by a competent scientific institution to those scholars who attain a required level of competence in this profession, thus warranting them a kind of immunity against an unqualified judgment. Whereas in the domain of fine arts, the title of Doctor *honoris causa* being only an honorary one, i.e., without a similar guarantee, all that is left to its bearers is but an unhealthy stimulation of his pride. This, in my opinion, is perfectly anomal [*sic*] and it is why I refused the acceptance of this title."[22]

Stravinsky demanded this kind of ironclad "immunity against an unqualified judgment" especially because he had been badly stung by the actions of an academic institution fifteen years earlier. In 1936 he was denied an important honor by the French Institute—an honor he wanted very much, and in being rejected was publicly embarrassed—and the memory doubtless contributed to a sense of retribution underlying these typically high-minded homilies. And as with everything else in his decision making, personal history and his own sense of propriety primarily influenced him. In 1965, the Netherlands offered the composer the Erasmus Prize, a prestigious award previously bestowed upon Marc Chagall, Charlie Chaplin, and other artists whom Stravinsky admired. But in his case it was to be shared with Benjamin Britten. On 15 November, Stravinsky politely declined, "for personal reasons," and then confessed in a letter that he hadn't accepted because the honor was being awarded jointly. "How tactless these Dutch," he wrote. A few years earlier, in 1959, Serge Lifar offered Stravinsky the "Prix Serge de Diaghilev" in commemoration of the fiftieth anniversary of the Ballets Russes. Stravinsky didn't even reply, although his recent collaborator on the ballet *Agon,* Balanchine, was being asked to share the award for his work as director of the New York City

Ballet. Not only was he unwilling to share the limelight with his old friend, by 1959 the composer's ties with French ballet and his friendship with Lifar had long ceased.

Stravinsky enjoyed the companionship of some of the preeminent writers living in or visiting Hollywood around the same time: T. S. Eliot, Aldous Huxley, Christopher Isherwood, Thomas Mann (explored more fully in Chapter 4). He shared several evenings with Mann, for example, and their conversations were often substantive, especially regarding religion. The composer's relationship with Huxley especially deserves study, for as different as they were in many ways, there was a deeper affinity that bonded them. Huxley considered Stravinsky a brilliant artist who not only understood the ins and outs of the creative process, but could shape its inexorable path with such authority as to construct the most beautiful, logical, persuasive, and expressive forms. Stravinsky's admiration for the writer was equally unbounded. He relied upon Huxley as a close friend and sage source who was capable of fielding questions most eloquently on most any matter. Whether the topic was art, science, history, or politics, the composer turned to Huxley for "answers" that Stravinsky seemed to accept implicitly.

Although Huxley purportedly recoiled at any mention of his *Brave New World* (so dwarfing was its renown in comparison with his other works), nevertheless he wanted to find someone to provide music for his adaptation of the book as a play. Naturally he first turned to his friend Stravinsky. As Huxley's biographer David Dunaway reports: "In the spring of 1957, Huxley offered this project to Stravinsky via Robert Craft, then to Leonard Bernstein. Both rejected it." Huxley wrote that he had prepared "a dramatic adaptation . . . not so much of a conventional musical, as of a play with music—a ballet or two and some songs." He hoped that Stravinsky might add "a little ballet music for brave new worlders and another piece for the Indians on the reservation," as well as several additional songs.[23]

When someone like Huxley was not approaching Stravinsky about a possible collaboration, the composer approached other prominent personalities in the hope of finding some joint venture. In the 1950s, he asked Tennessee Williams to provide an English translation for *L'Histoire,* and also made the same request of Orson Welles, Marlon Brando, and Thornton Wilder. Much earlier, Stravinsky had hoped to work with Noël Coward, but Coward's agent responded on 10 April 1931: "I am sorry I have been unable to persuade Mr. Noël Coward to enter into a collaboration with you. . . . At the moment I cannot think of any other English speaking man likely to form an effective union, unless it might be H. G. Wells." Stravinsky was also struck by Ingmar Bergman's 1961 staging of *The Rake's Progress* ("the most original and beautiful realisation of any of my theatre pieces that I had ever seen on any stage," he gushed), and he hoped that Bergman would make a film of the opera. But negotiations failed, largely because of Bergman's own enormous ego. "What has Stravinsky done for *me*," was the reply when the director's monetary demands were not met.

Shortly after *The Rake* premiered in 1951, Stravinsky wanted to do another opera, this time with Dylan Thomas. They met in May 1953 to discuss a libretto based on the idea of an atomic catastrophe that would precipitate, first, the complete annihilation of the planet, but then the subsequent rebirth of the human race—presumably a kinder and wiser race that had learned its lesson. It was a universal theme, and one, as we shall see, that continued to occupy Stravinsky during the 1950s and early 1960s. Unfortunately, Thomas died before they could carry out their plans.

Inasmuch as no new music came of countless unrealized projects, they are usually unceremoniously tossed aside by music historians as nothing more than inconsequential curiosities: no music, no value. But Stravinsky's desire to undertake such collaborations, to interact with those he saw as his artistic counterparts, reveals the larger sphere in which he wished to move, and certainly speaks clearly to his own self-image. His friendships and his ambitions helped to define who he was, or at least who he wanted to be. "For myself," he wrote in his *Poetics*, "I cannot begin to take an interest in the phenomenon of music except insofar as it emanates from the integral man. I mean from a man armed with the resources of his senses, his psychological faculties, and his intellectual equipment."[24] These unrealized works are part of the "integral" character of the composer; for they help to explain much about his senses, his psychology, and even his own estimate of just how far his intellect felt it must stretch to be fulfilled. Unquestionably Stravinsky was a committed, serious artist absolutely driven to express his ideas as forcefully and cogently as he could. But that in itself was not enough. Nor should it have been, especially given his enormous powers in envisioning collaborative enterprises more incisively than any other composer in the century. He needed to step beyond society's imposed role of what a composer should be, and thus step beyond what the public too often saw as the limited boundaries of music history. He wanted more because he was capable of doing more.

Stravinsky's image could be sold, so why not sell it? Not only did he work hard at being famous, those around him sometimes compliantly contrived whatever beneficial spin would bolster his marketability. Vernon Duke, the Russian composer turned Hollywood songwriter and arranger (of "April in Paris" fame), avowed in his egregiously hostile article "The Deification of Stravinsky," in 1964, that "the composer remained popular because of his own and Craft's clever business acumen." In spite of Duke's thinly veiled agenda, there is more than a grain of truth in the charge. But to accuse Stravinsky and Craft of outright deceit in gaining whatever advantage they might at any cost, as Duke implies, exceeds in the extreme how the composer cleverly handled the many opportunities that presented themselves.[25]

Closer to the truth, I believe, Stravinsky's image was as deftly orchestrated and choreographed as any of his ballets. He was a marketable commodity easily packaged and sold. Nowhere is this more honestly or eloquently addressed than in Claudio Spies's "Notes in His Memory," published in *Perspectives of New Music* shortly after the composer's death in 1971. "In time, the demands of his position as a public figure entailed ever further extensions and varieties of exposure: books appeared under his name, yet none of these were written by him. . . . More and more the public composer was trapped by the uncontrollably proliferating exigencies of publicity. . . . It is in his final two years that the limelight reaped its bitterest, crassest harvest of publicity. . . . His infirmity was subjected to outrageous public display, and his ensnarement was rendered the more appallingly evident through those reiterated projections of his 'image.'"[26]

Those "reiterated projections" are lodged in our memories. Lincoln Kirstein, the composer's ballet patron, concedes in his autobiography that "memory is unreliable, particularly when it tries to distinguish between what was hoped for, spoken of, read about, and what was indeed witnessed."[27] In large measure, of course, history's business is the questioning of such memories, the purging of fictions. In Stravinsky's case, whatever memory or whatever fiction was created often resulted from a team effort; nor in so saying should one rush to judgment. Given his often appallingly abrasive statements and beliefs, Stravinsky often had to be protected from himself. Beginning in the late 1940s, Robert Craft primarily provided the armor, often acting as an antitoxin to Stravinsky's sometimes venomous statements. But, consequently, what we know of the composer is to some extent the residue of a sometimes impoverished, expurgated, and selective memory.

Winthrop Sargeant once prophesied that a hundred years from now, Stravinsky's star would quickly descend. Olin Downes caustically brushed aside the composer as a "debatable genius" who had "succumbed utterly to aimlessness" after *Le Sacre*. But perhaps the most acerbic impeachment was hurled by the always outlandish Canadian pianist Glenn Gould, in his scathing "Music in the Soviet Union" address at the University of Toronto during the early 1960s.

> Stravinsky has . . . never been able to decide which things are pertinent to his spiritual being and which are superficial. . . . He has never been able to find, apart from this constant transition of fleeting identifications, the real personality of Igor Stravinsky. This, of course, is tragic. . . . What are the adoptions and renouncements of vows from one decade to another . . . if not the ultimate embarrassment of the man who recognizes that his enormous capacity and technique and perception are not enough, who recognizes that he is not made to play the part of one of the great men of history? And so he turns his life into a pathetic search for the identity and conviction and repose that he knows exists in the great world but which he knows too that he shall never find.[28]

Some might discard Gould's rhetoric as symptomatic of what many saw as his own dementia. Yet for all the hoopla that surrounded Stravinsky, and for all the laurels with which the world honored him, the composer knew what Gould and others were thinking, and it bothered him. Regardless of the shield Stravinsky often used to deflect the constant assaults on his works, it would be foolish to assume that he was not hurt by them. The criticisms of his music were explicit, and, rightly or wrongly, ultimately they were bridged to his being. Stravinsky, for all his wit, for all his astringent retorts, was a terribly sensitive man. His own self-image may never have recovered from a difficult and not particularly nurtured childhood, despite his efforts to cast aside whatever ghosts haunted him. His archives betray his fear that people were watching, judging, compiling his annals with every statement made and action taken. And with the release of these long inaccessible primary sources, the task of separating truth from illusion may now begin.

C·h·a·p·t·e·r ·2·

Rediscovering the
American *Apollon Musagète:*
Stravinsky, Coolidge, and the
Forgotten Washington Connection

Without stopping to describe my visual impressions on landing in New York—skyscrapers, traffic, lights, Negroes, cinemas, theatres, in fact all that rouses the curiosity of foreigners, and very rightly so—I want to begin by bearing witness as a musician to the fact that in the United States, side by side with a profound weakness for the freakish and the sensational, I found a real taste for the art of music, as manifested by the many societies devoted to musical culture and by the magnificent orchestras munificently endowed by private individuals.
—Stravinsky, *An Autobiography*

Stravinsky's impressions of America were recorded a decade after his first tour of the United States in 1925. But the composer had already become familiar with American music years earlier, while still a young man in St. Petersburg. In 1914 the rumblings of war forced him to retreat to Switzerland, and even as his nostalgia for Russia deepened during his self-imposed exile, his interest in America's music and culture grew. In a 1916 interview with the *New York Tribune,* Stravinsky spoke of his admiration for American "jazz," although the term was loosely understood to include ragtime, blues, boogie-woogie—any form of "music hall" popular styles. "It is a veritable art and I can never get enough of it to satisfy me," the composer reported.[1] In 1918, his friend Ernest Ansermet presented him with samples of American ragtime (probably obtained two years earlier while Ansermet was in the United States with Diaghilev's troupe). Stravinsky immediately found the music intriguing. Its "Negro origin" stirred his always acquisitive mind, just as his curiosity about the United States itself was piqued.

Still, until his first transatlantic crossing on the SS *Paris* in late December

1924, Stravinsky's early image of American music was almost exclusively formed through the eyes of others. When Serge Diaghilev returned to France after his Ballets Russes first toured the United States in 1916, the impressions he shared with the composer were less than kind. The dancer Tamara Geva remembered Diaghilev callously referring to the cultural wasteland of America's "Indians . . . bankers . . . and gangsters." They were no more than "cave people," he said. Similarly, Léonide Massine recalled that after the company's disappointing reception at its first performance in New York (which included *The Firebird*), Diaghilev promptly decreed that America simply was not prepared for his innovative ideas about ballet. Diaghilev, Massine reported, "told me that Americans still seemed to think of ballet as light entertainment, to be enjoyed after a hard day at the office!"[2]

Stravinsky originally expected to travel to the United States with Vaslav Nijinsky, the great star in Diaghilev's galaxy. Both were to join the Ballets Russes during its 1916 season. The invitation was to have come from the Metropolitan Opera, where Diaghilev's company was engaged. Yet only Nijinsky made the journey in February. Diaghilev's letters to Stravinsky from Chicago, Milwaukee, Cleveland, Pittsburgh, Philadelphia, and New York leave an endless trail of misunderstandings. The composer angrily charged that Diaghilev was not providing proper compensation for *The Firebird* and his other ballets being performed on tour. He chided his friend for failing to procure the funding that would have allowed him to make the voyage to New York. Certainly Stravinsky was eager to escape his musical confinement in Switzerland, especially given the instant notoriety he had tasted with Diaghilev's company in Paris only a few years earlier. While he would have to wait nearly a decade before undertaking his first tour of several American cities, as a pianist and conductor, by then his music was familiar to audiences across the United States.

More important, his image was already etched in the minds of American critics, composers, and concertgoers. It was generally a fond image too, even though reactions to his music were by no means unanimously favorable. While secluded in the Swiss town of Morges, the composer received monetary supplements from Americans who assumed his plight was worse than it really was—an impression that Stravinsky did little to correct. By 1924, Pitts Sanborn, critic for the *New York Evening Mail,* reported, "Inevitably the New York music season of 1923–24 will go down in history as the Stravinsky season. . . . Stravinsky's abiding fame we must leave to the years that are to come. The fact of prime importance in last season's record is that through it Stravinsky has 'arrived' in New York."

When Stravinsky actually did arrive in New York, in early January 1925, he was greeted as a musical celebrity. As the *New York Times* reported, during his very first evening in America the composer went out on the town "to dine and hear on its native hearth the dance music that the Old World has called American jazz." Exactly what kind of "jazz" Stravinsky heard is not clear. Fletcher Henderson, Duke Ellington, Bessie Smith, and Fats Waller were all active in the city. Louis Armstrong was also in New York playing with Henderson's band. Darius Milhaud had visited Harlem five years earlier and was struck with the "revelation" of hearing how different the music was when performed live, as opposed to the scores he had seen and the Black Swan records he heard (which he had purchased in Harlem). It is unlikely that Stravinsky would not have heard the music of black musicians in 1925, as just then they were an important part of the Harlem Renaissance exerting a powerful impact on both American and European composers. He also heard the music of George Gershwin during those first months in America and, shortly after arriving in New York, met him on 7 January at a party given in Stravinsky's honor. The next evening, the two composers met again at a reception following Stravinsky's Carnegie Hall concert. With several celebrities in attendance, including Fred and Adele Astaire, Stravinsky and Gershwin were coaxed to the piano and asked to improvise a duet. But they were reluctant and soon "retired to their separate corners," as Gershwin biographer Edward Jablonski tells it. By the time he completed his tour in March and returned to Europe, Stravinsky grandly declared that a knowledge of American jazz was absolutely essential to any serious composer. Its presence and power were inescapable.[3]

Only three years later, in a musical vein as far removed from American jazz as one could imagine, *Apollon Musagète,* a work now hailed as a classic in the annals of ballet, was first staged. During the pivotal period just before and after the composer's first American tour, the contrast in his musical styles is enormous. Stravinsky's earliest memories of popular music in America and his use of jazz idioms in such works as the Concerto for Piano and Winds of 1924 gave way to the writing of such marmoreal Greek-inspired compositions as *Oedipus Rex* in 1926. What happened? How did the composer get from his Piano Concerto, with its Gershwin-like piano figurations (*Rhapsody in Blue* was written the same year and premiered with the Paul Whiteman band just a few months before Stravinsky first played his new concerto under Serge Koussevitzky in Paris), to the extraordinary tranquillity of *Apollon Musagète*? How did he come to write, as dance historian Richard Buckle once aptly described it, such "holy music"?

Stravinsky's Piano Concerto, with the composer's own fingerings (Courtesy of the Music Division, Library of Congress)

The metamorphosis came from a particularly intense period of strife for the composer. Upon returning to France after his tour, Stravinsky again became an active communicant in the church; he studied the neoscholastic writings of the theologian Jacques Maritain in a quest to restore balance in his life; he struggled between loyalty to his wife and his desire to be with his mistress; and at age forty-three he weighed the course of his future from a midlife plateau. His self-reflection finds an analogue in Apollo's own transformation, as the young god matures and eventually assumes the role of "leader of the Muses." At one level, *Apollon Musagète*, or *Apollo*, as the composer came to prefer the title, is an achievement of sublime visual beauty, asking little explanation beyond what our senses immediately tell us. Yet the work is also an immensely symbolic statement, marking one of many crucial crossroads in Stravinsky's career. For that matter, the ballet represents no less a turning point in the life of George Balanchine, the choreographer with whom Stravinsky most successfully joined forces for more than forty years. *Apollo* is undoubtedly the nexus of this historic union. With uncharacteristic effusion, the composer sanctioned the newly merged partnership by publicly proclaiming his unreserved approval of Balanchine's elegant choreography. Without a doubt, *Apollo* is a milestone of collaborative genius.[4]

Yet in our rush to anoint the ballet as the embarkation of the Stravinsky and Balanchine collaboration, the actual premiere is consigned to a footnote. Most biographers and program annotators commemorate Diaghilev's Paris production of 12 June 1928 as the birth date on which *Apollo* was, as Andrew Porter once remarked in the *New Yorker,* "first shaped in mortal history on the stage of the Sarah Bernhardt Theatre in Paris."[5] While Porter justly ascribes such portent to the Diaghilev premiere, the forgotten American connection suffers an undeserved fate. The real first performance of the ballet took place six weeks earlier, on 27 April, not in Paris but an ocean away at the Library of Congress and choreographed not by Balanchine but by Adolph Bolm.

During the Jazz Age, Washington, D.C., was a city that had reached a crucial crossroads. Facing its own internal battle for artistic integrity, it hoped to lift itself to a higher level of cultural respectability by becoming, appropriately, a national mecca of the arts. One woman especially, Elizabeth Sprague Coolidge (1864–1953), was willing to lead a governmentally supported movement to remake Washington in the image of the older American musical centers of the eastern seaboard. But she would do so in her own way and through her own love of chamber music. Coolidge understood perfectly well that a composer with the visibility of Stravinsky could instantly bolster the image of Washington as a federal capital—a cutting-edge capital, she hoped, championing the cause of new music.

Apollo was a benchmark in many ways for both America and Stravinsky. It was the composer's first completed American commission; it was the first Stravinsky opus premiered in this country; and, perhaps most important, *Apollo* was, as Olin Downes wrote in the 6 May 1928 *New York Times* review of the American premiere, "the first time in history a major ballet work had its world premiere in America" (meaning a major ballet written by a renowned European composer).[6] Especially in light of those historically important milestones, why has the story of the Washington connection all but vanished? In this case, as in so many others, history is the victim of a distortion—one of many the composer did nothing to clarify.

On one hand, the genesis of *Apollon Musagète* presumably had absolutely nothing to do with Diaghilev and Balanchine; yet on the other, the ballet was, from its very first measures, tailor-made for the Ballets Russes principals. Such riddles are not uncommon in untangling the Stravinsky biography, for the composer was amazingly resourceful in juggling publicly professed and privately designed agendas. *Apollo*'s artifacts also provide an important biographical document in understanding the composer's view of contemporary American culture—a culture he would eventually adopt, or at least permanently append to his ineradicable Russian core. In this sense, the many unpublished documents addressing the Washington production provide a glimpse into Stravinsky's backstage machinations during the American *Apollo*'s development.

In observing these interactions, the shield with which history often guarded the composer is dropped. We are able to trace Stravinsky's penchant for adeptly shaping commissions; to witness his shrewdness in exacting what would serve him alone best; to understand the expectations of the American press and American audiences; to judge the state of classical ballet in the U.S. capital during the Roaring Twenties; and, perhaps most pertinent, to follow how Stravinsky consciously shaped his own biography, or at least perpetuated certain myths by permitting indisputable facts to evaporate. Equally important with regard to the musical and choreographical structure of the ballet, a study of the American *Apollo* is enlightening. In formative ways, the Washington commission significantly defined the compositional boundaries of the ballet's artistic dimensions—dimensions that Stravinsky was obligated to honor in creating the ballet and that Balanchine would immediately inherit and reconcile with his own conception of the work.

A search of Stravinsky's archives discloses an almost total expurgation of any association with the original Washington production. There is not a single document recording communications the composer exchanged either with Washington directly or through Gavril Païchadze, his representative. While Stravinsky normally saved virtually every scrap of information about the most meaningless events and the most insignificant performances, his file on the "American Apollo" is among the thinnest in his unpublished papers. Only a few documents survive, including a program from the original Washington performance and a program booklet from a much later Los Angeles performance of the concert version (Stravinsky conducted the work as a concert piece much more often than as a ballet). This memento was probably preserved because of its humorous reference to the premiere: "*Apollon Musagète* was written for the 1928 May Chamber Music Festival, with which Mrs F. S. Coolidge opened the music hall built by her as an annex and a gift to the Congressional Library in Washington D.C. Although the 'Leader of the Muses' has never invaded the floor of the House or Senate—most likely he would be ejected by the Sergeant-at-Arms as a lunatic—the compelling and yet delicate beauty of this work has nevertheless become a benefaction as much as the building it served to consecrate."[7]

Publicly, Stravinsky said little about the American commission. There seems to be no more than a single press release, in which the composer divulges nothing about the work other than its eventual deposit at the Library of Congress. Moreover there is no more than a passing reference to the Washington performance in his *Autobiography,* suggesting the dispatch with which his ghostwriter, Walter Nouvel, may have been directed to acknowledge the first performance: "My ballet, *Apollo Musagètes,* was given in Washington for the first time on April 27, with Adolph Bolm's choreography. As I was not there I cannot say anything about it. What interested me far more was its first performance in Paris at Diaghileff's theatre, inasmuch as I was myself to conduct the music."[8]

As with most everything the composer included in his *Autobiography,* Stravinsky's statements are consistently "brief and smug," as Virgil Thomson once characterized them, giving "one the feeling that Mr. Stravinsky has just swallowed the canary and doesn't mind our knowing it."[9] But Stravinsky's dismissive statement is informative, for, typically, it is both prevaricating and accurate. The excuse of withholding critical comment because he did not attend the performance is a charade. Absences from performances of his own music never stifled the irrepressible Stravinsky from speaking his mind, usually derogatorily. Yet he is bluntly honest and even a little cruel (for his comments would have been read by the Americans responsible for mounting the premiere) in conceding that it was the Diaghilev production on which he focused his attention, as if the Washington staging had been no more than a vehicle for his ulterior goal.

In fact, that is precisely how the composer treated the American production. Even years later, Stravinsky would recall only that Elizabeth Sprague Coolidge had underwritten a thirty-minute work—a work he carefully conceived "with the exactitude of a film composer." He added that he chose both the subject and the employment of a string ensemble in keeping with the "instrumentation appropriate to a small hall."[10] As the Basel compositional sketches confirm, the temporal pacing of the music was indeed methodically calibrated as it was composed, sometimes in segments as short as ten or fifteen seconds. But the actual contractual specifications of the commission were largely suppressed. Also, Stravinsky's gratitude for Coolidge's support was at best negligible, although his gestures of appreciation for anyone commissioning his works are hard to come by. He viewed each commission as a job to be done, and certainly not a favor or honor or anything other than a straightforward professional contract.

Diaghilev's annoyance with Stravinsky (at least as reported in *Dialogues*) for accepting the commission prompted the impresario to characterize Coolidge as *"complètement sourde."* Stravinsky raised little protest, responding only that even if she was "completely deaf," at least she was willing to pay. (The allusion to deafness no doubt stems from the fact that her hearing was impaired and she used a hearing aid.) A letter to Païchadze on 13 March 1928 clearly suggests that Stravinsky was intent on provoking Diaghilev—something he seemed to relish. There is no question that Diaghilev was peeved by Stravinsky's acceptance of the American commission, and consequently he was equally eager to annoy the composer. Trying to distance himself from the Coolidge premiere, Diaghilev wanted Stravinsky to change the ballet's title; but the composer was not about to budge. Such exchanges were symptomatic of the power struggle that marked their twenty-year relationship.[11]

Coolidge, the "fairy godmother of chamber music," as the British lexicographer W. W. Cobbett once portrayed her, was an accomplished pianist and composer, although until recently her own musical achievements have been largely ignored. It is her benefaction for which she is most remembered. Her offer to underwrite *Apollo* was a godsend, particularly since Stravinsky's flourishing career as a pianist and conductor increasingly carried him away from composition during the middle 1920s. Without Coolidge's offer, it is unlikely that he would have found the incentive, let alone sponsorship, to undertake yet another aloofly "Greek" work so soon after the tepid reception with which his and Cocteau's 1927 opera-oratorio *Oedipus Rex* was greeted in Paris.[12]

In establishing the Elizabeth Sprague Coolidge Foundation, the philanthropist boldly stated her goals in a letter to the librarian of Congress, Herbert Putnam, on 4 February 1925. She wished to promote the performance of music that "might otherwise be considered too unique or too expensive to be ordinarily undertaken." She was committed to "artistic rather than to economic values; and to opportunity over expediency." Along with her ongoing sponsorship of performances and the commissioning of new works, Coolidge provided sixty thousand dollars toward the construction of a commodiously designed small concert hall to be added on to the open courtyard of the Library of Congress, expressly for the performance of modestly scored chamber works. In fact, until the Coolidge Auditorium was constructed, Washington did not have a recital hall specifically devoted to music.[13] Coolidge insisted on an architect who would design a hall of "severe and chaste beauty," in her words, rather than "ornate display"—words, as it would turn out, that appropriately capture *Apollo*'s classical imagery. The same year the new auditorium was erected, the Coolidge Foundation inaugurated its contemporary music festival, the first and most important of several festivals that would grow amid the blossoming of the arts in Washington. It was for this festival that *Apollo* would be commissioned.

The nation's capital recognized that Coolidge was both determined and powerful. Samuel Chotzinoff wrote in the *New York World* the day after *Apollo*'s first performance: "As everybody knows by now, Mrs. Coolidge—the philanthropist, not the first lady of the land—has in recent years forced the participation of our National Government in musical affairs by the simple expedient of building a concert hall . . . endowing it handsomely and arranging for it musical matters of the first importance." Writing in the *New York Tribune* a few days later, Lawrence Gilman pointed out two seeming improbabilities: first, "If anyone had told us a few years ago that we should live to see the day when the United States Government would be caught in the act of commissioning a musical work by Igor Stravinsky, we should have laughed with as brutal a mirth as our sense of manners would permit"; and second (with notable misogyny), "Surely it is a vivid and suggestive commentary upon our American civilization, from which one may draw whatever moral one pleases, that it took a woman to persuade the United States Government to become a patron of musical art." Gilman is in error, of course, for the United States government had nothing to do with the Stravinsky commission. Yet Coolidge's largesse was often interpreted as meddlesome, as both Chotzinoff's and Gilman's loaded prose suggests. Her gifts were often seen as an attempt to pressure and embarrass the nation into endorsing a governmental patronage that many did not support. Especially as a woman, so the undercurrent went, it was not her place to lobby Congress, even indirectly.

Not only did Coolidge support dozens of distinguished American composers, she traveled often to Europe (even attending a performance at Bayreuth conducted by Wagner) and commissioned a constellation of important contemporary composers: Dallapiccola, Ginastera, Hindemith, Messiaen, Prokofiev, Ravel, Respighi, Schoenberg, Webern, and of course Stravinsky. She also realized, as she told Putnam, that unfamiliar new music would likely not be performed unless she provided for the public recital of contemporary works. But one should not assume that Coolidge necessarily approved of or even understood much of the music she sponsored. She was quite candid about her musical tastes. It is clear from her correspondence that whether or not she thought a new work would meet with her personal approval, she realized that bringing attention to significant new compositions was far more important.[14]

When Coolidge began actively promoting her agenda, Washington's status as the governmental seat of power was hardly matched by its meager artistic presence. Musically, the city had not measured up to the Parisian Beaux-Arts elegance first envisioned by George Washington, Thomas Jefferson, and the city's designer, Pierre Charles L'Enfant, in 1791. (The Library of Congress building, first occupied in 1897, was originally likened to the Paris Opéra.) Could Coolidge's sponsorship of important foreign composers and performers launch the establishment of an American tradition that would enhance Washington's status? Her support of non-American composers sometimes was questioned. Her response, most clearly articulated in a 1926 letter to Carl Engel (who had become chief of the music division at the Library of Congress four years earlier), spoke of "Americanism" as a policy that could only be advanced by insisting on musical excellence: "It seems to me that one of our highest needs in this country is of an honest reverence for quality; the only way to know and revere musical quality is to hear it," Coolidge wrote.[15]

With the election of Herbert Hoover in 1928, the same year as Stravinsky's ballet, the United States was riding the crest of unprecedented prosperity. New technologies were booming, the country's giddiness continued to bubble just before the crash of 1929, and Congress was funding public education for the nation's children at a rate more than that of the rest of the world combined. A case for serious music, and serious public exposure to it, needed to be made, especially in the federal capital. Coolidge understood the need for legislative intercession, even if this meant that she would need to provide a considerable subvention. In the principled spirit of the Kellogg-Briand Pact of 1928, wherein almost all nations agreed to "outlaw" war as a means of deciding foreign conflict, Coolidge hoped to enfranchise the idea of music as a universal language capable of cutting across cultural and political barriers. Her goal of a global community of musicians working together for world peace would probably have amused Stravinsky, who often pooh-poohed such grandly proclaimed humanitarian goals. The power of music rested in its intrinsic logic and force, he argued, in the immutable laws of compositional order and structural coherence. A piece of music was powerful in its own right without the appurtenance of politics. For Stravinsky, there simply wasn't any musical potion capable of bewitching warring countries into joining hands despite their colliding interests or ideologies.

Coolidge's link with Stravinsky was at best indirect, and given their contrasting views on such deeply felt issues, theirs was more of a misalliance than a connection. No extant correspondence suggests that the two discussed the commission in any detail, let alone Coolidge's more sweeping and lofty aspirations. Most of the business negotiations were entrusted to Engel; but while it is true that he was most often the intermediary for such commissions, Coolidge often maintained close friendships with the composers she funded. She personally knew, and seemed to be particularly fond of, several Italian composers (no doubt because of her association with the American Academy in Rome and her sponsorship of festivals there as early as 1923), including Alfredo Casella, Ottorino Respighi, and also the Spanish composer Manuel de Falla. All three were connected to the Washington festival at which *Apollo* was first presented. In Paris, Coolidge spent time with Ravel, in Vienna with Schoenberg, in Prague with Martinu, in London with Elgar. But nowhere in her recounting of her frequent European travels is Stravinsky mentioned.

While the composer's archives in Basel divulge no exchanges with Coolidge or Engel, several unpublished files in the music division of the Library of Congress allow a reassembly of *Apollo*'s evolution.[16] As early as 18 November 1926, Engel, writing to the ballet's choreographer, Adolph Bolm, first mentioned the unprecedented concept of an entire evening of ballets for the 1928 Coolidge Festival of chamber music:

> For the next Festival at the Library which will take place about the end of April 1928, we should very much like to plan a program of dancing or pantomime, and if possible, have your services on that occasion. As a matter of fact, we have written to de Falla asking him if he would accept a commission to write something for us, in the form of a pantomime for not more than three characters that would have its first performance in Washington.

The letter is instructive on many counts, including the intent to commission a ballet. Yet in his *Autobiography,* Stravinsky misleadingly declares that his control of the contractual stipulations included determining the actual form of the music.[17] Frederick Jacobi, who reviewed the premiere for the May–June 1928 issue of *Modern Music,* reported that "Stravinsky inquired for specific details: the exact dimensions of the stage and those of the orchestra pit," thus promulgating the common illusion that he was in charge. But this is fiction. It was Engel who was constantly placed in the unenviable position of tactfully but persistently reminding Stravinsky in letter after letter of the necessary limitations the commission imposed, especially regarding the issue of space. Further, the restriction to a maximum of three characters belies the composer's contention that he freely chose the number of Muses. Balanchine, as late as 1961, in an interview in *Horizon,* similarly suggested that Stravinsky, by his own volition, chose three Muses instead of nine because "nine are very boring—every Muse is the same." Nothing could be further from the truth. Stravinsky's options were almost entirely prescribed by Coolidge's contract.

The decision as to the ballet's musical design and number of players was determined by the Coolidge Festival only a few months before it considered inviting Stravinsky. From the start, Stravinsky had reservations about Washington as a venue for *Apollo,* although he was not about to pass up an opportunity to accept an American commission as a way of gaining a foothold in the country. During his three-month tour in the winter of 1925, Stravinsky performed in New York, Boston, Chicago, Philadelphia, Cleveland, Detroit, and Cincinnati, praising these "magnificent orchestras." Yet there is nothing to suggest that the composer wanted anything to do with the cultural outpost of Washington, a "background" city, as Henry James called it. Unfairly, Stravinsky considered Mrs. Coolidge a parvenue, certainly not part of the stylish, haut-monde inner circle of European patronesses with whom he, sometimes intimately, was involved—Misia Sert, Gabrielle "Coco" Chanel, and especially the American-born Winaretta Singer, heiress to the Isaac Merritt Singer sewing machine fortune, and known more familiarly to music historians as the Princesse de Polignac. Coolidge was an American who needed *him,* who needed his name, he would have reasoned, and of course he was absolutely right.

Engel's letter further discloses that Coolidge's friend, Manuel de Falla, was first invited to accept the commission. Other unpublished documents in the Bolm file reveal that not only was the popular Spanish composer actively courted but so was another Coolidge favorite, Ottorino Respighi, though nothing came of Engel's efforts to engage either. The fact is, Stravinsky was third in line in Coolidge's estimate (as eighteen years earlier he had been an alternate choice for Diaghilev's *Firebird*). On 13 April 1927, Païchadze informed Engel that the composer was interested in the proposition. A month later, in a 14 May letter, Engel reported to Coolidge: "Stravinsky is apparently eager to write a little pantomime for us. From other sources I learned that

Stravinsky is constantly in need of money. I offered to pay $500 on his accepting the commission and the other half on delivery of the material."[18]

By June Stravinsky had agreed to the terms of the commission, though with a clearly deposed condition (the fifth of nine contractual clauses the businesslike composer outlined) that he would be "free to offer the ballet to Europe and South America immediately after the American première." The language is more than standard boilerplate terminology, for it paved the way for *Apollo*'s immediate future. From the beginning, the composer's proviso was included with Paris in mind. He agreed to accept the thousand-dollar commission to write a chamber ballet, and in his written reply in early July, Engel included the five-hundred-dollar advance. All the terms seemed agreeable. The composer began sketching the music five days later, on 16 July. Most important, in the same letter Engel also enclosed a description of both the stage and the "sunken pit," as well as a photograph—all unambiguously graphic cues to impress upon the composer the severe spatial restrictions within which he was obliged to design the work's dimensions. Time and time again, Engel emphasized to Stravinsky the importance of this nonnegotiable point.

In his few public statements about the work, Stravinsky understated the commission's required chamber nature. Yet the library's insistence that whatever was composed comply in spirit and proportion with the festival's underlying chamber music mission was unequivocal and absolutely central in adjudging *Apollo*'s distinctively moderate tone and size. Craft reports in *Stravinsky in Pictures and Documents* that the composer may have somehow misunderstood the commission altogether, expecting the work to be heard by "a small circle from the White House," as he told one interviewer. Could it be that Stravinsky really thought the Washington premiere was to be in the nature of a private performance for only a few people, perhaps *"à la Maison Blanche,"* as the interviewer wrote?[19] Given the frequent correspondence between Engel and Stravinsky, including most obviously Engel's inclusion of a photograph of the theater itself six months earlier, how could the composer have possibly misunderstood? His remark to the interviewer reveals either the depth of his ignorance of the Coolidge Festival or his absolute indifference to the importance Mrs. Coolidge attached to the event as an American landmark—or perhaps his propensity for aggrandizing his own importance. Although the composer could be extremely perceptive in grasping the unwritten implications of a commission, he could just as easily toss them aside, focusing on what he intended to do while blocking out the expectations of others.

Given the stage's limited space, the dramatis personae would necessarily be limited too: no more than six dancers. Stravinsky was acutely cognizant of this condition, even drawing a picture of the stage on the cover of the *Apollo* sketchbook. As several unpublished documents suggest, had the stage been larger, the scenario would almost have certainly been quite different. These spatial restrictions are in fact the key to understanding the simple, elegant nature of *Apollo* today. As Balanchine's choreography unfolds on the cavernous stages of the New York State Theater or the Saratoga Performing Arts Center, one can't help but wonder how restrained the breadth of the dancing would have appeared in the Washington auditorium's tiny space. Its small size, with no wings for a dancer's entrance, had everything to do with Bolm's choices in choreographing the ballet.

The artistic constraints thus placed on the composer were considerable; but as always, Stravinsky found such impediments liberating rather than constrictive—a problem to be solved, he would have called it. There is evidence in the unpublished Coolidge files to suggest that Stravinsky originally contemplated including more than three Muses, but because of the space restrictions he abandoned the idea. The platform stage of the theater is only thirty feet wide and twenty feet deep (considerably smaller than many dance rehearsal studios) and obviously not conducive to the grand corps de ballet ensembles of a *Swan Lake* or the "Shrove-Tide Fair" scenes of *Petrushka*. Stravinsky's professed lack of interest in Washington notwithstanding, the Coolidge commission fundamentally shaped *Apollo*'s underlying dimensions in very formative ways. In describing the more well known Parisian production, Lincoln Kirstein once extolled Stravinsky and Diaghilev's brilliant decision to forsake the traditional "large *corps de ballets* as a background for [the] soloists," thus creating one of "the most surprising novelties."[20] But Kirstein's praise, here at least, was misplaced: in light of the library's personnel stipulations and the stage's spatial limits, a large corps wasn't even an option.

The orchestra pit was also extremely small and was thus critical in shaping the musical score of the ballet. Naturally the "chamber nature" (as Coolidge's contract emphasized) of the instrumentation reflects the onstage action. Stravinsky, of course, was wise enough to realize that the bond between the delicate balance of his orchestration and the modest dance and drama action had to be thoroughly linked. Thus the inventive way of scoring for strings was rooted not only in the composer's gift for orchestration but, just as important, in the cause of practicality. In his *Autobiography*, Stravinsky makes much of his employment of a string orchestra: "My music demanded six

The Coolidge Auditorium in Washington, D.C., showing the small stage on which *Apollo* was first performed (Courtesy of the Music Division, Library of Congress)

[string] groups instead of the quartet, as it is usually called, but, to be more exact, 'quintet,' of the ordinary orchestra, which is composed of first and second violins, violas, violoncellos, and double bass. I therefore added to the regular ensemble a sixth group, which was to be of second violoncellos. I thus formed an instrumental sextet, each group of which had a strictly defined part. This required the establishment of a well-proportioned gradation in the matter of the number of instruments for each group."[21]

Indeed it did, and despite conductor Hans Kindler's faultfinding with the string scoring, the mellifluous sextet writing clearly enriches the pristine, diaphanous "whiteness" (as the composer and Balanchine thought of it) of the ballet. However, the Basel sketches reveal that Stravinsky originally considered several instrumental combinations, including one employing both harp and piano. Given the centrality of the lyre in the Apollonian myth, the harp seems right enough, with its symbolic significance as well as its dulcet sonority. The surviving sketches for piano make sense too, especially since the keyboard was employed prominently in the opera-oratorio *Oedipus Rex*, the last composition completed before Stravinsky undertook *Apollo*. But the appropriateness of sound and symbol aside, such bulky instruments proved impractical for the auditorium's small sunken pit. Once Stravinsky finally conceded that the piano and harp were too unwieldy to include, his sketches— almost to the day that Engel's correspondence finally convinced him of how limited the space was—began to reveal a dramatic reorchestrating of the strings.

The composer struggled over their apportionment, often crossing out various combinations, as his sketchbook discloses. The precise number of violins, violas, cellos, and basses are notated, adjusted, constantly reconsidered, again almost solely because of simple logistics. The quiet intimacy, the transparency of this *blanc en blanc* ballet, as Stravinsky referred to it, has everything to do with his practical solution to a very mundane problem—the size of the pit. For the first time, sketches for strings written *divisi* (wherein the first violin section, for example, is divided into smaller groups, each with its own line) are employed as a very functional way of compensating texturally for the now forsaken harp and piano.

Any thoughts of later altering the balance for other, more spacious theaters, simply because larger orchestra pits could accommodate more musicians, would have upset such a delicate equilibrium. In his *Autobiography*, Stravinsky complains that in a rehearsal in Berlin the conductor Otto Klemperer doubled the number of strings called for, evidently because his theater had the space. "I was struck by both confusion of sound and the excessive resonance," wrote the composer, adding that once Klemperer restored the original proportions "everything became sharp and clear."[22] Certainly this was true; but it should not be forgotten that the "plasticity and clarity of the musical line," as he fondly described his "solution" in *Apollo*, originally arose from solving a specific compositional problem, a technical snag. And in his finding the solution to that problem, we recognize Stravinsky's masterful ability to deal with whatever limitations were imposed on him.

In revisiting the American *Apollo*, the importance of its choreographer, Adolph Bolm (1884–1951), must be considered. Unlike Diaghilev, Bolm felt comfortable in America, sensing in its possibilities "youth, naiveté, and mass culture, the very stuff of which the ballets of the future could be made."[23] Mounting an evening of ballets for the Coolidge Festival (a complete break from the more traditional programming of previous festivals) originally had

nothing to do with Stravinsky. Even after the composer accepted the commission, Bolm remained prominently listed in public announcements of the
opening Friday night program ("admission by card only"). As unpublished correspondence reveals, it was the Russian-born Bolm around whom Coolidge
first intended the festival to revolve. Raised in the Maryinsky tradition of St.
Petersburg, Bolm was the original Chief Warrior in Fokine's *Polovtsian Dances*
and frequently the partner of some of the company's prima ballerinas. Stravinsky had known Bolm since 1911 when he danced in *Petrushka*. He also later
danced and directed productions of both *The Firebird* and *Petrushka* in America. Early in this century, ballet in the United States was still very much under the influence of the repertory and tradition brought here by Mikhail Mord-
kin, Anna Pavlova, Diaghilev, and other Russian dancers and choreographers
such as Fokine and Bolm.

As early as 1907, Bolm and Pavlova became two of the first Maryinsky
dancers to break free and seek an international career. Bolm's dancing was
thrilling, winning fans everywhere and leading managers to trust his choreographic talents, as the Chicago Grand Opera did as early as 1919. He toured
with Diaghilev's troupe and, following its second American tour in 1917,
opted to remain in the United States, soon rising to the position of *maître de
ballet* at New York's Metropolitan Opera. Eventually he founded his own suc-

The choreographer Adolph Bolm and the composer
collaborating on a performance of *Petrushka* in Hollywood, 1943

cessful school in Chicago. Stravinsky seems to have held a mixed opinion of Bolm, as his unpublished correspondence reveals. There was an abiding bond, given their shared Russian heritage; such cultural underpinnings were always held dear by the composer. Yet at times Bolm seems to have irritated Stravinsky personally, especially because of what he considered Bolm's questionable artistic convictions. Stravinsky seems to have listened more to a reconnoitering Ansermet, who wrote to the composer in the fall of 1927 complaining that Bolm's staging of *Petrushka* at the Met was so inferior that he did not have the courage to congratulate him. Yet given our knowledge that at least two other composers were first invited to contribute a ballet to the 1928 festival, and knowing of Bolm's affection for his old compatriot Stravinsky, it may initially have been Bolm's rather than Coolidge's idea to approach the composer once others declined. Despite Stravinsky's reluctance to trust Bolm's abilities in preparing the Washington *Apollo,* the two remained close friends, with Bolm even writing a letter of reference for Stravinsky when the composer applied for American citizenship in the 1940s.[24]

As always, Stravinsky treated the commission with steely business acumen, fulfilling each contractual clause to the letter, but with minimal flexibility, let alone sympathy, toward those charged with mounting the ballet. He was in no hurry to deliver materials in a timely fashion, and as was customary for him, he composed according to his own pace. Engel, in a telegram to Païchadze on 27 December 1927, pleaded to know as soon as possible the details of Stravinsky's scenario. Naturally, Engel needed to arrange for the sets and costumes so that the festival could proceed. But Stravinsky would never accede to such requests. In a letter of 4 January 1928 to Païchadze, the composer promised the ballet's piano reduction within a few weeks, but he also instructed Païchadze: "You will copy it and send the copy to Washington together with the scenario which I will add to it. I do not think it will be possible to send the scenario before, since I have a great number of things to do and the scenario, as I envisage it, requires mature reflection."[25]

Not only was the composer not about to be rushed, his comments suggest how late in the compositional process the scenario was finalized. About a month later, in a letter to Coolidge dated 1 February 1928, a bewildered Engel related how he had learned the details of the ballet secondhand: "I have heard nothing from Paris in reply to my cable asking for the scenario and costuming. However, I read in a recent number of the *Musical Standard* that our piece is called *Apollo* and that it is scored for string instruments only. It is rather strange that this intelligence should reach us through a British magazine rather than directly through the composer or the composer's man of affairs."[26]

When the scenario did arrive in Washington a few weeks later, Bolm was immediately forced to adjust the program's order. Rather than featuring the ballet at the end of the evening, *Apollo* now had to be scheduled first because of the rigorous demands Stravinsky made on the dancers. It is clear from the directions sent to Bolm that Stravinsky even participated in laying out the choreography in rather specific terms (and by this time probably had already discussed part of the stage action with Balanchine in Nice or Monte Carlo). Practical matters of costume change and the dancers' stamina were involved. *Apollo* was one of four ballets to be performed, along with Ravel's *Pavane,* Mondonville's comic *Arlecchinata,* and the music of Beethoven's *Elf Wiener Tänze,* a pastiche of loosely constructed dances presented under the title *Alt-Wien.* Bolm not only choreographed all four of the ballets, he danced in each as well.

In spite of his repeated and bluntly worded statements to Stravinsky stressing the need for a modestly sized chamber work, Engel grew chary. It was evident that the composer's scenario was not going to fit on the small auditorium stage. Confirming Engel's worst fears, Bolm wrote to him on 8 February: "My reaction to the scenario of Stravinsky's ballet is not so very stimulating. I think it makes it obvious that your stage is too small for more than three Muses" (again inviting speculation that more than three may have been initially considered).[27]

Kindler, the conductor-cellist, aired his musical concerns, revealing that he studied the piano reduction with growing apprehension. Nor was he reassured once the instrumental score eventually arrived; in a February letter to Coolidge, he wrote, "The Stravinsky piano extract came and it sounds very ugly!" Kindler also complained bitterly to both Bolm and Coolidge about the scoring of the music, specifically Stravinsky's bowings, claiming that the string writing was especially unidiomatic. But of course it was nothing of the kind— only unusual in the ingenious string writing Stravinsky was compelled to create because of the spatial restrictions. The string writing in *Apollo* is among some of the most beautiful scoring the composer ever achieved, and surely it is the reason the ballet works very well as a concert piece. Kindler's reaction was altogether negative, and unbelievably, as Charles Rosen relates, he was so puzzled by the score's harsh dissonances that he considered them "mistakes of the copyist, and replaced them with blander harmonies" when he conducted the performance.[28]

Adolph Bolm as Apollo in the Washington, D.C., premiere, April 1928

Stravinsky's recalcitrance in complying with the festival's deadlines certainly didn't help matters. Only a month before the April premiere, correspondence between Païchadze and Engel reveals, there were unresolved questions about the most basic matters. In a letter of 16 March, Engel inquired, "Is Stravinsky's orchestration for strings and winds, or strings alone, and how many?" Still in the dark, Engel was placed in the impossible position of not knowing which instrumentalists to hire, or how many. Païchadze responded the very next day, sending the completed orchestra parts for twenty-five strings (not twenty as was being assumed). Even more revealing, Païchadze relayed Stravinsky's detailed remarks about the costumes the Muses were to wear:

> I would like to call your attention on this occasion to a little omission Mr. Stravinsky made in communicating to you the description of the costumes. In that description he wrote that the muses wore the traditional tutu and should hide it under light tunics during the prologue. It is clear that one can hide the tutu with difficulty under the tunic. Stravinsky forgot to add that the dancers should have on over the tunics, the leotard and the breast plate, and put on the tutus after having taken off their tunics, which only takes a few seconds.

Evidently Stravinsky wished to control the precise details of costuming and, to some extent, the set design as well. Yet he remained unhurried about forwarding stage directions. In an interview with J. Farron Mayoral on 25 March 1928, only a month before the premiere, Stravinsky spoke quite specifically about the stage décor he was seeking. According to Mayoral's report, for example, the "set design will portray the classical forest, palms, a temple. The first scene represents Apollo's birth [and] a chorus of goddesses hails the infant from Olympus." Jacobi's review claimed that "the composer indicated his desire that the first scene represent the birth of Apollo; that Apollo be born on stage, springing full-grown from the womb of his mother. However it was thought inadvisable to stage the parturition in just this way in Washington." Consequently, Gilman wrote in his 30 April review, Apollo's mother, Leto, was "unceremoniously scrapped."[29]

Actually, the audience would not have known that anything was scrapped, since it had no idea what to expect. Oscar Thompson wrote in his *New York Sun* review: "The absence of program notes conspired . . . to compel listeners to depend entirely on their own ears and eyes for what was going on in the orchestra pit as well as on the stage. Not so much as a synopsis of the visual action, much less a score, was available." Even Engel, Bolm, and Kindler (to say nothing of the dancers themselves) learned of Stravinsky's specifications only as the composer was announcing them in Europe. Engel's letter, moreover, implies that perhaps by necessity the three Muses were to participate in the Prologue, rather than enter only after what was originally designed to be Leto's birthing scene. Given the stage restrictions and limited number of dancers permitted, it is conceivable that Stravinsky originally intended the "Washington" Muses to double as Leto's handmaidens in the Prologue, then quickly (since it "only takes a few seconds," as he wrote) transform themselves into their solo roles.[30]

The staging of *Apollo* proved a nightmare for Engel, who dealt patiently

not only with Stravinsky's obstinacy but also with the often peevish performers themselves. The production was fraught with last-minute sniping, and the
turmoil that ensued tested the nerves of all involved. The dancers bickered
about billing; Ruth Page insisted that, as Terpsichore, her name should be
printed on a separate line from the less important Calliope (danced by Elise
Reiman) and Polyhymnia (portrayed by Bernice Holmes).[31] Bolm, of course,
danced Apollo. Kindler attempted to rearrange rehearsals during the very
week of the performance, all the while muttering about Bolm's indecisiveness
regarding the choreography and staging. Bolm complained about the rehearsal piano, the rehearsal pianist, the inferiority of the local string players,
the lack of adequate rehearsal time, and angrily charged Engel with not providing a sufficient budget for scenery, costumes, and personnel. Bolm was
compensated $4,200 for the performance—more than four times the fee
Stravinsky received, largely because Coolidge recognized how much added effort Bolm expended in pulling the production together.

The performance was almost completely derailed when at the last moment
the entire orchestra had to be imported from Philadelphia, doubtless af-
fronting the local string players in Washington. Kindler was forced to travel to
Philadelphia to rehearse the musicians, since Fritz Reiner was guest conducting there and had called added rehearsals for his own concerts. In fact,
no dress rehearsal with the musicians and dancers in the Coolidge Auditorium
ever took place, so the acoustical setting for Stravinsky's delicate string writing went untested. Only a few days before the premiere, it appeared that the
entire production was about to collapse. In uncovering this behind-the-scenes
imbroglio, what emerges is something akin to commedia dell'arte; but, at the
same time, it confirms Stravinsky's hesitancy in entrusting such a production
to an essentially freelance assortment of musicians and dancers. The seemingly imperturbable Engel ultimately succeeded in mediating all disputes, although his exasperation is evident by the end, as he quipped in a private note
to Kindler, "If we ever get through this I shall perform a dance on my own."

Writing in the Amusement Section of the *Washington Sunday Star* on 22
April 1928 (only a few days before the *Apollo* premiere), Helen Fetter provided
a contemporary account of both the hall and the festival. Her article depicts
the sociohistorical context into which the ballet was about to be born.

> The current week has a 'surprise feature' for its finale. It is quite the an-
> tithesis of grand opera. The annual chamber music festival presented under
> the auspices of the Elizabeth Sprague Coolidge Foundation in the auditorium
> of the Library of Congress will be held Friday, Saturday and Sunday.

A momentous decision affecting musical progress was reached when Mrs. Coolidge obtained permission by special arrangement to donate of her great wealth to the establishment of the Chamber Music Auditorium that bears her name. . . . Located on Government ground, invitation programs are offered to special audiences, sometimes drawn from congressional circles, sometimes from local music lovers, sometimes from music center groups elsewhere who are staying in Washington.

To have such a hall under Government supervision, where only the best of musical artists are presented in programs that revive rare ancient chamber music and premières may be given of new compositions, is an inspiration that might foreshadow the development in time, of an art or culture department by the Government.

In the Fall of 1925, the first Coolidge Chamber Music Festival was presented in the Library of Congress. The list of those invited comprised music critics, authorities, patrons, and musicians from all over the country, and even from abroad. With the limited capacity of 511 seats, it has not been possible, in the new home for these concerts, to extend the invitations much beyond the original limitations, but the number is always more than doubled from the overflow "waiting list." Carl Engel, chief of the music division, who is generally in charge of these events, announces that this year the response from musicians and patrons of music has shown that an unusually large number intend to come this year. Therefore, the margin of tickets available for local applicants is rather scant.

Fetter's remarks betray a society page elitism, breezy yet implicitly upper crust, and implying that only a well-bred plutocracy committed to "high art" would be party to the event. There is an air of provincialism in all the hullabaloo surrounding the occasion. Even Coolidge's direction that the ballet be short was consistent with what was envisioned as a glittery soirée. An evening of ballet was primarily an evening of entertainment, a visual spectacle employing musical accompaniment as nothing more than a pleasant diversion (just as Diaghilev had observed of American attitudes in 1916). That Stravinsky vehemently objected to such thinking (as clearly evinced by the uncompromising solemnity of *Apollo*) seems not to have bothered those in Washington. Whatever the understanding or expectation, it is no surprise that tickets were at a premium. Stravinsky's inclusion in any festival was news, but it was all the more so in the still young Washington musical scene.

Much was riding on the success of the 1928 festival. Stravinsky's score, and the prestige his name commanded, was meant to signal Washington's artistic arrival in the same way that the city's striking granite monuments architecturally proclaimed its identity as a world capital. Certainly it was no secret that for years Washington was facing an uphill struggle in attempting to organize a professional orchestra. After many unsuccessful attempts, the National Symphony Orchestra was launched in 1931, nearly a century after the New York Philharmonic Society was founded in 1842. It was hardly a coincidence that the Coolidge Festival planned to attract several prominent conductors, among them Howard Hanson of the Eastman School of Music, Alexander Smallens, director of the Philadelphia Civic Opera Company, Rudolph Ganz, conductor of the St. Louis Symphony Orchestra, and Fritz Reiner (who later became one of the few conductors Stravinsky trusted), then director of the Cincinnati Symphony Orchestra. It was to be Washington's moment in the sun.

The program was broadcast live over radio station NAA from the Washington Navy Yard. Coolidge was well aware of radio's influential range, providing for the transmission of her concerts as early as 1925; by the time of the *Apollo* broadcast, American households contained more than four million radio receivers. A composers' forum was scheduled the same weekend, again doubtless calculated to highlight Washington's pledge to the musical vanguard. Amy Beach, "perhaps the most universally admired, respected, and beloved dean of American women composers," as Helen Fetter wrote, was in town to perform her Piano Quintet with the Kneisel Quartet. Finally, the presence of prominent music critics among the invitees was also purposeful: Lawrence Gilman of the *New York Herald-Tribune*, Olin Downes of the *Times*, Alfred Frankenstein of the *Chicago Tribune*, as well as representatives from *Musical America* and other influential journals were all there, waiting to be convinced of Washington's emergence as a cultural force.

The list of attendees at the premiere reads like a Who's Who register from the worlds of music and societal privilege. An article in the *Sunday Star*, under the banner "Prominent Musicians and Writers Here for Festival," listed most of those in attendance, including Alfred Frankenstein, Edwin Hughes, Howard Hanson, David Mannes, Marion Bauer, Edward W. Bok, George Foster Peabody, H. T. Parker, Alfred A. Knopf, H. L. Mencken, Oscar Sonneck, Mr. and Mrs. Rudolph Wurlitzer, Rudolph Ganz, Aaron Copland, Wallingford Riegger, Fritz Reiner, Carlos Salzedo, Mrs. H. H. A. (Amy) Beach, Harold Gleason, Otto Kinkeldey, Olin Downes, Lawrence Gilman, Edgar Varèse, Oscar Thompson, and Mme. Olga Samaroff-Stokowski.

Conspicuously, Stravinsky's name is missing, and his decision not to travel to Washington for the premiere, even if it would have necessitated some rescheduling of the few concerts he and Ansermet were sharing in Amsterdam at the time, further hints at his apathy. There was no contractual obligation to appear, although in fact many of the composers Coolidge commissioned often were, noblesse oblige, in attendance. Alfredo Casella was there, performing one of his own chamber works on the Sunday afternoon recital of the weekend-long festival. Ravel was there too, attending rehearsals of one of his works that Bolm was choreographing for the evening. But it was primarily Stravinsky's notoriety as an internationally recognized composer that was meant to lend a crowning touch to the event's visibility. Yet there is nothing among his private papers that suggests he even considered making the trip. Even Vera Stravinsky's diary—usually a reliable guide to the daily events in the composer's life, listing almost every interaction with performers, publishers, friends—contains no mention whatsoever of any discussion or letters exchanged about Coolidge or Engel. If one were to rely upon those historical documents, it might be concluded that the event did not occur.[32]

Despite the high-society plaudits Washington won in introducing a major Stravinsky work, the reception the music received was unenthusiastic. The *New York Musical Courier* of 3 May 1928 published a review representative of those in many of the nation's newspapers: "There is not a great deal that can be said in favor of Mr. Stravinsky's latest creation. . . . The score is soft, simmering with a lukewarm hint that Mr. Stravinsky is either no longer deeply interested in originality, or prefers to rest upon past performances." Samuel L. Laciar's headline for the *Philadelphia Public Ledger* of 6 May 1928 exclaimed: "Stravinsky's New Ballet Proves Most Disappointing Feature." And even in Washington, where one might expect a partisan report, local arts critic Helen Fetter had to admit that of the four works performed, *Apollo* fared worst. Her 28 April review ("Ballet Program Charms Hearers," for the *Evening Star*) is worth reproducing, inasmuch as it provides one of the few documented local memories of the ballet's single Washington production.

> A brilliant and distinguished audience last night attended the opening program in the Festival of Chamber Music, presented at the Library of Congress under the auspices of the Elizabeth Sprague Coolidge Foundation. . . . Mrs. Frederick Coolidge, patroness of the events, was present. The little chamber music hall with its limitation of 511 seats was filled to capacity. Hans Kindler, renowned Dutch violoncellist, proved himself a highly capable leader of the Chamber Music Orchestra made up of men from the Philadelphia Symphony Orchestra.
>
> The four ballets presented were as different in mood and treatment as in the music. Charmingly modern settings, not bizarre, but colorful and imaginative, designed by Nicholas Remisoff, and equally delightful costumes con-

tributed as much to the charm of the entire ballets as the dancers and musicians. Adolph Bolm directed the dancers and devised the stage action, showing his mastery clearly in every case. He participated in each of the four numbers.

The ballet was especially written for this occasion by Igor Stravinsky, Russian modernist. The three lovely muses, Calliope, Muse of Epic Poetry, Polyhymnia, Muse of the Sublime Hymn and also of Remembrance, and Terpsichore, Muse of the Dance, appeared in graceful steps and postures about the lifting flame of an altar-urn. The prologue ended and the curtains parting wider showed the stage set with classical Greek exterior, in the background and M. Bolm, in martial appearing plumed helmet and garb. The music seemed flat, insufficient to the aloof possibilities of this theme of *Apollo Musagetes,* Apollo, leader of the Muses. It may be that this is the kind of music that requires "getting used to." The general opinion, however, seems to be that this music was far below the standards the composer had previously set so high in *Ouiseau* [sic] *de Feu* and *La* [sic] *Sacre du Printemps.*

The traditional steps of the ballet seemed oddly at variance with the music even though the rhythms allow many variations and combinations in postures that were frequently effective. Perfect, clean-cut technique would seem a prime requirement of this ballet making the slightest lack of practice or fumbling in a reverse pirouette readily noticeable.

Fetter's dilettantish remarks went on to praise more enthusiastically the Ravel work, since "his scores always offer an exquisite bridge across from the 'classics' to the 'modern' [as] represented by his Pavane." But she did accurately portray the public reaction. Olin Downes's preview article in the *New York Times* on 8 April had noted the unique departure from the Coolidge chamber music format: he wondered how any ballet could fit on such a small stage. (Downes also reported that Stravinsky had communicated to Kindler that the ballet's "melodies will not be the stuff of moonbeams and flowers, but of zinc," obviously attempting to forewarn the audience.) Subsequently, his 28 April review spoke of "a concert room suddenly turned theatre" in which the other three works on the program proved more satisfying than the disappointing *Apollo:* "The music was simple but expert . . . [a] rather tiresome procedure of harkening back to old forms. . . . As a consummate achievement in economy of material, the piece is worth hearing. But as Music that is either sincere or inspired, it is of very questionable quality [and] it does not stir or excite. The work is too anachronistic to give the listener confidence in the composer. . . . The reception was cool."

Downes's review further protested that the birthing of Apollo by Leto was ineffectively replaced "by a ceremony which begins with a tripod placed center stage before the curtain. The sacred flames ascend—3 Muses appear—then when the curtain opens, Apollo is discovered on an elevation with fantastic sets—Greco/Roman designs by Nicolas Remisoff."[33] In fact, the only positive words the critic offered were for Bolm's choreography. Otherwise, Downes pronounced Stravinsky's score an unmitigated failure. Yet it is important to recognize the lens through which he observed Stravinsky's music: *Apollo* was very far removed from *The Firebird,* which Downes had ravishingly reviewed during Diaghilev's Ballets Russes tour of 1916. In that case, every stereotyped preconception of what Russian music ought to be was faithfully realized. The "oriental" *Firebird* was a ballet whose score was overflowing with "music of essentially fantastical and racial quality," just as it should be, Downes noted in his review. No matter that by 1928 Stravinsky had performed such neoclassical works as the Concerto for Piano and Winds in various American cities (and in fact received a fairly positive review from Downes when he played it in Carnegie Hall during his 1925 tour); it was still only the "Russian" Stravinsky the public expected, even demanded, to hear.

A very young John Martin, perhaps the most perceptive dance critic of his generation, also praised Bolm's ingenuity. He, too, immediately comprehended the severe strictures Stravinsky had encountered in writing for such a tiny stage—a stage more appropriate for a chamber work such as *L'Histoire du soldat,* Martin acknowledged. But the review quickly turned to Bolm: "It is doubtful if he or any other choreographer has ever been faced with a ballet score offering any more difficulties." He questioned what he saw as the dichotomy of the "candy-coated" pseudolyricism of Vincenzo Bellini in contrast to the underlying "vicious rhythm and persistent irregularities" with which the dancers had to cope: "The ingenious fashion in which Mr. Bolm reconciled these two seemingly irreconcilable conditions furnished the chief delight of the performance. . . . Mr. Bolm's sense of style made stern demands on his dancers. Faces wreathed in lyric smiles, but they could be seen counting diligently!"[34]

Martin was sharp enough to realize that *Apollo* was not the blockbuster ballet the library had expected, and he was right. In several letters exchanged in the weeks just before the festival, Kindler, Engel, and Coolidge all privately bemoaned the music's blandness. Their reactions betray their disillusion with a phlegmatic score and scenario that caught them entirely off guard. Martin knew the yardstick with which Stravinsky's score would be measured, just as it was measured by Downes. It was the exotic Russian, not the emotionless "Greek" Stravinsky that Americans wanted to hear. They wanted color, scintillation, flair; they wanted the orotund spectacle of *Scheherazade* or *Le Sacre du printemps* all over again, and *Apollo* failed to produce. In his review, Martin amusingly remarked that now, fifteen years after the once scandalous *Sacre*, Americans came *hoping* to see a virgin sacrificed.

Stravinsky, sensing a disaster in the making, had distanced himself from the production as the Washington premiere approached. After the letter to Engel on 17 March, a month before the performance, the only further correspondence was a short, undated note from Engel to Stravinsky following the festival, assuring the composer that "*Apollon* was admirably realized by Bolm and conducted with excellence by Kindler, making for a wonderful evening."

It was the only time that Bolm's choreography was performed, but not because he did not actively seek additional performances. Two months after *Apollo*'s Parisian premiere (which also received mixed reviews), Bolm, back in Chicago with his own company, wrote to Engel on 13 August: "Thanks just loads for your letter with the Klingsois review of *Apollo*. . . . I have seen a few photos of Diaghilev's production and the postures and style looked very forced, like the rest of the ballets he is doing lately. I have always partly enjoyed the new ballets of Diaghilev's repertoire but I cannot help having a feeling that they made a supreme effort in order to be different. That is the reason people don't understand why he doesn't touch them as he did in previous years as there is a lack of sincerity." He immediately followed his transparent criticism with a request that Engel persuade Coolidge to sponsor a repeat performance of Bolm's production in Chicago with his own company in October. Knowing that Stravinsky would have nothing to do with it, Engel quickly closed the door, citing the exclusivity of the composer's contract (the right to use orchestra parts, among other things) as legally binding. The composer was entirely uninterested in any further American productions beyond his contractual obligation, and given the multitude of problems besetting the original Washington performance, by that point Engel had no desire to resurrect the matter either.

The voyage of Stravinsky's *Apollo* has been a long one. It was conceived in southern France, where he composed most of the work in 1927, in Nice; given birth in Washington, where it was unsuccessfully unveiled on 27 April 1928; introduced to Paris six weeks later, where it quickly matured under Balanchine's keen eye; arrived back in America in 1937, where it was soon restaged with his choreography, not Bolm's now completely forgotten version, on 27 April (nine years, to the day, after the sole Washington performance, coincidentally). Finally, the ballet gradually rose to its legendary status in the New

York City Ballet's repertory. Even for a Greek myth, the journey of *Apollo* remains a curious odyssey indeed. The Library of Congress, Coolidge, Engel, Bolm, and Kindler now receive only a nominal nod in an appendix to the ballet's history.

Likewise, this chapter of the ballet's evolution as a valuable record of the state of American culture in Washington during the late 1920s—especially as led by such visionary figures as Elizabeth Sprague Coolidge—is essentially closed. From the documentation that survives, it appears that Stravinsky never cared about how *Apollo* would be received in Washington; nor was he even remotely concerned about the importance of his ballet as a symbolic coming of age in the cultural growth of the nation's capital. From the start, his eyes were turned toward Balanchine, Lifar, Paris, and the Ballets Russes; and, in fact, the work was being shaped in the dance studios of Monte Carlo in preparation for its Parisian premiere even before Engel knew what performance demands the score would make. For all Diaghilev's complaining, the work virtually fell into his lap, courtesy of Mrs. Coolidge. A preservation of the ballet's roots served no useful purpose for Stravinsky. Therefore its history, as with so many other aspects of the composer's chronicle, has been all but expunged. After one performance, and to the near effacement of any memory of the ill-fated Washington premiere, Coolidge's *Apollo* instantly became Diaghilev's *Apollo*, forevermore.

C·h·a·p·t·e·r ·3·

Fathers and Sons:
Remembering Sviatoslav Soulima

> Nikolai Petrovitch went into the garden to his favorite arbor. He was over-
> taken by melancholy thoughts. For the first time he realized clearly the
> rift between him and his son; he foresaw that every day it would grow
> wider and wider.
> —Ivan Turgenev, *Fathers and Sons*

W
ritten twenty years before Igor Stravinsky's birth, Ivan Turgenev's 1862 sociopolitical novel offered more than a contemporary commentary on the wayward son Bazarov's nihilism. As Turgenev's friend Afanasy
Fet observed, it was a sweeping statement about ourselves, our ideals, the
rhythms of life, and, perhaps most poignantly, "the flowering and the fading
of love." *Fathers and Sons* is about ambivalence, about families in conflict, and
ultimately about resistance giving way to resignation. Along with the novels
of Aleksandr Pushkin, Mikhail Lermontov, and of course Tolstoy, Turgenev's
writings were certainly known to Igor Stravinsky's father, Fyodor, a bibliophile
whose operatic career at the Maryinsky Theater flourished during the last
quarter of the nineteenth century. Indeed Igor remembers that his father knew
the author personally. Moreover, the young Stravinsky became familiar with
Turgenev's prose early on. The author's *Sportsman's Sketches,* reports biographer Stephen Walsh, "had already been deemed a suitable tenth-birthday
present."[1] According to what Igor later related, as a young man he felt emotionally trapped by the same perplexities Turgenev thematically pursued
throughout his controversial novel. Fyodor's son, like Turgenev's characters,
was confused by equivocal feelings about his parents, especially the image projected by his intimidating father.

Yet it was primarily through Fyodor that Igor breathed in the exhilarating
world of music and theater. He browsed his father's library of Horace,
Flaubert, Dostoyevsky; at the piano he read opera score reductions of Mozart

and the Russian nationalists; he grew up in the ballet world of his father's friend Marius Petipa, the choreographer of *The Sleeping Beauty* and the other brilliant Tchaikovsky ballets of the period; and, most vitalizing, he was allowed to attend his father's rehearsals and performances. If not already genetically encoded, a sense of theater and theatricality seeped into the impressionable boy's blood. Yet for all this wonderment, the composer's memories of those formative years, as strewn throughout his late conversation books with Robert Craft, as well as his autobiographical remembrances, are marked more by a bitter fear of his father's authority than by any pride, let alone filial affection. There are dark memories tinted by a young boy's dread of how his father might angrily react in any given situation. Fyodor was temperamental, it becomes clear, and thus unsurprisingly he was capable of lashing out at those closest to him, including his immediate family. Regrettably, Igor's youth seems largely to have been touched by a coldness that turned into a deep revulsion. Eventually, he completely dismissed this period of his life with utter resentment: "My childhood was a period of waiting for the moment when I could send everyone and everything connected with it to hell."[2]

These public condemnations surely were proclaimed to wrest a measure of retribution for his father's refusal to acknowledge the son's nascent talent. Igor felt ignored as a child, less loved and cherished than his three brothers. By his mother's rather heartless admission, he was "the least favored" of her children. "I was very lonely," Stravinsky confessed in the opening pages of his 1936 *Autobiography*. He claims to have suffered the pangs of solitude William James once described as "the greatest terror of childhood." That "terror" was compounded by the young Stravinsky's anxiety over his physical appearance: he was short, gaunt, and made to feel the runt of the family. He later recalled that he was often the brunt of jokes and ridicule, and the typical teasing of childhood seems not to have been warded off so easily. Even within his immediate circle of brothers, the physically undersized but emotionally overly sensitive young boy had to compete within an almost exclusively male-oriented and at times brutish environment. It could not have been easy for him. Consequently, his resentment, easily traceable to the residue of his youthful loneliness, manifests itself in his later querulous and at times heretical behavior—behavior marked by a braggadocio orated with his own distinctive mix of humor and vitriol. His childhood memories were indelible, especially the confused emotions he felt toward his stern paterfamilias. Such unerasable impressions often continue to flash across one's mind into adulthood. Sadly, they are frequently bequeathed to the next generation, where the toll of inheritance can reverberate ruinously.

The Stravinsky family in 1901. The composer is second from the right; his future
wife, Catherine, is third from the left.

Can one imagine being Igor Stravinsky's son? I often asked myself that
question during the years I studied with Sviatoslav-Soulima Stravinsky
(1910–94), the third of the composer's four children. There can be no question that the weight of Soulima's burden was heavy, and it directly shaped his
life. Further, in profiling Soulima's father, the interpersonal dimension of the
composer's life must come into play, and nowhere is it more prominent than
in the father's aspirations, hopes, disappointments, and ultimately unresolved
feelings for his son.[3]

I first knew Professor Stravinsky while I was a graduate piano student at
the University of Illinois in Urbana. Thereafter I corresponded and visited
with him during the late 1960s and early '70s. During my studies I was not

fully aware that these years would be among the most personally disconsolate for my teacher, as his father's health deteriorated and their estrangement widened. From a distance of twenty-five years, I now see connections to Soulima's past that clarify how stiflingly conscious of his father he was. Those connections are traceable to Soulima's earliest memories of his father—memories astonishingly similar to those of his own father's troubled relationship with Soulima's grandfather, Fyodor. But they are also attributable to the extraordinarily unusual environment in which Soulima was raised, and to the choices he made—or perhaps drove himself to make—in building his own professional career. From his earliest years as a professional pianist, those with more distance than Igor could muster saw immediately that Soulima was pushing himself to the point of both physical and mental fatigue in attempting to emulate his father. He was often weakened by the deleterious compulsions of overachievement—once in Barcelona to the point of actually collapsing after a public recital, necessitating the cancellation of upcoming concerts.[4]

Every time I looked at Professor Stravinsky during those years, I admit that I couldn't help being aware (sometimes to distraction) of his birthright. I wondered what he and his father really felt for one another, what they discussed, how close they had been, and what eventually went wrong. What influence was consciously or subtly exerted upon Soulima by his "imperialistic father," as Nijinsky once described him? Especially for Soulima, the only musician among the Stravinsky children, what role did the father's own childhood experiences play in mitigating the course of his son's personal and professional life? Regrettably, but accurately, history is likely to characterize Soulima with the dismissive presumption that it would have been virtually impossible for any of Stravinsky's children even to approach, let alone match, their father's monumental achievements. Soulima and his siblings were saddled with a heavy and very public albatross. They had no choice but to survive "within and against the cage of reality," as James Baldwin once described the framework of our lives.

Cultural anthropologists argue that our sense of identity constitutes the absolute center of our being, and that ambivalence, conflict, a balance of dependency and independence, self-assertiveness and submission all contribute to our projection of "self." They argue that self-image is initially imposed on us from without, by our social context, most notably by those who first play the largest role in that context—our parents. "It is not our parents' loins, so much as our parents' lives, that enthralls and blinds us," writes the poet Thomas Traherne. So intense were the irrepressible qualities of Igor Stravinsky's persona that those around him could easily be gobbled up.

If Stravinsky's peers, many of them giants in their day, sometimes felt their self-sovereignty threatened, how much more difficult must it have been for Stravinsky's two sons and two daughters? Moreover, Soulima's father almost obsessively indulged in restless self-reflexivity. As a result, those closest to the angst-ridden composer would always pay a huge emotional price. Who would be more burdened by the composer's doubts and denials than his family, especially his impressionable young children? Even if only intuitively, they possessed the sensibility, if not the maturity, to wonder about his mercurial and sometimes even rash behavior. In the end, Stravinsky may have been honest enough to recognize his own ambivalence, at least privately, but not stoic enough to avoid inflicting it on others.

One must also realize that the composer's children were raised within a rigidly patriarchal family—a deeply Russian patriarchal family, Soulima was always quick to qualify—in which authority, tradition, submissiveness, and deference were inviolable. The children's lineage carried with it not only privilege but also conflict. Each of their individual searches for identity would be trying enough; but to inflame an already overwhelming propinquity by risking a career as a musician, as only Soulima dared, could only lead down a slippery slope. Or was it that his youthful exuberance in attempting to follow in his father's enormous footsteps was motivated by a need for approval, just as his own father had once hoped to win Fyodor's approbation? For Soulima it may have been both: a subconscious and simultaneous attempt to please and challenge his magisterial father. Unavoidably, from the moment he made the decision to pursue music, a Sisyphean struggle teeming with predestined comparisons and insuperable frustrations ensued.

Soulima told me that even after his father's death in 1971, *Le Sacre du printemps* remained the "crux" (to use his word) of his earliest image of his father. The 1913 premiere had frightened him. As a young child, he couldn't begin to comprehend the ballet's titanic impact, but he sensed that its message had rattled the world. Insofar as all children see the world from a self-centered viewpoint, it had alarmed him. He told me he overheard whisperings about the obscenities that the Parisian public hurled at his father that fateful evening of 29 May. He feared for his father amid the infamous riot the ballet incited. He couldn't make sense of the blurry line that sometimes separates villainy from heroism—and on which side of that line his father stood. He only recognized the power his father wielded. Soulima further remembered that his father came to look upon *Le Sacre* with "a kind of revulsion against his own creation."

Still, Stravinsky and Diaghilev immediately realized the cataclysm they had created, just as they had intended to do. Certainly Diaghilev was particularly pleased with the din of its public reception. For Stravinsky, the eventual cost was high: *Le Sacre* became an enormity from which the composer would never escape unless he forcibly shifted direction. Perhaps, Soulima implied, his father always felt "compelled to move forward, to explore in new directions," so as not to be held hostage by the iconoclasm of the tumultuous ballet.[5] In creating it, he had been "irresistibly pulled" by some inexplicable magnet, the composer mystically claimed, and he had served merely "as a vessel through which *Le Sacre* passed"; although hundreds of compositional sketches reveal there was much more to it than that. When the cultural history of the century is written, *Le Sacre,* incontestably one of the great gateways to modernism, will transcend the artifice music historians and analysts routinely erect in their eternal search for the holiest of grails, structural unity.

Viewed at its ritualistic base, *Le Sacre* is a chest-thumping eruption, flagrantly outrageous, defiant at every level, and every bit as exhibitionistic as the nude photos Stravinsky had made of himself and sent to his friends, Maurice Delage and Florent Schmitt, while he was working on the composition. Clearly he was quite proud of the ruckus he was causing—one that would draw the world's attention and, in very significant ways, serve as a new paragon, not only for music, but for how we think of artistic ideas and the limits of expressivity. No wonder the work initially startled his young son. Whether or not the ballet represents one of those bestial paroxysms of the "collective unconscious" that Jungians enjoy discussing, it shook the young Soulima terribly. He quickly realized that his father was capable of creating either an artistic marvel or a monster—he wasn't sure which.

Soulima was swept away not only by the paradox of *Le Sacre* but more broadly by the scope of his father's illustrious life. Yet his memories belie his own vacillation in accepting who his father was. In 1971, when his University of Illinois colleague Ben Johnston asked at what point Soulima first sensed how important his father was, the son responded: "Very early, because there were very important people visiting him all the time and I was aware of that [and] I knew. Children know much more than you suspect they do. I certainly knew that he was a very great person. This was so obvious that it was not discussed." Yet when he had been asked the same question twenty-two years ear-

Stravinsky the exhibitionist, summer 1912

lier, in 1949 (while his father was still very active, and at the same time that Soulima was attempting to break free by making a career for himself in America), he professed to have been completely oblivious to his father's fame: "The fact is that growing up in such a household, I had no idea that it was different." He added that he found it odd that people persisted in asking about his background, "expecting to hear glowing accounts of all the things that make an artist's household different from the ordinary home."[6] But how could it not have been different?

Already at age five, he remembered his father composing behind an always closed door. He recalled listening intently, and trying to imitate at the piano what his father had written (though he also recalled his mother reproaching him for playing his father's music before it was published). Soulima told me, with great delight, of accompanying his father to visit Camille Saint-Saëns, as the elderly composer shared and discussed with Stravinsky sketches for his most recent work. When he was a little older, Soulima regularly traveled with his father from Nice to Paris to see Diaghilev's newest creation. "I went backstage to embrace my friends Lifar and Danilova who were dancing like gods and they *were* the gods at the time," he wistfully remembered. Just as Fyodor's Maryinsky career left a lasting imprint on his son Igor, the world of dance, as vivified by the kaleidoscopic Ballets Russes, now made a deep impression on Soulima (enough so that he once considered becoming a dancer rather than a musician). He was charmed by the beau-monde sparkle of Paris. He remembered the circle of friends who visited his home—Ansermet, Auberjonois, Balanchine, Cocteau, Diaghilev, Boris Kochno, Lifar, Massine, Picasso—and he felt included in the ebullience of the time. These were imperishable memories, sure to whet the young boy's ambitions just at the moment his own talents were emerging.

Even earlier, when Soulima was only four, visitors to the Stravinsky home in Morges reported a portrait of domestic bliss. As the Princesse Edmond de Polignac recorded in her memoirs:

> I often saw Stravinsky, who had taken a house at Morges, where he lived with his wife and family and numerous pale, fair-haired young children. . . . I shall always remember the happy impression I had as Stravinsky took me into his house, for it looked to me like a Christmas tree, all brilliantly lit up and decorated in the warm colours that the Russian Ballet had brought to Paris.
>
> Madame Stravinsky was a striking figure: pale, thin, full of dignity and grace, she at once gave me the impression of nobility, of race and grace that was confirmed by all she did in the following years. In the warmth of her charming house she looked like a princess in a Russian fairy tale; surrounded by her delicate children, then, of course, very young.
>
> I can never forget the delight of that evening at Morges; the table brilliantly lit with coloured candles, and covered with fruit, flowers and desserts of every hue. The supper was a wonderful example of Russian cuisine, carefully prepared by Madame Stravinsky . . . making it a feast to be always remembered.[7]

But this idyllic description differs from Nijinsky's, who wrote in his diary that at home Stravinsky was prone to act "like an emperor and his wife and children are his servants and soldiers." Nijinsky had asked the Stravinskys to care for his daughter Kyra while he traveled to America to join Diaghilev in 1916, but Stravinsky refused, saying that he could not take on the added responsibility, though it was clear that Catherine Stravinsky was willing. Undeniably, Stravinsky, like many self-absorbed creative people, often endured his own children as necessary responsibilities.

As a five-year-old, Soulima was already puzzled by his father's quicksilver disposition. His earliest remembrance (cut from Tony Palmer's 1982 documentary, *Aspects of Stravinsky*) reflects his confusion in struggling to reconcile the mixed signals his father sent:

> Once I was given a little purse with a Swiss franc or a coin of some sort, and I was very happy; but as all children (I was five or six years old) I was careless and dropped it and couldn't find it again. My father asked, "I didn't see your purse recently. What did you do with it?" and I thought my stomach would go. I didn't know what to say. "I haven't got it." "That's the way you take care of things, well, you won't have another purse!" And I was miserable, but that's my first recollection of direct contact with him. I'm sorry it's the contact of a fearful child with a stern father, but he wasn't always stern. He could be very loving. And very rude when he was unpleased. We were too young to know exactly how to handle it, but later you learned not to—and my mother helped very much by telling us, "Don't go near him today, better stay away," and so we would know exactly what the situation was. But when he called me in his room one day, and he had written for me a transcription of a Glinka aria, and even then I knew how important it was. Imagine Stravinsky writing especially for his son a transcription of a very beautiful *cavatina* from *Ruslan,* twelve pages in a little clothbound book, and it wasn't for my birthday or anything—just like that.

Even more befuddling, how did Soulima and his brother and sisters cope with their father's prolonged extramarital relationship, begun when Soulima was only eleven and carried on even as their mother wasted away from tuberculosis? Much that Stravinsky did either personally or professionally (carefully planning performing engagements, for example, to avoid any potential contretemps) was at least partially determined by his not-so-secret affair. Still, Soulima and the other children initially concealed the relationship from their mother and their paternal grandmother. The composer lived in constant fear of being found out, not only by his wife, but—even more worrisome for Igor—by his own severe mother, the matriarch of the family who was then living in the same household.[8]

Stravinsky's relationship with his mother has all the makings of a novel. She, perhaps even more than her husband Fyodor, was particularly stern regarding her son's musical abilities. Anna Kirillovna Stravinskaya was a pianist herself, and her son remembers sitting at the family Bechstein with his mother when he was quite young. In one of the few kind remarks he ever made about her, Stravinsky suggested that it was his mother's sight-reading ability that he inherited. Moreover, Nicolas Nabokov suggests that Anna's regular playing of standard piano repertoire while Igor was a child must surely have influenced him, although he would never admit it. The relationship was always strained, continuing into the years his mother lived with him and Catherine in France until her death in 1939.

Once it became evident that Stravinsky was not about to end his relationship with Vera Sudeikina—to whom Diaghilev had introduced the composer in 1921, and with whom Stravinsky had immediately fallen in love—Catherine accepted her husband's infidelity, bearing it with a mixture of magnanimity, bitterness, and compassion. Given the nature of her marital relationship, Catherine's passive acceptance of her husband's indiscretion is not so surprising. She had always been submissive, viewing herself mainly as the wife of a great man destined to transform the musical world. What is surprising, however, is Stravinsky's self-absorbed assumption that Catherine would not only accept his affair but somehow willingly approve of it. The composer's unfeeling demands on his servile wife surely baffled Soulima and the other children. Powerless in an incomprehensible situation, they had little choice but to internalize their feelings; to raise the issue openly was unthinkable.[9]

When Palmer asked Soulima in the documentary about this peculiar arrangement (though most of the interview was never aired), the son spoke of a closeness with his mother—a closeness that could only have alienated him from the father he so admired as a musician. To complain of his father's absence, Soulima remarked, "would imply that my father had been a little unjust to [my mother] or didn't care, which was more complicated than that." Soulima further asserted that his mother's religious devotion "replaced something that she didn't have and that her heart needed." He added that history had treated Catherine badly, and that although life also treated her harshly, "she came through with an uncommon dignity" that deepened her unwavering concern for her children.

Soulima's younger sister, Milene, was reticent when Palmer asked about her father's secret life. She conceded only that it was a big problem for the children, and that her mother was the person her father "loved most in his life." She recalled that in his final years he said of her mother, "The minute I met her, I loved her and I still love her." There is the air of denial in Milene's refusal even to acknowledge Vera Sudeikina's existence or her father's love for the woman who would become his second wife. Soulima's response, when Palmer asked why his father had treated his mother so poorly, was less guarded, though still dispirited. "My father had a double life and that was it," Soulima answered. "He couldn't cope so it was a reflection of that and I am sure he suffered from the situation very much. . . . I have reasons to believe he must have felt guilty but he had a passion and could not cope with it."

This same uncomfortable mélange of ambivalence and guilt certainly hastened Stravinsky's return to the church upon returning from America in 1925, Soulima claimed, adding with undisguised resentment that religion had served his father only when it suited him. He remembered his father forcing the family to pray together in front of icons, and how uncomfortable he and the other children had felt. The son spoke of a deep dejection and the untenable tangle in which his family was trapped. "What would we have done? Go to our mother and turn our back on our father, or with our father, turn our back to our mother, which was unthinkable?" He also remembers that his father, naturally, avoided openly confronting the matter and would say only, "Well, things are like that and there is nothing you can do about it, that's all." Finally, in an unreleased part of Palmer's interview, Soulima suddenly reverses himself and, attempting to underplay the significance of his father's affair, tries to convince us: "We were not affected by this inner tragedy, because it is a tragedy. . . . We didn't have an unhappy life and we were not marked by something that could have marked other young people . . . especially at such a tender age where you never know how things are going to mark one. . . . My mother's extraordinary sensitivity and courage made it possible for us to accept what she accepted, with no scars."

No scars? When Virginia Woolf, writing in *A Sketch of the Past,* recalls the agonizing memories of her own "tyrant father—the exacting, the violent, the histrionic, the demonstrative, the self-centered, the self pitying [and] alternately loved and hated father," she openly airs her internal turmoil. Woolf tells of feeling "absolved" upon discovering Freud's theory of ambivalence. One feels her exhaling in relief (recorded in her 1939 diary) as she realizes that her once hidden and "violently disturbing" feelings about her father—"like being shut up in the same cage as a wild beast"—were not so abnormal. One wonders at what point Soulima recognized that he, too, would have to resolve so many deeply inured, competing feelings. Far from escaping unwounded, the ambivalence Soulima experienced was transfigurative.

Igor Stravinsky's resentment of his parents clearly stemmed from their dismissal of his talents. They seem to have regarded his musical efforts as unexceptional, even amateurish, and the composer took note of their rejection. The same, however, cannot be said of his own treatment of Soulima. The lean Swiss years of self-imposed exile during the period leading to the October Revolution forced an isolation on Stravinsky from which his children, at least, benefited. During this time Stravinsky wrote, or at least sketched, seven or eight nostalgic collections of children's pieces: Russian cradle songs, fables, and especially piano waltzes. I recall Soulima telling me that some of the happiest moments of his youth were spent playing these duets with his father, joining him in reading piano reductions of the standard classical repertoire, and later, when he was capable, assisting his father by grabbing some notes in rough compositional sketches that could not be managed with only two hands.

It was during this period that Stravinsky composed two sets of duets, in 1915 and 1917, respectively, in which the easier of the two parts could be played by a child. Officially, Stravinsky spoke of writing the *Three Easy Pieces* for his friends Casella, Diaghilev, and Erik Satie. But while these little duets do indeed carry a published dedication to the composer's compatriots, the elementary *seconda* parts also fit Soulima's young hands and, as Soulima told me, were actually written with him in mind. Even at age five, he could play the rudimentary ostinato figures without much effort. The slightly later *Five Easy Pieces* were, according to Stravinsky, written as elementary music lessons for two of his other children. There is a closeness apparent between father and children during this period of family music making—a trying period both financially and emotionally. The numerous pictures of the young Soulima and his elder brother, Theodore, posed with their father display an affection that, sadly, is often missing in later photographs.

Especially in Morges during Soulima's childhood, music was always in the house, and he began to study piano at age five. It was only one of many artistic sources to which the children were exposed, and his passion was drawing and, especially, painting. By the time he was eleven, however, his attraction to playing the piano and composing became evident. He was studying with Alexander Napravnik (himself the son of a noted conductor and pianist and perhaps, therefore, sympathetic to the boy's lot in life) and, by twelve, according to Soulima, he had "awakened to musical responsibility." It was just about that time that his father became aware of Soulima's resolve in pursuing piano and composition. In a 1921 letter to Ramuz, his collaborator in *L'Histoire,* Stravinsky affectionately referred to Soulima as "Nini" and spoke casually of the shift in his interests, how he had turned away from painting and drawing (just as his father did during his own childhood) as he became drawn toward making music. Igor went on to tell Ramuz of his son's elementary attempts to compose a waltz: "Two days in a row he sat before a piece of music paper with a calligraphic title, 'Petite Valse,' followed by nothing."[10] It is a curious comment, but nonetheless Soulima's effort to compose a waltz—no

Sketch for *Three Easy Pieces,* piano duet, scribbled on a calendar slip
(Courtesy of the Paul Sacher Stiftung)

doubt similar to the *Valse pour les enfants* published the same year by his father—suggests an innocent and touching try by an eleven-year-old to mimic
and thereby win the approval of his father.

Certainly Soulima wished to please him. Once it became clear that he was
committed to becoming a musician, his father interceded. And unlike his
own father, Igor did all he could in providing the best teachers for his son, both
in fundamental musicianship training and piano. The instructors chosen, as
one might expect, were steadfast disciples of Stravinsky.

Nadia Boulanger is deservedly praised as one of the master pedagogues of
this century, and it was to her that Stravinsky entrusted the musical education
of the young Soulima. She inspired a phalanx of distinguished American composers who made the pilgrimage to Paris or Fontainebleau to worship at the
altar of Soulima's father. Igor treated her almost as a family member; but she
also acted extensively and reliably as the composer's assistant, transcriber,

proofreader, faithful interpreter of his music, and confidant. At times her influence was remarkably strong, such as when she convinced the composer in the *Symphony of Psalms* to recast aspects of the textual setting and tempi—advice that Stravinsky, uncharacteristically, accepted.

Igor implicitly trusted her impeccable musicianship, and in return Boulanger remained an ardent advocate of his music—at least the music written before the mid-1950s, when the composer suddenly turned his attention toward the verboten Viennese dodecaphonists. Thereafter she disparaged Stravinsky's serial music in front of her students. By the time I studied with her, Stravinsky's later music was banned from discussion, probably (as some of his closest friends have told me) because she simply did not understand or appreciate the vocabulary or the beauty such techniques are capable of producing. In my youthful ignorance, when I first auditioned for Mlle Boulanger in 1971, I committed the unforgivable faux pas of playing Arnold Schoenberg's *Drei Klavierstücke*, Opus 11. She listened impassively, then spent the next thirty minutes berating first me, for my failure to distinguish between good and bad composition, then Mr. Schoenberg, for *his* failure to distinguish between musical tension and release. There was no middle ground in Mlle Boulanger's studio, no room for negotiation when it came to taste.

Loyalty was demanded of Boulanger's students in a cultist way, although some courageously resisted her amusingly doctrinaire maxim, "Very musical, but forbidden." She often imbued her pliant students with a rigor and confidence that enabled them to transcend what some saw as rigidity. Even Aaron Copland, one of her most devoted American students, would later profess that she was so close to Stravinsky personally that her teaching tended to be compositionally one-dimensional. For all the inspiration she instilled in her best students, Boulanger could also produce robotic Francophile clones who manufactured little more than insipid Stravinskyan reproductions.

Either way, questioning her authority—an authority that approached papal infallibility—was tantamount to excommunication. She was as intransigently wedded to her own prescriptive views as Stravinsky was to his (no doubt part of their rapport), and on musical as well as nonmusical issues ranging from *la grande ligne* to anti-Semitism, their minds were often one. But there is evidence too that Stravinsky, with typical purpose, used Boulanger to his advantage, and that the relationship deteriorated once she refused to accept the composer's serial interests. "According to Craft," write Louis Andriessen and Elmer Schönberger, Boulanger "the recently-deceased breeder of composers was just as destructive as she was influential: she preached the gospel according to Stravinsky and the rest was rubbish. Stravinsky more than slightly detested this lackey."[11]

Lackey, legend, or both, Boulanger may have been the worst possible choice as a teacher for Soulima. She watched over him tenderly, and perhaps excessively, though there is nothing to suggest that Soulima overtly questioned the value of his studies with her. It was during this period that the young pianist was learning his father's piano works (written for Igor's own public performances during the 1920s) as quickly as his father could write them. Unquestionably, Boulanger understood the contrapuntal foundations of those neoclassical works and thoroughly explained them to Soulima. She indoctrinated all her pupils in the esteemed French conservatoire tradition extolling the venerable, inviolable precepts of classicism. It was a closed circle, and one that rejected contemporary compositional innovations exceeding its own geographic or ideological perimeter—particularly given the politics of the day. And, importantly, it was in such an assiduous and circumscribed environment that Soulima's formative years were spent. Even if he did have a mind to do so, would he dare challenge the austerity and inflexibility of her teachings? Quibbling over any aspect of her methodical pedagogy was risky even for the most roguishly minded student, but for Soulima there existed an added layer of near familial allegiance. Implicitly or otherwise, in Boulanger's presence, Soulima must have felt obligated—so much so that he could not, naturally, ever admit it.

Stravinsky entrusted Boulanger with every aspect of Soulima's musical education. He excelled, for example, at counterpoint. I remember that many of my piano lessons focused on tracing the interlacing lines of most any composition, be it by Bach or Schubert. Soulima spent considerable energy in showing me how the tenor line of a passage migrated to the alto, and how I must honor that with my fingers, even in filigree passages that first seemed fundamentally accompanimental or subsidiary. Moving one's fingers to grab notes here and there was almost too easy for a pianist, he insisted, and risked a disengagement from the music. So he would ask me to sing one line while playing another, impressing upon me that I must musically negotiate leaps with my fingers with the same involved energy and precise attention as a singer must, and never mechanically. All these lessons, I was soon to discover, were learned from Boulanger, since she also regularly asked me to perform the same exercises in private lessons I had with her one summer. But what I remember most about Soulima's demands (I can even recall his rubbing his hands together in stressing how his fingers were his tools, just as his father once used the exact same expression) was that I should think of the pianist's hand as a choir, each finger with its own independent part to perform. It was much harder to sing a line than simply to drop one's fingers on the keys, and I must be always aware of this as I "connected" notes, he would say.

All this came back to me as I read a letter from 1929 in which Stravinsky informed Ernest Ansermet that Boulanger would now choose his son's principal piano teacher. There were earlier teachers, including Alfred Cortot, the pianist who had defended Stravinsky's much maligned piano music during the 1920s. But Boulanger now called upon her own conservatory colleague, Isidor Philipp. Like Boulanger, he was a predictable choice. Soulima's father had himself studied with Philipp a few years earlier in preparing to play his new and pianistically awkward Concerto for Piano and Winds, the work with which Stravinsky had introduced himself to the public as a pianist. As teacher of both father and son, Philipp's pedagogy should not be undervalued, for in very direct ways it shaped their pianism. His important *Complete School of Piano Technique for the Pianoforte,* for example, was a guiding influence for Igor's piano writing, although these etudes have now fallen out of favor and are hardly known. "I am building my muscles like Carpentier's—a substitute for physical culture," Stravinsky once remarked in an interview while learning the Piano Concerto with Philipp.

Soulima recalled that some of Philipp's teaching methods were unorthodox, but useful. He asked Philipp to help him with the ferociously difficult piano transcription of *Petrushka:* "To overcome the problem of these leaps Philipp advised me to place two books between my body and my upper arm, and to play the passages thirty times, working from my elbows only. . . . The result was that when I had performed this 'trick' thirty times, the normal playing seemed, by comparison, very simple." So, too, I vividly recall Soulima insisting that endurance (rather than relaxation) was the "trick" to overcoming the pianistic obstacles of technically demanding literature—a type of "grin-and-bear it" stamina that most teachers would immediately (and with good reason) reject.[12]

Moreover, Igor's copy of Philipp's exercises, also preserved in Basel, is abundantly marked. Exercises built on the chromatic scale, as well as those employing short arpeggios, octaves, and double sixths, were particularly helpful, and he carefully dated them to track his progress. While this valuable primary source demonstrates how seriously Stravinsky took his piano practice, it also helps explain the composer's unique compositional approach to the key-

Soulima Stravinsky, 1934 (Photograph by George Hoyningen-Huene;
courtesy of the Harvard Theatre Collection)

board. Those familiar with the Piano Concerto, and the slightly later *Sonata* and *Serenade en la,* will immediately understand; it is impossible to miss their reliance on Philipp's exercises as useful models. Many of the compositional sketches for these works reveal that Stravinsky experimented with various fingerings for certain sections that are similar to those found in his copy of Philipp's manual. Much of the idiosyncratic passage work of Stravinsky's piano writing in the 1920s owes greatly to Philipp's influence.

One of the great underestimates in Stravinsky scholarship is of just how important these pianistic, tactile models were in shaping the composer's writing during this period. Many of the textural figurations of Stravinsky's non-piano works—*Apollo* for example—are inextricably bound to the anatomy of his unusually large hands. (Soulima's hands were also quite large, specifically the thickness of his fingers—so thick that, odd as it sounds, he told me of avoiding certain pieces because his fingers actually "got in the way" of passages that were chromatically intricate.) And while some analysts are quick to argue for the novel spacing of certain orchestral sonorities, such "novelty" is often ascribable to how the notes fell under the composer's hands at the keyboard. He constantly improvised, Soulima remembered, searching for new

Soulima Stravinsky, around 1950
(The Fred and Rose Plaut Archives, courtesy of the Yale University Music Library)

spacings of the simplest of chords and looking for new "fingerprints," as he called them.[13]

In retrospect it may appear to have been premature for Soulima to begin concertizing only a year after first working with Philipp. Perhaps he was not yet ready to face the rigors of the concert hall, especially given what was surely on everybody's mind. How much Igor himself cajoled Soulima—ready or not—into taking the leap cannot be known for certain, but there is no question that the father was working behind the scenes in promoting his son's career. Whether he was confident that Soulima was up to the test or whether he was simply overly eager to have his son establish an independent existence is a matter of some speculation. He contacted his own agent and friends in seeking engagements for his son. He promoted him with zeal in the hope of convincing others that the time was ripe for Soulima to assume his rightful place on the concert stage. Yet the fact is it was Vera, not Igor, who attended Soulima's first public recital (at age nineteen) in Valenciennes, April 1930. Why Vera and not his father? Igor may have wanted to distance himself from his son as Soulima went about striking out on his own, and of course there was always his own career and his own carefully guarded time to consider. Vera, on the other hand, seemed eager to be supportive of all the Stravinsky children, although it does appear that Soulima was a favorite.

In the years that followed, she consistently demonstrated a genuine interest in his budding career as a pianist, attending performances when she could (although, given the delicate nature of her relationship with his father, she had to do so discreetly at times). Her diary records that she listened to radio broadcasts whenever she could, as did Stravinsky himself as well as Soulima's grandmother. Vera took a personal interest in Soulima too. Perhaps her motivation grew partially out of her desire to enfold herself into Igor's life as much as she could, but there seems to have been more to it than that. While Stravinsky and Sudeikina continued their affair throughout the 1930s, Soulima and she grew close. Even after the father departed in 1939 for America to assume the Norton Chair at Harvard, it was principally Vera's lengthy letters that kept him informed of his son's activities in France.

Later, while serving in the French army, Soulima would spend time with Vera whenever he was granted leave from his military duties, lunching with her, or shopping. Surely he must have wrestled with his own feelings in sorting out his fondness for Vera from his love and admiration of his mother. And, to a certain degree, he now fell victim to the same emotional balancing act that preoccupied his father. How much easier it would have been for Soulima to think of Vera as an intrusive, evil stepmother. But she was no such thing. In *And Music at the Close*, Lillian Libman writes: "It is a sad truth that, for the most part, the feelings of the Stravinsky children toward their stepmother were defined in terms of fairy tales, lacking only the adjective 'cruel.'"[14] While that may have been the case by the 1960s, certainly it does not describe the warm relationship between Soulima and Vera in earlier years, or Vera's earnest attempts to mend fences between father and son, even well into the 1960s. In fact, Soulima's aforementioned comments notwithstanding, it was not Vera but his own mother, especially during the 1930s, who became a source of considerable vexation.

Adding to what must have been a whirlpool of swirling emotions, Catherine Stravinsky's criticism of her son's musicianship was draconian. She monitored his recitals with unforgiving scrutiny, never failing to fault his playing. During the early 1930s, Soulima and his father regularly teamed as pianist and conductor. Not only did this allow Soulima visibility, but it also permitted his father to take the podium (a less arduous task than that of a solo pianist, Stravinsky admitted) and thus remain in the public eye. But Soulima's still largely untested public concertizing created risks, and he was not always up to the challenge. When Soulima momentarily stumbled in the first joint performance of the *Capriccio* with his father in Barcelona in 1933, Catherine's concern, as expressed in a letter to her husband, ran more to him than to her son. Still, whatever anxiety the father experienced, it was not enough to dissuade him from increasingly employing his son as his substitute in public concerts wherein Soulima often played both the *Capriccio* and the Piano Concerto.[15]

Father and son continued to perform the *Capriccio* regularly, however, winning praise for both the composition and their joint efforts. Ezra Pound's review of a Venetian performance a year later, in 1934, speaks of an unqualified success: "I have heard a great mass or mess of so-called 'piano concertos,' but I have never heard but one *composition* for piano and orchestra, namely Stravinsky's *Capriccio*—there the piano and orchestra are as two shells of a walnut. I sat in the top gallery in Venice, while Igor led and his son played the solo part, and while I have sometimes thought I could hear, or hear part of, the noise of a composition from looking at printed notes, on this occasion, I had the mirage of seeing the unknown score from the aural stimulae [*sic*] offered."[16]

Despite such gleaming receptions, in a letter of 11 February 1935 Catherine flatly told her husband, "Svetik very much needs a few more lessons from Philipp [and] on his return he'll study with Philipp again, but this time [on] technique which, in my opinion, he has neglected." She also related that Soulima was devastated by some of the reviews following his recitals, and how hopeless he felt competing with pianists like Sergey Rachmaninoff, who often played in the same cities and halls. By 1937 Soulima had toured a large part of Europe and South America, joining his father in dozens of private and public performances of the 1935 Concerto for Two Solo Pianos. From the genesis of the compositional process, in which Stravinsky tested his ideas "measure by measure with my son Soulima at the other keyboard," to their recording of the work in 1938, this concerto marks their closest collaboration. It was an uncompromising, even acrid work, making considerable demands on audiences, but also bringing father and son closer together. Written expressly for their use on tour, it was composed to fit their hands. The published score carries an inscription noting that the work was first performed "par moi et mon fils, Sviatoslav Soulima-Stravinsky"; it does not, however, bear a formal dedication to Soulima—something that both saddened and galled him, even when I knew him.

Igor Stravinsky and son Soulima, 1934 (Photograph by George Hoyningen-Huene; courtesy of the Harvard Theatre Collection)

It was also in relation to this Double Concerto, as Soulima called it, that he spoke most openly and insightfully of his father's views on interpretation. Igor told his son that pianists should realize that even though there are few indications in the score, "they should be a little smarter than that"—meaning that he in fact not only allowed but expected them to take some musical liberties. Soulima recalled that the "steady pulse" of the performance was absolutely nonnegotiable; and indeed their recorded performance of 16 February 1938 in Paris is generally true to the score's metronomic markings. The elder Stravinsky's earlier solo recording of the 1919 *Piano-Rag Music*, however, wanders both faster and slower than the tempo marking given, although the performance itself is quite thrilling in its improvisational liberties—just the kind of liberties the composer, in one homily after another, forbade other performers to take. Soulima's playing of his father's works in recital, as I recall, was always very steady, evincing much less tempo variance than one hears in his father's few preserved performances—which frequently accelerate headlong into very fast tempi.

A conflation of rapidly unfolding events dramatically affected Soulima during the decade of 1929–39. He was guided by the finest teachers in Paris, but they were subjugating teachers who decided what music he should and shouldn't like—teachers he dared not contradict because of their personal ties to his father; he was baptized into public performance while only in his teens, carrying with him every typecast expectation of his namesake; he performed in the role of concerto soloist under the baton of his father, thus providing audiences with a vivarium in which to make on-the-spot comparisons of father and son; he grew to trust and to some extent even depend on the close companionship of his father's mistress, a woman he probably felt he should by all rights dislike in deference to his mother; but she was a censorious mother who told him (perhaps too honestly for him to hear), that even though he had already toured internationally he still needed more piano lessons; he served in the army of a country that his father warned was on the verge of disaster and about to be occupied by the advancing Nazis; and, just at the moment that his sister, mother, and grandmother died, his father set sail in 1939 to pursue his own independent career in America, leaving his son in Europe, feeling abandoned—though perhaps also liberated. With so much baggage in tow, how could Soulima imagine himself being hurled into a future that might or might not include his father, whatever his jumbled feelings about him may have been?

He continued to perform his father's works in Europe during the war. By 1944 he had begun teaching the music in Paris. Vera, who by 1940 had become Mrs. Stravinsky, interceded, hoping to convince Igor to help his children emigrate. In the summer of 1948, Soulima finally left France, spending his first year in Hollywood only a few miles from his father in a rented cottage; but in the autumn of 1949 he moved to New York, where he hoped to concertize on his own.

Stravinsky eagerly supported Soulima's early career in the United States, often accepting conducting engagements on the condition that his son be engaged as the concerto soloist. Whether his continuing devotion to his son's career stemmed from obligation or a belief in Soulima's musicianship, Igor was not above angling for his son's success. When Soulima first arrived in America, he immediately accepted a position teaching piano at the Music Academy of the West in Santa Barbara. He also continued to concertize with his father, just as they had done in Europe. Soulima's first American appearance was in Colorado in 1948, where he performed his father's *Capriccio* before a huge audience of eight thousand people in the open-air Red Rocks Amphitheater near Denver. His father conducted an all-Russian concert beginning with the overture to *Ruslan,* as well as Tchaikovsky's Second Symphony, a work the composer often programmed. Howard Taubman's review in the *New York Times* of 25 July said that "Soulima looked like a young replica of Igor," adding almost as an afterthought that he also happened to play well. Taubman described his pianism as "detached," suggesting that it reflected the "objectivity" of his father's scores.

Igor retained every review, as well as brochures, concert flyers, and other memorabilia about his son, often questioning and correcting in the margins inaccuracies about Soulima's teachers and background. He was so concerned about his son's success that he uncharacteristically excused, or at least overlooked, criticism aimed in his own direction. Following a Boston Symphony Orchestra concert at Carnegie Hall a few months later, in which Soulima played his father's Piano Concerto, Stravinsky circled several words of praise for his son in a review by Olin Downes, even though Downes had ridiculed the work itself as "the very apotheosis of the insignificant." It was in fact at that same concert, Soulima told Ben Johnston, that he remembers having trouble playing the concerto under his father, for they had not played together often since Soulima's immigration, and during the interim his father had "changed his ideas on the tempo of the second movement. He wanted it very, very, very slow. So I felt not quite at ease."

By 1948 also, Soulima was becoming more active as a composer, and he published his conservatively conceived Piano Sonata in B-flat that year in London. The work was generally well received by the piano community. One reviewer in the July 1949 issue of *Music and Letters* wrote of its "striking and endearing quality," of a work that was "fresh and airy." But another, writing in the November 1949 *Music Review,* began with what was bound to be at least an implicit comparison: "Igor Stravinsky's son has produced a pleasantly limpid piece of writing that makes no pretensions to importance."

Stravinsky's letters to several friends during the late 1940s regularly praised Soulima, almost obsequiously, as if it were genetically inconceivable for *his* son not to excel. Every recital was a triumph, the father boasted, every audience enthralled, and, if the father was to be believed, the critical reception of each performance unrestrained in its enthusiasm. Despite Libman's suggestion that Stravinsky never found "intellectual companionship" in either of his sons (or daughters?), he worked hard to allow Soulima his own independent professional life, as did Vera. But Soulima didn't enjoy the critically acclaimed career that other pianists did in the 1940s and '50s. How could he? Vladimir Horowitz, Arthur Rubinstein, Sviatoslav Richter, Claudio Arrau, the charismatic young Van Cliburn—all these keyboard titans thundered through the Romantic warhorses with blistering showmanship. They easily conquered New York audiences ready to be swooned by increasing feats of pyrotechnical pianistic wizardry. Soulima, however, continued to play mostly his father's music, while also developing some notoriety as a Mozart specialist. Such a repertoire ignited too few sparks to compete with yet one more syrupy performance of Rachmaninoff's endearing Second Piano Concerto.

It wasn't that Soulima was uninterested in playing the music of other composers; on the contrary, he often tried to strike a deal between what agents expected him to program and what he wanted to perform. "I will play Stravinsky if I can also play some Chopin, Schumann, or Mozart," he told *Time* in a 1948 interview. He tried composing a ballet, *The Muted Wife*, based on his favorite Scarlatti sonatas; but he did so in a pseudo-styled reincarnation of *Pulcinella*—as if the comparisons with his father were not already debilitating. Predictably, critics were eagerly poised to measure him against his father with silly analogies too irresistible to pass over: "Soulima conducted with some of the flapping 'Firebird' motions of Igor Stravinsky," one review began, descending from there into further absurdity. Still, Soulima's ballet was a doomed endeavor from the start, and even the trustworthy dance critic Walter Terry panned the Ballet Russe de Monte Carlo premiere as "long, slow and not at all amusing."

All the while, Soulima witnessed his father's miraculous rejuvenation following *The Rake's Progress* in 1951. Approaching seventy, the amazingly resilient composer, now prodded by Craft to explore new directions, was just getting his second wind. Soulima must have wondered exactly what Craft's role in his father's musical and personal life was. Had he been replaced? Was he, the always devoted son, being pushed away by someone more musically in sync with the voices of compositional change, and more sensitive to his father's unquenchable pursuit of new ideas? Did Craft understand Stravinsky's compulsive need to remain in the foreground of contemporary music? And, most obviously, where was Soulima's own career as a pianist and composer headed as he entered middle age?

That question was clearly on his father's mind too, as events unfolding in the late 1940s attest. On 9 June 1948, Stravinsky wrote to his New York concert agent, Bruno Zirato, arranging a concert for the 1949 season in Urbana, Illinois, where he would conduct. The always opportunistic Stravinsky advised Zirato in a letter, "It would be also a good thing for my son to participate in this concert, playing either my *Concerto* or my *Capriccio*. But try to get a decent fee." Father and son gave two concerts at the University of Illinois, one in March 1949 and again in 1950. A letter to Stravinsky from the School of Music's director, John Kuypers, in January 1950 announced that Soulima would be asked to join the music department: "We will do everything possible to provide him with the conditions which he needs to flourish as a teacher, composer and performer." That same day, in another letter, Kuypers wrote to Soulima, offering him an associate professorship. The appointment owed directly to his father's intercession—doubtless urged by Vera, who remained particularly concerned about the welfare of Stravinsky's children. By the early 1950s, Soulima was a college professor. Whether this had been his life's goal or not, he was now destined to teach piano on the Urbana campus for the next twenty-seven years.

In 1954, the father-and-son performing partnership ended. Soulima continued to perform, of course, even joining Craft in Boston as late as 1957 for a performance of the *Capriccio* as one of three Stravinsky concerts arranged by Sarah Caldwell. Some of Stravinsky's friends who attended the performances suggest that this engagement was a turning point in the father and son's relationship, implying that Soulima's performance was still flawed (after many years of playing these same works) and that the elder Stravinsky had by now lost patience, realizing that Soulima's proficiency as a pianist, at forty-seven, had perhaps peaked. Soulima and his father still visited occasionally, but their correspondence discloses a growing alienation. Their letters are cordial, even chatty—trading political opinions on Joseph McCarthy, Robert Kennedy, Vietnam, or discussing family matters regarding the education of Soulima's son, house repairs, recent vacations—but one could hardly characterize these exchanges as warm.[17]

Yet as late as 1966, Stravinsky displayed interest in Soulima's musical life, suggesting, in an unpublished letter, that his son might consider performing *Movements*—Stravinsky's last large piano work with orchestra—in New York (although the performance never took place). Why, if the composer had lost faith in his son's abilities as a pianist, would he invite him to perform such an important and intricate composition? Was it because he still wanted to believe in his son, or was he perhaps encouraged to do so by Mrs. Stravinsky, who remained supportive long after the father apparently became exasperated by all

Igor and Soulima Stravinsky at rehearsal with members of the University of Illinois orchestra, Urbana, 1949 (Courtesy of the University of Illinois Archives)

of his children. By the late 1960s, as Stravinsky's health worsened, his relationship with Soulima grew colder, their visits more infrequent. As the final years further divided Soulima from his father, the strain on my teacher was evident, as I was able to observe.

I first met Soulima Stravinsky in the autumn of 1967. Just before beginning my audition for the graduate piano program at the University of Illinois, several faculty members filed into a piano studio in small groups, talking among themselves. Mr. Stravinsky entered alone and sat almost unnoticed in a corner. He was a slight man, smaller than I had imagined, although maybe it was just the name itself that prompted the first of many unfair expectations. When he was introduced, he nodded formally with a polite smile. After the audition, the faculty remained and, like good ambassadors, visited for a few minutes; but beyond a short farewell every bit as perfunctory as his greeting, Mr. Stravinsky offered no congenialities and quietly exited alone. I distinctly remember how sullen he appeared, and how distanced from his colleagues he seemed.

When I arrived the next fall, I was assigned to Professor Stravinsky's studio. I remember walking down the hallway to arrange a lesson time. As the studio door swung open, he welcomed me with a more friendly but still rather reserved greeting. As at my audition, I was immediately struck by his almost diminutive physical stature, except for hands so disproportionately large I wondered if the Picasso caricatures of his father were all that exaggerated. It reminds me now of Paul Horgan's description of the famous Picasso portraits as remembered in *Encounters with Stravinsky*: "The hands were in repose, they were exaggerated in order to portray the workman's strength which they commanded. The spread of the right hand was equal in vertical dimension to the whole head."

I was hardly alone in noticing the astonishing similarities of father and son in both physical appearance and the deep tone of their voices. It was instantly recognizable. Soulima, naturally, consistently denied any resemblance: "When I look at myself in the mirror, I can't see it," he once protested. But the physical likeness was so uncanny that, years earlier in 1948, when he first appeared before the American public as part of a *Time* magazine cover story on Igor, it included a physiognomic comparison of father and son. It seemed offensive in its simian detail: "They were almost dead ringers. Soulima's features seem to be just an understatement of his father's—the conical, coconut-shaped head and palm-frond ears, protruding nose with a stubble of sandy mustache above pendulous lips." How many times was Soulima made to endure such personal, physical scrutiny that unfairly consigned his own musicianship to little more than an addendum? How familiar it all sounds as one remembers his father's self-consciousness as a child. And as Professor Stravinsky spoke with me that first morning, explaining his views on piano playing and what we might accomplish over the next two years, I was guilty of the same tunnel vision, hardly hearing a word he said.

The ideas Mr. Stravinsky stressed during my studies, the methods he invoked, the criticisms and reactions he offered—virtually all the comments and suggestions he made—were rooted in either an endorsement of or reaction to his father's or Boulanger's influence. I was bemused, for instance, with his insistence that I not only practice but also perform in concert several of Carl Czerny's Forty Etudes, Opus 337. As Isidor Philipp required Soulima to concentrate on finger dexterity and endurance, I was now assured by my teacher that Czerny would help "keep my fingers clean, like a painter's brushes," in his analogy. And just as his mother demanded that Soulima develop a better technique, I was now advised "to go get more technicity" (a wonderful neologism, like so many of his father's), as if I could run out to the local pharmacy in Urbana and buy some. I understood the utility of etudes; but didn't everyone know that Czerny studies were really just mechanical "velocity" exercises, and certainly not serious piano literature? Evidently not. In retrospect, Soulima's notion about the panacean value of Czerny studies makes perfect sense, especially in light of his remembrance in 1949:

> We were then [around 1921] living in Biarritz and though I then had a teacher, there was nothing markedly distinguished about his method. I learned my lessons, played jazz, improvised, and amused myself musically. Then my grandmother, my father's mother who had lived all her life in an atmosphere of musical integrity, came to visit us. Hearing me play, she was horrified. She said I had talent and must be put to work! It was all very well to play *at* the piano, but it was better really to play the piano! There was a family discussion as to what to do with me, and where to send me for serious study; but I solved the problem by deciding to stop "playing" and to work by myself. For six months, I put myself through the most exacting course of study of Czerny, and thus laid the foundations of a sound technique.[18]

Although Soulima never referred to it directly, his father had, with typical fanfare, crowned Czerny "the greatest composer for the piano." Czerny supposedly imbued Igor with "keen musical pleasure . . . for not only was [he] a remarkable teacher but also a thoroughbred musician." I found in Stravinsky's library in Basel his greatly worn copy of Czerny's Opus 337. It was bountifully marked with his fingerings, along with his own metronomic calibrations, methodically charting his daily progress toward attaining the optimum speed Czerny designates. Even more relevant, several of Czerny's figurations provide a clear pianistic model for Stravinsky's *Capriccio*. Indeed, the 1929 opus virtually lifts passages from Czerny that the composer obviously studied and marked. And like the Philipp exercises, several of Czerny's etudes (all bearing the composer's notations) had provided Stravinsky with an important compositional prototype for the earlier Concerto for Piano and Winds in 1923.

I once asked Professor Stravinsky if I might work with him on this same Piano Concerto. Hardly anyone would know the work better, and surely he could provide some special insight. He abruptly dismissed the notion. Was it because it was too painful, particularly at that moment, to deal with works loaded with so many personal memories; or was it because even then he heard footsteps? Seldom did he teach his father's works to his students. University teaching was perhaps the most visible, individuating characteristic that allowed Soulima an independent professional life. His father's always obstreperously voiced views on the perils of teaching were not shared by Soulima, who either by choice or necessity devoted a large part of his life to working with students. He made no secret of declaring pedagogy his jurisdiction, not his father's: "Something which helped me enormously was my teaching," he once commented. "Now that I have begun to work out of my father's reflected glory," he told an interviewer soon after arriving in America, "I want to stay out." His professorship permitted a needed autonomy, a control over what he would or would not permit once one crossed the threshold and entered the private domain of his studio. Why compromise that control by inviting his father in? Whatever the reason, for me at least, the door was closed. If I really wanted to do some twentieth-century literature, why not Hindemith, he suggested, or better still, I was surprised to hear him say, Schoenberg.

If any composer intrigued Soulima at the time, it was, of all people, the Viennese serialist. I remember his working very thoroughly and unusually enthusiastically with me through the serial intricacies of Schoenberg's *Klavierstücke*, Opus 33a and b. Soulima's love of this music was evident, as was his fascination with the structural basis on which each piece is built. It was not that he was familiar with such concatenate theoretical vocabulary as hexachordal segmentations, combinatoriality, or other analytical constructs that led to a richer understanding of the compositional techniques employed; but his musicianship came through nonetheless. He meticulously marked notes to be stressed, or hidden voices to be uncovered, with his ever present red and blue pencils—the first correction in blue, and if further reminders were needed, then in red. Each of these colorful emendations was entered with great calligraphic attention, and I can remember how slowly and carefully he literally drew each mark. As such, they were reminiscent of the same red and blue observations, criticisms, and various marginalia found throughout his father's library books, letters, and manuscripts in Basel, where, similarly, they are added for emphasis or redressing some wrong.

Professor Stravinsky spoke more fondly of Schoenberg's Violin Fantasy (which he was then performing frequently with his longtime violin collaborator, Roman Totenberg) than any of his father's music. Perhaps this was another concerted effort at emancipation, for now he was free to teach the music he wanted—the very same "boche" music Boulanger was still assailing well into the 1970s. But by the 1960s it was safe for Soulima to discuss Schoenberg with his father. To do so earlier would have been impossible: there were simply "certain issues," he once told me, that would not have been "proper" to raise with his father. Several unpublished letters from son to father, dating from the early 1960s, specifically mention Schoenberg as an awakening interest: "Your little note complimenting me on my joint recital to come with Totenberg gave me pleasure too. I hope we will succeed in presenting this fine music with all the artistry it requires. I have been teaching the piano works of Schoenberg 'et al.' for the last ten years. I wish my average audiences were better prepared to receive them! They soon will be."

The strongest memory I retain of my study with Mr. Stravinsky during that sensitive period was his explicit effort to sever any attachment to his father. Whenever discussing such works as the *Serenade en la* or the piano version of *Petrushka*, Soulima always referred bloodlessly to the composer of those works as "Stravinsky," almost as Leopold Mozart in his later days referred to his estranged son Wolfgang merely as "Nannerl's brother." Never were there references to their many performances of the Concerto for Two Solo Pianos or their frequent conductor-soloist collaborations. Nor did he even once refer to his "father" as such, let alone offer any personal anecdotes about these collaborations. But in his effort to distance himself from his parentage, he brought attention to the very issue he wished to skirt. As rather naive and self-indulgent students, we found the avoidance puzzling. Who better to teach us about the elder Stravinsky than the person who played, recorded, edited, and knew these piano works intimately from their very origins?

On one occasion, after relentless badgering on my part, Professor Stravinsky did agree to hear my wife and me play the 1932 *Duo Concertant* for violin and piano. Finally, here was an opportunity to tap some hidden wellspring. We arrived at his studio ready to learn some closely guarded secrets about his father's music—secrets that only Soulima would know. He encouraged us to play the jagged lines of the thorny first movement more "metallically," as he put it. We should aim for the sound of "quacking geese." Now, as I listen to his father's 1945 recording of the work with Joseph Szigeti, I understand what Soulima meant. His observations were insightful and helpful but, to my dismay, disappointingly impersonal. I couldn't detect any difference in the way he approached this work compared with any other. As I thought about the session, what lingered most was the dispassion of his coaching. I expected more and, selfishly, I felt cheated. I wanted him to share some privileged arcanum that only he and his father knew. I narrowly cast Soulima in the role of a courier. Why would I assume that he would willingly act merely as the messenger of his father's view, without regard to his own interpretive understanding of the piece? It was a subordination he was made to confront daily; and consequently, I believe, it prompted him at times to respond peculiarly.

Soulima could say and do things that initially appeared narcissistic. He performed the complete set of Chopin Mazurkas (more than fifty of them) in piano literature class one very long afternoon, but with virtually no comment, and without any evident purpose. Once he played the Liszt Piano Sonata two times consecutively, pausing briefly between his back-to-back performances to point out some of the work's prodigious pianistic hazards, vowing to correct in his second playing some of the technical problems he had stumbled over the first time around.

He also devoted considerable time to Mozart, the composer with whom he was most associated beyond his father (in fact, he and his father once recorded the Mozart Fugue in C Minor, K. 426—a rarity, since the two almost exclusively played the father's music in recital). But he did so in a way that focused attention on himself rather than the literature. He asked me to learn the orchestral reduction of a very early Mozart concerto for a class demonstration; but as we rehearsed, I couldn't help thinking, why play what was obviously a very feeble work? If the intent was to demonstrate just how inchoate Mozart's early piano concerti were, why plow through the entire thing? But play it we did, start to finish. Shortly thereafter, Professor Stravinsky addressed Mozart's much more important Piano Concerto in C Major, K. 503. Rather than using one of the many standard recordings available, he instead played a private tape of his own performance given years earlier with one of the European radio orchestras. We assumed he wished to highlight his own interpretation of the work; but we never reached that level of discussion. Not only were there distracting technical mishaps throughout, but Soulima couldn't resist supplying a running apology, alerting us to each misstep in advance ("here comes a little memory slip," and "in this section I get a little off").

These were curious actions—whether vain or pitiable, we weren't sure. When he placed himself at the center of such performances, did Soulima really feel that we would better benefit from his Liszt interpretation than, say, that of Emil Gilels? Or was it the other way around? Were such personalizations symptomatic of a deeper insecurity—one fueled by the realization that, beyond playing his father's music, no one was going to acknowledge his wider abilities, so he must do it himself? If the latter, was saturating us in Chopin enough to convince us that he knew more than just his father's *Capriccio*? And why, we prattled among ourselves, would he play a conspicuously flawed tape, exposing himself to the kind of ridicule students are quick to inflict? Besides, it seems nearly incredible that the approval of a small, captive class of student pianists could provide the affirmation he needed. But the source of approbation evidently made little difference to him. Why else would Soulima, an otherwise kind and meek man, engage in a self-serving display of bravado more typical of his father?

Soulima's father enjoyed stretching whatever envelope of propriety tradition deemed acceptable. His mischievous delight in baffling others led him to champion the most outrageous positions imaginable. How utterly different was Professor Stravinsky's manner in the years I knew him. Remarkably temperate in speech, dress, mannerisms, and, most important, in his music making, the flamboyance his father embraced was inimical to him. Was Soulima's imperturbable disposition an acquired antidote to his father's impetuosity? His moderation came across subtly in his criticisms of my playing, which he always offered sensitively, honestly, and with a consistently even temper.

Sometimes, as I entered his studio, I caught Soulima gazing out his window, his mind obviously elsewhere. His sense of privacy during those years bordered on reclusiveness. He wasn't unfriendly or haughty: he was simply immersed in his thoughts, and his disheartenment was transparent. In *Fathers and Sons,* Turgenev gradually shapes Bazarov into a tragic but unlikely hero fated to seek the consolation of his own self-imposed isolation. Did Soulima feel similarly imprisoned, or victimized, or maybe protected by the sanctuary of academe? Or did he see his academic position as a consolation prize? Whatever his feelings, there was a perceivable distance in his eyes, and one could feel him jolting himself back to reality to deal with each day's routine demands.

His aloofness becomes understandable in light of the lamentable events occurring beyond Urbana during that period—events directly involving Soulima and his relationship with his father. Craft has recorded in some detail the ruinous debacle in which he and the entire Stravinsky family found themselves during the late 1960s and '70s.[19] I won't attempt to address any of the knotty legal issues or personal positions involved; I mention it here only as a means of understanding the preoccupation Professor Stravinsky exhibited when I knew him. If he projected some indifference, if he appeared taciturn, nonetheless he remained professional in his relations with students. It is difficult to imagine how he managed to function at all. When I graduated in the summer of 1970, he was as I first met him nearly three years earlier: formal, withdrawn, even morose.

If there was any uncertainty that my teacher's dark mood was largely attributable to the deteriorating condition of his father and his own failure to reach a reconciliation with him, that question was resolved when I next saw him, in the summer of 1971. It was only a few months after his father's death in April, but there was a palpable change in Soulima's demeanor. I was in Fontainebleau that summer, studying theory with Mlle Boulanger and piano with the likable Jean Casadesus. Soulima arrived to play a commemorative recital of his father's music. I was stunned by his playing that day. He performed with astonishing vigor, attacking such fiercely taxing works as the early Four Etudes, Opus 7, and *Petrushka* with a recklessness I had missed in previous performances. As he played, I became aware of this transformation as it unfolded in his playing. What had caused such a noticeable change? Was it the mixture of remorse, relief, guilt, freedom, closure, renewal, loss, liberation and, most of all, the ambivalence that children sometimes experience at such a crossroads—especially children who have for so long been emotionally entrapped? When I spoke with Soulima after the performance, there was a surprising affability about him. He introduced me to his brother, Theodore, who had come from Switzerland to visit him, and he simply chatted. There was a responsiveness in his eyes I had never before seen.

I next visited Mr. Stravinsky in the fall of 1973 back in Urbana. Without hesitation, he now spoke about what had previously been unspeakable. As I sat in his living room that November afternoon, he discussed his father with a candor I scarcely thought possible. He was less formal. No longer did his eyes look down or away. His speech was as animated as his playing had been in Fontainebleau two years earlier. He invited me to examine some of his father's manuscripts kept upstairs in his study. He forcefully asserted his ideas without being urged, insisting that I stress certain of his points. "Be sure to put *that* in your doctoral dissertation," he would say, pointing at me for emphasis. He spoke of a closeness with his father that was all the more touching given the estrangement of the last years. But he would neither acknowledge nor gainsay the existence of his separation from his father during that difficult period. This was still a sea not to be sailed. There was no reason for him to invite me into the murkier waters of the 1960s when the musical and familial relationships had begun to erode. At the time, I did not know the details of their dissolution. Nor did I know the disposition of the litigation over the archives being argued in the New York Surrogate Court by an army of lawyers hired by individual family members. Ignorance served me well that day; otherwise I might have bolted headlong into questions that would surely have offended my former teacher and embarrassed me.

Soulima continued to teach at Illinois for the next few years before retiring to Sarasota, Florida. It was hardly a retirement though, for now he had the time to compose regularly. As he wrote to me during the summer of 1981, he was most proud of composing the first of what would become three string quartets, whose recording by the Florida String Quartet won acclaim. Predictably, there were attempts to compare his writing with that of his father. "I do nothing to resemble him because it would be foolish," Soulima once said. But at the same time, "I do nothing to turn my back on the wonderful things he has taught us through his music." Yet inevitably, comparisons continued, even long after his father's death. One gratuitous publicity ploy promoting these same quartets included a photograph of Soulima superimposed over a picture of his father, with a caption asking, "Like father . . . like son?"

Likewise, many of the obituaries appearing after Soulima's death, on 29 November 1994, unjustly summarized his life almost solely in terms of his relationship with his father:

> His life was dominated by his relationship with his father who was a tyrant to his children—particularly to Soulima because he shared music as a profession. . . . The prickly relationship between father and son came to a head during the Second World War when Stravinsky was in the United States, while Soulima remained in France and gave recitals to collaborationist audiences; he also sought engagements in Germany. . . . Igor seemed anxious to patch up the relationship and arranged Soulima's American recital debut at Red Rocks, Colorado in 1948. . . . Between 1950 and 1954 father and son appeared together on three occasions, but their relationship had cooled, and they saw progressively less of each other.[20]

Even in death, Soulima was first and foremost the son of Stravinsky, and in this case, a despicable tabloidism insinuates that he was a disreputable son at that, playing concerts he should have refused (as if during the 1930s his father was any different). Soulima's own independent accomplishments were quite respectable, yet even when eulogized, they were often completely stigmatized by his father's ghost. The yardstick by which history measured him was simply too large.

He was a patient man, quietly and constantly trying to resign himself to what fell beyond his control. Still, he was beleaguered, and acutely aware of his fate. He once admitted that ("like all healthy and normal people," in his words) he had rebelled against his father's music as a way of challenging his father himself. When Tony Palmer interviewed the seventy-year-old Soulima in 1980, the question was posed as pointedly as it had ever been—perhaps a bit too directly, for the exchange that followed ultimately was cut from the documentary. His mood in this excised film clip should not be misconstrued as an expression of anger or petulance; it is more exasperation than anything, delivered with the same kind of forbearance I observed daily during my piano studies with him in the late 1960s. Palmer began: "But for you, sir, it must have been a problem, I mean, you were an excellent musician, and there you had a father who was another musician, I mean that must have been a problem." To which Soulima responded: "There were problems only with not very sensitive people, and you encounter many in your life. That was always a problem, always irritated me and still does to a certain degree, and when people think of you, of your father, before they think of you, you think it's not right. One should be correct and have at least minimum interest in me. I might have something to offer too."

In *The Devils of Loudun*, Stravinsky's friend Huxley wrote, "We participate in a tragedy; at a comedy we only look." Throughout his life, Soulima was forced to take part in a tragedy not of his own making, and not because he failed to accomplish anything. But in trying to establish his identity, he was hopelessly trapped in one of the epic dramas of twentieth-century art—a zeitgeist powerfully shaped by the towering image of his father. Sadly, his life was lived under a microscope, and perhaps more than anything else, it was destined to be viewed as a footnote to his father's biography. The ultimate irony is that a profile of Soulima finds its way into a book about his father. Some contend that Soulima was a compliant participant, that he willingly capitalized on his father's fortunes. Perhaps, but even so, Soulima engaged in a massive battle all his life, not knowing how much of his heritage he should retain, borrow, or reject, and unsure of the best way to strike an elusive balance. Consequently, he was fated to wrestle with the resulting ambivalence that often forms the core of tragedy. Indeed, it was the same kind of ambivalence that Turgenev described to a friend in an 1862 letter about *Fathers and Sons*. "Did I want to tear Bazarov to pieces or to extol him? *I don't know that myself,*" Turgenev stressed, "for I don't know whether I love him or hate him."[21]

Like Bazarov, Soulima's battle for identity, for independence, is symptomatic of a larger struggle—a struggle that marks the evolution of twentieth-century music as part of our cultural history. The sheer force of Igor Stravinsky's being was as overwhelming for his son as it was for generations of composers and, more broadly, creative artists. His celebrity was so ubiquitous, so enormous that his every move spawned a response. He spoke and acted with ex cathedra authority. Whether one's position bespoke advocacy or denunciation of Stravinsky's most recent work or latest edict, it was sure to elicit a reaction.

One simply had to deal with him, just as the world had to deal with Picasso or Einstein or Freud. Composers either "sounded" like Stravinsky, or they consciously worked at *not* sounding like Stravinsky. Either way the reality of his presence was inescapably felt—just as Soulima felt it every day of his life.

I remember the last time I heard Soulima perform while I was his student. He closed his recital with Beethoven's Piano Sonata in E Major, Opus 109, a transcendental work known for the range of emotions it summons. The concluding set of variations culminates not with a majestic fugue or grand finale but by restating the tranquil, unadorned theme that introduced the movement. With such a simple, direct reiteration, the profound cycle of emotions Beethoven explores comes full circle. The composer ends where he began, but transformed by the journey. His recital over, Soulima was called back to play something more. But, surprisingly, he didn't launch into the kind of empty virtuoso display typical of an encore. Instead, and as introspectively as ever, he sat motionless at the keyboard and, with an almost eerie remoteness, simply repeated the same closing eight measures of the sonata he had played only moments earlier. It was a gesture of quiet eloquence, and of resignation. There was nothing more to say, nothing else to be done—and I believe Soulima Stravinsky understood that more than most people ever could.

C·h·a·p·t·e·r ·4·

The Would-Be Hollywood Composer: Stravinsky, the Literati, and "The Dream Factory"

> I tried to take refuge in my pride. After all, this was movie-work, hackwork. It was something essentially false, cheap, vulgar. It was beneath me. I ought never to have become involved in it. . . . I was betraying my art. No wonder it was so difficult.
> —"Christopher," in *Prater Violet*

There are few more penetrating critiques of the film industry than Christopher Isherwood's 1945 novella *Prater Violet*. Through his sharply drawn characterizations, Isherwood autobiographically explores the nature of movie making and the dilemma creative artists face in reconciling their artistic principles with a crassly commercial world. The author's biting social commentary of 1935 Vienna spans a spectrum of issues he also confronted in Hollywood. *Prater Violet* brilliantly satirizes the often illusive distinction between image and reality—a distinction that characterizes not only the art of film but also Stravinsky's carefully sculpted public persona. Stravinsky knew all of Isherwood's Berlin stories, and the author presented him a copy of *Prater Violet*, signing it "from the Camera" (a reference to Isherwood's *I Am a Camera*, a 1951 play based on the author's Berlin stories as reformulated by John Van Druten; Stravinsky attended the premiere with Marlene Dietrich). The composer would remain suspicious of Hollywood, and suspicious of those who considered movie making an important form of artistic expression. But given his own turbulent relationship with Hollywood filmdom, Stravinsky's dismissal of filmmaking is mainly self-exonerating. The fact is, despite Isherwood's involvement in the world of film, the composer and author were kindred spirits in many fundamental ways.

Stephen Spender spoke of Isherwood's facility at juggling various "masks." The same could be said of the composer, whose confident-sounding music, brimming with conviction, often disguised the interior doubts just below the surface. Always publicly on the offensive, both Isherwood and Stravinsky were privately, and mercilessly, self-critical perfectionists. Both immigrated to the United States in 1939. By then, Isherwood had already produced several film scripts, and he was determined to succeed in the highly remunerative Hollywood studios. After enduring a Manhattan winter, just as Stravinsky did in Boston, Isherwood set out for southern California, joining his British compatriots Gerald Heard and Aldous Huxley. Isherwood "had every reason to believe he might be able to find work in the Hollywood studios," Katherine Bucknell relates. So did everyone else flocking to Hollywood, including Stravinsky.[1]

In selling their services to studio bosses, writers and composers often felt morally compelled to distance themselves from their work. While in one sense they disowned their efforts, they still accepted them as a necessary but alienated brand of labor—just as *Prater Violet*'s "Christopher" dismissed his scripts as "vulgar." Such palliation eased the conscience. Equally defensive, Samuel Goldwyn and other studio kingpins considered themselves the only reliable arbiters of cultural taste. They, not the artists, were the true speakers for the American people. Isherwood and Stravinsky frequently would clash with such potentates as Goldwyn. Shortly after landing in Hollywood, Isherwood recalled, "Goldwyn sent for me in his office. . . . He asked, did I think him a stupid, obstinate hick who knew nothing about writers and couldn't appreciate their work? If so, it was just too bad because although he was only a plain business man, he knew a good thing when he saw it." Isherwood understood the filmmaking métier. The cynicism piercing every page of his prose, as well as his spirited repartee with Stravinsky about the complicity of quid pro quo arrangements with studio producers, helped forge their friendship—a warm one that extended into Stravinsky's later years.[2]

What brought Isherwood and others to Hollywood is traceable to the late 1920s. When Al Jolson, in *The Jazz Singer* (1927), uttered those forever memorable words first spoken in a movie, "Wait a minute, wait a minute. You ain't heard nuttin' yet," he was almost right—literally. Other than a few scenes of synchronized singing that mark the film as milestone, there was no real dialogue in the historic talkie. It was only the next year that Warner Brothers released *The Lights of New York*, the first genuine full-length talking feature. No longer could studios get away with the stilted scripts of silent movies. It was a turning point, for telling stories not only with images but now with spoken words meant finding playwrights who could provide believable dialogue and effective drama. Equally problematic, these imported "hired hands" were serious authors in the business of carefully choosing their eloquent words. But if they hoped to draw a paycheck in Hollywood, they would need to adopt what became the catchphrase of the day—the "cinematization of prose." Isherwood, Huxley, Thomas Mann, H. G. Wells, P. G. Wodehouse, and others would now have to confront this conflict of ethics.

In September 1938, Neville Chamberlain agreed to Hitler's need for more "living space," and Germany's annexation of the Sudetenland was bartered in exchange for a guaranteed peace. A year later, on 1 September 1939, Hitler invaded Poland. Britain, France, Australia, and New Zealand declared war two days later. But the harbingers of a world war were apparent long before. Beginning in the mid-1930s, European authors opting for self-imposed exile in isolationist America quickly transformed themselves into screenwriters. Stravinsky, as well as a host of literary argonauts, streamed into California in anticipation of what lay ahead politically. Writing for *Horizon* in 1947, Isherwood tempered the optimism of what many believed was America's West Coast land of milk and honey:

> California is a tragic country—like Palestine, like every promised land. Its short history is a fever-chart of migrations—the land rush, the gold rush, the oil rush, the movie rush, the Okie fruit-picking rush, the wartime rush to the aircraft factories. . . . Most of us come to the Far West with somewhat cynical intentions. Privately, we hope to get something for nothing. The movie industry . . . is still very like a gold mining camp slowly and painfully engaged in transforming itself into a respectable, ordered community. Inevitably the process is violent. The anarchy of the old days, with every man for himself and winner take the jackpot, still exercises an insidious appeal. . . . The original tycoons were not monsters; they were merely adventurers. . . . Their attitude toward their employees, from stars down to stage-hands, was possessive and paternalistic. Knowing nothing about art and very little about technique, they did not hesitate to interfere in every stage of film production—blue-penciling scripts, dictating casting, bothering directors and criticizing camera angles. The spectre of the box-office haunted them night and day.[3]

Nevertheless, Isherwood sensed an industry capable of forging an imaginative artistic and cinematic synthesis. Whether cinema would prove to be all that Isherwood envisioned (let alone the "tenth muse," as Cocteau predicted), Hollywood offered the seduction of stardom. Stravinsky understood that as well as he understood anything. Why would the image-conscious composer *not* want to be affiliated with a medium that daily reached a larger and more diverse populace than could any concert performance or recording? When the young heartthrob Rudolph Valentino died in 1926, his body lay in state in New York while thousands of delirious fans filed by the catafalque, as if the country had suffered the loss of a national dignitary. The phenomenon of the "magic lantern" was immensely popular. At the height of Hollywood's golden age, motion picture ticket receipts reveal that over 75 percent of the United States population attended the movies weekly. When the composer arrived in America in 1939, Metro-Goldwyn-Mayer's epic *Gone With the Wind* and the technicolor world of *The Wizard of Oz* were about to mark two film industry landmarks. Hollywood became known as the world's "dream factory," grinding out more films than all other countries combined. Through the Great Depression and into the war years, film was America's ultimate escape, be it the slapstick antics of Charlie Chaplin, the dimpled innocence of a tap-dancing, ringlet-haired Shirley Temple, or the torrid romance of Vivien Leigh and Clark Gable.

Stravinsky's 1940 transplantation to the tinseled movie world of southern California seemed completely out of character. One cannot deny the irony in the often pontificating, artistically haughty Stravinsky finding in Hollywood a natural habitat among a clique of power brokers whose business revolved around turning a profit above all else. Yet Stravinsky genuinely thrived there, and home movies from the period reveal a portrait of domestic bliss. Both the composer and his new wife putter around their house, are seen in their garden, and quite simply seem to be enjoying the stability of a home together for the first time—and free from the turmoil gripping Europe. In another film clip cut from the Palmer documentary, Soulima remembered that while many people "scorned Hollywood's superficial glamour of the stars [my father] didn't mind it at all. He would show me the halls of Hollywood Boulevard. . . . He liked it. It was his town." In another portion of film, Stravinsky's daughter Milene recalls that her father reluctantly left California under protest to return to New York in 1969 for what would be his final few years.

Long before coming to America, Stravinsky was well aware of film's potential. The great Russian filmmaker Sergey Eisenstein released his path-breaking *Battleship Potemkin* in 1925, the same year Stravinsky first toured the United States. Even earlier, the composer was acquainted with the rich tradition of filmmaking in his motherland. In her early years, Vera Sudeikina was closely associated with Russian cinema, having appeared in several films produced in Moscow around 1914–16. Her role as Helen in Yakov Protazanov's film adaptation of *War and Peace* was especially admired. Stravinsky traced his first exposure to moving pictures to when he was a university student. By 1912, he was a fan of Mack Sennett's "Keystone" comedy shorts, regularly shown in St. Petersburg. In 1913, while *Le Sacre* was upending the European art world, Cecil B. DeMille was shooting his first film in California,

The Squaw Man. The first of many feature-length westerns, it initiated a film genre glorifying the rugged Wild West cowboy as an icon of America's history, just as *Le Sacre* dramatically symbolized (accurately or not) the primitivism of prehistoric Russia.

While Stravinsky was exiled in Switzerland, several French filmmakers sought permission to use some of his existing, popular ballet scores. The novelist Blaise Cendrars wrote to the composer on 7 October 1919, suggesting that Stravinsky's music might effectively underscore a projected film version of *Don Quixote.* He strongly encouraged the composer to contact "Films Abel Gance" in Paris, because Gance was eager to involve Stravinsky in his grand plans. Shortly thereafter, the curious composer answered from Morges indicating his interest, but cautiously, with the proviso that the proposal would have to be in accordance with his own strongly held convictions about the conjunction of music and film. He informed Cendrars that the idea of setting *Don Quixote* might be problematic since the project initially seemed at odds with his own ideas. More important, the letter confirms that despite his reservations the composer seriously contemplated movie music long before his Hollywood days. It also demonstrates that he had given considerable thought to his own concept of filmmaking's relationship to music—a concept he regularly enunciated during his early Hollywood years. Gance apparently was interested in creating film segments based on the music of two of the composer's most well known ballets, *Sacre* and *Firebird.* Ultimately, however, this early proposal became just one of many that would come to nothing.[4]

Initially, Stravinsky found the Hollywood cinema world alluring. As early as 1932, a letter from Adolph Bolm (who by then had relocated to Hollywood from Chicago) unabashedly glowed with the spoils of West Coast success and prosperity, boasting of his partnership with the stars of the film colony: "I am in California for two seasons making a film with John Barrymore and two seasons at the Hollywood Bowl." The finances available to mount expensive productions surely caught the eye of a composer who even then still scraped for a living while old compatriots of lesser abilities were striking gold in California. When Bolm concluded with the disclosure that "personnes proéminentes au Cinema" were providing a large subvention to offset the costs for his dance troupe's upcoming tour, certainly the composer's eyes must have widened.[5] Artistic integrity aside, is it any wonder that sooner or later he would have at least flirted with the motion picture trade? Several years after the composer's death, in an audio clip from a 1975 documentary, *Igor Stravinsky: The Man and His Music,* by Educational Media Associates, Vera Stravinsky admits that her husband was particularly eager to prosper in the years immediately following his immigration to America. And why not? After years of being cheated of his due, the composer felt, it was time to be compensated for his work, and if working for Hollywood provided a measure of financial restitution then he was more than willing to join his literary friends in such an "arrangement."

A commercially driven Hollywood knew there was money to be made by using the name Stravinsky. More than one producer tried to entice him to write film scores, offering enormous sums of money just for allowing his name to be used on music written by others. While the composer rejected such backroom finagling, the challenge of actual film scoring appealed to him. There was a sense of excitement, of solving another kind of compositional problem—precisely the kind of puzzle Stravinsky always found tantalizing.

Nor could the ever curious composer resist the enchanting, mysterious way that moving images could transport one into the simultaneously magical yet realistic world of Isherwood's *Prater Violet*. More than any other art form, film defines the cultural evolution of creative enterprise in the twentieth century—a marriage of technology and aesthetic expression graspable by an almost unlimited audience. As Huxley wrote in *Heaven and Hell*, "The twentieth-century equivalent of the magic lantern show is the coloured movie. In the huge, expensive 'spectaculars,' the soul of masque goes marching along—with a vengeance sometimes, but sometimes also with taste and a real feeling for vision-inducing phantasy." The capturing of recorded images, of retrievable movement, now enabled by the technology of the age, was just the kind of modern marvel Stravinsky always found beguiling. Furthermore, the fundamental delusion of this kind of "masque," of leading people to believe something was there that really wasn't, would have amused the composer. Wodehouse's wonderfully disarming exposure of the basic Hollywood hoax, wherein "the languorous lagoon is really a smelly tank with a stage hand named Ed wading about in a bathing suit," would have delighted a man who adored this kind of chicanery.[6]

Stravinsky regularly attended American movies released in Paris beginning as early as 1927. He enjoyed the films of Buster Keaton and is known to have attended an early screening of Chaplin's *City Lights*. Having settled in California in the early 1940s, the composer saw Chaplin's controversial picture *The Great Dictator*, but was unimpressed. Nor did he care for the films of such highly successful directors as Cecil B. DeMille, whose *Reap the Wild Wind*, for example, struck Stravinsky as so much claptrap. Stravinsky was not interested in sermonizing movies boorishly portending some hidden message, some "Rosebud" riddle to be contemplated; rather, he enjoyed the divertisse-ment of pictures meant merely to entertain. He preferred comedies, extrava-ganzas such as *Ben Hur,* and the James Bond series. In those that held a so-cial or moral message, as in many of Stanley Kramer's films urging racial tolerance and acceptance, Stravinsky seemed to miss it. Kramer's *Guess Who's Coming to Dinner* was of interest to Stravinsky and Vera mainly because of their fondness for Katharine Hepburn and Spencer Tracy, according to Lillian Libman, "but neither could understand the fuss over the central problem."[7]

Even in his late years the composer frequently watched the most mediocre films with childlike amusement, especially westerns. The thought of the el-derly Stravinsky, one of the most distinguished bards of our age, trekking off to the local movie house like anyone else may seem slightly bizarre. It flew in the face of what the public expected of its eminent cultural icons. Stravinsky should have been at home laboring over a masterpiece, not at the local movie house watching a 007 thriller or a spaghetti western. The composer's en-chantment with movies, like the general public's, arose not only in seeking a temporary respite from reality; Stravinsky was drawn to the big screen for the very reason that the movies are, quite literally, exaggerated in every dimen-sion—an apt description for a bigger-than-life composer whose own thoughts and actions were always cinemascopic.

Among his private papers, Stravinsky retained an interview he gave in the *Manchester Guardian* of 22 February 1934 in which he addressed filmmak-ing's potential, just as Isherwood did. The composer was mulling over direc-tions music might take in the developing cinematic field, and from the tenor of his comments, he was not about to burn bridges before they were even built. Publicly, at least, he kept his options open: "I believe that music has a most important part to play in the art of the cinema, which is a separate art form, only the cinema does not yet recognize the fact. As drama plus music makes opera, so film plus music will make—what? I do not know, but I feel sure it will be something vital to us, something new." Privately, Stravinsky's feelings about the matrimony of music and film were quite clear. He did not consider the interaction of sound and visual images to be an interaction at all. There simply was no real, deeply intertwined connection. Both arts must remain in-dependent—a sentiment strikingly similar to his view on the relationship of ballet and music.

By the 1930s studios had established a standard routine that narrowly and inflexibly defined the task of film composers. Typically, it was not a single com-poser who would be assigned to a score, but rather a music director who was placed in charge of assembling individual film sequences based upon the patchwork contributions of several in-house composers and arrangers. All of them pooled their forces, and usually at the very last moment. Writing for *Modern Music* in 1935, composer and commentator George Antheil described this collective, hurried, and often disjointed effort: "Every studio keeps a staff of seventeen to thirty composers on annual salary. They know nothing about the film till the final cutting day, when it is played over for some or all of them, replayed and stopwatched. Then the work is divided: one man writes war music, a second does love passages, and another is a specialist in nature stuff, and so on." The final soundtrack carried the name of the music director and was marketed as an "original score." But the Hollywood concept of matching score to film was changing, Antheil continued. Studios were beginning to realize the benefits of appointing a single composer to write the entire film score, just as European filmmakers and composers had been doing for years. The advantages were obvious, especially in terms of a much-needed artistic coherence. And with that advance on the horizon, Antheil sensed that film scoring could become a powerful form of artistic expression. Constant Lambert, Antheil added, was right in proclaiming that "films have the emotional impact for the twentieth century that operas had for the nineteenth. Pudovkin and Eisenstein are the true successors of Moussorgsky."[8]

Also among Stravinsky's unpublished papers is a clipping of an interview from 1937 in which Alfred Frankenstein probes the rumor that the composer was considering writing for Hollywood. The rumor was true, as frequent correspondence with Paramount from that year establishes. Both parties attempted to arrange a meeting. His American agent, Richard Copley, wrote in a letter of November 1937 that he wished to reschedule Stravinsky's proposed 1938 American tour so that the itinerary would allow "two or three weeks there [in California] to keep in touch with the picture people." According to Frankenstein, Stravinsky was "making plans and laying the groundwork for a unique new kind of picture." In the interview, published in the *San Francisco Chronicle* of 22 March 1937, titled "Just Where Is Stravinsky?" the composer himself announced his plans: "I shall not compose music in accompaniment to a photoplay. The story and the setting and all the rest will be written around the music, and the music will be composed in terms of the sound film. Thus the whole production will be conceived as a unit. I am not able at the present time to reveal the theme of the picture, but it will not be a Russian folk story."

If he had to comply with Hollywood's standard contractual terms, he publicly announced, he would refuse the project. He would write the music with total independence, and "Hollywood will take it or leave it." With character-istic pertinacity—or incorruptibility, as he saw it—Stravinsky adopted an in-flexible stance diametrically counter to that of other successful classical com-posers writing for films. That he honestly believed in his position was part of it, but also it sharpened his image as a maverick unwilling to cave in. Not only would Stravinsky have nothing to do with music "punctuating" films (as the English composer William Walton once described the secret of his own suc-cessful film scoring), he further declared that the success of any film project in which he was involved would not be measured by the vox populi. A success "with the public is not a matter of grave concern," he asserted. But ultimately it made no difference, for the public was never to have the opportunity to judge Stravinsky's proposed mystery project. Such a "take it or leave it" ultimatum inevitably provoked stern resistance from equally bullheaded studio bosses who held all the cards.

A January 1937 interview in the *Toronto Evening Telegram* (also saved in the same unpublished file) reported Stravinsky's love of Hollywood cinema. He claimed to prefer American movies to European ones; yet in the next breath he remarked that he "didn't find Mickey Mouse more than interesting for the same reason that I wouldn't care to write music for the moving pictures. Too much repetition. I have a feeling that Mr. Disney rests too much on his for-mula." Formula or not, Stravinsky soon entered into a much publicized busi-ness association with Walt Disney. It was a natural news maker. With notable ballyhoo, the pop-classical alliance was covered nationally by every newspa-per, complete with photographs of the two men jovially discussing some fu-ture project. On one hand was Disney, creator of *Steamboat Willie* and Mickey Mouse, the ubiquitous cartoon character who was not only emblematic of American cinematic animation at its most successful (and also immensely popular throughout France during the 1930s) but also a veritable symbol of all that was right and good in this country. In contrast was the famous for-eigner Stravinsky, the great "Russian" composer of the magical *Firebird*. The expatriated Stravinsky, it was obviously implied, had fled his distant homeland (meaning Russia, naturally, since living in Europe for two decades didn't seem nearly as romantic) to come to these shores and pursue the American dream.

Frequently the references were amusingly contrived. In a newspaper arti-cle from the *Cincinnati Enquirer* (clipped and marked in red by Stravinsky) of 22 November 1940, the composer noted the most preposterous attempts to fabricate a link: "Stravinsky likes Disney's general idea . . . to the point that he has signed a two-year contract to collaborate on film versions of some of his other ballets. America yet may see Mickey Mouse liberating the princess in the *Firebird.*"

Stravinsky wanted to be accepted as thoroughly Americanized. The last thing in the world he needed, as he futilely stressed in almost every interview, was to remain indelibly branded as a composer narrowly associated with Russian folk stories. The caricature of the eccentric little man who grew to become a Russian musical giant was just the kind of grist American tabloids relished. Stravinsky was heralded as a genuine Hollywood coup. With more than a subtle hint of jingoism, the composer's immigration was flaunted as yet another Yankee triumph over the artistic restraints of a creeping totalitarian menace then spreading across the world. By settling in California, the celebrated Russian also helped to reinforce an implicit belief: if the greatest composer on the face of the earth freely chose to live there rather than anyplace else, then truly Hollywood must be the epicenter of the artistic universe.

Stravinsky never completed an original film score for Disney's studio, but Disney did use the composer's most popular Russian music for a few of his

Stravinsky with Walt Disney, *left,* and George Balanchine, *center,* discussing some of the miniatures for *Fantasia*

movies. The negotiations and heated skirmishes that ensued reveal two obstinate men maneuvering for position. The Disney incidents of the early American years certainly colored Stravinsky's attitude—which became increasingly
ossified, ultimately leading to total obduracy in negotiating any reasonable
concessions with future film producers about using his music. Even before
Stravinsky's photo sessions with Disney in late 1939, he was indirectly in
touch with Disney's staff. The composer wrote to his publisher Willy Strecker
in May 1938, detailing the possibility of "writing something original for [Dis-
ney], i.e., for animated cartoons." In the same letter, he mentioned that negotiations about *The Firebird* were under way.[9] But before anything regarding
a proposed film adaptation of the popular ballet was resolved, a more tempting prospect arose in 1938 whereby *Le Sacre du printemps* would be used to
complement the groundbreaking phantasmagoria of Disney's innovative film
Fantasia.

Twenty years later Stravinsky recounted the events leading to what became
a hostile, protracted quarrel. He charged Disney with misleading him about
everything from finances to artistic rights, while Disney maintained that
Stravinsky had fully agreed to all contractual terms. Stravinsky claimed that
Disney approached him with a thinly veiled threat, implying that since the
music was unprotected by copyright, Disney did not "owe" the composer
anything. The score was there for the taking. Therefore, the composer complained, what choice did he have but to accept Disney's financial terms—
meager as they were. Even more embittering, Stravinsky charged, Disney
unilaterally decided to rearrange the order of the ballet's individual sections
from the way the composer had originally planned them. And when Stravinsky attended a prescreening, he was apparently horrified. As for the film's animation itself, a by now thoroughly disgruntled Stravinsky could not resist attacking the Disney project by completely dismissing it as a silly concoction
rising no higher than nincompoopery.

When the issue resurfaced in 1960, Disney, responding in the *Saturday
Review* to Stravinsky's allegations, countered that the composer had originally
been excited about the project. He further contended that Stravinsky had liked
the prescreening so much that he enthusiastically volunteered to the press
that Disney's matching of *Sacre* and *Fantasia*'s prehistoric creation-of-the-
world sequence was "really" what the composer had in mind when he originally conceived the ballet. When Stravinsky later reversed his position, railing about Disney's entire misconception, Disney responded bluntly. "What
turned [Stravinsky] against us," he argued, was harsh criticism of the film by

"intellectuals" who simply found cartoon animation foolish. Disney charged that the composer had been invited to participate in the ordering of the film sequences and clearly "agreed to certain cuts and rearrangements." Stravinsky later responded in the *Saturday Review,* attempting to discredit Disney's allegations one by one.

The comedy of it all is that both men, assured of their respective places in history, engaged in nothing much beyond schoolyard name calling. Both embellished their cases. Stravinsky's original contract with Disney survives, although the terms of the agreement have not been released. Little wonder. Stravinsky's uproar centered on the idea of producers, editors, and directors usurping what he assumed would be his musical jurisdiction: he wouldn't suffer any encroachments, and certainly nothing should be changed without his explicit approval. But the contract unequivocally states that he was required to release the music, unconditionally, to the Disney staff: "The said music may be used in whole or in part and may be adapted, changed, added to or subtracted from, as shall appear desirable to the Purchaser in its uncontrolled discretion." What could be clearer? Though Stravinsky undoubtedly regretted agreeing to such license, there was no case to argue, legally or otherwise, and this surely would have flustered him all the more.[10]

Justifiably, Stravinsky was greatly troubled by the film's wholesale tampering with the sequence of his music—especially since the precise sequencing of musical materials constantly concerned him, as sketches for almost all his works show. But it appears that the composer raised no objections about this during the prescreening of *Fantasia.* George Balanchine accompanied Stravinsky during this December 1939 studio visit; Aldous Huxley and his brother Julian, in the company of Stravinsky, also saw the rushes that same month. But nobody recalls the composer voicing any complaints. If Stravinsky was really as incensed as he later claimed, he remained silent. After viewing a prerelease version of the film in October 1940, he was still on cordial terms with Disney, and the two men even attended several ballet performances together.

After the film's release, however, the composer gradually distanced himself from the project, especially when the public's reception of it proved decidedly cool in comparison with that of Disney's first fully animated feature, *Snow White and the Seven Dwarfs,* in 1937. Stravinsky was also offended by the film's vitiating lack of taste, particularly the inclusion of Leopold Stokowski, whose conducting in *Fantasia* Stravinsky found repugnant. He clipped a review about Stokowski's role in the movie, in which an outraged critic's in-

dignation over the film's dark message was absurdly overdramatic: "Mr. Stokowski collaborated to the holocaust of the masters he adores in a performance of Satanic defilement committed before the largest possible public. . . .
All I could think to say of the 'experience' as I staggered out was that it was
'Nazi.' Nazism is the abuse of power, the perverted betrayal of the best instincts, the genius of a race turned into black magical destruction, and so is
this *Fantasia*."[11]

Professional jealousy surely contributed to Stravinsky's maligning of the
popular, self-absorbed conductor. Stokowski was a big-ticket item in Hollywood—an "egocentric," by his own admission—and willing to play along with
movie producers on any matter. As Norman Lebrecht writes in *The Maestro
Myth*, "Stokowski deliberately put the con in conducting. Preoccupied by his
public impact, he was part-showman, part-shaman, part-sham."[12] Stokowski
had also appeared in two earlier films, *The Big Broadcast of 1937* and *One Hundred Men and a Girl*. He was on a mission with Hollywood to bring classical
music to the masses, although in the process his own image as a "star" naturally would ascend even higher. Metro-Goldwyn-Mayer signed Stokowski to
play Richard Wagner in a production about the composer's life, at a time when
Hollywood was considering making several movies about classical composers.
His top billing in *Fantasia,* and for that matter as the personification of what
Hollywood thought classical music should be, certainly contributed to Stravinsky's disparagement of the conductor, the producer, and the film itself.

If ever there was a visually oriented composer, it was Stravinsky. The emphasis accorded the "retina" of his memory (as he once referred to it) is encountered repeatedly in his remembrances. "I have always had a horror of listening to music with my eyes shut," he wrote. "The sight of gesture and
movements of the various parts of the body producing the music is fundamentally necessary if it is to be grasped in all its fullness. All music created or
composed demands some exteriorization for the perception of the listener."[13]
There was an instinctual excitement about the phenomenon of movement, especially the visual realization of physical movement, or "exteriorization," as
the composer says. Not only did it manifest itself in ballet, but Stravinsky's
lifelong fascination with the concept of movement—as evinced by his own hy-
perkineticism—drew him to moving images as well. He regularly recounted
his life in terms of memorable visual images, including his interactions with
others, his initial conceptions of musical thoughts, and particularly his childhood memories. These snapshots exhibit an abiding interest in the human

body's physical energy, both in theater and in dance. It was an appeal that was as consuming as his preoccupation with religious rituals and images, and it was an appeal that took root early and grew.

With the notable exception of his partnership with Balanchine, Stravinsky's temperament did not lend itself to the elasticity required in any collaboration. Within the totally interdependent art form of cinema, his tenacity proved self-destructive. The composer could not be bridled by the demands of compromise. In *Composing for the Films,* a book Stravinsky kept in his library, author Hanns Eisler underscores the process of amalgamation as the cornerstone of the movie maker. There is an absolute need for the integration of "picture, words, sound, script, acting, and photography." Eisler also describes the composer as most successful when the music is supportive but "unobtrusive."[14] But Stravinsky would have bristled at such demagoguery. In his estimate, music must never be unobtrusive. It had to be meaningful, forceful. It had to be central.

One senses his general mistrust of others—implicitly questioning the competence of anyone other than himself to bring a task to fruition. Stravinsky's recognition and respect for the skills of others, especially in areas where he possessed little or no expertise, had nothing to do with his irrecusable opinions. Psychologically there was an embedded imperative to permit nothing to pass beyond his immediate control. Therein lies the nub of the composer's animosity in rebuking the equally willful gods of the Hollywood film industry. They would make the decisions, not Stravinsky—a condition that was totally unacceptable. From the moment the composer decided to live in Hollywood, he placed himself in an untenable position; his unwillingness to bargain with the captains of the film world immediately led to unresolvable confrontations. As this impasse became evident, the composer issued public disclaimers meant to separate him from what he considered the industry's philistinism. He made himself clear in an interview with Alfred Frankenstein for a *Modern Music* article, "Stravinsky in Beverly Hills," in 1942.

> "Film Music? That's monkey business, and for monkey business my price is too high." Thus, Igor Stravinsky, when asked if his going to live in Beverly Hills meant what it usually does with a composer. Of course Hollywood could use his experience and resourcefulness at fitting music to action and action to music. It still remains to be seen whether Hollywood will wake up to his presence, and, if it does, whether Hollywood will let him work as he wants. Stravinsky's ideas, while they can be paid for, cannot be bought. . . . Thus the two polar op-

posites of modern music, Stravinsky and Schoenberg, having been torn out of their natural environments, have come to roost in Filmtown, and the lessons of Stravinsky's rhythmic, nervous, polytonal neoclassicism now vie with the twelve-tone row.

In a 1948 diatribe aimed at Stravinsky, Schoenberg's disciple Rene Leibowitz suggested that even though the two composers resided in the world's film capital, neither wanted anything to do with motion pictures. Schoenberg displayed public contempt for the concept, especially in his outspoken 1940 article "Art and the Moving Pictures." He confessed that around 1928, film had intrigued him as a viable artistic forum, and that he had expected nothing less than "a renaissance of the arts." But he soon realized how wrong he had been, remarking that films (both in Isherwood's Berlin and now in Hollywood) completely thwarted creativity and opted instead for a mawkish pedestrianism catering only to mass appeal. With a supercilious ring reminiscent of his neighbor Stravinsky, Schoenberg complained that studios were not interested in serving the needs of highly educated viewers, nor did true artists covet the materialistic gratuities associated with Hollywood stardom. Shortly before Schoenberg issued this statement, Stravinsky had become irritated by Paramount's negotiations with the Soviet government in 1936 for the "loan" of Shostakovich, who produced more than a dozen film scores between 1928 and 1944 for the important Lenfilm studios. Sergey Prokofiev earned even greater notoriety with films like *Lieutenant Kizhe* (1934) and *Alexander Nevsky* (1938). Both musically and politically, it is hard to think of anything that would have annoyed Stravinsky more than the Soviet realism of these two composers.

While Shostakovich and Prokofiev were being praised for their successful film scoring, Stravinsky considered a proposal by Charlie Chaplin during the mid-1930s. The composer always revered the actor as an artist he considered his equal. He admired Chaplin's films as early as 1915. In *Memories and Commentaries,* the composer confesses, "I was touched . . . by the moral point of each Chaplin episode. . . . The Chaplin touch is in the moral ending. For me, Chaplin *is* Hollywood, in its brief age of art."[15] Moral endings indeed, and it is easy to see a common ground between Stravinsky's examination of morality, via Greek tragedy, and Chaplin's, through his touching, bittersweet comedy. Between 1935 and 1938, composer and filmmaker discussed doing a movie project together. Stravinsky was skeptical about what appeared to be an "extremely naive" concept and a story he considered blasphemous. Chaplin related one of their encounters in his autobiography, hinting that Stravinsky remained eager to find a suitable scenario even after the project had been abandoned.

> While dining at my house, Igor Stravinsky suggested we should do a film to-
> gether. I invented a story. It should be surrealistic I said—a decadent night-
> club with tables around the dance floor, at each table groups and couples rep-
> resenting the mundane world—at one table greed, at another hypocrisy, at
> another ruthlessness. The floor show is the passion play, and while the cruci-
> fixion of the Saviour is going on, groups at each table watch it indifferently,
> some ordering meals, others talking business, others showing little inter-
> est. . . . At a nearby table a group of business men are talking excitedly about
> a big deal. One draws nervously on his cigarette, looking up at the Saviour and
> blowing his smoke absent-mindedly in His direction. . . . I explained that
> putting a passion play on the dance floor of a night-club was to show how cyn-
> ical and conventional the world has become in professing Christianity. The
> maestro's face became very grave. "But that's sacrilegious!" he said. I was
> rather astonished and a little embarrassed. "Is it?" I said. "I never intended it
> to be. I thought it was a criticism of the world's attitude towards Christianity—
> perhaps, having made up the story as I went along, I haven't made that very
> clear." And so the subject was dropped. But several weeks later, Stravinsky
> wrote, wanting to know if I still considered the idea of our doing a film together.
> However, my enthusiasm [had] cooled off and I [became] interested in mak-
> ing a film of my own.[16]

Stravinsky and Charlie Chaplin in 1937

During the period that Chaplin and Stravinsky discussed working together, the American composer and outspoken commentator George Antheil previewed Hollywood's coming attractions. Writing in a 1936 issue of *Modern Music,* Antheil spoke of forthcoming movies about both Wagner and Chopin, the latter to be produced at Columbia Pictures and directed by Frank Capra (who had just won his second Academy Award, for *Mr. Deeds Goes to Town*). Antheil added that these "are only several of a whole batch of 'musical' films." Producers were beginning to understand, he said, that evocative musical scores translated into larger box office receipts. Such film music spoke to Hollywood "in its own language—the language of money." Classically trained composers from both America and Europe, desperate to earn a wage, were being lured to California as "picture music—a new art form—is coming into its own."[17]

Once they arrived, they were often perturbed by movie tycoons treating them as chattel. Aaron Copland visited the studios in 1937 and wrote to his friend Victor Kraft: "Hollywood is not nearly as composer-conscious as Antheil's articles make one think. The whole idea of their wanting 'different' music comes solely from Morros' [Boris Morros of Paramount Studios] playing around with the idea of Stravinsky, Schoenberg, et al. The conditions of work are very unsatisfactory. . . . The only thing for sure is there's money here."[18] Two years later, Copland became a studio success with the acclaimed documentary *The City.* Almost immediately after completing that score, Copland swiftly composed the music for Lewis Milestone's screen adaptation of Steinbeck's *Of Mice and Men* (1939). In 1940 the evocatively set score for *Our Town* further established Copland's reputation as a first-class film score composer. Perhaps most helpful in achieving instant credibility on the Hollywood lots, Copland was capable of spinning out notes with the kind of quick turnaround producers demanded. Once a film was shot, the composer was required to provide suitable music sometimes within two weeks. "Everybody is in a frightful hurry," Copland complained in a 1940 *Modern Music* article, "valuable time is passing and the studio has visions of the money it is losing each day that the film is not in the theatre."

Stravinsky saw *The City* in the early 1940s and went out of his way to praise it in public. Copland and Antheil visited him in 1943, when Stravinsky was again negotiating with several studios. He, too, was quite capable of writing music rapidly, but he would not be rushed by any deadline, nor was he willing to entrust his music to an intermediary music director or studio producer. In an often told exchange between Stravinsky and movie mogul Louis B. Mayer, the composer is said to have demanded $100,000 for completing a film score. Mayer readily agreed, admitting that Stravinsky, as the greatest composer of the age, was well worth it. But when Mayer asked how long it would take to produce the score, the composer asked how much music was needed. Forty-five minutes, came the answer, and apparently after some swift calculations, Stravinsky determined that he would need one whole year. That would delay the production and release of the film far too long, answered Mayer, and the negotiations ended abruptly. Copland was more adaptable: "There is no sense in denying the subordinate position the composer fills. After all, film music makes sense only if it helps the film [and] the music must be secondary in importance to the story being told on the screen"—not words Stravinsky was likely to heed.[19]

The two composers' paths eventually crossed on a film when Stravinsky was commissioned to score *The North Star* (with lyrics by Ira Gershwin and a script by the much sought-after Lillian Hellman). As with so many movies produced during the war years, the picture was intended to portray the triumph of the human spirit over the forces of aggression. In this case, the movie would depict the defense of a small Russian village, so it seemed obvious to have the thoroughly Russian Stravinsky (as Hollywood continued to categorize him) compose the score. He wrote music for the proposed film beginning in late 1942 and well into 1943, carefully timing and marking sections just as he did when composing ballets, since he was quite sensitive to pacing in such projects. But ultimately he was unable to reach a contractual agreement with Sam Goldwyn, even though much of the music was written by the time the composer's participation was abandoned later that year, mainly because of unresolvable differences over the script. "Neither Goldwyn or Igor will compromise," Vera recorded in her diary, "and Igor is pleased that the film project will not be realized." Copland became the composer for the film, and he quickly produced an Oscar-nominated score.

As Stravinsky consistently did with his aborted film scores, he recycled the already completed music into another usable form. In this case, he converted it into a score for Paul Whiteman's popular big band, which had access to substantial funds specifically for commissioning recognized "American" composers such as Stravinsky, Bernstein, Copland, Gershwin, and others. Actually Whiteman had offered the composer a commission as early as 1925, while Stravinsky was on his first American tour. Now, nearly twenty years later, he accepted a new commission and turned to the abandoned film score. He named it *Scherzo à la russe* (a title stolen from Tchaikovsky), and the work was first performed on the widely broadcast Blue Network Programme as a "jazz piece," then subsequently reorchestrated in a more successful symphonic form in 1945.

Stravinsky's *Scherzo,* a delightful piece of folk fluff, is based entirely on a collection of Russian folk songs the composer had purchased in Los Angeles, thinking the tunes would be useful in scoring what was to be Goldwyn's film. (Balanchine later choreographed the *Scherzo* for the 1972 Stravinsky Ballet Festival, with an ensemble of elaborately costumed dancers in full Russian peasant garb.) Stravinsky now declared that the music had originally been intended for Whiteman, suppressing the truth that it initially stemmed from his interest in scoring *The North Star.* It was just one of many black holes into which Stravinsky's memories conveniently vanished in an effort to protect his image.[20]

Vera's diary of 1942 records numerous meetings and negotiations between her husband and film industry executives. Stravinsky was actively courted. He met frequently with Mayer, Franz Werfel, and Salka Viertel to discuss possible projects, including *The North Star.* Her diary entries are telling, repeatedly expressing hope that one of the on-again, off-again movie proposals might ultimately develop into something definite: "June 13: Cohen and Louis B. Mayer here from 2 to 6 p.m. The film business seems to be materializing." But it never did, and this must surely have frustrated Stravinsky more than he was willing to admit. He continued to seek other opportunities, all the while professing indifference. Vera's commentary further suggests that each failed project relieved her husband; but he must have been nonplussed at what amounted to his exclusion from a community where his contemporaries were prospering. If it relieved him so, why did he continue to listen to one proposal after another?[21]

He even insisted on listing himself as a working film composer. When he filled out gas rationing forms during the war, he explained (as recorded in Vera's diary) that as a music composer and conductor, he had to travel regularly to motion picture studios. Later that same summer Stravinsky met with Warner Brothers to consider doing a film about George Gershwin in which he would play himself in a scene meant to reenact a famous encounter in Paris, as reported by Gershwin's biographer, Edward Jablonski. Apparently Stravinsky and Gershwin had met at the home of the violinist Paul Kochanski, and Gershwin could not resist asking Stravinsky if he might study with him. Stravinsky inquired how much Gershwin earned annually. Taken aback by the question, Gershwin quickly calculated that he earned "a sum that ran into six figures." Stravinsky immediately responded, in a characteristic quip, "In that case . . . I should study with you." Of course Gershwin never did study with Stravinsky, nor did the film that was eventually made about Gershwin include a cameo appearance by the elder composer.[22]

It is difficult to determine exactly how many film proposals Stravinsky seriously considered, let alone to track the music he began but never finished. In at least five cases, there are documented conversions of film-born scores into symphonic works or other musical forms. The unfinished film music that he turned into the *Scherzo* for Whiteman was not the first commission the composer had received. In 1941 he was asked to score a film about the invasion of Norway. It was, like *The North Star,* one of many "authentic" war films—authentic in that the casting included refugees and military forces that had actually been involved in the incident as a way of lending a sheen of historical realism to the movie. Stravinsky incorporated Norwegian folk tunes as a way of thematically connecting the work, but his score for the movie (eventually titled *The Commandos Strike at Dawn* and released in 1942, featuring Paul Muni, with music by Louis Gruenberg), was never used. Instead the composer salvaged the music, rewriting it as an orchestral concert suite of four pieces under the name *Four Norwegian Moods,* one of Stravinsky's lesser known works.

Another movie, *The Song of Bernadette* (1943), was based on a novel by Werfel, who was a friend of Stravinsky; several of his other Hollywood friends were cast, including Vincent Price and Jennifer Jones. Certainly the composer was motivated to be part of the Werfel-inspired project, admitting that "I was attracted by the idea and by his script." But once more he could not reach an agreement, since the contractual conditions were "so entirely in favour of the film producer," and his inability to work with the required flexibility film scoring demands again brought his participation to a halt. Alfred Newman completed the Academy Award–winning score, one of four Oscars the Henry King–directed film garnered. The highly successful Newman admitted his own frustrations in working with Hollywood's autocrats. He constantly skirmished with "musically ignorant directors or producers, trying to dissuade them from spoiling their pictures with banal, conventional, or ill-chosen approaches to their scores," according to Robert R. Faulkner.[23] As with earlier projects, Stravinsky completed a large portion of the score, eventually employing music written for the movie's "Apparition of the Virgin" scene as the middle movement of his Symphony in Three Movements, which was first performed in 1946 by the New York Philharmonic Orchestra.

Stravinsky originally intended the composition as a pure symphonic work, and the first movement was actually finished before Werfel approached him about the film project. The composer confirmed that the work came as close to being a "war symphony" as anything he wrote—and certainly it is as programmatic a piece as any he completed—especially in the first and last movements, which he said were intended to portray the grim casualties of war. The opening movement reflects his response to a documentary film depicting the "scorched-earth tactics in China," as Stravinsky described it. The third and final movement was also inspired by his viewing of newsreels and documentaries—grim footage of the ravages perpetrated by Hitler's war machine.[24] The fact that the music separating these two programmatic movements was conceived as an accompaniment to a film based on a religious theme could never be guessed. And while the music was a "failure" for Hollywood, it makes perfect sense as one of "Three Symphonic Movements," as Stravinsky once dubbed the symphony, thinking it a "more exact title."

Other sketches found in the Basel archives are among the manuscripts for what eventually became the Sonata for Two Pianos, completed in 1944. Sections of the work were originally drafted for orchestra and again first conceived as a film. The Russian folk melodies pervading the little Sonata are drawn from the same collection of folk songs Stravinsky used in preparing music he thought would be used for *The North Star*. But he did not begin sketching the work until after negotiations for that movie failed, leading one to believe that he may have immediately sensed that some of the same music might now be transplanted to another film project—perhaps the one discussed with Warner Brothers six months or so after Stravinsky broke off negotiations with Goldwyn. Once that possibility also failed to materialize, the composer may have reworked the material into a piece for two pianos, a medium with which he was quite comfortable. While it seems perfectly reasonable to use the music in a new form rather than forsake it entirely, it also suggests that the original scores Stravinsky wrote for all these unrealized projects were not so integrally bound to their film plots; otherwise they may not have been so easily disassembled and rewritten as concert music. Certainly such refurbishing attests to the composer's resourcefulness; but it also hints that the original scores may not have been appropriately accompanimental to begin with—and that is likely what directors and producers missed when they found the music ill-suited for their cinematic purposes.

Of all the music refashioned after film negotiations collapsed, the most interesting is the 1943 *Ode*. Its interest arises not from the composition itself (a secondary work, although it was performed by Koussevitzky and broadcast over the Blue Network) but from the circumstances leading to its conception. It began at the suggestion of Orson Welles, whose *Citizen Kane* in 1941 had impressed Stravinsky. A new cinematic technology allowing cameras to shoot with greater depth, producing more realistic shadowing, added to Welles's already powerful award-winning film. Stravinsky was struck by Welles's vision, and they agreed to work together. Welles's next project was David O. Selznick's *Jane Eyre*. The appeal was all the greater for Stravinsky as his friend Aldous Huxley was preparing the screenplay with Robert Stevenson and John Houseman.

Additionally, the composer remembers being intrigued by both the book and the Brontë sisters. His library included many of their books, which he procured in preparation for writing the film score. One even senses an empathy between Stravinsky and Charlotte Brontë as she outlines her views in the novel's original 1847 preface—views that Stravinsky would have endorsed: "Conventionality is not morality," Brontë writes. "Appearance should not be mistaken for truth. . . . The world may not like to see these ideas dissevered for it has been accustomed to blend them. . . . It may hate him who dares to scrutinise and expose . . . but hate as it will, it is indebted to him." Brontë's wariness in forewarning her readers was just the kind of preemption Stravinsky regularly invoked in introducing new compositions. Even the novel's main character has a Stravinskyan defiance about her. Her way of avoiding hell's pit of fire was simple: "I must keep in good health and not die." She questioned Brocklehurst's authority; she dared to "judge" the opinions of her lord and master, Edward Rochester; and, above all, she chose self-sufficiency at personal cost rather than curtsy to anyone. Through characters like Jane, Charlotte Brontë communicated a mix of emotionalism and rationality that the composer understood.

In consulting the various unpublished papers and sketches in Basel, it comes as no surprise that the conscientious Stravinsky undertook the film with characteristic diligence, reading many of the Brontës' books and even studying analytic commentaries about the significance of their writings. The idea of the newly immigrated composer, whose English was by no means fluent, throwing himself into writing music for a thoroughly English scenario seems rather peculiar; but if nothing else it presented an ideal opportunity to defy Hollywood's bias that Stravinsky could only write Russian music. He immersed himself in a study of source materials that he thought would help him prepare for the film. His library contains a copy of *The Melodist*, an anthology of English, Scotch, and Irish songs, and his unpublished sketches disclose that he meticulously transcribed nine models in preparing to enfold several of these folklike tunes into the film. The sketches show that Stravinsky chose tunes that were easily identifiable with the "landscape" of the film—just the kind of superficially programmatic association about which Stravinsky always protested but the producers demanded.

Even more poignant is an unpublished draft of Stravinsky's struggle to translate, sometimes in Russian and French, colloquialisms such as "by and by," "to and fro," "as of old," "whither." The composer also synopsized specific parts of the screenplay for his own study. In contemplating how he might envision the music for certain sections, he summarized such key scenes as Jane standing at the top of the steps in Thornfield Hall. Here his notes reveal that he planned a "lady's solo followed by a duet." And in another famous segment, which in the 1944 film shows Joan Fontaine (with whom Stravinsky was quite taken) playing the piano, Stravinsky had initially thought about drafting an "accompaniment in spirited style." If Stravinsky believed, as he publicly claimed, that film music should not stoop to merely mimicking the action or mood of a scene, there is no evidence here. On the contrary, these unpublished materials reveal a conciliating composer working hard to make very explicit associations between musical and cinematic elements. In this case at least, Stravinsky was interested in winning the producer's approbation, and he was therefore willing to write "background" music.[25]

Stravinsky wrote music specifically for the film's crucial hunting scene, whereupon Jane first meets Edward Rochester. But the music was never used for the Twentieth Century–Fox production. The scoring was probably too well-developed, too prominent in competing for the viewer's attention. The camera took as its priority Welles as the Byronic-looking Rochester, who literally gallops into the story. Negotiations once again broke off, and none of the composer's music was used in the film. Since the score was unusable for the film, Stravinsky rewrote the music under the new title of "Eclogue," inserting it as the central movement of his *Ode*. The revised orchestral work was premiered by the Boston Symphony Orchestra later in 1943.

From that point on, and with notable supererogation, his public rancor over the execrable nature of film music steadily grew. Yet despite his captious gibes at the industry as a whole, Stravinsky maintained congenial relations with some of the leading actors, actresses, columnists, and directors of the '30s and '40s—lunching with Marlene Dietrich, dining with Hedda Hopper,

Bette Davis, Cecil B. DeMille, being seen at parties with Katharine Hepburn, consulting with *Casablanca*'s music director, Max Steiner, attending charity golf tournaments with Bob Hope and Bing Crosby, trading jabs with Groucho Marx. While music history is quick to dismiss Stravinsky's early Hollywood years as an interregnum marked by glad-handing parties and a series of failed film scores, it was in fact a period of considerable cultural broadening. Far more relevant than some of the negligible music he salvaged from would-be movie scores, the composer's inclusion in a community of distinguished literati in Los Angeles was critical to Stravinsky's American acculturation. The camaraderie he enjoyed with some of the foremost authors of the day soon grew into stimulating, long-lasting friendships, influential and as puissant in shaping his time in America as those of earlier years in St. Petersburg and Paris. W. H. Auden once referred to Stravinsky's cronies in those early California days as "the Oxford literary gang," and Stravinsky was welcomed into the circle. This coterie deserves special attention, as does the context of events and ideologies to which the composer was exposed.

The steady exodus of refugees from Germany, France, and England, situated squarely in Hitler's warpath, brought an amazingly diversified and distinguished émigré community to southern California. Isherwood was only one of several gifted British writers who took up screenwriting as a livelihood. Because Stravinsky's earlier European visits to a sanitarium in southern France had temporarily alleviated his persistent lung problems, his relocation to Los Angeles (then still with smog-free air) seemed advisable. Others did the same. Thomas Mann, whose tubercular wife, like Catherine Stravinsky, had spent extended periods of recovery in Swiss sanitariums in the early 1920s (experiences that led to Mann's *Magic Mountain* in 1924), also found California's salubrious climate inviting. Stravinsky knew Mann from the early Diaghilev days, and they renewed their friendship in the 1920s in Switzerland. While history principally associates Mann with Arnold Schoenberg, in *The Story of a Novel* he mentions discussing Schoenberg's music with Stravinsky. It was shortly after doing so, in fact, in the spring of 1943, that Mann began writing *Doctor Faustus*.

Similarly, sunny California attracted Huxley, who purportedly moved there to repair his failing eyesight. The growing colony of European artists around Los Angeles also served as a powerful magnet for Huxley, H. G. Wells, Mann, Stravinsky, and many others. To understand fully Stravinsky's desire to be a part of the film world, one must recognize the composer's sympathetic feelings for an elite cadre of professional writers forced to turn their energies to churning out humdrum scripts. This is especially so in the case of Huxley, whose relationship with Stravinsky was very influential.

Huxley, in fact, had been trained as a pianist even as a boy. He studied the standard repertoire, including Bach, Chopin, and especially the composer he held in higher esteem than any other, Beethoven. Like Stravinsky, apparently, he enjoyed improvising and found it difficult to discipline himself to stick with a printed score until it was mastered. Because of his impaired vision, he often learned scores by Braille, slowly but eagerly acquainting himself with a wide array of music, including piano reductions of Wagner's operas. It is little wonder that his youthful love of music later manifested itself in so many of his short stories, such as the *Farcical History of Richard Greenow,* or in his more widely known novels, including *Point Counter Point.* Nor should we forget the more than sixty articles and reviews he filed in 1922–23 for the *Weekly Westminster Gazette* as its resident music critic—perceptive and sometimes blistering pieces that proclaimed his viewpoint with a nonnegotiable certainty that Stravinsky would have admired. Huxley was, declared Basil Hogarth in *The Musical Times,* "in some respects the most remarkable literary man who has ever written on musical subjects."

Perhaps, but even so, Stravinsky would surely have bristled over Huxley's early swipes at some of his music. Indeed, with the exception of his scorn for Bartók (a minor composer, he declared—a sentiment with which Stravinsky may well have agreed) Stravinsky was his favorite target. Reviewing a performance by the Ballets Russes of the composer's 1922 opera buffa, *Mavra,* Huxley found the work "depressing in spite of its gaiety . . . depressing because [of] its prodigious triviality." He blamed Stravinsky, as a principal rabble-rouser, for encouraging an interest in jazz—an interest that expresses itself in "every shade of all the baser emotions, from a baboon-like lust to a nauseating self-commiseration, from the mindless mass hysteria of howling mobs to a languishing masturbatory *träumerei.*" The composer's own *Ragtime,* for instance, was soulless and mechanical. And in one sweeping dismissal, he confidently asserted that history eventually would be amazed that young French composers of the early 1920s such as Stravinsky would be remembered "as anything more than a bad joke. Some of us even now are astonished."[26]

They first met in 1928 in London, where, coincidentally, they attended a film together (Tolstoy's *Resurrection*). Huxley came to the United States in 1937, a particularly pivotal year in how the United States looked at itself and its shrinking hopes of isolationism. The prospect of war increasingly intruded

on the thinking of Americans. While that same year Picasso graphically captured the horrors of fascism in the massive *Guernica*, Huxley took an altogether different direction, presenting a series of lectures on the corrosion
of human civility. For many, his relocation to Hollywood, like Stravinsky's,
seemed derelict and money grubbing. Americans were offended by Huxley's
grandiloquent homilies on global obliteration brought about by the reckless
abuse of governmental powers and the rise of technocracy. But he offered his
voluble observations even as he himself enjoyed a comfortable living far away
from the mounting deprivation and tragedies of the late 1930s. It was a common dilemma that many expatriate artists faced, and one with which Stravinsky certainly identified.

Spender addressed the problem in a *Horizon* article of January 1940 titled
"How Shall We Be Saved?" With the waning prospect of political compromise
as a peaceful means of preventing further atrocities of war, he argued that "not
only writers but all thinking people [were] in a position of comparative isolation." Spender cited the recent release of four timely books by Wells, Gerald
Heard, T. S. Eliot, and especially Huxley, with *After Many a Summer,* as well-
meaning attempts to deal with the impending "catastrophe" of the world. All
pleaded for global disarmament. Two years later, in June 1942, the razing of
Lidice by the Nazis horrified the world; Dwight D. Eisenhower landed in London; and the U.S. War Department launched the Manhattan Project. Spender
valiantly rose to the defense of Heard's and Huxley's decision to tackle such
momentous issues from the asylum of their adopted California residence.
Long before the Woodstock generation of the 1960s, Spender endorsed
Heard's and Huxley's mysticism, their supernatural experiences, their Yoga
philosophy, their Zen-like desire to attain enlightenment through meditation,
their Bloomsbury lifestyle, and their hope to seek "timeless eternity."

Of course Hollywood did not care in the least about anything so vaporous
as "timeless eternity." The industry functioned in the present tense, and bot-
tom-line economics was all that counted. "MGM wanted the luster of Huxley's fame," writes David Dunaway in his informative monograph about Huxley's California years; "the name alone was impressive, indicating that Hollywood could buy anything it wanted." It is apparent from a 1937 letter by his
wife, Maria, that he considered relocating to California primarily because
"writers made royal sums in the movies." In a subsequent letter, Maria Huxley admitted that her husband would consider such work only if he were to be
"fabulously paid . . . and even then Aldous is horrified, though fascinated, by
the prospect of being tied to this horrible life."[27] By 1940, a growing number

of critics charged that Huxley had sold out twice: first, by fleeing his country under what some complained was a fanatical but opportune adoption of pacifism, and second, by becoming engrossed with show business solely for profit. They were the very same accusations that shadowed Stravinsky.

Auden's self-styled libertine politics during the 1930s challenged social iniquities from capitalism to fascism. His views were pugnacious by design, endearing him to a composer who always placed a premium on bedevilment. He collaborated frequently with Isherwood during those years and was hailed as the greatest British poet since Yeats (who died in 1939, the same year Auden arrived in America, after having married Mann's daughter a few years earlier as a way of providing legal passage for her from Britain). Auden's strict upbringing in a devoutly Anglo-Catholic home left a deep imprint: he was awed by the "exciting magical rites" of religious ritual—yet another deeply rooted commonality with Stravinsky. His writing ranged over topics from religion to psychology, and he too became part of Stravinsky's literary circle and later collaborated with the composer on *The Rake's Progress*.

A contrarian by nature, Stravinsky relished the company of these impassioned men of letters. He recalled that he and Isherwood went to the beach once a week and got drunk; but Dunaway adds that they did so in an area of Santa Monica Canyon known as "'Queer Alley' where gay bars predominated."[28] Yet the homosexual lifestyles of Isherwood, Heard, Auden, Chester Kallman, and their partners didn't seem to concern the moralistic composer in the least; although occasionally his homophobia had surfaced in his puritanical remarks about Diaghilev's various lovers. The composer, moreover, either out of temperance or genuine curiosity, tolerated Huxley's beliefs in parapsychology, even his experiments with mescaline.

He listened to Heard's and Isherwood's fervent espousal of the powers of meditation and the need of humanity to be "one with the universe." He willingly engaged in Mann's eristic discussions of religion and eschatology. And, most certainly, he identified with Auden's strident criticisms of anybody and anything. Whatever his innermost beliefs, Stravinsky was overwhelmed by his friends' intellectual compass, and he valued their zeal. Perhaps at the root of their friendship was a bond of strongly expressed convictions in what they pursued—regardless of the topic—especially in the face of significant public ridicule. They were all willing to take a stand. The passion of these bohemian thinkers provided not only impetus but also a network of support for Stravinsky as he crossed his Rubicon from the neoclassical works of the 1940s to the less accessible nontonal music of the 1950s following *The Rake's Progress*.

Huxley's and Stravinsky's American years, particularly the 1940s, are often disregarded as creatively inferior (a pronouncement that irked both men). But their commiseration provided a further unity. If Huxley could be called one of the "most prodigiously learned writers not merely of this century but of all time" by the *Paris Review* and still write scripts for cartoon characters like Mr. Magoo (as he was asked to do in 1957), then who was Stravinsky to find fault? If European authors were grinding out screenplays, as were American writers of the caliber of William Faulkner, F. Scott Fitzgerald, and James Agee, then why couldn't Stravinsky compose movie music for the American populace—whose existence functioned on "the lower animal levels," as Huxley derisively remarked. Fitzgerald summarized Hollywood during his own brief career as a screenwriter toward the end of his life: "You either have credits, or you don't have credits."

Huxley deprecated the industry's shallowness while simultaneously worrying over his own acquiescence to those in power. As Isherwood remembered: "Huxley found it harder [as time went on]. It embarrassed him somehow, I always felt. I say this with total authority because I not only worked with him, but we were intent on earning our livings. We always got interested of course; the only real side of total 'no-goodness' is when you aren't interested in your work. He could live with it. You see, wise, braver, nobler people than any of us were doing it, and hating it far more than we did."[29]

George Balanchine also had his run-ins with the movie world. His association with Hollywood provides an interesting foil to that of his close friend Stravinsky. Balanchine loathed yielding control as much as anyone, particularly to arrogant studio heads whose sense of artistic value often rose, in his estimate, no higher than whatever decadence could be quickly and profitably turned. Still, Balanchine was in many ways a more realistic sort than Stravinsky. He didn't brood about uncontrollable issues as much as Stravinsky was apt to do. Like the composer and his author friends, Balanchine was a commodity that Hollywood could utilize. He added an air of polish and decorum to dance productions. Yet Balanchine's achievement, if not a glittering Hollywood success story, is all the more remarkable given the equally restrictive boundaries in which he was forced to work. The outspoken choreographer was accustomed to having his way, and he was greatly impeded by such production shackles as budgets, limited studio space, and rehearsal schedules. When the opportunity presented itself to return to New York, Balanchine did so eagerly, but without apology for his passing fling with the mass culture mentality of the movie world. It served its purpose, and like so many journeyman jobs the itinerant Balanchine was forced to take over the years, he tossed the experience off as just that, then moved on without the flagellation Huxley and others inflicted upon themselves.

Such forbearance could never be so easily accepted by the perpetually tormented Stravinsky, whose every decision bespoke a self-inflicted anguish almost amusing in its excess. The slightest change was bound to throw the linearly oriented Stravinsky into a whirl. For others to cut even a single measure of his music as part of a film score was nothing less than the most barbarous trespass imaginable. Balanchine, by contrast, partly because of the nature of dance and partly because of his laissez-faire attitude, was infinitely more capable of adjusting on the spot.

Stravinsky did not concede anything graciously, and if unsuccessful at something he felt wounded. Reflexively, it seems, mortification quickly led to deflection; if he did not succeed, it was because of the ineptitude of an unsophisticated public, the incompetent critic, or, in the case of film, the ignorance of producers failing to grasp the higher mission of music. The composer's memory was long, and there surely remained a residual bitterness about not having "made it" in the film world, especially since Balanchine, Huxley, Isherwood, and others had. Nowhere is his sourness more vituperative than in a September 1946 *Musical Digest* article in which he was interviewed by his assistant Ingolf Dahl, who taught a course on film music during the 1940s at the University of Southern California.

> Film people have a primitive and childish concept of music. Music explains nothing, music underlines nothing. When it attempts to explain, to narrate, or to underline something, the effect is both embarrassing and harmful. I have been asked whether my own music, written for the ballet and the stage, would not be comparable in its dramatic connotation to music in the films. It cannot be compared at all. . . . My music expresses nothing of a realistic character, and neither does the dance. Dancers have nothing to narrate and neither has my music. My music for the stage, then, never tries to "explain" the action, but rather it lives side by side with the visual movement, happily married to it, as one individual to another. The mass adds nothing to art. It cannot raise the level, and the artist who aims consciously at mass-appeal can do so only by lowering his own level. . . . Music cannot be helped by means of an increase of the quantity of listeners, be this increase effected by the film or any other medium. It can be helped only through an increase in the quality of listening, the quality of the individual soul.[30]

But in the next breath the composer rapidly backtracked, for even in 1946, after so many failures, he knew better than to occlude future opportunities: "All these reflections are not to be taken as a point-blank refusal on my part ever to work for the film. . . . There will be nothing shocking to me in offering my professional capacities to a film studio for remuneration." It did not take long for Hollywood to retaliate. A rebuttal appeared in the same magazine in January 1948 by David Raksin, a formidable film composer himself. The article, "Hollywood Strikes Back," included caricatures of Stravinsky and Raksin, swords drawn, about to duel. This was the kind of copy tabloids lived for, and the exchange was publicized and reprinted extensively in national newspapers and journals. Raksin's refutation first defended the legitimacy of film composing: "At least he works as a composer and does not wear himself out teaching dolts, concertizing or kowtowing to concert managers, dilettantes and other musical parasites." Point by point, Raksin unshrouded the paralogism of Stravinsky's argument. He poked holes in the obvious rationalizations the composer offered, and ridiculed Stravinsky's waffling. Raksin argued that music served several functions, accompaniment being one. Stravinsky had written—supposedly to signify its deific power—"Music probably attended the creation of the universe." If that were the case, Raksin rejoined, then it must have been "background music."[31]

The article rankled the composer, as the Basel archives demonstrate. Stravinsky took considerable time to analyze Raksin's reply, copiously marking his own copy in response to its criticisms. Again quite typical of the composer, he wrote in a letter to Dahl shortly thereafter, on 9 February 1948: "It is not my intention to answer his misunderstanding and misrepresentations of my ideas. . . . If Mr. Raksin thinks that passages from *Firebird* . . . lend themselves to a tap dance accompaniment, it only reflects on the private matter of his own attitude and taste." Stravinsky's unequivocal banishment of Raksin as artistically tasteless was to be expected. He would often conveniently dispatch those with whom he disagreed. Why bother replying to such trifling comments? he aloofly implied. Yet, as his unpublished papers disclose, he did just that, even if only within the privacy of his own studio.

David Adams, of the music publisher Boosey & Hawkes, asked Stravinsky in a letter dated 18 August 1952 if he would "write and direct the music for a one-hour full-length film." It was to be based on a fable in the form of a ballet, with choreography perhaps by Agnes de Mille and narration by Helen

Hayes. Adams wisely assured Stravinsky that "the music itself will play a very important part in the film presentation." Having read the script, Stravinsky responded to Adams that while "it is a rather pleasant, gay, and surrealistic affair," still the story was "not quite enough to let me commit myself to the project off-hand." The unpublished sixty-six-page script is titled "A Fable of Fortune," by Robert Shapiro. Stravinsky did not mark the script. The estimated production cost was $300,000 and the choreography was to be done, at Stravinsky's behest, by Balanchine, who considered but then turned down the project. "If Balanchine is not going to be the choreographer after all, then who is going to be, and what does he or she intend to do?" asked Stravinsky in an unpublished portion of a 26 September letter. Anthony Tudor was mentioned next, but after numerous exchanges with Boosey & Hawkes, Stravinsky rejected the proposal.

The composer considered a more tempting film collaboration on the subject of the *Odyssey* shortly afterward. British film director Michael Powell wrote to Stravinsky through Ernst Roth of Boosey & Hawkes in January 1953. Powell referred to his friendship with Isamu Noguchi and Dylan Thomas (who was being asked to write the "libretto"), and told Stravinsky that he wanted songs, dances, hymns, and an overture for the film. Even more relevant, his unpublished letter continued: "The feature-film as we know it, of unblessed memory, is nearly finished. New forms of entertainment are coming. . . . I would like a scene from our projected *Odyssey* to be one of the Tales. How do you fancy the Nausicaa episode on the sea-shore? It could be a fabulous scene if truly Mediterranean." Stravinsky responded to Roth on 16 January, "I ask you to enter into negotiation with him for me," requesting $12,000 for twelve minutes of music and promising the completed score by 1954, though again the deal was never made.[32] The "Nausicaa episode" was much on his mind in those days, as he was also having discussions with Lincoln Kirstein about a ballet based on this theme, which eventually resulted in *Agon* in 1957.

Even more enticing, television now loomed as a possibility. Roth wrote to Stravinsky: "There is no doubt that a new approach to the problem of film is necessary in view of television. . . . It may even be that television, with its impact on the film, may force the film into that artistic standard which it has vainly tried to achieve in the past." By the early 1950s, as Roth suggests, the lines dividing the Hollywood film industry and the novelty of television were beginning to cross. Stravinsky's ambition of becoming a successful Hollywood film composer led nowhere. What had first appeared a promising new venue for composition ultimately proved only a platform to preach about the flawed culture of the film industry—just as Isherwood's character Bergmann does in *Prater Violet:* "There are secrets which everybody knows and no one speaks of. . . . It lies and declares that the pretty Danube is blue, when the water is red with blood. I am punished for assisting in this lie. We shall all be punished."[33]

Stravinsky never did write an original film score—or even part of one—although it certainly wasn't for lack of trying. The closest he ever got was in the use of *Le Sacre,* when it was already nearly thirty years old, in *Fantasia,* and in his reworkings of music written for but never used in films to turn them into orchestral scores. The reasons he failed to make it as a film composer are many. Stravinsky's advocates would insist that, unlike Bergmann, the composer was above participating in "the lie." Perhaps—but it is difficult to avoid questioning whether Stravinsky's nobility in censuring the film industry was merely a pretext. He may well have dickered with studio bosses if he had known how; but relinquishing control ran counter to his nature. Intractable as ever, the composer reasoned that since the film industry was incapable of seeing things his way, it must be artistically barren. Yet he did not entirely give up the idea of creating music to go along with moving images, nor did others for whom he had great respect. Stravinsky's friend T. S. Eliot was now working in television after being disillusioned by the film industry's production in 1942 of *Murder in the Cathedral.* In 1952 (just about the time Stravinsky was approached about writing for television), Eliot's *The Cocktail Party* was telecast, drawing an estimated audience of more than three million viewers. If Hollywood didn't have the good sense to furnish a viable artistic forum for visually realizing Stravinsky's ideas, perhaps the emerging world of television would.

C·h·a·p·t·e·r ·5·

Television and *The Flood:*
Anatomy of an "Inglorious Flop"

Seldom has a television show been glorified with such frantic advance
ballyhoo. . . . Lyrical columns of publicity predicted an earth-shaking
event, but what transpired was an inglorious flop—an all-time dud. Noah
and the Flood proved to be as emptily pretentious as the shenanigans
which surrounded it.
—Albert Goldberg, *Los Angeles Times*

I remember turning on our television set on Saturday night, 14 June
1962, eager to watch the telecast of Stravinsky's newest work. As a fifteen-
year-old, I knew little of his music, but I did recall seeing him on one of
Leonard Bernstein's *Young People's Concerts,* so I suspected he must be somebody important. I was fascinated by the one-hour CBS broadcast that evening,
although apparently my parents did not share my enthusiasm, for they quietly
sneaked out of the room after the first five minutes or so. What captivated me
was the novelty of the production: the horrific alien-looking masks the players wore, the surrealistic sets, the abstractness of the dancing, the bizarre visual effects, the avant-garde flavor of it all, though in retrospect, of course, it
was hardly that. What I remember least was the music, perhaps because I
didn't understand it. I had no knowledge of this wonderful composition's elaborately structured serial underpinnings.

The commentary introducing the performance was, however, perfectly
clear. Actually it was more a homily than an introduction. A somber, tuxedoed
Laurence Harvey, standing against an empty black backdrop, told of aborigi-
nal flood myths as old as the Babylonians and the Incas; about Zeus sending
forth waters to purify the earth; about an obedient Noah's faith in God's
cleansing of the world, and the chance for life to begin anew. Harvey spoke
apocalyptically about "the Bomb," and the tense, uncertain times in which we
lived. They were familiar warnings—warnings ominously sounded in contemporary movies like *On the Beach, Fail-Safe,* and *Dr. Strangelove.* Such

The Flood, 1962, production design by Rouben Ter-Arutunian
(Courtesy of the Dance Collection of the New York Public Library
for the Performing Arts)

movies were more serious, more believable than Hollywood's rubber-suited nuclear monsters and mutants of earlier 1950s sci-fi B-thrillers, about which we could chuckle. Sputnik had launched the Space Age in 1957; the range of ICBM warheads was rapidly increasing; and with more than one hundred thousand bomb shelters built in the 1950s, the world had become a frightening place in which to live.

Stravinsky's new work was meant to reflect the gravity of the day. I may not have understood the composer's music that June evening, but the work's message and the resonance Harvey's words aimed for were anything but subtle, even for a teenager. *The Flood,* like many of Stravinsky's earlier theater compositions, looked to the past to moralize about the future. Harvey told us—or rather instructed us—that we were about to hear music by the world's "greatest living composer." We should consider ourselves fortunate, he lectured, since Stravinsky specifically had chosen TV as his medium, hoping to make his music available to the widest possible audience. Then suddenly the screen faded to black, from which soon emerged a stiff, hesitating Stravinsky, saying in his sometimes less than perfect English that he was glad to present "a very dear subject for audiences who can surely appreciate the drama. I don't want to speak you more, I want to play you more." Thus began the first and last televised performance of *The Flood.*

Recently, I watched once more the grainy black-and-white thirty-five-millimeter film, which is preserved in the Dance Collection of the New York Public Library for the Performing Arts at Lincoln Center. I was struck immediately by its artifice: the constant fading in and out of the cameras, the disjunctiveness of the scenes, the static quality of the production. How well did Stravinsky, the "architect of time," as Balanchine once dubbed him, really understand the specifics of film time and the need for seamless transitions between visual images that changed rapidly? As I now viewed the production, it was precisely the glaring seams that compromised the work's continuity. The "modernity" of the piece, as I had naively thought it in 1962, had evaporated.

Television's primitive efforts to bedazzle the audience with special effects—angels falling from the sky, the touching of silhouetted male and female hands in a simulated act of procreation, miniature figures of Noah's menagerie of beasts lifelessly photographed, grotesque-looking extraterrestrials, dancers emerging from a rippling blanket meant to represent the flood itself—all these contrivances now appeared archaic. Moreover, the production was sliced into short segments divided by shampoo commercials, thus severing whatever flow existed. Finally, television's attempt to frame the composition with both introductory and post-performance commentary seemed more forced than I had remembered. As the performance ends, Stravinsky is shown coldly staring into the camera, as if we could look directly into his mind's eye. Then the elocutionary Harvey reappears, reminding us that every epoch produces great men—great men like Stravinsky: "His works have changed the musical ears of the world." Craft and Stravinsky are seen discussing the problems of the public accepting the composer's newest ideas on the eve of his eightieth birthday. There are also wonderful shots of Stravinsky vigorously rehearsing the orchestra (in Los Angeles, where the score was recorded), and of Balanchine demonstrating portions of the ballet sequences for his dancers (in New York, where the choreography was filmed). These eye-catching clips would surely have worked more effectively at the beginning rather than at the end of the production, where they appeared as so much filler.

As I watched the film, I caught myself thinking about the uproar the production had originally precipitated. My parents were not the only ones who left their living rooms that evening. The Nielsen ratings reported that more than four million homes had tuned in, but by the end of the telecast that number had dropped drastically. *The Flood* was quickly judged a disaster. Unfairly, I believe, it was branded a "flop," and it has never fully recovered. Music historians often contend that the work is flawed, attributing its imperfections to the scourge of television (that "vast wasteland," as Kennedy-appointed FCC chair Newton Minow described the industry in 1961). Ostensibly *The Flood* had been taken out of the composer's control by television executives preoccupied with their own commercial aims. But was anything ever completely taken out of Stravinsky's hands, or is this another illusion intended to absolve the composer of responsibility by portraying him as a victim?

History has never known quite what to do with what many musicians see as the Stravinsky work that most resists easy categorization. It simply does not seem to fit any template. The structural boundaries framing Stravinsky's instrumental works are often intentionally, and almost always brilliantly, blurred. Though never abandoning their underlying classical design, the composer often transmogrified traditional sonata, concerto, and symphonic forms into something new and fresh. But it was in the laboratory of the theater that Stravinsky most consistently and imaginatively challenged accepted orthodoxy, as in *Renard, L'Histoire du soldat, Les Noces, Pulcinella, Mavra, Oedipus Rex, Perséphone,* and even to some extent *Babel, The Rake's Progress, A Sermon, A Narrative and a Prayer,* and *Requiem Canticles.* The composer's distinctive mixing of ritual, myth, cantata, dance, narration, melodrama, oratorio, and opera was never easily classified. His hybrid creations often left listeners reeling. They exposed Stravinsky to charges of inconsistency. Yet each of his theatrical experiments was refreshingly innovative, forcing listeners to stretch their own conceptions. Was *The Flood* the one exception, a momentary stumble in a long series of successful experiments?

Some commentators think this "dance-drama," as Stravinsky thought of it, was "artistically indecisive," "confused in its musico-dramatic action," and marked by a "naivety [that] is almost shocking." Why exactly was it such a "dud," as Albert Goldberg criticized? Even assuming that the harshest criticisms of what detractors saw as a musical-visual jumble were true, the work is still as much a chapter in the composer's chronicle as any of his revered masterpieces. How can so many biographers conveniently place it aside simply because it was not another *Sacre du printemps*? The work exists as a historical document. *The Flood*, written a half century after *Le Sacre*, stands at one of those transitional historical moments wherein a work's broadly viewed biographical sum is greater than its compositional parts. Just as *Le Sacre* cannot be detached from the context of Paris and Diaghilev's Ballets Russes, *The Flood* should not be decontextualized from the phenomenon of American television.

An untangling of the multiple influences shaping Stravinsky's work is therefore essential, for it illuminates his only compositional encounter with the venture of television, one of the most powerful cultural symbols of the electronic age. The behind-the-scenes politics and machinations of television as an enterprise in American culture place in proper perspective what music historians have often overlooked in declaring Stravinsky's work bereft of artistic merit. Some writers have argued that his participation in such a commercial project pitched to the masses was unimaginable. But given what we now know about the real rather than the fictionalized composer, it is not difficult to imagine at all. Tracing the evolution of *The Flood*, and to some extent the history of television at that moment, clarifies the extraordinary process set in motion the moment Stravinsky agreed to work in a cash-conscious medium— a medium tied directly to the same mass culture he had routinely and publicly denigrated over the preceding twenty years. More than just another Stravinsky composition, *The Flood* would test the waters of the consumer age.

As early as 1928, the same year as Stravinsky's *Apollo*, the first issue of *Television*, the journal of the British Royal Television Society, contained articles like "The Invisible Ray" and "How to Make a Simple Television." By the time Stravinsky arrived in America in 1939 to present his Harvard lectures, Franklin D. Roosevelt had appeared on television, speaking at the opening of the New York World's Fair. By the early 1950s, and still under siege from the House Un-American Activities Committee's censuring of "the Hollywood Ten," the golden age of the old Hollywood film industry was fading rapidly, just as television's star was rising. Ticket sales for Hollywood films plummeted at an astonishing rate of ten million a week. Why should people pay money to see bad films, Sam Goldwyn conceded, when they could stay home and watch bad programs for nothing. In 1946, there were an estimated sixty-five hundred television sets in the United States. By 1948 there were more than a million, and by 1950, four million. In 1948, 60 percent of all television sets purchased were sold on credit to middle- and low-income families; television was about to change the fabric of American life. As one critic complained: "The housewife who is accustomed to listen to [radio] soap operas while she washes, irons, and does the housework, cannot watch a visual program while she does her chores." The *New York Times* TV critic added that because of television, "The wife scarcely knows where the kitchen is, let alone her place in it."[1]

Not only is 1962 remembered by musicians as the year of Stravinsky's much anticipated new made-for-TV composition, but it was also an especially significant year in the history of America's newest information highway. And while it is true that Hollywood still was competing for audiences by offering "adult" films, such as the titillating screen adaptation of Vladimir Nabokov's *Lolita* in that year, the battle was already lost. Though more prudish than Hollywood, TV's range was enormous, its influence staggering. The same year as *The Flood,* the networks covered astronaut John Glenn's orbiting of the earth. It was the year of Armageddon, many felt, as John F. Kennedy boldly staged his publicly televised showdown with Nikita S. Khrushchev during those fourteen days in October, risking nuclear winter. Walter Cronkite, who later became the "most trusted man in America," began his stint as anchor for *The CBS Evening News.* The year also brought the all-American boy Johnny Carson to NBC's *Tonight Show,* and it gave us a royal tour of the White House with America's own queen, Jacqueline Kennedy. Within such diverse programming of news and entertainment, television also spoke specifically to the growing confrontation of classical art and artists with American populism at a volatile time—a time when, as now, creative license and artistic integrity were increasingly incriminated by a growing media audience wanting not so much to be uplifted as to be briefly updated on the news, or mindlessly entertained by endless sitcoms (a term first used at about this time).

Broadcast across the country that June, *The Flood* was billed as a momentous event in the early years of network television. It was meant not only to celebrate the astonishing vitality of Stravinsky the octogenarian but to mark an American cultural milestone. Network television, still suffering in the aftermath of the *$64,000 Question* quiz show scandals of the late 1950s, was eager to establish itself as a legitimate purveyor of American taste. Attempting to reverse its image, television would not scrimp in its efforts at redemption. It devoted a huge amount of funding and more programming hours to documentaries than ever before. Artistic productions, too, were seen as a symbolic gesture of TV's beneficence. An unprecedented media blitz touted Stravinsky's newest work as a major historic event. A month before its airing, Congressman Edward P. Boland regaled the House of Representatives with a lengthy tribute to shampoo baron John H. Breck for his vision in sponsoring this pioneering broadcast. The *Congressional Record* praised the endeavor for its "cultural high-mindedness." And the political gods did not fail to note that Stravinsky, still publicly flaunted as a trophy that America had wrested from the Russians, was now working for American television—a powerful blow against the "Red Menace," right in the middle of an increasingly heated Cold War.

So-called high culture, often taken by Americans as a defining mark of class distinction, was blandished by television as an easily attainable, passive acquisition. Participating in a meaningful artistic experience was becoming as simple as driving to the local Sears & Roebuck and buying one's very own tube. The prescription was painless: a half hour or so of exposure each week to whatever channel was broadcasting something "arty." It was all as easy as convenience shopping—easier really, since programs were magically transmitted right into forty-six million homes, nearly 88 percent of all American households. It was just this kind of fast-food appeal that television sought in commissioning Stravinsky. Yet many creative artists felt as conductor and commentator Richard Franko Goldman did: "Somewhere along the line, the 20th century forgot that artistic endeavors were based upon a two-way communication requiring sophistication and sensitivity on the part of the viewer."[2]

Sophisticated or not, television was wildly successful. Although he would not admit it, Stravinsky was a fan of television, often watching comedies, animal shows, and almost anything that was diverting. More important, he was acutely aware of the young industry's potential. Its success was not limited to comedy and variety shows in the style of Milton Berle's *Texaco Star Theater* and Ed Sullivan's *Talk of the Town*. Well-conceived artistic ventures such as *Omnibus*, whose support by the Ford Foundation permitted producers to program artistic events without having to appease commercial sponsors, showed great promise. In its first season alone, the program offered six filmed ballets, and later began producing live dance performances. When the foundation's subsidy of the show expired in 1957, television critic Jack Gould rightly predicted that programs would now be forced to become more popular.[3] As *TV Guide* (whose readership outdistanced those of *Time* and *Newsweek*) reported, Americans were not interested in "anything that smacks even a little bit of intellectualism." Television became an "amusement park," wrote Paddy Chayefsky: "We're in the boredom-killing business." If an artistic enterprise was to survive, a broader, more palatable conception of what constituted serious artistic entertainment would need to be sought, for more people would now have to be tuned in if sponsors were to prosper.

Leonard Bernstein's popular *Young People's Concerts* in the late 1950s and early 1960s virtually catapulted the naturally telegenic conductor to the status of American icon. Might television provide Stravinsky with the same celebrity that Hollywood had earlier promised? As the world's "greatest living composer," Stravinsky's name carried substantial weight; and just as Hollywood had initially sought to parlay that notoriety for its own commercial gain, television now wagered that Americans, whether or not they had ever heard (let alone understood) anything beyond *The Firebird,* would probably at least recognize the composer's name and therefore the event's artistic significance. When Laurence Olivier played Hamlet over the airwaves, TV boasted that the audience of fifty million people exceeded the total of everyone who had seen the play ever before. Across the heartland of America, television burst forth as the new demagogue. If Walter Cronkite said it was so . . . then it was so.

The electronic box hypnotized viewers into believing that if Stravinsky's music was important enough to be beamed into their living rooms, they'd better sit down and listen. Sylvester ("Pat") Weaver, one of American TV's early leaders, grandly declared that the nation must be exposed to the glories of fine art through widely broadcast shows: "To program for the intellectual alone is easy and duplicates other media. To make us all into intellectuals—there is the challenge of television." A leviathan challenge indeed, and one whose chances of succeeding were about as good as Hollywood's convincing Stravinsky that filmmaking was a team sport.

Initially, some producers were hopeful of inveigling a new generation of composers to write expressly for television. Opera particularly promised the kind of spectacle viewers might appreciate. Gian Carlo Menotti became an overnight star in 1939 when NBC radio commissioned his opera *The Old Maid and the Thief*. Ten years later his incredibly successful *Amahl and the Night Visitors* was commissioned specifically for television. The popularity of *Amahl* was unparalleled. By 1984 an estimated five hundred performances had been televised across the country. Olin Downes reviewed *Amahl* in the *New York Times* on 12 December 1951, ardently claiming that Americans, "through blurred eyes and emotions that were not easy to conceal," surely understood Menotti's "rare art." *Amahl* set the standard for what televised opera should be—and it was surely what the sponsors had in mind when they approached Stravinsky.

But the teary-eyed, sentimental display of emotions evoked by *Amahl* ran completely counter to Stravinsky's aesthetic. He was well aware of Menotti's hit, and quite jealous. In the early 1950s he entertained thoughts of staging his forthcoming *The Rake's Progress* on Broadway, knowing full well that his opera could never compete commercially with *Amahl's* unqualified triumph. When Rouben Ter-Arutunian (the designer of *The Flood*) approached him in the 1960s about having Menotti redesign and produce *The Rake's Progress* at the Metropolitan Opera, an incensed Stravinsky would have nothing to do with it. In a letter of 8 January 1967, fearing that a restaging of his "opera" would again fail, the composer confessed that he would prefer that Menotti not revive the work, "especially if it were played between *Lulu* and some jazz-integrationist rubbish."

In spite of Menotti's easily digestible hits, some critics felt that mounting a musical production for TV was, from the start, a bleak prospect. The visual stimuli engulf the senses so rapidly that any other components, including the music, are likely to be crushed. Given Stravinsky's similar dicta regarding the primacy of music over visual images, as well as his sentiments about the musically illiterate masses making up the target audience of television, how did he see himself fitting in? "A televised concert is a great bore," he said in a *Saturday Review* interview the week *The Flood* aired. "Yes, of course you can see timpani and the trombone and the oboe person by person as they play, but what is the interest of that?" Yet two weeks later in a follow-up article, Stravinsky claimed that the real mystery about televising music was the balance between the visual and musical experiences. "I feel that television is the greatest medium for a new musical form, and if I decide to write another opera myself, I know that it will be for the electronic glass tube. . . . The one 'specific' of the medium that guided me in my conceptions of *The Flood* [was that] visualization can be instantaneous."[4]

Why, given Stravinsky's equivocation about television, did he want to become involved with such a mass media vehicle in the first place? Perhaps his motivation stemmed at least partially from a Bernstein or Olivier complex— the prospect of having his music and name more widely circulated than he could ever have imagined. Perhaps, too, his falling out with Hollywood still disturbed him, and he needed to prove that his music was expressive enough to touch anybody. But his interest was also buoyed by close literary friends such as Huxley and Isherwood, who, while jeering television as a venue for serious art, recognized the benefits of its high exposure. ("Good heavens," exclaimed Noël Coward, "television is something you appear on, you don't watch.") Stravinsky's implantation into the culture of television would also further his efforts to "Americanize" himself, something he had been trying to do since he first came to the United States. As Isherwood noted in a diary entry in 1960, Stravinsky still felt absolutely driven to be a highly visible public figure since "he is so accustomed to being a great celebrity." What better way to guarantee this than to ride "the magic carpet," as television was then called, into everybody's living room?[5]

Isherwood himself, his diaries reveal, was quite hopeful of writing television scripts, including one intended for Hermione Gingold in 1959 that never materialized, and another a few years later for a television series. In the late 1950s, when he and Stravinsky were close Hollywood friends, Isherwood appeared regularly on Oscar Levant's West Coast television show. Just how deeply involved Isherwood hoped to become with television is apparent in an entry from March 1960 in which he listed as possible projects a film documentary on Gandhi with Shelley Winters and Tony Franciosa; a film for Lincoln Kirstein's *Sleeping Beauty*; Jerry Lawrence's TV series; a projected television show with Aldous Huxley; and most especially "Bob Craft's idea that I should narrate something for a Stravinsky composition—in 1962!" which, of course, was to become *The Flood*, although in fact Isherwood was never to be involved.[6]

From the outset, Stravinsky was both cautious and unsure of his mission in writing for television. Even as the composition was taking form in his mind, he insisted on making the point that his newest work was neither an opera nor a ballet. In fact unpublished correspondence confirms that Stravinsky was not even sure the work could be thought of in terms of theater. Writing to his friend Rolf Liebermann on 29 January 1961, he complained that Liebermann, like others, had entirely misconstrued the intent of the composition. Again the composer took pains to emphasize that the new opus would not be operatic in the traditional sense (as Liebermann assumed), but a work pointedly targeted at taking advantage of television's potential. Stravinsky further revealed to Liebermann that although there would not be a great deal of singing, there would be a mixture of narrative dialogue and some choreography, the balance of which had not yet been determined. Liebermann responded on 3 February, asking if *The Flood* could be presented on 17 June 1962 as part of Stravinsky's eightieth birthday anniversary. He hoped to persuade Stravinsky to stage the work as an opera in Germany, and in fact did so. Yet a week after Liebermann's response, in another unpublished letter, Stravinsky remarked that he still was not yet sure of the new work's form, nor when it would be completed. He also expressed his reservations about the wisdom of presenting it as an opera. All he was sure of was that Balanchine would prepare the ballet for the television premiere.

Stravinsky continued to quash reports that the composition would be an opera, as if to scuttle any comparison with Menotti; he expressed greater concern about the work's mistaken identity as an opera than he did about its suitability for television. He also showed his exasperation with the frequent misstatement of the title as *Noah and the Flood,* and he regularly crossed out the incorrect "Noah and" whenever he saw it. He remained almost oblivious to the comparison with Menotti, perhaps for fear of appearing to adapt his music to the idiosyncrasies of the medium. Certainly he would not permit the visual aspect of the work to become the shaping force. Yet Stravinsky declared with some assurance that television might indeed someday serve as a viable platform for a new expressive art form. Nor would it be a simple retooling of the fundamental dramatic precepts of opera. Rather, while disclaiming any interest in "the musical life of television," he hoped it would make possible an entirely new "musico-dramatic form," as he called it. He sensed that the capacity of television to focus on different aspects of the dramatic action in rapid succession—perhaps a camera zooming in here, another panning more widely—would allow a true rethinking of old ideas. It would invite a fresh, innovative approach full of diverse images that would strike the eye and ear in a completely new way. Moreover, it was "the saving of musical time [that] interests me more than anything visual," he wrote in *Dialogues.* And most revealing, he remarked that it was this "new musical economy," that served as his guide in plotting the architecture of his new work.[7]

Choreography was envisioned from the first. Balanchine was often involved in a variety of television shows during the '50s, and his frequent interchanges with Stravinsky sensitized the composer to both the advantages and problems of the new medium. Since the days of *Apollo,* Stravinsky had trusted his friend's eye. Balanchine's role in the production was much more significant than the choreographer professed. The visually sensitive Balanchine was far more conversant than the composer with television's possibilities, as well as its limitations; and Stravinsky seems not to have hesitated in entrusting this dimension of the new opus to his friend.

Balanchine was no newcomer to television. Even in the medium's infancy in the late 1940s he was creating dance sequences for CBC Television in Montreal. He arranged a made-for-television version of *Cinderella,* first broadcast on 25 April 1949 for CBS (with Tanaquil Le Clercq as Cinderella), based on excerpts from the three early Tchaikovsky symphonies. Balanchine's *One, Yuletide Square* was broadcast on Christmas Day, 1952, on NBC, again featuring his wife Tanny Le Clercq in this abridged version of the 1870 *Coppélia* ballet. For the popular *Kate Smith Hour* on NBC, the choreographer presented yet another made-for-television ballet, *The Countess Becomes the Maid* (1953), based on excerpts from *Die Fledermaus.* And on Christmas night, 1958, Balanchine himself played Drosselmeyer in a widely viewed and highly praised version of *The Nutcracker* for CBS. But certainly his most ambitious televised achievement was *The Magic Flute,* expressly prepared for television and based on an adaptation by W. H. Auden. Balanchine was completely responsible for the stage direction. First telecast on 15 January 1956 on the popular *NBC Opera Theater,* the cast featured a young Leontyne Price; the choreographer also prepared dance sequences for the "Queen of the Night's Three Ladies."

Ever since Maria Gambarelli, the first dancer to appear on television in New York on 26 May 1931, had been forced to confine her movements to a five-foot-square space so that she would fit on the small screen, choreographers had been skeptical of the medium's ability to capture unhampered dance movement. Twenty-five years later, Edward Villella's athletic soaring across the TV screen was big business, reaching all corners of the country. When Villella was invited to dance on *Omnibus* in a 1958 program conceived by Gene Kelly ("Dancing Is a Man's Game"), Balanchine objected. He had little regard for the medium and, as Villella recalls, felt that "quality, development of an idea, the investigation of how a dance could be adapted to the medium, were not given a high priority." Balanchine complained that regardless of the artistic efforts devoted to such productions, regardless of what was agreed to, the program itself never quite jelled the way it was envisioned. The medium impeded the art of dance, and inevitably viewers were left with a distortion. If music placed a "corset on the dance," as Balanchine once stated, then television placed manacles on it. He always felt obliged, he confessed, to preface any of his televised choreography with the caveat that viewers were about to see something "really pretty awful. . . . It's not going to be at all what ballet can be. . . . You'll have to imagine it."[8]

Still, Balanchine was a practical man, and he understood the gains to be won in being seen by such a diverse audience. Nor did his feelings change over the next four years, even though he relented and agreed to work with Stravinsky on the new project. During the taping of *The Flood*, he carefully studied the television monitor, making adjustments as needed. And while Stravinsky was busy refuting assumptions that *The Flood* was operatic, Balanchine was busily countering the notion that it was a ballet.

> This is a miracle play more than a masque. As I see it, it's a church play or a choreographed oratorio. Most importantly it's *not* a ballet. *The Flood* could have been produced with actors speaking, or with singers and actors, or it could have been an opera. Our version is a musical composite. It's all done in gesture by dancers and objects. The most important thing about it is that it's Stravinsky. It's his work. His music is not accompaniment for the dance. Actually it's about Stravinsky himself, as a composer. And we are not trying to interfere with his music. The most important thing for me is for his music to be heard.[9]

His apprehension naturally spilled over into *The Flood,* and, in truth, it was out of deference to Stravinsky that he accepted the challenge—one that the realistic Balanchine knew would be greatly hobbling. Regrettably, though perhaps predictably, only "a rough draft" (in his words) of his conception was televised. Moreover, Stravinsky's and Balanchine's longtime associate and financier Lincoln Kirstein was ruthless in his public derision of the medium: "I've never owned a television set; the few times I've watched . . . I've been amply confirmed in my distaste." His disparagement, reminiscent of Stravinsky's earlier condemnation of film and mass culture, signifies the gulf often separating creative artists from American populism. Kirstein continued: "Commercial TV directors and their staffs always start by admitting they know nothing about ballet, but are experts in TV, which means they know next to nothing about any visual aspect important to choreographers. What they know about are the conditions imposed by advertising, which is the sole reason and support for cash one can earn by the medium, except token prestige occasionally thrown in to sweeten a smelly pot."[10]

Such vilification only exacerbated the widening fissure between television and the arts. Misunderstandings and incendiary overstatements abounded as each camp staked out its territorial rights. Doubtless this wedge had an impact on Stravinsky when in 1959, with the influential thoughts of such trusted friends as Huxley, Isherwood, Kirstein, Balanchine, and others in mind, he was first approached about writing a work for television. Naturally he recalled the unresolvable clashes with Hollywood; only now, especially with the diplomatic mediation of Robert Craft (whose role in the creation of the work has been grossly underestimated), he was better prepared to negotiate.

The producer of the proposed project, Robert Graff, suggested W. H. Auden as a possible librettist, but Stravinsky was more interested in T. S. Eliot. Coincidentally, Eliot and Stravinsky were just then corresponding about the possibility of an entirely different collaboration, an opera. In an unpublished letter to Stravinsky, dated 19 March 1959, Eliot stated his understanding that an unidentified organization was interested in pairing the two of them, for twenty thousand dollars each, in collaborating on an opera. Eliot confessed that he was unsure of his abilities to prepare a libretto, nor did he have any immediate ideas about a story. But rather than shutting the door completely, he added that before refusing he would like Stravinsky's thoughts. Further, Eliot ventured, "To be quite frank, I was not happy with Wystan Auden's libretto for *The Rake's Progress*." Eliot became aware of Stravinsky's music as early the 1920s, and indeed was moved by such iconoclastic works as *The Rite of Spring*. It is well known too that Stravinsky often read Eliot, freely quoting the writer in his own articles, interviews, and lectures during the 1940s. Eliot's works, such as *Sweeney Agonistes: Fragments of an Aristophanic Melodrama*, written in the mid-1920s, were later to have a direct impact on Stravinsky's ballet *Agon*. These two creative giants did not meet, however, until the mid-1950s.

As letters in the Sacher archive in Basel establish, the composer replied on 8 April that while he was not interested in writing a traditional opera, perhaps they could "invent something interesting together . . . a cantata or a static stage piece . . . more suitable to my present non-operatic musical thought." On 6 August, he wrote again to Eliot outlining the origins of what would eventually become *The Flood*. The composer reported being contacted by NBC television about commissioning him to write something for an audience in "categories that they know—ballets, operas, plays—and I do not propose to write in any of these." Instead, he proposed to Eliot the story of Noah told dramatically with narration ("what delightful animal rhymes you could do," he suggested), a chorus, solo voices, and choreography, all following the form "of a medieval morality play."[11]

The Stravinskys with T. S. Eliot, London, 1958. Robert Craft appears in the center.

Apparently Stravinsky was fairly confident that Eliot would accept his invitation to collaborate on the work—at least enough that when he responded to the network on 2 August (four days before his letter to the poet), he felt free to use Eliot's name: "I have been considering your proposition with Mr. Balanchine as he is at Hollywood at present. . . . I do have in the mind a theatrical work with scenic and choreographic elements, and with a story or myth subject ancient and known to everyone. . . . I hope and expect that the author of its text will be T. S. Eliot and I intend to meet with Mr. Eliot in London at the beginning of next month to begin work."

But Eliot's answer, on 16 August, further retreated from the idea, and now hinted that he wasn't interested in pursuing the matter. His judiciously written letter stated that he could not do the project since he had "no vocation as a librettist," adding that "apart from the fact that as soon as I am free from other commitments, I shall want to be turning my mind to a new play." Stravinsky persisted, although he sensed the likelihood of a collaboration slipping away. When the two finally did meet in London a few weeks later, the project apparently went unmentioned. Still, even months afterward the composer continued raising the matter in subsequent correspondence, but to no avail. When Eliot wrote again to Stravinsky on 8 December (kindly but minimally volunteering to offer some textual suggestions for the work), the response was firm, ending any hope of a collaboration. Stravinsky would do better to seek another partner, Eliot concluded.

While the composer now needed to find a librettist immediately, confusion as to the nature of the work continued. Stravinsky seems to have formed no more than a vague concept of what he had in mind for *The Flood*. Certainly he must have given at least some preliminary thought to the balance of dance, music, and narration, although there is no evidence that at this early date he had planned an overall architecture. What the balance would be, how the individual numbers would be structured, how many dancers were to be used— all these questions remained up in the air. In fact, twenty-eight members of the New York City Ballet were ultimately employed. Arthur Todd reported in his article "What Went Wrong" that the dancers worked "valiantly and heroically for endless hours . . . [giving] the impression that these dedicated artists were toiling solely to produce a birthday garland for Stravinsky in gratitude for all of his great ballet scores."

Not wishing to incur Stravinsky's easily stirred wrath, cautious negotiations dragged on triangularly among the composer, his publisher Boosey & Hawkes, and Graff, whose television production company, Sextant, commissioned the work for broadcast on the CBS network (not NBC, as Stravinsky regularly misstated in all his correspondence). The exchanges themselves disclose how quickly the composer's short fuse could detonate, and just how deep the chasm was between him and the industry. Sextant originally announced to the press that the work would be a one-hour ballet, but a bilious Stravinsky quickly corrected Graff, informing him that he had no idea whether the piece would take that form. Stravinsky also made it clear that if Sextant's seeing the libretto was a condition of the contract, then there would be no contract. When the contract did arrive a few weeks later, Stravinsky, as always, studied the agreement closely, writing "impossible" next to clauses specifying that the work was to be completed by June 1961, and that television would hold the production rights for the next twenty years.

According to Lillian Libman, Stravinsky's secretary at the time, he was unsure of his ability to complete the work in such a short time since he was "not young enough" to deal with the pressure. But it is doubtful that age had anything to do with fulfilling the commission, given the composer's completely uncurbed creative powers. When he responded to Graff through Libman, he explained that he had "only about eight weeks to compose in 1960." In truth, Stravinsky did continue to juggle a frenetic schedule of conducting and recording that left little time for composing. He would sign the Sextant contract only if he could have until January 1962, and he candidly added, "I can't finish by then either, but there is no penalty for me in the agreement if I don't finish." Graff agreed and the contract was signed in May, presumably bringing a mutually satisfactory end to the business aspect of the work.

But as was frequently the case with Stravinsky, such negotiations took on added convolutions that regularly caught all parties off guard. Boosey & Hawkes was unaware that Stravinsky was already in the process of negotiating a television contract. In a letter of 5 July 1960, held in the Basel archives, Ernst Roth of the London branch of the publishing house immediately wrote to Stravinsky, hoping to avert a potentially serious breach: "I was profoundly shocked [with] the terms of an agreement you intend to make with some people called Sextant who are entirely unknown to me. . . . I implore you not to sell your youngest child into slavery." He complained that Stravinsky was completely "out of order" in making any "arrangements for television or stage or, in fact, any other type of performance." Roth further implied that Stravinsky had promised "exclusivity rights to Sextant for 20 years," which, he argued, simply meant "an unqualified guarantee that there will be next to no performances either on television or on the stage," as it was unlikely the work would be another *My Fair Lady*. But Stravinsky was primarily interested in obtaining as large a commission as he could and seemed unconcerned about his publisher's rights to control subsequent performances.

The commission stalled. A year passed, as Graff grew more anxious. Stravinsky refused to discuss the work with him, disdainful of network concerns about scheduling both rehearsals and the actual telecast. In the autumn of 1961, Graff unwisely attempted to prod the composer into submitting an update. Stravinsky would tolerate no infringement on his work or schedule by, of all people, media executives. That October, Roth replied to Sextant on Stravinsky's behalf. It was the only response the producers received. Stravinsky thoroughly proofed Roth's dispatch, writing on the draft: "Very Good Letter." As it demonstrates, little had changed since the composer assumed his doctrinaire stance with the Hollywood film world twenty years earlier. It was all or nothing:

> It is clear that Sextant has to change their attitude. . . . They cannot deal with Stravinsky as they might deal with any routine composer who could produce things made to measure as far as the character of the work and the time of de-

livery is concerned. If Sextant would now like to cancel the whole agreement there would be no ill-feeling on Stravinsky's part. . . . Stravinsky cannot be influenced in any way in any artistic matter: he cannot be hurried and cannot be induced to change any artistic plan in order to comply with requests which are outside his own artistic conception.

Having lost Eliot as a librettist, the composer turned to Craft. Libman wrongfully trivializes Craft's contribution by contending that he only compiled the texts, as history generally assumes. But this is a stupendous underestimate. From start to finish, Craft played a more critical role in the evolution of *The Flood* than in any other Stravinsky opus. The well-known "Working Notes," published in *Dialogues,* primarily address the discussions between Stravinsky and Balanchine during the final stage of the work's development. But they also suggest that Stravinsky, Balanchine, and Craft were actively involved in designing the look of the production. There are constant references to desired special effects: "the screen is filled with a 'celestial effulgence,'" there were to be "animation and graphic arts," as well as such phantasmic images as "hands sprouting grass from the fingers." Even the flood itself "might be supplemented by an electronic effect suggesting 'atmospheric disturbances, or by a pure noise, like a sinus tone.'"[12] Craft divulges how central his role was, suggesting that he advised Stravinsky as to how certain pieces could be structured, and what formal models might be applied. He further reports that after Stravinsky's death, as he was examining the composer's sketches, he discovered that Stravinsky had indeed taken his suggestions so seriously that the composer had actually inserted some of his notes directly into the manuscript. So disturbing was this finding, Craft goes on to report, that he "immediately tore them out," and only later realized that Stravinsky had wanted the world to recognize him for his important contribution to the work. As the Basel archives reveal, Craft's notes were indeed substantive, dealing with fundamental matters running to the core of the piece, both in compositional terms and regarding the playing out of the scenario. Craft himself mentions that he had, for example, suggested "the music in the film sequence in *Lulu* as a model retrograde for the biblical storm scene in *The Flood.*"[13]

Stravinsky owned a paperback edition of *Everyman and Medieval Miracle Plays,* which Craft used as a basis for the libretto. Eliot had suggested the book to the composer while their collaboration was still being discussed. Craft inserted a small piece of paper in the book on which he drafted a possible scenario beginning with "The Creation & Fall—the Fall of Lucifer" and leading eventually to "Noah's Flood." Individual parts of the work are outlined for speakers, chorus, and dancing. All the notations are in Craft's hand. He studied the text carefully, underlining certain sections in the introduction referring to the plays dealing with salvation themes; highlighting "a rib coloured red," which was part of the inventory list from the 1565 Norwich Grocer's Company performance (a deus ex machina device actually used in the sixteenth century); and deleting certain words and lines of the text. This clearly is the genesis of the composition, and it is just as clear that Craft personally molded the project rather than only perfunctorily transcribing the text.

In *Expositions and Developments,* Craft asks the composer for his description of the work. And while to some extent the statements are useful, Stravinsky, probably with Craft's aid, presents a kind of clever, humorous, even slightly glib account of the composition's problems and evolution—just the kind of response so typical of the writing found through the conversation books.[14] These carefully scripted statements tell only the side of the story intended for public consumption. Another unedited primary source is more instructive. Between the time Stravinsky notified the producer in April 1960 that the deal was off if it hinged on Graff's and Sextant's authorization of the libretto and the time the contract was actually signed in late May, Craft met privately with Graff in New York to outline the scenario and assuage the producer's growing anxiety. The network expected a traditional work, one that would be immediately graspable by the American television audience. Knowing virtually nothing of what Stravinsky was planning, it is no wonder Graff was nervous. Even more important, Craft discreetly responded to Graff's appeal without having to involve Stravinsky directly.

Craft's unpublished notes on his conversation with Graff leave little doubt as to his pivotal role. He clearly outlines the intent of Stravinsky's new opus, providing considerable detail on the sources of the scenario and the specific action that would unfold. He addresses what were surely Graff's concerns about how the audience would be able to relate to Stravinsky's musical language, and the textual language as well. Craft makes a special effort to assure the producer that the work will be approachable, that is, it would be conceived from the start in terms of what would be appropriate for television. There are allusions to the biblical story of Noah as a metaphor for contemporary concerns—concerns with the uneasiness surrounding the nuclear age in which we were living. This comes as no surprise given Stravinsky's earlier exploration of a similar topic with Dylan Thomas (the two artists had considered collaborating on an opera a decade earlier). Finally, with amazing specificity, Craft suggests very clearly defined ideas about the architectural plan of the music, the interaction of narration, dance, and music, and other details that in fact do ultimately manifest themselves in the work's final conception.[15]

Craft's summary of his meeting with Graff demonstrates a concerted effort to quell the fears of an edgy producer who had been left in the dark. But beyond this, he addresses several technical matters that were absolutely critical, including the use and positioning of cameras. This is central, since there is very little evidence to suggest that Stravinsky ever directly concerned himself with such matters, probably deferring to Balanchine and others to shape this aspect of the production. Indeed, as late as eighteen months after the meeting, a New Zealand newspaper quoted the composer flippantly declaring that it did not concern him that the work was being made for TV: "I don't know what TV is."[16] Stravinsky's feigned ignorance was just the kind of quotable sound bite calculated to show that both he and his music stood high above the medium for which the work was expressly commissioned. Suggesting that the composition was conceived entirely in television terms and at the next moment claiming he didn't know a thing about the medium was pure Stravinsky. He liked keeping all parties baffled.

Perhaps even more revealing is another source held by the Sacher Stiftung in which Craft outlines and indeed specifies in even greater detail the very core of the work's architecture. This undated, unpublished document must surely have been drafted and submitted to Stravinsky long before he actually began to write the music. Moreover it is clear from this remarkable précis that the work's overall length, as well as specific sectional durations, had already been determined. Not only does Craft suggest timings for each of the composition's individual sections, but he provides a running commentary on such matters as camera positions, instrumentation, suggestions for scenery, and even several different musical "styles" in which portions of the work might be cast (everything from Verdi to John Cage to the operas of Alban Berg).[17]

Craft's influence in charting a compositional blueprint for Stravinsky to follow is indisputable. He assumed the multiple role of collaborator, librettist, attaché, and agent to the television producers Stravinsky viewed so contemptuously. Had it not been for Craft's intercession, especially after Eliot's bowing out, it is likely *The Flood* would have been abandoned as were so many of Stravinsky's aborted film projects; it is questionable whether it would even have been undertaken at all. The final score demonstrates that Stravinsky followed most of the textual and even musical recommendations made by Craft.

Stravinsky never missed a deadline, but in this case he cut things uncomfortably close. Between 14 and 16 March 1962—only two weeks before the production was taped, he and Balanchine worked together in California on the final version of the scenario. A 27 March entry in Stravinsky's diary reports, "From now on every day, John McClure [of Columbia Broadcasting] and TV people for *The Flood*." The work was finally recorded at the CBS studios in Hollywood on 31 March. Craft conducted the orchestra for the audio taping (although the televised program led the audience to believe that Stravinsky himself was on the podium), and Leonard Bernstein helped as well. A week later the composer wrote to McClure in New York, providing specific instructions for a passage to be recorded by Leonard Bernstein. Stravinsky had telegraphed the conductor a day earlier, asking him if he would be willing to do a "great favor" and record "the three snippets John McClure has from *The Flood*."

Stravinsky addressed the question of who conducted which passages in his letter to McClure on 6 April.

> The solution to the conductor credit problem seems less satisfactory the more I think about it. If *The Flood* were for two orchestra [*sic*] like Stockhausen, then two conductors could be used. It seems to me you invite speculation and call undue attention to a problem by saying two people conducted and not saying who conducted what. Therefore, leave out the word "conductor" *entirely*. Say "recording supervised by the composer." I will also make R. Graff say "Musical performance under the supervision of the composer." This at least is not fraud. And, certainly, no one is going to buy the record for the conductor.

(In fact, Columbia Masterworks released the recording even before the televised performance.)

On 15 April, Stravinsky and Balanchine wrote jointly to Graff: "We are now absolutely clear in our minds that nothing should be changed, cut, or repeated and that the work should be heard exactly as it now stands." They reassured him that the work would take twenty-five minutes, but this would be achieved only "by the lengthening of pauses . . . not by the repetition of unrepeatable music." Where Stravinsky had persistently argued before that the work was not a ballet piece, here he reversed himself by saying, "We have worked out a choreographic visualization . . . and your earlier publicity releases about *The Flood* calling it a Stravinsky-Balanchine ballet are now more precise than we at that time thought."[18]

Some of the unpublished compositional sketches in Basel further confirm how late decisions were made. Several measures were added, deleted, shifted, repeated, and some passages were even taped into the score at the last moment, especially in the dance sequences. Typically, the composer carefully timed every fragment. Durations marked as precisely as "seventeen seconds" were not unusual. Nor was it uncommon for Stravinsky to work with Balanchine in this way: on earlier ballets, especially *Orpheus* and *Agon,* he was willing to adjust the music's pacing to accommodate choreographic conceptions. The sketches also establish that the music was not completed until 14 March, the same afternoon Balanchine arrived in Hollywood to begin blocking the stage action.

The actual script for the performance is heavily marked by Craft with suggestions for revising the wording of certain sentences, advising the speaker to deliver the text with specific pauses and nuances, and specifying enunciation and inflection. Of course all the concerns with timing, how fast the text should be read, when and how quickly to make entrances and exits, were now precisely regulated to insure that the program would not run over or under the allotted broadcast slot. How much Stravinsky himself was involved in these refinements is unknown, but certainly there is nothing to suggest that he either initiated or objected to Craft's guiding hand in these matters. The composer and the choreographer continued to assure Graff that the work would be twenty-five minutes long. Yet the matter was still unresolved after Stravinsky and Balanchine concluded their discussions in March. Incredibly, Graff wrote to Stravinsky in a letter on 2 April that he must now lengthen the work— or, more to the point, that Craft would have to: "I would appreciate your aid in guiding Bob to such extension of the work which would permit a dance presentation in excess of 30 minutes. This will insure the success of the premiere." Everything now seemed rushed.

Earlier, Stravinsky had been growing more tentative about the production's chances of succeeding. Writing to Graff in February, he requested: "I would like to see what your writer has done by way of introduction to the show and I would like to see Arutunian's sketches. The success of the show will depend to a great extend [sic] *on the narrator.*" The composer's apprehension intensified; he presciently wrote to his friend Liebermann on 22 March: "In a few days I am recording *The Flood* which I finished a week ago . . . Happy I finished it and I hope *The Flood* will not be *A FLOP.*"[19]

The production was videotaped and the commitment to televise the program was made. The tape was not previewed until only two days before the telecast, by which time it was too late to pull the program. *The Flood* aired as scheduled. Stravinsky, who was touring in Germany, didn't see the telecast. It was just as well. He received the first report from Graff in a telegram dated 19 June: "Flood played to enormous audience network. Notices generally unfavorable. Have no doubt work will be replayed many times. Hearty congratulations, many bravos." (Stravinsky underlined the word *unfavorable*.) But the final verdict could not be suppressed forever, and as the reviews from across the country accumulated during the next two weeks, it became clear that Stravinsky's fears had been well founded. On 9 July, Graff wrote to him again, now finding nothing more encouraging to say than "it is my humble opinion *The Flood* will assert its tremendous strength little by little, longer and longer."

The sponsorship had gambled on the lure of Stravinsky's name. An enormous financial investment underwrote a publicity campaign to promote the venture, especially the work's artistic significance. But the public outcry following the broadcast was overwhelmingly negative. With one voice, the public defiantly shouted that television was no place for such artistic dada, and no place for Stravinsky's empty dialectics about the world's impending nuclear calamity. Emily Coleman of *Newsweek* observed that "somewhere along the way somebody underestimated the American public." Clive Barnes spoke of television as the "first truly democratic culture" entirely governed by what people wanted to see. The "terrifying" problem, Barnes noted, was precisely what it *was* that they wanted to see. No matter how famous Stravinsky might be, the public was not about to pull itself up to his music. The composer suffered the brunt of such denunciations—unsurprisingly really—for he was an easy target for critics aware of his constant carping about film, television, and the entertainment industry in general. Indeed, the public reacted with "vulgar merriment," one critic added, for the composer had been brazen enough to attempt to force viewers to become intellectuals, as network executive Sylvester Weaver had once proclaimed television would do.

Every aspect of *The Flood* came under attack: Balanchine's choreography had been "restricted and dark" (certainly the lighting as televised was horribly dim), Ter-Arutunian had gone "overboard in the sets, costumes and props," the overall production was little more than "an electronics show put together to be seen in a box" and "an excess of electronic hanky-panky," one newspaper after another charged. Press reviews reveal how deep the chasm was between the "people" and the "artist." Jack O'Brien, television critic of the *New York Journal-American*, was one of several writers reviewing the production through the eyes of a television rather than music critic. His yardstick measured what made for "good TV entertainment." O'Brien complained about the "corps de BVD . . . one huge underwear ad with all models en pointe," and went on to charge the production with "artistic larceny." The *Baltimore Sun* critic couldn't resist a watery metaphor: "Noah and the Flood . . . was less like a deluge than a leaky faucet. It's now painfully obvious that in television

[Stravinsky] is a whale out of water." One viewer from Hagerstown, Maryland, wrote that he was so baffled he could only admit his own confusion: "The only thing I understood was the commercials." Even the titles of several newspaper reviews were awash with cynicism: "Noah Almost Got Drowned," from San Francisco; "Noah's Ark Had Enough Trouble," and "Noah Submerged," from New York; "Igor and Noah Sink in the Flood," from Los Angeles.

Because of a barrage of pre-telecast commercials, viewers fully expected to see more dancing. Edward Villella, Jillana, Jacques d'Amboise—all young stars in Balanchine's company—were publicized as having important roles and were given individual screen credits, but their parts were so small (to say nothing of the overwhelming masks and scenery making them unrecognizable) that they were almost entirely missed. In his New York Times review of 25 June, Allen Hughes wrote perceptively: "We must assume that Mr. Balanchine had no effective control over Noah and the Flood." A review from Philadelphia spoke of the "artistic chaos" and the regrettable fact that "Balanchine's choreography was not well served by a feeling of constriction and by dark photography." Perhaps the most dispassionate review was filed by dance critic Walter Terry for the Herald-Tribune, who viewed the telecast from another angle.

> The dancing in Noah and the Flood is frankly incidental but the sequences of action and even the fragments of gesture which George Balanchine has created contribute handsomely to the tenth and the latest collaboration between Stravinsky and Balanchine. . . . Mr. Balanchine does not treat the building of the ark in terms of representational movement or pantomime; rather does he present his dancers as celebrants at a dedication and only through their patterns of interweaving do we find a hint of the act of creating or building. . . . There are also some mime passages—the dancers wear masks—and at the close of the work in the "Covenant of the Rainbow" section, there is a very brief but stunning adagio passage. But then, Noah and the Flood is a short work and, it follows, the dancing comes in quick, episodic fragments. Incidentally . . . not only did we catch a glimpse of Stravinsky rehearsing but also Mr. Balanchine working in the studio with his dancers. I was especially delighted to hear Balanchine inform one of the dancers who had had difficulty mastering a flowing, sea-like movement, "I guess I'll have to take you to Atlantic City." Choreographically, Noah and the Flood does not represent the most exciting and meaty of the Stravinsky and Balanchine collaborations but, during its brief course, it gives us a few very special images of movement beauty which only Balanchine could devise.[20]

Stravinsky saved more than sixty press reviews in a file marked "American critics about The Flood, June 1962." Musicians usually place little stock in the

Jacques d'Amboise (Adam) and Jillana (Eve) in the CBS production of *The Flood*
(Courtesy of the Dance Collection of the New York Public Library
for the Performing Arts)

views of critics (most of them, it is true, are ludicrously uninformed), but the fact that Stravinsky read so many is telling. His files confirm that he closely monitored reactions to his work while publicly dismissing them. Yet he read every review, correcting those that erroneously referred to the work as *Noah*, as if the gesture itself retained for him a certain bittersweet vestige of control. For a composer who claimed immunity from public opinion, especially the opinion of critics, such documents testify to strong feelings of hurt. That hurt erupted in a 24 June telegram that Stravinsky wired to the *New York Herald-Tribune*, which the newspaper published. The composer was retaliating for a damaging review by the paper's critic, Paul Henry Lang. Among several unjust swipes, the well-respected musicologist had criticized "the junior high school quality" of the work's prologue. Stravinsky angrily replied: "Of hundreds of reviews of my New York work, most of them, like every opus since 1905, were gratifyingly unfavorable. I found only yours entirely stupid and suppurating with gratuitous malice. The only blight on my eightieth birthday is the realization my age will probably keep me from celebrating the funeral of your senile music columnist."

With that notable exception, the composer attempted to conceal his bruises about the work's reception. Still, his facade of indifference is belied by his undisclosed retention of several fan letters, including one from a fifteen-year-old high school student who with youthful innocence tried to compliment the composer: "I think that when the music and choreography were combined that they created a fascinating effect." That the preeminent composer of the age would need to record such an assurance speaks to a susceptibility in his nature that remained carefully hidden from the public. For Stravinsky to admit concern over what others thought of his music might allow for too much exposure and, by extension, too much scrutiny of him as a person rather than of the composition as a product. With a public tribunal of millions watching—an audience forewarned that it absolutely must be edified by the significance of *The Flood*—Stravinsky's vulnerability was obvious. He was put on the spot, especially amid the hype of the televised promises of a "milestone" moment. There was too much risk of public degradation. How much safer publicly to divest any stake in whether people would respond to a work the composer himself privately hoped would be popular.

One of Stravinsky's advocates rose to the embattled composer's defense. Attempting to undercut the criticisms, composer and music theorist Benjamin Boretz wrote a rebuttal, published in *The Nation*—a journal that had almost always been sympathetic to Stravinsky's music—suggesting that the clever composer delighted in this confrontation of serious music with popular culture. Stravinsky "seems to take a special pleasure in carefully fulfilling the letter of such a commission so that the commissioner gets precisely what he has asked for but hardly what he expected," Boretz wrote. He justly charged that the producers "crushed the refined music" between a "pseudo-profound anthropological prologue" and a "long, disorganized totally inappropriate review of the Stravinsky-Balanchine collaborations." And with a final barb, Boretz concluded that "however extensive the damage done to mass culture . . . a new and interesting Stravinsky work . . . slipped past the heavy-footed promoters."[21]

Boretz's response was meant to demonstrate that both the allegedly unethical producers and the show's provincial viewers had been bamboozled by the crafty composer. But was this what Stravinsky really had in mind from the outset? If Boretz was right, hadn't Stravinsky been disingenuous in claiming "I tried hard to keep *The Flood* very simple as music: it was commissioned for television after all, and I could not regard this commission cynically"? Did Stravinsky really intend to hoodwink the sponsors, or was Boretz (speaking for many Stravinsky supporters) merely grasping for some retaliative defense? Boretz's contention was that the "refined music" had been "crushed" by frequent insertions of unrelated, nonmusical addenda, so as to stretch the show for the entire hour. He was absolutely right, of course. Balanchine was even more direct, charging that the sponsors "smothered the work by a whole goulash of other things they dumped into the package to fill it up." The choreographer complained that the package was "sickening and patronizing" in browbeating the public over the intrinsic value of "high art."

Stravinsky knew that there would be introductory material, and he was even invited to participate more fully in it than he did (although his archives reveal that his appearance would have come with an added financial charge). He also knew that the hour would include inserted footage, such as Balanchine rehearsing the dancers and his own rehearsing of the orchestra. That such filler disrupted the music's continuity was undeniable; but if it was all that disturbing, why did he go along with it? The question was raised by television analyst Jack Gould in a review that Stravinsky considered important enough not only to save but to mark for his files.

> Would the composer consent to a concert appearance without a full awareness and agreement on what would occur before and after his participation? Hence the quandary. In the media in which Stravinsky and Balanchine are normally engaged, it could be assumed that *"Noah and the Flood"* would not see

the light of day in anything like the manner in which it was offered on television. . . . If the giants of the arts in effect make the fundamental concession that television is a world apart, an irascible stepchild of creativity, can they then disassociate themselves from the consequences of their own example? . . . It would seem incumbent on major artistic figures to recognize that while expedient acquiescence may be entirely understandable, it simply cannot simultaneously be hailed as impressive artistic leadership. What television needs most desperately is the vigorous help and guidance of such persons, not their resigned compliance.[22]

Gould's exhortation might well be interpreted as mere proselytizing, offered to ward off the common accusation that television was an "idiot box" incapable of producing anything of artistic merit. Even so, some musicians worried about the meaningfulness of the production. Richard Franko Goldman wondered about Stravinsky's intent: "*The Flood* has nothing to do with belief, nor is it believable. It is merely . . . 'significant,' yet it signifies nothing, except the ultimately vain attempt to sanctify the pretense that art can exist for itself alone, as an object, in a vacuum, not to be loved or believed, but merely to be admired or consumed." Goldman applauded Gould for his directness and confessed his "distress that an artist of Stravinsky's genius and influence did not wish, or was unable, to make something less dismal of the production."[23]

There is little evidence, in fact, that Stravinsky felt any social responsibility as a "giant of the arts." He simply wanted to write what he wished, and then find somebody willing to commission it. Whether he really cared about *The Flood* being offered up as a benediction, or a paradigm for what television might be, is doubtful. He told the press, "My first composition for the medium of television was highly stimulating," but one wonders what else he could have said. Was he concerned about how the telecast would look once he, as Boretz suggested, "fulfilled the letter of the commission," then departed for Hamburg and a festival of his music? Did he even acknowledge the artistic stewardship with which Gould was charging him? Certainly he felt a singular, even profound responsibility to himself as an artist to write the best music he could. But whether he was genuinely concerned about his music being fundamentally capable of speaking intelligibly to the "illusory mass," as Gould dubbed the TV audience—that was quite another matter.

Successful programs such as *The Voice of Firestone*, showcasing opera divas singing emotionally overflowing arias, or beautiful ballerinas performing in the elegant white tutu tradition of a *Swan Lake* were doubtless the kind of entertaining fare the audience thought it would see as it settled back for its weekly dose of Saturday night culture. After all, this is what the American television audience had come to expect in the 1950s. Viewers wanted something that was clearly defined and in accord with their comfortably packaged ideas about art, and that is exactly what the sponsors expected Stravinsky would produce. But the composer was never comfortable with easily consumable fare. The artistic amalgam—or, from the audience's armchair perspective, garish hodgepodge—that confronted TV land that evening was simply too unfamiliar for viewers to accept.[24]

Yet even if the sponsors of *The Flood* baited the public with misleading commercial promotions as to what they might expect, the best production imaginable would surely have fallen on unreceptive eyes and ears. Television viewers were totally unprepared to deal with a canting miracle play set to music in a still unfamiliar—and to them "unmelodic"—compositional style. Stravinsky and Balanchine were always energized by a natural contrariness that resisted convention. How could the producers of *The Flood* not have known this? Did they really expect the sugary pabulum of *Amahl*? In the end, *The Flood* drowned in its own homiletics, and its failure cannot be dodged so easily by blaming this "inglorious flop" entirely on the poorly produced broadcast. The unbridgeable abyss that separated what artists of range and imagination saw as communicative from what the reality of American television already had become was horrendously misjudged by everybody involved, even though the musical score itself is as cohesive and imaginative as the composer's other works from that period.

What *The New Grove Dictionary of American Music* calls "possibly the most spectacular failure among television opera performances" cost Stravinsky dearly. The composer has often been portrayed as a craggy, unflappable iconoclast, staunchly secure in his creative powers, immune to public ridicule. But he was not. At age eighty, Stravinsky must have been injured personally and publicly through the far-reaching lens of the television camera. It is unlikely his own premonition of a "flop" was swallowed as easily as he and others would have us believe. Other television commissions were to come along, but his experience with Hollywood, and now television, taught him that there were more productive and more controllable paths to follow. Perhaps the power of television could somehow be harnessed for his own personal gain—harnessed in ways that would not force him to concede any part of his beliefs, or of himself. Maybe it was the colorful, even endearing crustiness of his individuality that could be most beneficially marketed over the airwaves for musically unsophisticated but naturally curious audiences. Maybe Americans, with their spoon-fed conceptions of how eccentric, creative people should act, might actually be more interested in the persona of the man, his image as an icon, rather than in the indecipherable message of his still richly expressive music. Perhaps the cameras should focus, not on his music, but directly upon him.

C·h·a·p·t·e·r ·6·

Film Documentaries:
The Composer On and Off Camera

> The documentary idea, after all, demands no more than that the affairs
> of our time shall be brought to the screen in any fashion which strikes
> the imagination and makes observation a little richer than it was. At one
> level the vision may be journalistic; and at another it may rise to poetry
> and drama. At another level, again, its artistic quality may lie in the mere
> lucidity of its exposition.
> —John Grierson, *The Story of the Documentary Film*

In describing film's capacity to visualize the critical events of our
time, John Grierson coined the term *documentary*. A teacher by profession,
the British filmmaker was committed to educating the general public about
the social, economic, political, and other contemporary forces shaping our
world. Grierson wished to engage his viewers in a novel way: his films would
forgo an exact recounting of history's pivotal moments in favor of a "creative
interpretation of actuality."[1] By the 1950s, television was flooding the airwaves with its newest brainchild, the documentary drama. It was a decade in
which TV programming saw the concept of "creative actuality" emerge as an
effective way of melding entertainment, art, and history.

At about the same time, Stravinsky's status as the world's greatest living
composer was being even more aggressively promoted. Finally, after years of
no more than moderate financial success, the composer was in a position to
capitalize on his image—and to do it in a way that his notoriety deserved.
Hailed as a national treasure, how much would Stravinsky involve himself in
sculpting his own image? How might his life story be "actualized," as Grierson might have said?

The United States was producing film documentaries as early as the
1930s, including Louis de Rochemont's *March of Time* series, produced by
Time, Inc., and released beginning in 1935. Shown in movie theaters around
the country, the series had a visceral impact on how people viewed current
events. *Time* magazine defended screen journalism as "fakery in the allegiance

of truth," and films like "Inside Nazi-Germany" in 1938 shook America, exposing the monstrousness of Hitler in searing visual images. The storm troopers depicted in the shocking sixteen-minute reel, however, were not Nazis at all but loyal German-American citizens who, during the hardship of the Great Depression, took whatever work they could find; and these costumed, makeshift actors were filmed not inside Germany but in New Jersey. Other early ventures often amounted to a conglomeration of newsreels, narrative, and interviews—a mixture of truth and embellishment—aimed at bringing the public in closer contact with the world.

The form caught on quickly. It was employed globally, not as a tool to report the events of the day objectively, but as a weapon of propaganda. Even in the early 1900s, glimpses of the Bolshevik revolution were filmed with an eye toward visually stirring emotions. In the 1930s, Hitler's National Ministry of Public Enlightenment and Propaganda, created by Joseph Goebbels, used film extensively as an especially effective means of convoking support for the Reich. America retaliated, employing documentaries to promote its own war effort. Walt Disney joined the rallying of the troops by producing several films, as did Frank Capra in the popular *Why We Fight* series (1942–45). Grierson himself attempted to draw a reluctant and neutral United States into the war, knowing that Hollywood was "the greatest potential munitions factory."

Even after the armistice—and continuing to evolve as a highly expressive art form—the American documentary was used to rouse patriotism. NBC's 1952–53 *Victory at Sea* compilation series, with twenty-six half-hour episodes set to the music of Richard Rodgers as orchestrated by Robert Russell Bennett, won artistic as well as political acclaim in graphically demonstrating how the brutality of war could almost be touched through filmmaking. Many composers wrote for documentaries during the 1950s and '60s, including the Americans Paul Creston and Morton Gould, as well as two members of Les Six, Georges Auric and Darius Milhaud. On more than one occasion, Stravinsky was invited to score a documentary, although he regularly declined. CBS's *The Twentieth Century* presented the biographies of the "great men" of our age: Churchill, Gandhi, Mussolini, FDR, Woodrow Wilson, and others. The contributions of artists to society were addressed in CBS's "Paris in the Twenties." The film was introduced by Walter Cronkite and focused on Janet Flanner, the *New Yorker*'s Paris correspondent, who had written several perceptive articles about Stravinsky. Flanner spoke of the halcyon days of Picasso, Fitzgerald, Stravinsky, Gertrude Stein, and other artists who gave birth to one of the most artistically fertile periods of our time.

Documentaries became an "instrument of transportation," as Edward R. Murrow remarked, capable of bringing viewers right into the homes of the very people who were writing our history. Moving from radio and his *Hear It Now* broadcasts, Murrow's own legendary television series, *See It Now* (begun in 1951, the same year as Stravinsky's *Rake's Progress*), would often casually blend narrative and armchair commentary with fact, leaving it to the viewer to sort one from the other. It is, of course, Murrow's unshrinking assaults on McCarthyism, aired over several confrontational telecasts during March 1954, that are remembered most. But there were documentaries about artists too. That same year, Murrow did an October program titled "A Visit to Flat Rock—Carl Sandburg." The venerable poet, seated in a rocking chair, spoke directly and plainly to the camera without much prodding or interference from Murrow. The impact was captivating. The CBS network annually presented nearly eighty hours of documentaries, including successful series such as *Eye-Witness to History, Face the Nation,* and especially *The Twentieth Century,* which often focused on the cultural contributions of writers, artists, and musicians.

While increasingly well-defined programming strategies were evolving over the commercial networks, Stravinsky too was undergoing a revitalizing transformation. After *The Rake's Progress,* his music took an unanticipated turn—one steered by Craft's presence in the composer's life. Arnold Schoenberg's death in July 1951 came only a few months before *The Rake* was premiered in Venice. Almost immediately, Stravinsky rescinded his earlier denunciations of Schoenberg, embracing the previously maligned tenets of Viennese serialism. For those who felt Stravinsky had been wandering artistically since arriving in America a decade earlier, it was the end of his Odyssean journey. He now made a commitment to a compositional style that would serve him for the rest of his life. Whether or not this once unthinkable about-face was really a logical next step (as the composer rather defensively contended, claiming that he had always been a "serial" composer), the backlash was predictably hostile. Stravinsky had capitulated to the enemy, and even such old loyalists as Ansermet and Boulanger shook their heads at his adoption of what they considered repellent models. The circle of musicians who comprehended his newest works (some of the most brilliant pieces he would write) largely comprised admiring academics and composers familiar with the works of Schoenberg's pupil Anton Webern—until then a largely unknown composer in this country.

In the decade between *The Rake's Progress* and *The Flood,* American culture changed dramatically. Allen Ginsberg's 1956 poem *Howl* heralded the

Beat generation; McDonald's changed the country's eating habits; Detroit's assembly lines produced more cars than ever before during the golden age of the tail fin; and Eisenhower initiated the interstate highway system, enabling Americans to move quickly from place to place. All the while, television's new commitment to the documentary drama enjoyed a surge of popularity. It presented history in a pictorial nutshell to an audience wanting only the TV-dinner version of the truth. Attention spans shortened, people grew more hurried, and audiences became increasingly dependent on the visual images that now were part of everyday routine, thanks to television's cultural invasion. Meanwhile, Stravinsky's stature as the ranking composer of the age continued to grow. It did so, curiously, despite his music's dwindling accessibility to the American public. Even more ironically, whatever the reasons for his unsuccessful Hollywood filmmaking attempts, television networks were not dissuaded from popularizing him as a subject of numerous documentaries. During the 1950s and 1960s, Stravinsky became the most filmed, the most marketable, the most "documentable" composer of the twentieth century.[2]

Music aside, Stravinsky's whole life was a docudrama, requiring little ornament. While leaving many former supporters in his wake, his post-1950 serial works actually heightened his mystique. Comprehension and notoriety do not necessarily go hand in hand, and it was perfectly fine for the public not to deal with or understand what he was writing. His music was pronounced "esoteric" by many, but this only created the impression that he was light-years ahead of contemporary composers half his age. Actually, nothing could have been further from the truth. By the early 1960s, Stravinsky's music could hardly be counted among the wave of "New Music" composers that included the texturally imaginative and montagelike works of Pierre Boulez, Krzysztof Penderecki, Luciano Berio, and others. Still, for the general public, the unapproachable nature of Stravinsky's serial music mythologized the already hallowed composer all the more, and in the way that Americans like to lionize their creative artists. Here was this enigmatic "elder," who continued to rock the world with each new creation. *The Flood* may have been a flop by television standards, but nobody was willing to deny that the old fox was still turning heads, still eager, still capable of igniting controversy.

Television producers in Europe and North America found him attractive for a variety of reasons. He was the ideal film personality: funny, droll, quick, eccentric, quirky, controversial, contentious, yet still pedestaled as the epitome of the not-to-be-deterred rebellious hero so many admired. It was a time when Americans enshrined restless, nonconformist film icons like James

Dean. When Marlon Brando's Johnny comes riding into town on his motorcycle in Laslo Benedek's 1953 film *The Wild One,* we know he means business. When asked what he is rebelling against, the leather-jacketed tough guy snaps, "What have you got?" Brando's bad-boy character had an attitude, and so did the always spunky Stravinsky. Into his eighties, he was still upsetting applecarts, still doing things his way, still defiant; and it really made little difference whether people understood just what he was being defiant about. By birthright, he was a natural performer who needed and commanded the spotlight. His heavily accented basso voice added to his aura, and the broad grin and twinkling eyes radiated a buoyancy that should have vanished years before. The cameras portrayed him as a cultural hero, and most documentaries purposely tilted more toward hagiography than biography. They also left many of the composer's flaws on the cutting-room floor, and those clips that were printed often were carefully scripted and prescreened.

How vital and sanguine Stravinsky appeared on screen compared with the sullen images of Rachmaninoff, Shostakovich, Schoenberg, Bartók, and other contemporaries visibly worn down by wars, governmental strictures, and life's vagaries. He was the embodiment of everything producers desired, a caricature of himself, almost as if some clever Hollywood screenwriter had conjured up this made-to-order character. Stravinsky loved the attention (while denying that he did), and he became pliant in his willingness to mug for the camera. Eager to cash in on his showbiz visibility, he literally starred in numerous film ventures, many of which were either destroyed or are now mostly forgotten. The camera became his constant companion. Every time his plane touched down in whatever city or country he happened to be, his arrival was recorded on film. Yet despite several extant (albeit not easily obtainable) documentaries, filmed testimony of Stravinsky is a dimension of the composer's biography generally ignored.

Nor is it a dimension that is easily analyzed, for it is often difficult to separate the private Stravinsky—the Stravinsky that lived beyond the probing lens of the camera—from the public man who knew precisely what to say and how to charm an audience with disarming aplomb. Thanks to his status as an icon, an immense amount of footage was shot of the composer engaged in a variety of interesting and entertaining activities: conducting, responding to questions, participating in interviews wherein he skillfully interacted with the press, and exchanging views with such colleagues as Balanchine and Nabokov. He was, quite literally, a master of "ceremony" in the broadest sense. Nor should the importance of reel after reel of such historical footage be undervalued. The fact is, with our own eyes we see Stravinsky more than we have seen any other composer of the century, and that in itself becomes a not-to-be-ignored aspect of biographical interpretation in drawing a fuller portrait of the man.

Curious viewers were allowed a peek into the private lives of celebrated performers and composers. During the mid-1950s through the 1960s, the three major American commercial networks, as well as the newer noncommercial educational stations, filmed performances, master classes, and offered special profiles on Pablo Casals, Jascha Heifetz, the Juilliard Quartet, Herbert von Karajan, Yehudi Menuhin, Arthur Rubinstein, and others. Composers, too, were featured, including Bartók and Jean Sibelius. Stravinsky was seen on television as early as 1954, when Chicago's WGN broadcast one of his orchestral concerts. He also appeared as a guest conductor on Bernstein's *Young People's Concerts* in January 1960. Not only did such telecasts keep Stravinsky in the public eye, but they required little preparation while proving financially profitable. A letter to the composer from his New York attorney in late 1962 included a two-thousand-dollar check, in effect a royalty fee for a recent television repeat of Bernstein's "The Creative Performer." The show was a telecast of the New York Philharmonic; Bernstein, doing all the talking, introduced Stravinsky to the audience. The composer then came on stage, took the podium without a word, and conducted the final portion of *The Firebird*. It was a bittersweet irony indeed, following the disaster of *The Flood*, which had been shown on the same network only a few months before.

In fact, it was *The Flood*'s producer Robert Graff who had assembled the very first television documentary on the composer for NBC in 1957. Graff's commissioning of the 1962 opus owed greatly to his collaboration with Stravinsky and Craft on this earlier project. Stravinsky's correspondence indicates that he originally liked and trusted Graff, and he accepted the commission for *The Flood* on the basis of their work together on the 1957 documentary, adding that he was looking forward to their close collaboration. Graff produced several successful documentaries, including the highly acclaimed *Valiant Years* (1960), a monumental series of twenty-six half-hour segments based on Winston Churchill's epic prose as delivered by Richard Burton, with music by Richard Rodgers. The achievement of this docudrama stemmed from Graff's earlier experience on NBC's *Wisdom* series of 1957, of which the half-hour documentary showcasing Stravinsky became part.

In an article in the 15 June 1957 issue of *The Nation*, Lincoln Kirstein confidently prognosticated that Stravinsky would never be party to such documentaries: "Stravinsky has always resisted canonization! He will not license his 'wisdom' to be documented on an 'educational' TV short with mood music from his more familiar recordings. He may be 'great,' but the aura of bard, mage, oracle is not of his choosing." But Stravinsky wanted very much to be seen as an oracle, and virtually everything that Kirstein proclaimed was dead wrong. Graff's contract specifically stipulated that the show would be "educational," that it would use snippets of his familiar music, and that the purpose of the series was to share the "wisdom" of great people with everyday viewers. Kirstein's remarks reinforce the image of Stravinsky as a fiercely sovereign genius who would never stoop to selling his notoriety. But Stravinsky's unpublished file, marked "NBC Television, June 1957," demonstrates that his image was very much for sale at the right price. Kirstein's argument notwithstanding, why shouldn't it have been? Celebrities, musical and otherwise, were profiting from their public images, so why not him?

Stravinsky's attorney, as was often the case, served as his intermediary, and several letters exchanged with Graff over the next month reveal detailed and hard-fought negotiations regarding an appropriate fee. The composer asked for a sum that Graff found unacceptably higher than "other persons equally eminent." But eventually a deal was struck and the NBC television crew arrived at the Stravinsky home on 12 June. The footage was assembled quickly and within a few days the twenty-eight-minute film was shot.[3] The title itself—*A Conversation with Igor Stravinsky*—replicates the dialogue format that Craft and Stravinsky were just then initiating, and which eventually led to the popular series of conversation books. The opening moments of the program originally suggested by Graff were even scripted to simulate an impromptu chat between the composer and his assistant. As the unpublished scenario by Graff outlines:

> We find Maestro Stravinsky at the piano in the small room adjacent to the living room. He is busy reworking a musical phrase or working on a composition in some stage of completion. He strikes notes on the piano. He proceeds normally. Shortly he resolves the musical problem and decides to ask Mr. Craft's opinion. He calls Mr. Craft who enters from the door by the bathroom. The two men sit side by side on the piano bench or Mr. Craft stands by Maestro Stravinsky who is seated, or whatever arrangement is natural. Mr. Craft asks how the composing goes (or a remark pertinent to the situation). Maestro Stravinsky answers and the conversation is under way.

Graff's stolid staging was followed to the letter. The telecast opened with Stravinsky seated at the piano, plucking away at his most recent composition, the ballet *Agon*. Before long, the composer pauses, then calls "Oh, Bob"—and in true out-of-the-blue 1950s television style, Bob miraculously appears right on cue. He joins the composer at the piano and assists the maestro in playing a passage requiring four hands. Then, sticking to the forced dialogue, Craft asks a few questions. The two then nonchalantly walk to an adjoining room where the composer, on the spur of the moment (so it appeared), exhibits several manuscript sketches for the camera, "and the conversation is under way," as Graff's script directed. It was all very much in the style of the popular Murrow interviews, wherein celebrities sauntered around their homes completely unconcerned that a camera just happened to be filming them. Who would have guessed that Stravinsky would go along with this phony staging, forcing him into a rigidity completely alien to his natural spontaneity?

Moreover, the laughable notion that Stravinsky would actually compose in front of an audience for all the world to see (as Picasso had done two years earlier in the 1955 film directed by Henri-Georges Clouzot, *Le Mystère Picasso*) could only have been imagined in the make-believe world of television. How seriously Stravinsky took the project is even suspect. Yet, amazingly, he seemed willing to be used as little more than a prop. He was adept at quickly shifting to a wholly devised television actor mode, following whatever contrived directions were given, without raising an objection. One can easily detect such casualness among the light-hearted answers Stravinsky originally penned to a set of questions Graff initially provided.

> *How do musical ideas occur to you?*
>   Well, sometimes in the bathroom.
> *Do you write them down?*
>   Sometimes.
> *Does chance or accident play a role in musical ideas?*
>   Of course.
> *Do you think of yourself as a creative artist, or as an artisan?*
>   [Stravinsky circled "as an artisan" and added the word "only."]
> *What brought about your use of serial techniques after World War II?*
>   The need for discipline.
> *Which of the older composers do you like best?*
>   The older the better.
> *Do music critics perform a useful function?*
>   They think so.
> *How does a composer of serious music survive economically in our time?*
>   The same as in any other time—very badly.[4]

None of these replies were used in the film, even though they were right on the mark in capturing the composer's dry wit. Such sardonicism was a bit too irreverent for the "family values" of 1950s television. Yet Stravinsky seems not to have objected to Graff's editing of his comments. In fact, he seems not to have protested being scripted at all. Throughout the program the composer interspersed familiar bromides that amounted to little more than canned answers: "Craftsmanship reminds me of a very great word, 'homo faber'—a man who makes things and for things to be made he must invent them." "Diaghilev was furious because the triumph of *Sacre* was not in his ballet [but rather in Stravinsky's later orchestral performance in Paris]. So I went on and composed something which has far more importance than the people think about it, that's *Apollon Musagète*. I think of *Apollo* as the beginning of something new in my music . . . the technique was new."

Craft asks Stravinsky to define music—perhaps the question most frequently posed to the composer ever since his inscrutable (and, for many, intentionally inflammatory) maxim uttered almost twenty years earlier in his *Autobiography*: "Music is powerless to express anything at all." Stravinsky now defines it exactly as Schopenhauer did: "And the musical tones inhabit and form a universe of their own in which the human mind has created the materials and reduced them to order." Both of these replies are accurate, even informative to an audience largely unaware of the composer's often expressed dicta. Yet they reflect only his public image. Seldom does the film transmit Stravinsky's ageless vigor.

Occasionally, though, his less inhibited temperament does manage to slip by the documentary's artificiality. When Craft asks why Stravinsky spends so much time conducting, the composer forthrightly enumerates: one, he is the son of an actor and the theater is in his blood; two, he wishes his music to be interpreted correctly (implying of course that no other conductor could); and, three, he earns a great deal more money conducting and "being seen" by the public than he does composing. At one point in Graff's film, Stravinsky demonstrates and guides Craft in conducting *Agon*, showing him what to emphasize and what to ignore. That kind of exhibition employs television in a way that no monograph, newspaper interview, or even audio recording could duplicate as effectively. For those who never actually saw Stravinsky during his many active years, Graff's documentary in this respect is quite valuable. In reviewing the film, *Time* declared it "an uninterrupted half hour of discerning intimacy and directness." It was hardly that, but, nevertheless, as the earliest documentary devoted to him, it is a source that remains uniquely instructive in portraying what television thought Stravinsky's public image should be.

The composer knew that appreciable financial gains could be realized by surrendering to the will of documentary producers. Such a concession would not in any way compromise what he wanted to write, and preserving that integrity was most important to him. By the 1960s, those around him were becoming progressively involved in commercializing his life to an unprecedented degree. Interviews, articles, as well as several conversation book sequels with Craft, now appeared regularly. Every personal testimony was built around immortalizing the accomplishments and sentiments of the composer while he was still alert enough to recount them with his inimitable flair. Yet for all these discursive accounts, the television documentaries from the 1960s preserve his legacy most dynamically. American producers were not alone in their desire to film him, either. Correspondence in Basel reveals that in May 1961, Louis Applebaum, TV consultant for the Canadian Broadcasting Corporation, inquired about a possible film project. A fee was negotiated and Applebaum named Franz Kraemer as the producer. The film was three times as long as Graff's earlier documentary. Applebaum knew exactly what he wanted, and he had asked the composer to "think in terms of a television show" that would incorporate all the ingredients that would appeal to a public audience. Certainly that hope was realized to a far greater extent than in the 1957 NBC film.[5]

Another documentary, titled simply *Stravinsky,* was produced for the CBC in 1965 by Roman Kroitor and Wolf Koenig. It is billed as "the definitive profile of the great Russian composer/conductor." The film takes as its focal point Stravinsky actually recording the *Symphony of Psalms* with the CBC Symphony Orchestra and the Festival Singers of Toronto. Interspersed among footage of his conducting are wonderful interviews and anecdotes not to be found elsewhere. Some sequences seem to have been filmed without Stravinsky aware that he was being recorded. There is a supposedly spontaneous discussion with Julian Bream (he just happens to be in the concert hall), who literally serenades Stravinsky with his lute while the CBC orchestra gathers on stage for a rehearsal. Stravinsky listens intently, telling Bream that the lute is his favorite musical instrument because it is the "most personal" of all. Bream suggests the composer write a piece for the lute, but Stravinsky answers candidly that he hasn't the time.

Memories of Stravinsky's association with the world of dance, especially the Ballets Russes, are also included. The film's narrator speaks of Diaghilev having a servant who did his praying; of Picasso and Stravinsky being arrested "when they relieved themselves outside the Naples Opera" around the time they collaborated on *Pulcinella;* and of their being stopped at the Italian border when the police thought that a sketch of the composer by the artist was a clandestine plan of attack. Nicolas Nabokov speaks of the unfairness the composer was made to suffer because his three early "best-sellers" (meaning of course the three early Russian ballets for Diaghilev) were not under copyright, and how, in fact, Stravinsky really was forced to eke out an existence in Switzerland while such composers as Maurice Ravel and Richard Strauss became wealthy on one or two works. Craft recalls for the camera that Stravinsky saw the "big Tchaikovsky ballets" when he was only eight. By the age of ten, Craft continues, the composer knew all the classical positions and was generally quite at ease with ballet technique—down to the way he learned to bow in the Maryinsky tradition.

Especially valuable is a very rare sequence of Balanchine rehearsing dancers from the New York City Ballet in preparation for a Stravinsky premiere. There are exquisite moments in which the choreographer—the "perfect collaborator," Stravinsky calls him—is caught with his head bowed and eyes closed, deep in thought as he envisages the piece. Though the footage is brief, a very young Suzanne Farrell and Jacques d'Amboise are shown during a rehearsal of Stravinsky's *Movements,* apparently filmed a few years earlier, in 1963, when the work was first staged (and televised as well, on CBS). Balanchine can be seen watching very carefully and quietly offering suggestions ("Don't shake it in there," he says) as Farrell and d'Amboise work through a passage.

Balanchine's observations in both CBC films made during this period are not to be found elsewhere. He traces Stravinsky's ballet lineage to Tchaikovsky, but he also stresses the importance of time and order in Stravinsky's music—the two most fundamental ingredients of creative dance. "We are representing art of dancing, art of body movement, in time, in space," Balanchine contends. "It is the music, it is really time more than the melody, and our body must be subordinated to time—because without time, dance doesn't exist. It must be order—it's like a planet. . . . If it's not precise, it falls to pieces." But Balanchine also adjures an interviewer who asks for specifics: "It's not for the public to know how, what technique to use."

The Balanchine–Stravinsky connection is further addressed in another documentary, *A Stravinsky Portrait,* filmed mostly in March 1965. Produced for Norddeutscher Rundfunk Television in Hamburg, the film was directed by Richard Leacock and Rolf Liebermann. Liebermann proposed the documentary to the composer only a month before it was shot. Leacock was one of a new breed of documentary filmmakers who wished to record the "naturalness" of action as unobtrusively as possible by using hand-held cameras. This cinema verité, as the technique was known, left a significant imprint on the look of documentaries, and the NDR film was the most informative and candid Stravinsky footage shot to that point. The composer is shown in his home in Hollywood, chatting with Pierre Boulez and talking fondly of Beethoven's symphonies and Wagner's operas—music that he claims he had finally grown to like by 1965. There is footage of him preparing his recent *Introitus* (in memoriam T. S. Eliot) at the piano, just composed for his friend who had died on 4 January. There is also a brief segment (filmed a few years earlier, evidently) in which Aldous Huxley visits with Stravinsky in the composer's living room, asking him if anything can be said about the creative process, if it can be understood at all. The composer answers, "I don't know if there is a creative process as such," and then adds, in true *homo faber* style, that simply doing something is all that is important: "I like to compose more than to listen to the music."

But most significantly, there is rare footage of both Stravinsky and Balanchine working individually in preparation for a ballet performance of *Apollo*. An entire reel survives, showing Stravinsky leading the Hamburg musicians in an orchestral rehearsal (without the dancers) as they prepare to make a recording that Balanchine will use later. This is a genuine working rehearsal, not one intended to entertain a television audience. The filming reveals a thoroughly focused conductor very much concerned with determining the kind of musical details most viewers would find dull. Only selected excerpts from this precious can of film (absolutely invaluable to conductors interested in Stravinsky's rehearsal habits) were included in the final print. In subsequent documentaries, clips of the composer conducting seem concertedly aimed at amusing the nonmusical viewer and perpetuating the image of Stravinsky as a wisecracking maestro. The Hamburg film sequences of him rehearsing here are unparalleled; there are also equally matchless segments of Balanchine rehearsing *Apollo*.

The camera records Balanchine and Stravinsky in a casual conversation as the choreographer suggests that *Apollo* moved too slowly for Diaghilev; there was simply not enough action. But now the work has become so familiar, Balanchine contends, that "people whistle it in the street." Stravinsky retorts, "Not always in the street, maybe in the bathroom." He then offers Balanchine more to drink, saying, "Let's be drunk . . . you are not dancing, and I am not dancing." All of this bantering could not have been better designed for the camera, yet the footage, farcical as it is, reveals an ineffable bond between the two—an affection that is impossible to express in words. More seriously, in another segment filmed in Stravinsky's absence, Balanchine listens to the audiotape of *Apollo* just recorded by the composer and the Hamburg musicians. Balanchine stands at a piano with some of his New York City Ballet dancers gathered around, telling them that the tempo of this new recording is incredibly faster than when he first choreographed the ballet almost four decades earlier—so fast that he admits he will need to adjust the choreographic patterns. He complains about the speed of Stravinsky's new interpretation, recalling that originally Stravinsky himself sat at the piano in 1928 and very accurately set the tempi at a much slower pace.[6]

There are irreplaceable sequences of Balanchine rehearsing Suzanne Farrell, who by the time of this film had taken her place as the choreographer's latest muse. During the Polyhymnia variation, Balanchine turns the *Apollo* recording off, takes his place at center stage, and sings the whole variation himself as he coaches one of his dancers. He dances the parts of all three Muses, always bestowing special attention on the young Farrell. When audiences think of Farrell today, most tend to picture Balanchine's "alabaster princess," or the later, mature ballerina at the pinnacle of her stunning success. But here, at age nineteen, Balanchine's "Dulcinea" appears innocently naive and hesitant—as would any teenager—even diffident in the presence of the patriarchal choreographer.

Often the camera cuts from Farrell dancing to Balanchine observing, as he follows her every move with a "blind infatuation" that Farrell herself remembers making her feel somewhat uncomfortable.[7] The camera follows her rehearsing the Terpsichore variation, as she makes faces, picks at her fingernails nervously, covers her face timidly, and clowns around awkwardly when she stumbles over certain steps. She listens to Balanchine's suggestions, but with her head turned away so as to avoid eye contact. A fixated Balanchine seems hopelessly smitten, his attention exclusively concentrated on the young ballerina. While the other dancers are rehearsing on stage, Balanchine escorts Farrell off to the side and works with her privately, oblivious to everyone else. The camera occasionally focuses on other members of the company standing around, clearly unamused by Balanchine's preoccupation. None of these reactions are included in the released print. Such footage betrays the mesmerizing influence Farrell had on Balanchine during these years, as he tailored so many dances with her in mind. The sometimes vested accounts about Balanchine, offered in a profusion of recent memoirs by several of his dancers, are quickly eclipsed by these rare and instructive clips, most of which, regrettably, were cut.

By 1965 Stravinsky was a global symbol of classical music "made in America." He was a phenomenon, still composing at eighty-three, still maintaining a transcontinental concert schedule unrivaled by musicians half his age. As a living legend he was beseeched by the media. His fame was now inextricably linked to his longevity, as the camera took pains to point out. He had simply outlasted everybody, and people liked that. He may have slowed a little physically, but he still had fangs. Yet now his scathing wit was no longer construed as caustic so much as winsome. He was no longer maligned as obstinate but admired for his pluck. He now consented regularly to serve as the subject of films, rather than safeguarding his once all too brief composing time. This reversal spoke for itself. There were the obligatory allusions to Stravinsky's uninterrupted schedule, to his creative stamina; and indeed his magnificent *Requiem Canticles* was yet to be written. Generally though, documentaries tended to emphasize past accomplishments, and his respected status as the grand sage who had already changed the course of contemporary music years earlier. Stravinsky, however, did not want to be consigned to the past, particularly at the price of conceding that he had nothing left to say. Yet it was chiefly the past that now primarily drove the filmmaker's agenda. Documentaries are in the business of historical recall; but for Stravinsky, who throughout his life had argued so vehemently that doing was more important than having done, there is a certain melancholy in viewing his compliant participation in these often staged retrospectives.

Nonetheless, he was perfectly cognizant of his role. Only a week before Liebermann discussed the proposed NDR Hamburg film, Stravinsky dined with David Oppenheim in New York, on 5 February 1965, to discuss what would become another important documentary, this time for CBS. Liebermann's filming began on 16 March, and within a few weeks CBS also was recording Stravinsky, as he arrived in Austin, Texas, and traveled to the University of Texas campus (escorted by a motorcycle brigade, no less) to speak and work with students. Stravinsky now balanced the scheduling of filming commitments just as he skillfully continued to juggle compositional commissions.

He fully capitalized on his notoriety. When CBS offered ten thousand dollars for the television documentary, Stravinsky balked. He had done his homework. He knew that the network had recently paid the same amount to Pablo Casals, and he contended that he was worth far more. After all, as his agent advised CBS, Casals was merely a performer, not a composer—and not a particularly trustworthy performer at that, since he played "Bach in the style of

The composer with David Oppenheim, producer and director of the 1966 CBS documentary *Portrait of Stravinsky* (The Fred and Rose Plaut Archives, courtesy of the Yale University Music Library)

Brahms," the composer complained. Who in 1965 could remember who the performers had been during Beethoven's lifetime? Casals, it was implied, would be no more than a historical footnote two hundred years hence, known principally as an egocentric who placed himself above the music. Stravinsky's compositions, however, would endure. CBS readily agreed to pay the composer fifteen thousand dollars, a sum nearly five times that for his first documentary only eight years earlier for NBC. Even more eye-opening, the fee approached the asking price of his compositional commissions. He was now earning as much being seen as having his music heard.

The film, *Portrait of Stravinsky,* was produced and directed by Oppenheim and narrated by Charles Kuralt. The shooting was done over an extended period beginning in late March 1965, and it first aired on CBS on 3 May 1966. Mrs. Stravinsky's diary entries during April record the continuous and often disruptive shooting. The Stravinsky family sailed for Europe in early May on the *Kungsholm*. Oppenheim would often scout locations, working closely with Craft in preparing interviews and the filming of various concerts, and the producer even joined the family on the ship, where they all continued working on the film while they sailed for Europe.

I spoke with both Oppenheim and Kuralt about the making of the documentary. Kuralt claimed that in this film, as opposed to many of the other documentaries in which he participated, he was strictly a narrator—that is, the post-production overdubbing was "dropped into" the program after it had been completed. Whereas Kuralt usually wrote his own scripts for such televised projects to accommodate his manner of delivery and add his well-known "color," here he followed what he was handed. The only occasion on which he and Stravinsky spoke in any detail was when the composer tried to explain the compositional vocabulary of Schoenberg's "seriality" to him. The fact is, the longtime CBS commentator had very little interaction with Stravinsky himself—nothing more than some publicity photographs for promoting the documentary. But he also recalled that virtually every aspect of the film was handled by Craft, who continually guided Stravinsky through the entire shooting.

Oppenheim, himself a musician, had known Stravinsky for years, and the two often made music together. Although the usual story is that CBS originally approached Stravinsky about making the film, Oppenheim remarked, when I asked him, that instead it was the composer who sought out the network. Though naturally unwilling to admit it, Stravinsky had seen the Casals film shortly before contacting Oppenheim, and he felt that a similar documentary about him would make an interesting project. Were there any restrictions, I inquired, regarding what could be filmed? None, according to Oppenheim, and he said that Stravinsky, his wife, and Craft cooperated fully in permitting the cameras to roam freely. Stravinsky had no say in what was to be used in the final print, for it was network policy to work without restrictions. But Oppenheim recalls that Stravinsky did not object to anything, and if he had, "I would have fixed it."

Of the hundreds of rolls of film that were shot over the year, most of the footage naturally could not be included in the forty-two-minute documentary. The decisions on what to include were left to the editor, Patricia Jaffe, who made cuts seeking to balance the events of the composer's life with the entertainment value for the viewing audience. So extensive and intense was the filming across the world—from Texas to New York, Rome, Warsaw, and through the Swiss towns where Stravinsky had lived fifty years earlier—that the Stravinskys and the documentary crew became a "family," as Oppenheim put it. Stravinsky did prescreen the final print, according to the director, but "was not wild about it" or particularly impressed, thinking that it was more a film for the masses than an accurate or full portrait of his life.

The CBS documentary opens with a shot of Stravinsky composing, as Kuralt repeats the familiar Stravinskyan declaration, "The interest of my life, my intellectual life, my everyday life, is to make. I am a maker." The composer is joined by his son Theodore in retracing his footsteps in Clarens, the Swiss mountain village where much of *Le Sacre du printemps* was conceived. Like a sacred pilgrimage, he leads the camera up the steps to the very room in which the "beautiful nightmare," as Debussy once called it, was composed. Kuralt announces: "That the music was created here, that such power—one pictures Igor Stravinsky at the piano holding handfuls of volts—was unleashed in this dingy anteroom, is wondrous." At the piano, the composer gleefully pounds out *Le Sacre*'s most famous chord—indeed one of the most celebrated chords in all of music history—as he works the camera and enthuses, "I like this chord." Stravinsky is at his thespian best, and with a sense of timing that only great storytellers possess he recounts the creation of a ballet that changed the musical world. He recalls that Diaghilev thought the composer was "not serious" in repeating the chord over and over. "How long will the chord last?" Diaghilev purportedly asked. "Until it is done, my dear," Stravinsky supposedly responded, as he grins for the camera's benefit. If ever there was any question that theater ran deep in the composer's blood, surely this performance puts such doubts to rest.

He visits Léonide Massine and a troupe of young ballerinas in the Théâtre des Champs-Elysées, where he shows the camera where he sat in the audience the night the infamous riot erupted during the ballet's premiere. There are wonderful clips of the Warsaw Opera Ballet performing *Sacre*, including a brilliant performance of the "Sacrificial Dance," with Elizabeth Chardon as the "Chosen One." Regrettably, the performance is almost entirely forgotten, and even though it is not Nijinsky's original choreography, the production is striking in its use of skeletonlike figures wearing death masks, wielding canes, and converging upon Chardon as the ballet ends. The performance also cuts occasionally to Stravinsky, in concert tux and conducting the pit orchestra, although this footage was shot separately and added later.

At the Vatican, Stravinsky receives a commendation while the camera records him genuflecting before Pope Paul VI as the *Symphony of Psalms* plays in the background. (Other composers were being honored, too, Craft recounts, including Milhaud and Gian Francesco Malipiero, but they were relegated to off-camera seats so as not to steal any focus from Stravinsky.) He is filmed in Paris, where Alberto Giacometti ("one of the best sculptors in the world," Stravinsky declares) sketches him while the composer simultaneously sketches Giacometti. Then it is on to Warsaw, where he had not been since 1924. He conducts *The Firebird* and is shown touring the city's streets, saddened, Kuralt tells us, by the ravaging "scars of war." Also in Warsaw, he led the *Symphony of Psalms* in concert, although all the rehearsals were conducted by Craft, as several reels of unreleased film demonstrate. There seems little question that CBS skillfully prepared each segment of the film with an eye toward portraying Stravinsky in a certain light—a light that would appeal to the general public. And the composer, by now a veteran before the cameras, played his role to the hilt.

Whatever the scripting, the CBS documentary is informative and entertaining—just as Grierson originally envisioned the docudrama's mission; whatever television trickery exists in arranging for certain scenarios to unfold, Stravinsky's on-camera demeanor was no different from that of other biographical figures in similarly produced documentaries. The real gold mine of this film, however, is buried in the segments that were ultimately excluded. As Oppenheim told me, hundreds of hours of film were shot on both sides of the Atlantic, as well as during the transoceanic voyage. Much of the footage is worthless: some is too candid, and most had to be trimmed to keep the length of the film manageable. Yet some of the outtakes are quite informative, and it is from them that we learn the most.[8]

Oppenheim shot wherever and whatever he could. He followed Stravinsky from city to city as he lectured, gave master classes, rehearsed, recorded, performed, chatted with friends in hotel rooms, had dinner in restaurants, and told stories from his cabin during the ocean crossing. There are even clips of Stravinsky, his wife, and Craft recorded by a camera mounted in the front seat of a taxi and aimed at the trio seated in back, as the cab traveled through the streets of New York. In this charming trans-Manhattan sequence, the composer is unknowingly filmed as he speaks his mind. "Newspapers are as incompetent in music as in politics," Kuralt quotes Stravinsky in the released print; but during the unused taxi sequence, the composer has much more to add as he saltily berates the endless stream of interviewers with whom he must constantly contend. As Mrs. Stravinsky and Craft sit quietly (permitting the composer to vent, they stare passively out the cab's windows), he reviles one interviewer as insulting, another as humiliating, and a third as "polite . . . stupid, but polite."

Oppenheim's crew shot two reels in early May during a difficult crossing from New York to Warsaw, the composer's eventual destination. Craft records in his diary that a rough sea forced Stravinsky to take to his cabin, and none of the footage shot was usable. Still, one of the cut segments shows a frail, recumbent Stravinsky resting in his cabin room (surrounded by his well-known pharmacy of various elixirs) as the interviewing team prompts him to recall his youth. Sitting halfway up with his hands propped behind his head, Stravinsky seems unusually relaxed, or perhaps just exhausted, as if unaware or unconcerned with the camera's constant intrusion. He speaks of his parents, slowly and somberly. This was not the "on-camera," prankish Stravinsky who delighted in jousting and exaggerating. Even his manner of speech seems subdued, pensive, as he tells of a father who was "severe and unappreciative." "I never was on good terms with my father until after I had pleurisy and was dangerously ill as a child," he recalls. It seemed to have been a turning point in their relationship. "The sickness put a stop to the anger." Still, the composer maintains, it did little to heal the distance between them. "I could say many things about my father but I wish to forget them. I will never speak about it."

Such uncensored admissions are certainly useful in explaining Stravinsky's often contradictory feelings about his childhood. As for his mother, the composer's memories were similarly impersonal: "I was never close to either of my parents. . . . I always tried to be out." And after his eldest brother's death in 1897, Stravinsky remembered his mother taking little interest in anything; she thought only of her lost son. "I was never very close to my mother," he says with an expressionless voice. This was not the first time the composer alluded to these painful memories; some had been aired earlier in his conversation books, although just how reliable his recollections were in that format is increasingly being questioned by such scholars as Richard Taruskin and Stephen Walsh. Here, seen through the unedited and direct impact of the film, Stravinsky resurrects these memories dispassionately, and consequently his remembrances seem all the more telling. It is all very grim, and one gets the feeling that it is closer to what really happened. It is likely that because of its somberness—a somberness that is deeply penetrating as captured on film—the footage was cut. It was the kind of intimate confession the producers probably judged unsuitable for inclusion in a television program meant primarily to entertain a general audience.

The composer describes his marriage to Catherine in 1906, and he touchingly remembers that he will "soon" be married to her sixty years. It is apparent that he still thinks of her in some sense as his wife, beyond his very happy life for the past forty-five years with Vera. There has not been much said about Stravinsky's first wife, either by him or others, until recently.[9] How many of his memories and feelings for her stemmed from guilt, love, or a mixture of both, one can never know; but there is absolutely no doubt, as one views this poignant unreleased film sequence, that she remained present in his private thoughts—thoughts that here, for just a moment, slip out.

Stravinsky ranges over a variety of topics in response to perceptive questions posed by Oppenheim and intended to elicit something that might be incorporated into the documentary. In the privacy of his cabin room, the composer speaks openly about issues that rarely surface in other image-proofed biographical sources. Of Rimsky-Korsakov, Stravinsky remembers that he was disagreeable, and that he was jealous about Tchaikovsky's music. Every time Stravinsky would mention something favorable about Tchaikovsky, Rimsky-Korsakov would counter with something even more unfavorable. Stravinsky recounts that they discussed the music of Wagner regularly, since Rimsky-Korsakov respected the German's instrumentation. They spoke too of Beethoven's orchestrations, especially the symphonies, and here, more than anywhere else on record, Stravinsky glowingly reveals his admiration: "For me, Beethoven is an architect." He remembers that Rimsky-Korsakov admired the "academics," but only because he was not an academic himself, according to Stravinsky, and therefore was envious of their learning. To deny this, Stravinsky remembers, Rimsky-Korsakov belligerently preached an anti-intellectualism to his impressionable student. When asked what was the greatest lesson he learned from his teacher, Stravinsky says, "how to use an eraser."

He remembers his close friendship with Debussy, but he adds that the French composer became "horrified" when Stravinsky divulged that he was impressed by Schoenberg's music. He also admits that their friendship cooled after 1912, just as Stravinsky's music was finding its own voice. He speaks too of his memories of the Polish ballet visiting St. Petersburg and the pride he still has in his Polish blood. And finally, he admonishes, all that has been said about him in writing, in interviews, and in conversations is not necessarily accurate.

The filming had begun in Austin in late March 1965. Stravinsky is greeted, or rather ambushed, at the airport by a group of yipping cowboys as he hoists the gift of a ten-gallon hat on his raised cane for all to see. He is pronounced an official Texas cowboy, and without missing a beat he responds that he cannot think of any greater honor. This is priceless footage in TV terms—and just the kind to which some critics objected as distorted—reinforcing the kind of genius-with-the-common-touch image producers surely had hoped for. He had come to the University of Texas to give a lecture and master class, and the CBS telecast included footage from a question-and-answer exchange with students. Stravinsky and his wife were seated on stage as he responded (sometimes with the help of Vera providing certain translations or American expressions) in what was designed to look like an extemporaneous session. But the unreleased film establishes that the exchanges were far from unprepared. These ostensibly unrehearsed dialogues were in fact reshot several times over a two-day period. Before the filming of the second day's shooting officially started, Stravinsky, unaware that the camera is rolling, jokingly advises the students, "Ask me good questions that I can answer." They did, and portions of this segment were included. All these "retakes" naturally are part of the film-maker's job, and Stravinsky patiently went along.

Another session is even more enlightening, showing Stravinsky conducting a master class with several student musicians. Where else can the composer be seen actually instructing students, offering criticisms on how his music should be played? He sits on stage as several young performers play his works. The quality of musicianship is high, and Stravinsky is clearly taken. It is one of those rare occasions when he seems to have momentarily forgotten that *he* has to perform for the camera. He sits impassively, listening intently, and without any trace of emotion. He seems completely absorbed in the performance of the music, blocking out the camera's presence. One young man plays the Three Pieces for Clarinet, and Stravinsky takes a considerable amount of time to coach him in very specific terms. The composer is remarkably kind, solicitous, even complimentary to the student. Perhaps he was on his best behavior here, but there is no evidence of the tyrannical composer— as he was often depicted—eager to pounce on any performer foolhardy enough to interpret his music. He is all business, obviously devoted to the moment. Regrettably though, all his very instructive comments about articulation, dynamics, phrasing, breathing, and tempo are simply too detailed to make entertaining TV. Consequently, none of it was included in the CBS portrait.

The composer recorded his *Ebony Concerto* in New York with Benny Goodman, and CBS filmed several rehearsal sessions. Again the camera rolled freely, and although only a few moments were included in the televised documentary, at least two more hours of additional footage exists. Stravinsky is shown in these forgotten rehearsals, as he was in Austin, working with a very deliberate, professional purpose. Surely aware that the union clock is running, he is careful to accomplish his job as efficiently as possible. During all the rehearsals, Stravinsky remains surprisingly calm, even stoic, and quite focused on his task. Seldom does he lift his head from the score, and never does he launch into unnecessarily prolonged explanations to make a simple point. There is none of the theatrical hamming that had become almost obligatory for a segment to survive editorial trimming. Stravinsky willingly takes suggestions from recording producer John McClure; McClure, in turn, is guided by Craft, who sits next to him in the recording booth. Their conversations in the unreleased portions of the film are revealing as they debate which takes will be used in the audio recording. Although Stravinsky seldom would relinquish control, here, rather remarkably, he seems to trust Craft's and McClure's advice.

If one of the musicians in the orchestra makes an obvious mistake, Stravinsky simply stops. He never lectures, or even takes time to correct the musician. It is clear that there is a problem; he respects the professionalism of the performers; and the passage is done over without fuss. Nowhere are there the famous tirades that the composer supposedly inflicted on hapless performers. Were these fictional outbursts simply part of a more quirky, and thus more marketable, image? The film captures a Stravinsky entirely at odds with the portrait we have inherited of the intemperate, martinet conductor.[10]

In several excised portions Craft can be seen standing just behind Stravinsky, who leads the ensemble. But the musicians look to Craft, who is also conducting, thus confirming what many suspected or already knew. Finally, during a break in the rehearsal, the camera catches Stravinsky actually coaching Benny Goodman as he plays a few passages from the same Three Pieces for Clarinet played in the Austin master class. Here Stravinsky is much more critical than he was with the student, and not at all reluctant to criticize Goodman's interpretation, firmly but kindly. None of this survives in the televised film. The few clips of Stravinsky and Goodman that are included are voiced over with narration by Kuralt.

There are also portions in which Craft is notably bold, some might even say brusque, with his criticisms and opinions. As they leave a rehearsal of Stravinsky's *Variations* (written for Aldous Huxley), filmed in Chicago where the premiere was given, Craft and the composer are sitting next to each other in a car as the camera eavesdrops on their conversation. Stravinsky remarks that he arranged the orchestral work's instrumentation according to the number of strings he was told he would have in Chicago. If he had known, for example, that the orchestra included so many violas he would have orchestrated some sections differently. Craft makes a few specific suggestions as to what can be done to improve the orchestral balance, and after pausing a few moments as he peers out the car window, the composer responds, "Perhaps you

Stravinsky with Benny Goodman, rehearsing the *Ebony Concerto* before television cameras in 1965 (The Fred and Rose Plaut Archives, courtesy of the Yale University Music Library)

are right." What cannot be denied in such private moments is the freedom that Craft felt, and apparently Stravinsky encouraged, to give advice in matters one might have presumed off-limits. Throughout the hours of filming compiled, it is clear that both Stravinsky and his wife depended heavily on Craft.

In his Chicago hotel room, Stravinsky is asked to discuss how he composed his new *Variations*. He obliges by displaying the sketchbook for his "pre-compositional ideas" (his term). Here are the serial rows and charts Stravinsky plotted before he actually started to write. Yet in almost the same breath, he declares that his very first idea for the work was absolutely not a premeditatively constructed row but rather a pure melody, which he only later discovered, almost coincidentally, had twelve different notes. Stravinsky stresses this extraordinary compositional evolution with notable pride, knowing that most would doubt such an unlikely sequence of events. He wants to make it clear that he was not controlled abstractly by dodecaphonic matrices and other academic paraphernalia: "The melody was first, then came the charts. I can repeat two notes but not three in a series." He flips through several pages of his sketchbook, commenting as he goes, and making certain that viewers realize they are watching the actual creation of the work right before their eyes. But alas, there was no need to worry about his viewers here, for the entire segment was cut. Such shop talk would have been meaningless for the targeted viewing audience.[11]

During another filming session in Chicago, Stravinsky is asked about performances of his ballets, and choreographers. This, too, did not survive the editing process. "I'm very curious to see what Robbins did with my *Noces,*" he says. "He's a *very* talented man, *very* talented [the composer took pains to stress]. I spoke about him with Balanchine. He likes Robbins very much. He said Robbins is an American but he understood so well the Russian gestures, not the official Russian gestures, but the musical gestures, so well." And, regarding the composer's reactions to the 1913 premiere of *Le Sacre,* he confirms his often stated belief that it was not the music that caused people to riot "but what they saw on stage. They came for *Scheherazade,* they came to see beautiful girls, and they saw *Le Sacre du printemps,* and they were shocked. They were very naive and very stupid people."

Finally, just before departing for Warsaw, Stravinsky visits the New York State Theater at Lincoln Center—all on film, and almost all cut. As he and his wife exit their limousine, Vera says, "Now we will see what we will see," to which a glinting Stravinsky replies, "Now we will see the girls." He is taken backstage where he is joined by Balanchine and Suzanne Farrell. Composer and choreographer converse while Farrell stands demurely with her eyes cast down, not saying (or being invited to say) a word. "I find that music is more useful than statements," Stravinsky offers; Balanchine agrees, adding, "A statement is a cliché because it lasts longer and everybody repeats it and they don't know what it means." Balanchine had recently choreographed *Variations,* preparing it especially for Farrell, and it was about to be premiered in March 1966. The composer thanks Balanchine for choreographing his music so wonderfully: "To say that I was very happy with what you did with my music is not enough." He then approaches Farrell, formally shakes her hand with his familiar courtly bow, and says, "I thank you for what you do, for your danc-ing." Farrell, as timid as she was in the NDR filming of *Apollo*, answers almost inaudibly, "I enjoy dancing," then quickly turns away with an obvious gesture of relief at having survived the moment. One sympathizes with the young dancer, understandably intimidated by the presence of the great composer. The filming then cuts to Stravinsky seated on stage watching Balanchine work with Farrell, clearly for the camera's benefit, as the choreographer poses her in various positions for Stravinsky to observe. Choreographer and composer walk offstage together, speaking in Russian, leaving the young ballerina to trail along, unsure where she should be or what she should be doing. In her auto-biography, Farrell relates the scene somewhat differently:

> It was at this time that I had my last encounter with the composer himself. Stravinsky was visiting the theater one afternoon, and Mr. B suggested I dance *Variations* for him, an impromptu private performance. While Mr. B stood qui-etly to one side, Stravinsky perched on a little stool in the center of the stage near the footlights, cane in hand, chin leaning forward—he looked so small to be such a musical giant—and I charged through *Variations*. Afterward, while I was in my dressing room, George knocked on the door to say "Igor" was leav-ing and I murmured, "I so love his music." George said conspiratorially, "Tell him, tell him," so I chased down the hall after the disappearing little figure, shouting "Mr. Stravinsky, Mr. Stravinsky." He stopped and turned and I said meekly, "I just want to thank you. I so love dancing to your music." He hugged me and said, "Oh yes, dear. I can tell."[12]

While the cameras reveal that the encounter may not have unfolded quite as Farrell describes it, the romancing of the story is harmless enough. Such accounts are typical of the aggrandizement that often develops when stories about Stravinsky and his circle are garnished for the public's appetite. These expurgated film clips are particularly useful in throttling the kind of revision-ism that often accrues when biographies of public figures are marketed. Re-instituting some semblance of reality (particularly in the case of Stravinsky, who did little himself to curb the inflation of his own image) will constitute one of the principal tasks historians must embark upon in the years ahead; and certainly such lost film clips will partially provide certain checks and bal-ances in drawing a sharper, and therefore truer, portrait of the composer.

David Oppenheim's film set a new standard. So useful was the footage that portions of it were routinely incorporated into later documentaries, of which there were many. Unpublished correspondence from 1966 reveals that Her-bert von Karajan expressed interest in doing a film of Stravinsky in which the composer might be shown conducting sections of *Le Sacre* taken from the CBS footage recorded in Warsaw (though the project was still to focus on Karajan himself). Karajan was almost as attractive a TV personality as Bernstein, and a natural for television productions. Craft remembers that CBS filmed Stravinsky repeatedly conducting certain portions of *Le Sacre* in an empty auditorium. The idea was that various slates from the videotaping could eventually be pieced together so that the end result would produce the illusion of Stravinsky, dressed in tails, actually conducting a full performance of the Warsaw Ballet.[13]

Several other video and audiotape documentaries were made, and these can be quickly summarized. A Canadian company made a film of Stravinsky rehearsing *L'Histoire du soldat* in 1967. An unpublished letter from CBS Records, dated 18 September 1968, requests that Stravinsky permit his voice—as recorded from six earlier "films for television shows"—to be used for a Columbia Masterworks "bonus record . . . given free of charge to purchasers" as part of a six-record set of the composer's major works. Even after the composer's death in 1971, oral histories and films continued to appear. Thirteen television episodes of oral history, titled *The Life and Times of Igor Stravinsky*, were produced by the CBC and broadcast in 1976.[14]

Another was a little-known (and now almost entirely forgotten) series of ninety-minute audio recordings titled *Igor Stravinsky: The Man and His Music*, produced by Educational Media Associates of America in 1976. Several of the composer's young American musician friends were included in making these recordings, although not all of them were used. Lukas Foss reports that Stravinsky never traveled to India because everyone there was poor and, in his judgment, "The poor are not interesting." Claudio Spies speaks to the Stravinsky-Craft conversation books, saying, "The tone of [Stravinsky's] conversation is impossible to convey in any prose, so that none of the books that purportedly are his conversations are in fact his conversations at all." Lawrence Morton contends, "I think basically that Stravinsky's music is very sexy . . . it appeals to certain basic rhythmical things that people feel in their own bodies." In fact, this may be as basic and cogent an explanation as any of the composer's wide appeal. People could simply feel the energy of the music without really understanding pitch control or the other compositional techniques on which the works were built. Certainly by Balanchine's admission it was this physical, rhythmic power that drew the choreographer and his dancers to the music. Craft mentions in the same tape that Stravinsky simply could not tolerate "music that was better than his music, or greater, or bigger than his music," although it is a strange statement given Stravinsky's heuristic study of so much music that would eventually serve as models.[15]

Nearly a decade after his death, Stravinsky still served as the subject of several audio and video retrospectives. A particularly odd documentary aired in 1980 on National Public Radio, titled *A Question of Place: Igor Stravinsky— A Portrait in Sound.* In its dilettantish pandering, the production was image tweaking at its worst. Those in charge knew exactly what an uninformed populist audience wanted to hear about its great composers, and the made-to-order script delivered. The hour-long broadcast opened to the sounds of chirping birds in the background as the narrator (supposedly Louis Laloy, a critic and personal friend of Debussy) describes Stravinsky running madly down the boulevard to catch Debussy—as if it were happening just at that moment. He was hurrying to catch the French composer so that he could join him in a four-hand performance of *Le Sacre* on a player piano. From there the script descends, indulging in a series of quotes from Stravinsky's *Autobiography* and elsewhere. Several of Stravinsky's French and Russian friends happen by, all reading familiar passages with clichéd, exaggerated linguistic inflections. The tape tries to create the impression of a documentary unfolding in strict chronology beginning with the early Russian ballets and moving through the serial works of the 1960s. But the quotations employed are hopelessly out of order, and obviously interspersed for effect. Historical context, let alone accuracy, seems of little concern (we are told, for example, that Stravinsky delivered his Norton lectures at Harvard in 1947). Particularly outlandish is Theodore Bikel's typecast portrayal of Stravinsky himself. He orates several of the composer's most quotable pronouncements in a stereotypically Russianized intonation that perpetuates the worst affectation imaginable.

Then just at the moment that the tape appears little more than a bad joke, who should jump in but Elliott Carter, one of the most respected composers of our day, and an astute critic of Stravinsky's life and works. "Hearing *The Rite of Spring*," Carter remarks, "made me decide to be a composer. It established the wonder of music in a way no other piece had ever done." Since Carter seldom consented to interviews, his words are worth noting. He speaks of Stravinsky's imagination in specific terms, referring to aspects of the music's sound in a way that is absolutely engaging. But as quickly as he appeared, he now vanishes, as a scripted re-creation of the infamous riot that greeted the premiere of *Le Sacre* (complete with simulated caterwauling) interrupts. And so the tape continues for most of the hour, although Carter does resurface, this time with his equally insightful colleague, the pianist-scholar Charles Rosen. They chat informally but instructively about the many misprints that continue to mar Stravinsky's published scores; about the central importance of Medieval and Renaissance models in the composer's adoption of serialism; about how Stravinsky was able to transform models with the most minimal of changes, yet in a way that made the sound of his music unmistakably individualistic. Rosen presents a comparison of Stravinsky's Piano Sonata with the second movement of Beethoven's Opus 54 Piano Sonata in F Major. Carter speaks about Stravinsky's *Movements* and how the composer explained to him how strict adherence to a particular tone row was less important than other musical considerations. In the end, the audiotape provides a hodgepodge of worthless anecdotes and inaccurate information alongside valuable and otherwise not to be found observations by Carter and Rosen. For the latter alone, the broadcast was worth the effort.[16]

Easily the most expansive documentary was released during the centennial celebration of Stravinsky's birth by British filmmaker Tony Palmer. *Aspects of Stravinsky* was originally produced for London Television Weekend and aired in England over Easter weekend, 1982. Shot over two years, it was a prodigious attempt to cover the whole of Stravinsky's biography on film. A two-hour documentary was first planned, but the filming was so extensive that the picture ended up three hours long, and it was telecast over two days for London Television. Even so, this version includes a fraction of the total footage shot and edited. Palmer agreed to make the film on the condition that Stravinsky's three surviving children, and Craft, appear in the documentary—not an easy hurdle to leap given the tensions surrounding the Stravinsky estate throughout much of the 1970s. The film includes previously compiled footage from as early as the 1920s (and virtually unavailable elsewhere), and, as with the CBS documentary, all of Palmer's outtakes survive. It is these that provide the most informative glimpses into Stravinsky's life.[17]

This dichotomy of image and reality was addressed by Craft in his diary notes, written 22 November 1982, on Palmer's film. Craft noted that the sumptuously shot film was "a delight to the eyes [though] the best comments of the interviewees seem to have been edited out." He also questioned Palmer's editing. Viewers were hoodwinked into believing that Stravinsky himself took part in the filming. But of course he didn't, and the illusion is accomplished by employing an actor (George Pravda) to read some of Stravinsky's commentaries of earlier years. Familiar excerpts are often read as the audience views old footage of Stravinsky—footage from other places and other times.

These are mixed with a script containing lines that are "doctored excerpts from the composer's books," Craft adds.[18]

Palmer, however, contends that it was Craft who originally proposed the use of some of Stravinsky's recorded tapes, but because the voice quality was poor he agreed to have a surrogate read certain lines; this seems hard to believe, though, in light of Craft's objections in his diary entry. The filmmaker also claims that Craft rewrote parts of the recorded speeches to accommodate Pravda's reading style. The condition that Mrs. Stravinsky endorse such an "impostor" was fulfilled, according to Palmer. Whatever actually happened, certainly Craft is justified in questioning the inclusion of several segments that lapse into narrow accounts of the interviewees' lives with little relevance to Stravinsky's biography. Unlike all the earlier documentaries, Craft seldom appears in Palmer's film; yet several trims survive in which he relates episodes about Stravinsky's life that are not available anywhere else in his extensive writings about the composer.

In one slate, Craft speaks about Stravinsky's recognition that his early autobiography was woefully incomplete, especially in its neglect of the composer's formative years. He speaks of Stravinsky's early occupation as an accompanist and later his pursuit of a law degree at the university, where he specifically studied to be a judge. Craft also addresses in some detail Stravinsky's love of the stage—a love that the composer attributed to watching his father at the Maryinsky. Indeed, in another slate that was cut, Stravinsky's son Theodore confirms that his father "loved to be in contact with the public, he adored it, he needed it."

Craft ranges widely over topics that include Stravinsky's close personal identification with his pieces and his need to have people like his compositions, despite his frequent disclaimers. He speaks of the composer's daily reading of Bach at the keyboard as a way of stimulating the compositional process. He recounts Stravinsky's sometimes embarrassingly captious behavior in his treatment of old friends such as Ansermet and Monteux, although none of this is really new information. Yet there are comments that help to dispel certain long held assumptions. For example, Craft speaks of Stravinsky's indecision about instrumentation—a wavering that sometimes continued until the last moment, as with his last-minute decision to use a harpsichord in *The Rake's Progress*. We are reminded that the composer always worked at the piano (at least until the last years of his life) as a result of Rimsky-Korsakov's early directive. In contrast, Rimsky-Korsakov's granddaughter Tatiana reveals in an interview cut from the film that her grandfather's study had no piano: "He never composed sitting at the piano. He did not need it." The composer also, she continues, "had a gift for being oblivious to everything and sinking himself into his music—exterior sounds and interruptions didn't bother him": quite different from Stravinsky, whose concentration was broken by the slightest distraction.

In other segments cut from the film, Craft displays some of Stravinsky's manuscripts, describing them for a panning camera. He exhibits a section of a compositional sketchbook for *Oedipus Rex,* indicating where Boris Kochno added some sections of the text. (Kochno's hand is also evident in a sketchbook for *Apollo,* where his calligraphy is often mistaken for Stravinsky's.) In addition to the 1922 one-act opera *Mavra,* Stravinsky and Kochno, with Diaghilev's enthusiastic support, had considered doing another opera together— an updated *Barber of Seville,* apparently—as Kochno recalls in his own informative, but regrettably, discarded clip. He remembers that he and Stravinsky visited Seville in 1921 where they listened to flamenco music and frequented cabarets nightly where they studied the movements of the dancers.[19]

Especially enlightening are Craft's comments regarding the composer's 1931 Violin Concerto. He speaks of the work's internal divisions matching the amount of time ("minutage," as Stravinsky referred to it) that could be accommodated on a side of a record. The assertion is easily confirmed by examining many of the composer's manuscripts, wherein he regularly calibrated the length of a passage or movement around four minutes, so that it would be suitable for recording purposes. Craft speaks of Stravinsky's cache of stopwatches, which, as is also readily confirmed by examining almost any of his sketchbooks, were an integral part of the compositional process. Although many of Craft's comments are stated elsewhere among his own prolific writings, some—especially those dealing with discussions of the composer's music and often its very practical genesis—are invaluable. In that regard it is indeed unfortunate that more of his insightful comments were not included in the film. In reviewing the documentary, Craft himself wondered why more had not been included. But as Palmer told me, his reasons for excluding these portions were the same as for footage snipped from earlier documentaries: while its value to the specialist might be considerable, its appeal to a general audience would be limited.

A performance of the last two movements of the Violin Concerto was included in the Palmer film. The segment is positioned at the end of a section dealing with Stravinsky's 1939 European departure (and at the end of what became the first of two separate commercially available videotapes). In his diary, Craft questioned the rationale of the clip's inclusion. (The violinist is Kyung Wha-Chung, in a stunning performance.) Craft is justified in his concern, especially in the chronological context of the film, since the concerto, written eight years earlier, seemingly has nothing to do with Stravinsky's leaving France.

The explanation lies in an excluded segment with Louise Dushkin, wife of Sam Dushkin—with whom Stravinsky had collaborated on the Violin Concerto and who often performed the work. According to Dushkin's wife, as Palmer related the story to me, Stravinsky confessed unusually personal feelings about one of the work's elegiac movements ("Aria II"). When she sat with Stravinsky in the audience, as she often did when her husband performed the solo part, Stravinsky would openly weep. When she asked him about this uncharacteristically emotional reaction, Stravinsky confided that he had written the movement for his wife Catherine. It was, he said, "the only way I could think of to apologize"—a reference, of course, to his relationship with Vera Sudeikina. Palmer chose to use this memory-laden composition at the film's dividing point, to mark 1939 as a pivotal time in Stravinsky's life—a time of family loss, as noted earlier, and a time to put the past behind as he began his new life in America.

For many historians, Stravinsky's contributions to the world of ballet may well stand as his most significant achievement. Many interviews with key people in the Diaghilev-Stravinsky world are included, but given the nature of documentary filmmaking, several are, unfortunately but necessarily, very brief (including those with Alexandra Danilova, Tamara Geva, Serge Lifar, Alicia Markova, and others). Certain illuminating interviews are missing entirely. Marie Rambert, who danced in the original production of *Le Sacre,* describes Nijinsky as a "taciturn" man who was completely unable to explain any dance movement in words: "He was ready to do the movement twenty times . . . he just showed you the movement as it has to be done." Rambert, or "Rhythmitschka," as she was dubbed, speaks in some detail of Diaghilev's consultation of Emile Jaques-Dalcroze, the "inventor" of eurythmics, though all this is cut from the finished film.

> Diaghilev came and found me working in Dresden. . . . I didn't take any notice because at the time I was absolutely devoted to Dalcroze. . . . I saw a tall man with a small man, and that's all I saw, but I was only interested in what Dalcroze had to say. . . . I was very surprised when the next day Dalcroze said to me, "You know Diaghilev wants you in his company." By that time I had worked three years with Dalcroze and I thought that would be fun, I wanted

to travel. So I came to Berlin, that's when I saw the first rehearsal [of *Le Sacre*]. . . . All Nijinsky wanted to do is to try and translate every note into movement, which is a bad system. But he was hell-bent on translating every note into a movement.

A lengthy interview with Serge Lifar is almost completely cut. Typically, given the dancer's vainglory, he speaks more of himself than Stravinsky, although Palmer's questions are aimed toward exploring Lifar's memories of the Diaghilev ballet world. Despite his self-absorption, Lifar offers a broad context in which both Diaghilev and Stravinsky may be viewed from the perspective of an important dancer in the midst of the company's activities. Not only are Lifar's comments extensive and worthy of a separate discussion, but those of other Diaghilev dancers likewise deserve a fuller treatment. It would have been impossible, however, for Palmer to include all their stories in the three-hour documentary.[20]

Some portions were surely too painful for television audiences to watch. Only a few moments of Vera Stravinsky are included, except toward the end of the film where she repeats a few often told anecdotes. Her health is obviously in rapid decline, and the images of this once vital woman are sadly disturbing—images caught in words, rather than pictures, by Stephen Spender when he visited her in the fall of 1980:

> [Vera's] nurse-companion took me into her large drawing room. . . . Vera was sitting in an armchair at a table on which there were, I think, some painting things. "Here is Stephen," said her nurse. Vera looked up at me, not recognizing me but seeming to realize I was a friend and not a stranger. . . . "I don't know what this room is," she said, looking round her. "I am sure these are not my things. Anyway I don't want them. One ought not to have any things. One should give them all away."
>
> She wondered where we were. The nurse suggested New York. "No, I don't think we are in New York," she said, "and it's not Paris either."
>
> At this point I stupidly allowed tears to trickle down my face. . . . There was plenty to cry about, if one thought about the wonderful festive life, like an endless succession of gifts, borne in on concert platforms, gondolas, good company, fame, wit, laughter, rage, passion, wine; of the life of Igor Stravinsky, Vera and Bob Craft.[21]

Spender's words are achingly descriptive of Vera's "big life . . . a life full of dead people," as she recalls it for Palmer's camera. But mostly she is seen, rather than heard, in a few filmed segments: sitting in the park, painting, walking around her apartment. By the time she was interviewed, she had already suffered a stroke and was no longer lucid. She speaks in German, falls asleep, and, regrettably, seems mostly incoherent. Footage survives in which attempts are made to draw Mrs. Stravinsky into a conversation. She is urged to retell a few anecdotes or at least to say something that might be usable. But these efforts are futile, and in the end, except for a few comments caught on film, Mrs. Stravinsky is seen but not heard.

Other interviews conducted by Palmer raise disquieting questions about the composer's welfare. As recorded by the filmmaker, some friends intimated that toward the end of his life Stravinsky was making too many compromises. He continued to make appearances, for example, when he really should not have. One of the composer's closest friends told Palmer that at the State University of New York at Stony Brook, on 27 April 1969, Stravinsky appeared completely disoriented and unable to recognize those around him. Was it that he continued to feel it was his duty to attend concerts of his music as a way of remaining in the spotlight? Why else would he have pushed himself, risking injury to his already frail health? Although such questions were raised in the Palmer interviews, ultimately they were cut from the film's final print.

Such observations were prohibitively frank. They might have invited too many questions, too many doubts about a Stravinskyan image methodically plotted in so many frames of so many films. There is the distinct risk of a one-dimensional view. For the most part, documentaries had intended to portray the composer and those who knew him in a certain way, and through judicious editing the image they sought was resourcefully achieved. We are fortunate to have the footage that has survived; but the sequences that were released sometimes do nothing more than reinforce the mythmaking long associated with the composer.

Assembling an accurate profile of any public figure with the notoriety of a Stravinsky is always risky, especially for one who welcomed the attention and often acted, along with his friends, as his own biographer. The documentaries as televised usually present a monolithic view. But much of the composer's story, left on the cutting-room floor, has been conveniently swept away. The docudrama as an art form, in reality, was often only a half-truth to begin with. In its quest to engage an audience, the reporting of events was obligated to be as persuasive and compelling as possible. As John Grierson himself admitted, the function of the form was "to make drama from life." The agenda, explicitly stated or not, was not only to inform but also to convince, or at least influence. The outtakes from the Palmer film and earlier documentaries are particularly crucial, as they allow one to know—without filters or partiality—

what Stravinsky and those closest to him really thought. In this sense alone, the unaltered transcripts of these edited segments should rightfully take a place alongside Stravinsky's unedited and unpublished correspondence, as well as other primary source materials such as his library and manuscripts. History deserves to draw its own conclusions based not only on what has been said and seen but, perhaps more important, what has been edited and snipped. Through such sources, the "curtain of protection" to which Isherwood alluded throughout *Prater Violet* will be drawn. The Stravinsky that we will eventually see is likely to be somewhat different from the celluloid image preserved through the televised documentaries that survive. Grierson hoped that documentaries would stimulate our imaginations and enrich our observations. In Stravinsky's case, they certainly have, although, as always, the line that separates the fictional Stravinsky from the real one too easily becomes blurred.

C·h·a·p·t·e·r ·7·

Letters, Books, Private Thoughts: Reading Between the Lines

> The explicit order to destroy this letter I did not obey. . . . I did not obey it, in the first instance because I felt the need to read again and again a piece of writing at first run through so quickly; to study it, not so much read as study, stylistically and psychologically. Then with the passage of time, the moment to destroy it had passed too; I learned to regard it as a document of which the order to destroy was a part, so that by its documentary nature it canceled itself out.
> —Thomas Mann, *Doctor Faustus*

Following Stravinsky's death in 1971, more than a decade of protracted litigation dragged through the New York courts in deciding the final disposition of his archives. Several American universities, libraries, and private foundations tendered bids. Zubin Mehta issued a passionate call to arms: "We cannot allow the Stravinsky archives to leave these shores." But despite a multimillion-dollar offer from New York's Pierpont Morgan Library for the outright purchase of the archives, it was determined that the Stravinsky collection would go to the Paul Sacher Foundation. On 14 June 1983, a settlement was reached, sending the composer's manuscripts, correspondence, and other primary sources to Sacher, Stravinsky's old friend, a noted conductor and philanthropist. The Sacher Stiftung in Basel, Switzerland, now holds the Stravinsky *Nachlass,* the most important and comprehensive collection of the composer's source materials.[1]

On 30 August 1983, the Stiftung received 116 boxes of documents, including thousands of letters to and from the composer. As described in the Sacher Foundation catalog: "The boxes of letters are divided into three parts: business correspondence with publishers, record companies, and music agents; letters covering all domains of public and private life, from Debussy to Boulez and Stockhausen, from Diaghilev to Balanchine, from Cocteau to Giacometti; and finally a third group, in chronological order, with special reference to his works and their performances." Cataloging the sheer volume of materials was arduous enough, yet it was complicated by the scattering of misdated and undated letters into various folders, often filed in no particular chronological— or for that matter, any perceivable—order. As overwhelming as the correspondence is, it is only a single part of the *Nachlass*, which also includes an important library of books, recordings, and scores, as well as the treasured centerpiece of the archives, the manuscripts and compositional sketches of most of Stravinsky's music.

Many of the letters address routine business matters. The composer constantly stewed over the particulars of a commission, sometimes changing his mind even after an offer was accepted. In a letter to Mark Schubart, director of the Juilliard School, on 10 July 1947, Stravinsky agreed to write a new work for the Juilliard Quartet for one thousand dollars, cautioning that it would be a while before he could complete it. Three years later Schubart discreetly inquired about the work's progress, since the composition was to be premiered at a 1951 Stravinsky festival. The composer's reply was surely not what Schubart wanted to hear, but at least it was forthright in stating that he had not even begun the work, adding that he could not say "if and when" he would be able to write it. No doubt sensing a catastrophe in the making, Schubart quickly replied that it was probably best to withdraw the commission and consider renewing the offer at some later date. On 15 June 1950, Stravinsky wrote across Schubart's letter, "Withdrawn."

The composer was in a position to reject various offers. One of the more curious commissions that he passed over involved Clare Boothe Luce. In a letter of 27 April 1950, the conductor Bruno Zirato wrote to him that Mrs. Luce had recently completed "a script for a ballet entitled *St. Francis of Assisi*." She specifically wanted Stravinsky to compose the score, and had gone so far as to stipulate that the length of the ballet "will not be over twenty or twenty-five minutes." Zirato suggested that accepting the commission—at not too high a fee, he added—would be a good idea, especially since Luce had recently joined the board of the New York Philharmonic. He strongly encouraged Stravinsky to speak with her, but nothing came of the project.

At about the same time, Stravinsky actively promoted the sale of his manuscripts, although he encountered difficulty finding buyers willing to meet his price. Returning several of the composer's works, the publishing house Broude Brothers, in an unpublished 1950 letter, informed him that a purchaser could not be found at the prices Stravinsky had set for *Perséphone* ($7,000), *Mavra* ($4,500), the Violin Concerto ($4,500), and the Piano Concerto ($4,000). Even with his reputation secure, the composer constantly had to work, often unsuccessfully, at selling himself. During the late 1940s and early 1950s Stravinsky was getting played and recorded, but many of the commissions he was offered were not particularly appealing. He was making a living largely by conducting what people still wanted to hear most—the old Diaghilev ballets.

The composer would threaten to pull out of commissions at the last moment. As the *Canticum Sacrum* neared its 1956 premiere at St. Mark's Cathedral in Venice, Stravinsky almost walked away from the project. He wrote to Alessandro Piovesan, director of the Venice Biennale International Festival of Contemporary Music, which had awarded him the commission:

> I seem to understand that you have been deceived by the fact that my *Canticum Sacrum*—to which I am now putting the final touches—will be of a duration of 16 minutes. Apparently this is less than you expected. If you and your organization ever expected a substantially longer piece it shouldn't have been commissioned from me at this time because the contrapuntal line of my music today . . . makes it a must to keep the duration of a composition strictly within rigid limits. This is due to the requirements and possibilities of the human ear and because this kind of music is of the densest kind. . . . I refer you to the works of Schoenberg, Webern, etc. . . . Because of the basic misunderstanding when we originally signed our contract . . . I suggest that we face the situation very bluntly and realistically. We have two ways out of the present impasse: 1/-either we stop where we are, forget the whole thing, and cancel our plans 2/-or we have to come to a new agreement at once.

The presentation of the "situation" is typically Stravinsky in its churlish either/or tone. Also bemusing is the composer's invocation of the once shunned serial gods, now embraced as old buddies, in defending the work's musical logic. Three months after this ultimatum, in another unreleased letter, Stravinsky rattled his saber more loudly: "Unless I receive immediate telegraphic acceptance all points paragraph 2 my letter . . . I am canceling my voyage to Venice. You have avoided committing yourselves while I made all possible concessions—[this] situation must end." Subsequently, Stravinsky suggested another solution: simply repeat the *Canticum Sacrum* after intermission, a programming practice he endorsed in earlier years (although in fact the *Canticum* was not repeated). But Stravinsky was not entirely unjustified in his objections, for communications with the festival were always difficult. Still, the bluster evident here is indicative of the confident composer's readiness to operate with the same kind of free-agent machismo more typical of today's superstar athletes than a classical composer. He knew his clout, and he wasn't shy about using it.

That, coupled with his notoriously freewheeling style (unilaterally making deals without the knowledge, let alone permission, of agents or publishers), made business negotiations always chancy. The composer's way of handling these dealings becomes quite apparent in examining in the incredible farrago surrounding negotiations between Stravinsky and his publisher-agent regarding the 1951 premiere of *The Rake's Progress*. The composer had been offered five thousand dollars for the premiere in Central City, Colorado, but the Venice Biennale festival offered twenty thousand dollars. "They were willing to do it in English," Stravinsky explained to his publisher, "and had given all guarantees, as well artistically as materially. . . . I could not possibly overlook such an opportunity inasmuch as by giving me the financial means to accelerate the completion of my work . . . Venice was the only one wise enough to put their money on the table."[2] In reply, an annoyed Ernst Roth of Boosey & Hawkes protested in a letter of January 1951: "I must confess that I had a shock when I received [the cable]. I only wish I had known that you were negotiating European performances yourself. . . . Undoubtedly you are aware that the situation for us is extremely awkward. I think you were informed that we had promised the European first performance to Covent Garden in December 1951, to be followed almost immediately by the Scala in Milan. The Scala especially would take great exception if the premiere went to Venice and there is no doubt that neither the Scala nor any other Italian Opera would perform the work for quite some time."[3]

The response reflects the simmering tension underlying many misunderstood communications with Stravinsky over a ten-year period, often owing to the composer's autonomous actions. Roth often felt cornered. His letters typically began: "I was profoundly shocked," "I was perturbed," "I was totally surprised," "I was bewildered." As earlier unpublished letters regarding *The Rake* confirm, Stravinsky knew that contracts had already been signed. Betty Bean, also of Boosey & Hawkes, was placed in the awkward position of undoing the havoc Stravinsky had wreaked. She, too, responded to the composer, on 27 January 1951, after learning that he had offered the premiere to Venice instead of Central City: "This is the first intimation I have had that such negotiations were even under consideration. From your general correspondence in the past I had long assumed that a premiere in Italy was out of the picture. This most recent development has come as rather a surprise for Nagy and the financial representative of Central City who were in the midst of attempting to encompass *The Rake's Progress* into their present budget as far as singers, etc. go."

Stravinsky wrote back to Roth in early February, first feigning innocence, then offering a meretricious five-page defense. It is vintage Stravinsky in its sophism. Although he attempted to bolster his ex parte stance by quoting himself from his own October 1950 letter, his position was clearly indefensible. It now fell to Roth to extricate both composer and publisher from the imbroglio that Stravinsky's private negotiating had precipitated. Much correspondence (most of it unpublished) ensued over the next few months. In March, Roth actually flew to Milan and Rome "to try and prevent a scandal." Another letter from Roth, on 23 March 1951, concedes his failure to placate the affronted Italians. "Dr. Ghiringhelli made it clear to me," he wrote, "and I had to admit that it was correct that we still have an obligation to offer your opera to the Scala before offering it to any other theatre on the European continent." Apparently a Venetian premiere would be permissible only if musicians from La Scala were imported. "Under the circumstances, this is the only way in which the Venice performance could be realized," Roth continued. As his letter attests, this solution would be considered, but "if the Scala and the people in Rome do not agree, there will be legal procedure by the Scala and Dr. Ghiringhelli made it plain to me that he would not refrain from a big scandal and from bringing the matter to the notice of the Italian parliament particularly as regards the payment of the 20,000 dollars. This is a very serious prospect for all of us."

At Roth's urging, Stravinsky finally pleaded nolo contendere, writing to La Scala and inviting the opera company "to associate itself with the premiere in Venice." The composer surely realized he was in the wrong, although his pride could never allow him to admit it. In a letter to his son Theodore in April, he complained, "Boosey & Hawkes seem to be in hot water, having promised the premiere left and right without telling me." But Stravinsky understood his predicament, and he informed Roth in a telegram: "Am cabling and writing Scala and Rome warmly encouraging them to get together. Thousand Thanks." The fact is, La Scala's involvement in the opera arose out of a last-ditch, face-saving tactic to avoid a shambles.[4]

There was not always smooth sailing with W. H. Auden, either. Questions arose about the first performance, the division of fees, and, most important, the subsequent adjustments to the staging following the Venetian premiere. This restaging, in large part, cannot be understood without considering the role of Auden's co-librettist, Chester Kallman. His proposed revisions of 27 January 1952 (intended for staging at a Metropolitan Opera Company performance, and painstakingly outlined in perhaps the lengthiest letter ever written to Stravinsky) survive in the Sacher archives. Given the debate over what has always been viewed as a problematic subdivision of the opera's stage action, Kallman's suggestions are worth reprinting in full.

Wystan has gotten me up-to-date on the *RAKE* negotiations with Bing [Rudolf Bing, director of the Metropolitan Opera]. On the whole, everything sounds fine. I must admit, however, that I have grave doubts about the new alignment of the scenes. Leitner [Ferdinand Leitner, responsible for La Scala's chorus and orchestra], as you know, suggested it at La Scala, and after thinking about it there, I came to the conclusion that whatever advantages it might have, they were more than counterbalanced by the disadvantages. Besides, Leitner wanted to make cuts in order to shorten what would have become a rather lengthy second act. But that, of course, is hardly at the core of my objections; we should, naturally, have no cuts in New York. What I feel is that the *unity* of the Rake, depending as it does a great deal on the balance between its parts, is certain to suffer slightly by shifting the Auction to the end of the Second Act. Musically, dramatically and scenically, the Second Act seems to me so absolutely to run in the classic a-b-a form, with its highest point of intensity, in the trio of the second scene, that the Auction could not but seem to be tacked on to it, if placed immediately after. And the brilliance of Sellem's scene, wonderfully effective as the opening of an act, would, since it does not really advance the auction, be in the nature of a parenthesis if played as the opening of a fourth scene. I do think that a parenthesis that late in what had been, up to then in the act, a continuous action, runs the risk of being, at least, mildly irritating. Also, to follow the brio of the Rakewell-Shadow duet with the brio of the Auction scene prelude must inevitably diminish the effect of the second. And the link between the Auction scene and the Cemetery scene, the offstage ballad-tune, will be lost in the intermission that should, in my opinion, serve rather as marking the months of Baba's sleep. To discover her still seated in her place in a new act is surely more effective than discovering her a moment later. And the poor mezzo-soprano certainly wants a few minutes to breathe in and take a bow. Further, I think the back-stage chorus (Ruin, disaster, shame) a shade too striking a device to place between two scenes; it is so much a call to attention for the opening of an act, a post-intermission device. Moreover, the original act endings were in the nature of two precipices: Anne on the edge of going to London and finding Tom, Tom on the edge of his financial ruin. Shifting the auction scene would mean that the suspended action at the end of the second act was the same as that of the first: Anne seeking her tenor again, "I go, I go to him." Also, I understand that in order to get the stage prepared in time for the cobwebs and dust of the auction scene, it will be necessary to play the end of the Rakewell-Shadow duet, in front of the drop; which means that the lines: "I have no wife . . . etc." are sung *without* Baba's visual presence to give them point. Surely that particular finale insists on what the progressive school teachers used to call "visual aid"; or so, at any rate, I think. Probably my objections might be answered simply by the fact that the auction scene has a more effective curtain than the other; but really, does that balance all the disadvantages? And is that the kind of effectiveness we want for the Rake? I have no doubt that the Stuttgart mob, from what I could gather from Leitner and the photographs he showed me, got some pretty startling effects on their own; but I also gathered that the effects had damned little to do with us and could only in the long run, give an erroneous impression of the opera and establish mistaken traditions for its performance. Just as I noticed, after the Venice production, that the critics who most highly praised [Robert] Rounseville's singing and acting [in the part of the Rake] and [Carl] Ebert's direction were the ones who liked the opera least. They too had their "effective" moments. The point of all the meandering on my part is that I feel, more strongly than any of my other objections, that it is necessary for us at certain points, to *flout* the theatre a bit. To say, in effect: Yes, we have our big curtains, our finales with grand gestures; that's easy. We can afford to throw them away because the effects we want are, in the end better, truer and, as a matter of fact, bigger. Wystan and I have already started that terrible and exciting work of getting our ideas in order for the new libretto; but until things are much clearer in our minds, we're maintaining a mysterious and, we hope intriguing, silence. New York is big and gray and damp, like Bruckner. I long for Italy.

Love to you and Vera.

Stravinsky responded to Kallman within a few days:

Your whole reasoning makes sense, indeed, but I do not quite agree with your estimate of the advantages compared to disadvantages in either one solution. . . . As you know, when I left, all minds seemed quite set on the solution of 4 scenes in the Second Act.

If the original staging of 3 scenes per act is to be observed, Armistead [Horace Armistead, who prepared scenery and costumes for the production] and Balanchine must know it once and for all before anyone in order to make their own plans adequately now. I must insist and warn you that *I will not accept* any stops between scenes as it was in Venice (this was also one of the reasons for Leitner's plan of switching the auction scene to the second Act so as to give enough time to prepare the churchyard scene). Please do let me know shortly what will be decided.

Stravinsky forwarded his reply to Balanchine, who was to direct the new production. Balanchine, who seldom wrote to Stravinsky because they often saw each other, responded on 6 February. He thanked the composer for the update while also informing him that he had already met with both Auden and Armistead. Balanchine addressed the proposed revision specifically: "I think it would be better divided as you yourself composed it. But don't be afraid of changes because unless we can find a way to do it very fast and smoothly we won't do it." He concludes by assuring the composer that the change should not be of much concern since the Met stage was large and "there should be no delay between scenes. We can prepare very carefully in advance."[5]

Following *The Rake,* unpublished letters of late 1951 and 1952 establish that several inquiries were made in the hope of commissioning a second opera, this one to be cast in one act, with Auden again as the librettist. Juilliard was approached, as were the Aspen Music Festival and the University of Southern California, though nothing came of these attempts.

Ernst Roth was only one of many publishers, agents, and lawyers who sparred with Stravinsky. In spite of all the time such commercial and legal matters consumed, the composer could not relinquish his grip. Consequently, and rather oddly, his immersion into such business affairs invited his attorneys to offer more than legal advice. In a letter of 20 August 1948, one of Stravinsky's lawyers obviously felt no hesitation in suggesting some rather drastic revisions to *The Rake*'s scenario. The story was too reminiscent of Faust, the attorney volunteered, and consequently lost the qualities of the Hogarth etchings that had first caught Stravinsky's eye. He objected to the portrayal of the bearded Baba, feeling that it was "unwholesome" and approached a rather cheap type of comedy. He also suggested that the speeches ran on too long, although he liked the famous Bedlam. And as with many of Stravinsky's critics, he wondered about the wisdom of including an epilogue, suggesting that perhaps a prologue would work better "in the style of the astrologer in *Le Coq d'Or.*"

But why would Stravinsky care what his attorney thought? The oddity is, he frequently welcomed such nonprofessional advice, readily investing it with the authority of objectivity—at least whenever it fortified his position. He regularly employed lawyers and publishers as conduits through which he could channel his fulminations. They served not only as legal counselors but therapists. In a 1957 letter to another of his lawyers, Stravinsky complained about Lincoln Kirstein: "As for Lincoln, I am very disappointed and even not a little humiliated that the Stravinsky Festival has dwindled to nothing. . . . I do not blame Lincoln for not being able to find the money, but for his very peculiar actions to ourselfs [*sic*] who are his old and dear friends." Yet this is pure sulking on the composer's part, and typical at that. Not only did his lawyers and others provide a catharsis, but they were safely distanced from the real dramatis personae participating in the artistic creation, underwriting, and production of a work. Griping to them carried no repercussions.

Stravinsky seldom relied on the counsel of other established composers—especially those he viewed as competitors. He would share his unpublished scores with younger composers, who naturally were awed by the master and thus reluctant to criticize. Their role, it seems, was to reassure him by allaying any doubts. Letters in the Sacher archive establish that Stravinsky would sometimes send prepublication drafts of his new scores to younger composers who had befriended him. Even compositions that had not yet been orchestrated were offered in preview, as in the case of his ballet *Orpheus*, sent in December 1947 to Harold Shapero, one of the few composers Stravinsky actually dubbed "promising."

Stravinsky was besieged by a constant stream of aspiring young composers eager to study with, or just attach themselves to, him. Typical is one young man's unpublished 1959 letter, accompanied by a composition, asking Stravinsky to evaluate it and perhaps take him on as a student. But Stravinsky gruffly replied: "Don't ask me things I am not in measure to fulfill. I have no time to examine and give my opinion about compositions I continuously receive from everywhere. And your case is by no means an exceptional one." At other times, he could be quite supportive of younger composers admitted into his trust, and would willingly share his views with them. Lukas Foss, in the audio oral history *Igor Stravinsky: The Man and His Music*, remembers the maestro's views on orchestration: "Stravinsky did away with orchestration and substituted writing for instruments as he called it. He would say why did you give that to the trumpets?" Foss remembered that if an idea made sense as a "trumpet tune," Stravinsky would insist that it be given "to the violins, which reveals something about his approach to orchestration."

Given Stravinsky's masterful control of orchestration, several primary sources, particularly his books and marginalia, deserve a few words. Frequently the image we have of Stravinsky as the consummate orchestrator arises from the assumption that his concept of "sound" came instinctively. But as his library demonstrates, he was often unsure of the color he wanted, and sometimes he traveled a considerable distance in arriving at a final instrumental assignment. Indecision sometimes persisted until the last moment, and, as many of his manuscripts show, the composer would even change his mind once a work was apparently considered finished. He even occasionally rethought certain orchestral decisions after the score was actually in print.

Moreover, his interest in learning all that he could about how instruments—even odd ones—worked, is evident in browsing through his library in Basel. He carefully studied Hugo Herman's *Einführung in die Komposition für Akkordeon,* a book about the possibilities of the accordion (even marking a section dealing with "harmonics"), even though Stravinsky never wrote for the instrument. His library contained method books on saxophones, guitars, even banjos. He purchased sheet music of popular songs to study the arrangements.

He also owned a copy of Charles M. Widor's famous treatise *Technique de l'orchestre moderne* (1910): the manual was thoroughly marked by the young Stravinsky.[6] The author listed several composers whose works for flute should be studied, including Gabriel Fauré and Camille Saint-Saëns. But Stravinsky underlined in red other flute composers Widor mentioned—Peter Benoît, Giulio Briccialdi, Cesare Ciardi, Hamilton J. Clarke—and wrote in the margin, "en effet très 'moderne'!" Widor also questioned Carl Maria von Weber's use of the flute in *Oberon,* reporting that Weber employed the second flute in an inappropriate range, to which Stravinsky responded in the margin, "C'est absurde!" He also placed an *x* next to Weber's name and added, "à Mozart aussi alors!" He inserted a handwritten bookmark labeled "Sarrusophone" in the section dealing with that instrument, and another marker where Widor, in speaking of Mozart's orchestration of *Don Giovanni,* suggested that trills for trombone not be used in symphonic orchestras. "Pourquoi pas?" wondered Stravinsky. Indeed, he questioned many bits of Widor's advice: when to use the harp, saxophones, when harmonics for the double bass are allowable. The composer even added his own fingerings in suggesting how the bass might negotiate harmonics, suggesting that he experimented with finding a way to produce the sound he wanted. Finally, Stravinsky corrected misprints in Widor's citation of Mozart's *Magic Flute* (restoring the correct clef for the glockenspiel), and also in some passages by Giacomo Meyerbeer, further revealing how closely he studied the examples. These are the markings of a composer who worked hard at orchestration, who studied the literature carefully and knew when and how to break established conventions. Yet they are technical matters, part of the craft of composition, and therefore almost never mentioned in his letters to friends and associates.

The composer's personal relationships with others often surface in the correspondence. His archives include an impressive file of recommendation letters for Guggenheim applicants, including Milton Babbitt, Jean Berger, Dahl, Vittorio Rieti, Claudio Spies, and many others. He took the time to write to Paul Horgan, recommending Luciano Berio for a lecturing appointment at

Wesleyan University in 1964 ("Signor Berio is, I believe, the most gifted of living Italian composers and with Boulez and Stockhousen [*sic*] a leader and direction-finder in the younger musical world today"). Sometimes applicants were asked to write their own recommendation letters so that Stravinsky could simply sign them. A particularly peculiar request came from his early biographer Boris de Schloezer asking him to recommend Aleksandr Scriabin's daughter, Marina, as a candidate for an international seminar at Harvard (Schloezer had written a biography of Scriabin). But it was Schloezer who actually wrote the letter. Stravinsky had it typed and signed his own name—but he couldn't resist scribbling a few changes, such as scratching out Schloezer's description of Scriabin as "the very famous" composer, leaving it to read simply "composer."[7]

Stravinsky received countless far-flung requests and bulletins from every walk of life: an eight-year-old from Philadelphia named her puppet "Petrouchka" and wanted him to know; students sent theses and dissertations to the composer, seeking his opinion; fans mailed blank pieces of paper for his autograph, some even asking him to compose a few bars of music to go along with his signature. A letter from the Tuscaloosa, Alabama, Music Study Club asked him to suggest recordings and to autograph a few excerpts from his scores that best express "your present musical philosophy or emotion." A letter from the National Catholic Welfare Conference in April 1960 was exceedingly clear in requesting that Stravinsky write a specific kind of hymn for its convention in June: "The music should spark inspiration. It should be majestic, attractive and suitably religious. It cannot be overly difficult since it is designed for group singing. It cannot be trivial or 'popular' yet it should have a common touch." The letter concluded with the postscript that little money was available. Telegrams seeking immediate help were also common. One desperate student literally preparing an eleventh-hour term paper posted a cable just before midnight in March 1958: "I am a student at the University of California Riverside studying your *Symphony of Psalms* and having difficulty. I cannot find a book on the subject. I cannot buy the record. Would you please call me so I can talk with you on the telephone concerning your *Symphony.* Phone Overland 4 . . ."

Stravinsky would spend precious time responding in lengthy, patient letters to requests and questions of most any kind. Advice for ballet was an especially popular item. In a 1941 letter to the composer, one aspiring choreographer resurrected the apparition of *Petrushka*: "Last night I heard your *Third Symphony in C* and it became a ballet for me—here is the idea. The staccato form of the greater part of the music suggests puppets. Couldn't you set the scene in a puppet theatre?" Long before Balanchine used the music of Stravinsky's 1929 *Capriccio* for the "Rubies" section of his 1967 ballet *Jewels,* a woman from Tonawanda, New York, wrote to the composer, in 1952: "Having been struck afresh by the ballet possibilities of your *Capriccio* . . . I should like to have your permission to work with it. I have in mind an allegorical theme, which I should carry out in the decor and costumes . . . and for reasons of economy the score would need to be reduced. Perhaps two pianos and another instrument for additional color." And, amazingly, Stravinsky took the time to answer: "I appreciate your interest in my *Capriccio* but I am sorry to say I disagree with your idea of using the music for a ballet. My feeling is strongly against it, notwithstanding the fact that I do not approve either of any tampering with my instrumentation."

He was consistently resolute on this last point, whether it was Eugene Ormandy wanting to do a reduced version of *Le Sacre* or Harvard University asking if *Oedipus Rex* could be done without orchestra. Nonetheless, the oddest requests and letters about ballet kept coming. Some correspondents attempted to unmask the roots of Stravinsky's models. In a 1949 letter, a fan wrote, "I have just listened to the *Orpheus* ballet music. My curiosity is aroused. I wonder if you have ever visited Georgia. Forty years ago I heard sounds strikingly similar to your ballet music in the trucks of a little train we used to call the picayune that ran between this city and the village of Harlem up the country from Augusta." Seeing no causal link between the "picayune" and Ovid, Stravinsky put a series of question marks around the statement— yet he still kept it in his file. Upon seeing a 1961 performance of another Stravinsky and Balanchine ballet, *Agon,* a fan sent a poem, suggesting specifically that it be read before and not during future performances of the work. The poem begins: "This is my *agon,* my battle, my competition of mind-being and metaphysical-being and challenged combat of unquiescent material-beings in conflict of all rhythms of life." Again Stravinsky responded, this time with an autographed photo and inscription: "Touched by your *Agon* inspired verses."[8]

Of all the ballet proposals the composer received, none is more interesting than Jerome Robbins's suggestion, offered in a letter of 23 February 1960, that he stage a new version of *Le Sacre du printemps.* "I have been wanting to choreograph *The Rite of Spring* for so many years," Robbins wrote. "It has been my life's dream to do this work." He went on to say that he had been asked to stage the work at the Royal Theatre in Copenhagen, "but that certain architectural problems," meaning the orchestra pit, were a problem. The pit was simply too small to accommodate the orchestra for which Stravinsky had scored the ballet. But Robbins was persistent: "I hope and pray most fervently that you will give us a solution and allow them some version of your wonderful score. I feel I can do a ballet of which you would be very proud and happy." In response, Stravinsky wrote to H. A. Brønsted of the Royal Theatre two days later: "I am very sorry not to be able to help you in this, especially as I am a very sincere admirer of Jerome Robbins, and I would be happy to know him staging the SACRE, but we must accept the fact that the re-writing this work for a smaller ensemble is already a 45 year old headache without result."

Stravinsky's publisher, Ralph Hawkes, also fancied himself a critic of both opera and ballet, as his unpublished correspondence with the composer reveals.[9] Sometimes Stravinsky landed in the middle of feuds between his attorney and Hawkes. In a handwritten note to the composer, Stravinsky's lawyer questioned Hawkes's opinion regarding the concert version of one of the composer's ballets: "He thinks that *Orpheus* is too long and repetitious for concerts and urges you to indicate when cuts may be made." Cuts? Not the best topic to raise with Stravinsky, given his hands-off policy when it came to tampering with the actual music.

Still, he enjoyed watching a swarm of business partners scurry for his attention while he himself ultimately controlled the outcome, turning to his confidants for advice before making decisions. His old friend and publisher Willy Strecker provided counsel well into the 1950s. In June 1951, as *The Rake* neared its September premiere, the composer asked Strecker to review his contract with Boosey & Hawkes. In response, Strecker stated that he was sorry not to share the attorney's "opinion regarding the position of your publisher as 'trustee of your opera.'" There followed a lengthy explanation of American copyright law, indivisible and absolute transfers, the rights to the assignee, and other legalese that Stravinsky probably studied with a magnifying glass. Strecker suggested that a potential record contract with Decca be delayed until after "a definite number of contracts with theaters were definitely affixed." Radio broadcasts of live performances from Venice and other cities would also be useful in promoting interest, but to release the recording too soon would be an ill-advised marketing strategy. "This is the best advice I can give you in your own interest as a friend, and not as a publisher," Strecker concluded.[10]

Stravinsky's early study of the law left an indelible imprint. Also, without copyright protection for his early and successful ballets, he suffered an inestimable loss of royalties. No wonder he did not completely trust the various attorneys and agents who came in and out of his life. The revenue lost on his earliest ballet, *The Firebird,* was in itself enough to make him circumspect. Once the work was under copyright in the United States, he and his lawyers monitored its royalties carefully. One of his attorneys wrote to Leeds Music Corporation on 31 March 1961, "It astonishes me that a firm of your repute should be so extraordinarily remiss in fulfilling its contractual obligations, especially when it is your privilege to be dealing with the world's greatest living composer"—just the kind of hard-line approach that Stravinsky demanded.

His problems with Leeds were traceable to the 1940s, when he sued the publisher over its publication of a melody from the ballet for a popular song titled "Summer Moon." A letter to Aaron Goldmark, attorney for Leeds, on 22 August 1947, argued: "It is your wish to publish this composition with the lyrics and to exploit it as a popular song on the commercial market. It is interesting to think of the thousands of people who may perhaps be humming or whistling this melody from the Firebird Suite all over America, much as they hummed and whistled and sang the famous Andante from Tschaikowsky's Fifth Symphony, after it was adapted from one the world's great classics. I am fully in accord and do hereby authorize you to exploit *this melody* from the Firebird Suite, with the lyrics by John Klenner. You have my complete endorsement."

The Stiftung holds a signed contract with Leeds dated 28 May 1947, complete with a listing of the royalty distribution. But the arrangement of the "tune" did not conform precisely to Stravinsky's understanding of what would be done, so the lawsuit was filed. (He finally lost the case in 1949, as reported in the *New York Daily News* under the headline "Igor Mortis.")[11] The importance here arises from a pattern, or more to the point an obsession, in Stravinsky's life: both in personal habit and certainly regarding the performance of his scores, he insisted upon exactness without the slightest liberty for individual interpretation or digression. For the compulsive and often suspicious composer—suspicious with good reason inasmuch as he was robbed of what he was rightfully owed—the smallest variance was strictly prohibited. This being the case, the often aggrieved composer felt unrestrained in changing his mind as a matter of conscience. And change it he often did, as evident in one further piece of business with Boosey & Hawkes.

A letter from the firm's David Adams in 1963 sought clarification about the recipients and division of monies for a scholarship to be given in Stravinsky's name. The composer had originally suggested splitting the award among the students mentioned but later changed his mind. Among his handwritten objections in the letter's margin: "I no longer wish to give money, or have money given in my name, to rich universities." "Why should I be impartial and put $1,000 into the pocket of some hostile student electrician in the Princeton Music Department?" One final note reveals, "I asked Bob to compose this answer." It didn't take much to irritate Stravinsky, and his response often came almost reflexively in this kind of reversal. Here, Craft merely did what he was told to do; but increasingly he became more than a dutiful secretary limited to wording tactful replies. He now served as an indispensable mediator.

Stravinsky expected homage, and at times even sycophancy, from those who surrounded him. He was personally affronted by those who violated his code of basic courtesies. Ingolf Dahl understood that, as he wrote in an unpublished letter of February 1966 to Stravinsky upon his receipt of the ASCAP Stravinsky Prize: "As an obligation to keep faith with whatever creative work I am capable of; as an obligation to stay as much in tune with the musical present as you are; and not the least, as an obligation to continue to serve your music with all my capabilities—this music which has helped shape today's world as much as it has helped shape myself." Another young composer, upon receiving the Lili Boulanger Memorial Award for composition, graciously thanked Stravinsky in a letter from April 1961. He praised him as "the greatest composer of the century," and especially applauded his recent serial works as inspirational models.

It was just the kind of admiration Stravinsky expected. Even Kirstein was not above reproach when the composer felt slighted: "Did you see *Agon*?" he asked in a 1957 letter to his attorney. "I received many wires and a telephone call from Balanchine and not a single word from Lincoln Kirstein (to whom *Agon* is dedicated)." David Diamond, who provided East Coast reconnaissance for Stravinsky, reporting on performances, informing him of any unapproved liberties conductors were taking with his music, and running errands for him with his publishers, committed the cardinal sin of addressing the composer as "Dear Igor" in a letter on 25 May 1949. In the margin Stravinsky wrote, "Why 'Igor' and not Stravinsky?—a strange familiarity." In an unreleased section from the Palmer documentary, composer and friend Alexei Haieff states that Stravinsky "hated familiarity. If somebody called him Igor that would be the end. He would hate that man, he'll remember him for years. . . . 'That awful upstart. How dare he call me Igor!'"

Just as Stravinsky was not above invoking the authority of his name, he would often casually allow its exploitation. When Lucia Chase, director of the

Ballet Theatre, invited him to join the company's board of governing trustees in 1945 (along with Agnes de Mille, A. Conger Goodyear, and Moss Hart), Stravinsky answered that he would "give my consent for the use of my name . . . however I will not assume definitely and absolutely any obligations or participation financial or artistic. If this condition is not acceptable to your Board we shall dismiss the matter."

Likewise, unpublished documents in the Boulanger file in Basel disclose Stravinsky's complicity as a judge in the annual competition for the Lili Boulanger Memorial Award. The truth is, Stravinsky never took part in judging the competition; he wasn't even sent the competitors' scores. Rather, he received only the ballots, with specific instructions as to how he should vote. In 1959, after he had already voted, Boulanger changed her mind about the winner, so naturally Stravinsky was told to change his. Boulanger's secretary Winifred Johnstone sent Stravinsky a new ballot, explaining, "As soon as I am in receipt of the enclosed vote, signed, I shall destroy the earlier vote you signed." By 1963, Stravinsky didn't even know for whom he was actually voting. Johnstone wrote: "I have left the name of the candidate blank on your vote . . . please sign and return at your earliest convenience." Well, after all, Stravinsky was a busy man.[12]

But as his archives demonstrate, he was never too busy to take an active interest in the performance of his own scores. With his well-known "composing is more important than having composed" stance, he often shrugged off his completed works as unimportant: "I don't care about my works, I care only about composing." It was a favorite saw, and one that many creative spirits share. John Steinbeck was no different in declaring that he really did not care about his books once they were completed: "The book dies a real death for me when I write the last word. . . . The line of books on the shelf are to me like very well embalmed corpses. . . . I have no sorrow for them because I have forgotten them."[13] As a performance art, music is quite a different matter, and despite Stravinsky's disclaimers, he cared deeply about both composing and how his works would be performed. How could a person so programmed to exercise absolute control indifferently walk away from "embalmed corpses"— or, as Stravinsky described his finished compositions, "his children"? Rather than release them, he guarded their lives like an overprotective parent. The letter of the law ruled—his law, of course, as laid down in his scores and recordings. As with nearly everything he undertook or espoused, his anxiety about the evils of interpretation approached fanaticism. "To speak of an interpreter means to speak of a translator," the composer warned in his *Poetics of Music.* "And it is not without reason that a well-known Italian proverb, which takes the form of a play on words, equates translation with betrayal."

The composer embarked on a performance career in the 1920s, partly as a way of making a living but also "to clarify and establish my intentions in a precise manner." As Boulez stated in a 1960 Darmstadt lecture ("Time, Notation, and Coding"), the issue was of such paramount interest to Stravinsky "that he concentrated all his attention on a coding so precise that it obliged the performer to reproduce the composer's message as exactly as it was originally communicated to him."[14] Just how precise is demonstrated in Stravinsky's infatuation during that period with the pianola (an instrument that attracted the interest of Marcel Proust, and Diaghilev too, who employed it in rehearsals for the Ballets Russes). He vowed that the mechanical piano transcriptions he laboriously prepared would faithfully register a living testament to his wishes. As he wrote in his autobiography, he wished to prevent the "distortion of my compositions by future interpreters," initially with the mechanical piano rolls, later with gramophone recordings. Once phonographs became available, around 1928, he quickly moved into the recording studio and spent a large part of the remainder of his life there; although in the end he characterized it as a "horrible industry" and by 1968 called recording no more than "embalming a performance on tape."

With the advent of phonograph recordings, Stravinsky, at least at times, seems to have compositionally planned and even adjusted the timing of individual movements to accommodate neatly the separate sides of records. He was conscious of this consideration as early as the mid-1920s (with the aforementioned *Serenade en la* in 1925, for example). Notations among several of his sketches are revealing in their careful calculation of a passage's or movement's duration, designed to fit "Side One," or "Side Two," of a record. Writing to the Columbia Recording Corporation twenty-five years later, he planned four sides of a forthcoming release, while expressing concern over which violinist would join him: "The Maiden's Song for Violin and Piano from my Opera *Mavra* which should be on one of the *Ode*'s sides (the *Ode* as you know, has but 3 sides) and which we planed [sic] to record this summer with Nathan Milstein [but] to my great disappointment he will not be here in California this summer. Now, what shall we do? Shall I talk personally to Szigeti asking him to work on that piece? Who else with a name could be asked?"[15]

Stravinsky's performances and recordings with Szigeti were among his best collaborations over the years with several violinists. In 1924, Szigeti played for the composer in Leipzig, and they found they were well suited to each other.

Stravinsky at the Pleyela, 1922, preparing a piano roll
(Courtesy of the Paul Sacher Stiftung)

Like Stravinsky, Szigeti was all business, and he was willing to shun the histrionics of public performance in the cause of interpreting the music as the composer wished. Stravinsky performed the *Duo Concertant* with Szigeti in Carnegie Hall on 8 February 1946. A few months earlier, over a three-day period in October, Szigeti had recorded the work with the composer in Hollywood. Among the historical recordings that Stravinsky made, it is one of the finest. Szigeti plays the prodigiously difficult "Gigue" with an appropriate harshness and bite that many contemporary violinists would find "unmusical." But it is exactly what the composer wanted. Stravinsky's playing, too, is marvelous in its energy and precision—much cleaner and more convincing than many of his solo piano recordings.

Szigeti's remembrance of their rehearsals at his southern California home speak to the composer's often misinterpreted attitude about performance:

> While playing, replaying, and discussing certain unorthodox devices of mine (to reinforce the G-string passage in the Gigue of the Duo), Stravinsky professed with utter simplicity his love for the physical roots of musical realization. As if he needed to explain the roots of this attitude of his, he added: "Vous comprenez, my father was an interpreter, he was a singer. I grew up with the consciousness of the executant's essential part in bringing our written music to life." . . . It is this awareness of Stravinsky's of what the executants of his

Aeolian Company pianola roll of *The Firebird,* indicating the composer's approval of the performance (Courtesy of the Music Division, Library of Congress)

music do, his interest in the instrumental "know-how," that makes working with him so delightful, even if sometimes pretty strenuous. . . . Stravinsky, in order to make his intentions realistically clear, is quite willing to disregard and often contradict commentators' dicta that have been read into his music; sometimes he will even deviate quite considerably from his own pronouncements.[16]

Stravinsky first saw recording as an opportunity to hand down his personal thoughts, once claiming that the worst of his own recordings were still useful to other performers. The saga of those recordings overshadows almost any other part of his various commercial enterprises. The documents detailing this history are marked by bitter exchanges with agents, performers, and audio directors—all of whom, the composer contended, failed to market him or his music effectively.[17] The summer of 1948 was particularly tense, as evinced by several frosty exchanges with Goddard Lieberson of Columbia Recordings over how performances were made and released. Stravinsky wrote to Lieberson on 5 June:

I can't refrain from telling you my utter disappointment in your failure to release my recordings. . . . Such a delay may be due to some specific commercial stunds [*sic*] which I am unable to grasp.

When I signed the contract with you, I firmly believed in your enthusiasm to present to the public the genuine aspect of my compositions before those of my numerous misinterpreters who so unscrupulously cripple my works on concerts and records. Alas I was mistaken.

As to your usual refrain that you are hampered in your intentions by the ineterferance [*sic*] of your "bosses," I consider it a fallacy, nothing else. It is unbelievable that any President or Vice of a powerful Corporation, such as yours, would not be able to produce important works of the contemporary musical output, be it only due to a lack of a wish to do so. . . . Charming!

To which Lieberson responded on 15 June:

I was very unhappy, troubled and a little shocked by the invective in your letter, which I suppose was in a way its intention.

You write as if I conduct a one man cabal against you and quite the opposite is the case. It seems to me that you have very little to complain about in regard to either me or Columbia. . . . We have no intentions of suppressing your unreleased recordings; quite the contrary, since they represent a large investment on which we have had no return whatsoever. . . . We cannot limit

Violinist Joseph Szigeti with the composer in 1946 (The Fred and Rose Plaut Archives, courtesy of the Yale University Music Library)

ourselves exclusively to Stravinsky and we have been issuing in the last years recordings of music by Alban Berg, Milhaud, Villa-Lobos, Charles Ives, David Diamond, Bela Bartok, Menotti, Copland, and many others, too numerous to mention.

Now let us turn to the case of Stravinsky, which I am sure interests you most: not only is he the best represented on our records of all contemporary composers but he has been fortunate enough to have his later works recorded, even if they had not reached a point of public acceptance, which is the *usual* criterion on which record companies operate. In other words, if it were only the "hits" we were interested in, we should have in our catalog "Firebird," "Petrouchka," and "Sacre," no doubt performed by Leopold Stokowski, copyright free, and be satisfied with only that!

But Stravinsky was not about to accept Lieberson's curt reply, writing to him again in July and accusing him of "your usual kind of alibies." Nearly twenty years later, Stravinsky continued to participate in every aspect of a recording's production. When John McClure of Columbia Masterworks was producing a new recording of the composer's *Capriccio* and Piano Concerto, Stravinsky raised an objection. He did not want to be listed as the conductor—"it is extremely dangerous to pretend that I conducted." He further complains that Philippe Entremont was not the pianist he would have chosen. And, unable to resist exhuming an earlier grievance from 1961, he reminded McClure of his disappointment in a recording of his Violin Concerto. He had objected to having his photograph taken with Isaac Stern, especially because "he never played the *Concerto* before or since recording it and he had hardly done me the respect of learning it then"—although one suspects this is one of the composer's frequent overstatements.[18]

Tempo was always Stravinsky's gravest performance concern. Once, when asked, "Whom do you consider the best of your interpreters," he replied, "Those who least of all mutilate my tempos." His son Soulima recalled shortly after his father's death: "First, the basic laws of correct music playing had to be observed, that is, correct rhythm and tempo relationship. That he was absolutely merciless about. You had to keep the tempo and be in the just tempo. You could vary, but the whole thing, the pulse, should be right. . . . Function normally and keep the steady pulse—that was his advice."[19]

The composer's personally marked scores are revealing. The published version of the *Duo Concertant*, for example, contains several fingerings, but many more are marked in Stravinsky's own copy. These would be instructive to performers, especially given Stravinsky's idiosyncratic piano writing. Just as Bee-

Stravinsky with Goddard Lieberson during a recording session for Columbia Records, early 1960s (The Goddard Lieberson Papers, courtesy of the Yale University Music Library and Mrs. Brigitta Lieberson)

thoven's piano fingerings illustrate how the composer wished to phrase a passage or stress a certain note, so too do Stravinsky's unpublished fingerings provide insight into his preferred reading. The composer also marked errors in his personal score—errors that persist in published scores. Perhaps most important for the would-be "executant," Stravinsky marked where to take a little time, what to accent, where the music should move faster or slower than the metronomic markings indicate. Even the violin part (marked by Sam Dushkin) indicates where the performer should take an up-bow or down-bow, and where harmonics might be employed or octaves dropped (even where Stravinsky originally wanted them). Such documents reinforce just how badly accurately published editions of Stravinsky's music are needed if contemporary performers are to abide by the composer's wishes.

Stravinsky was particularly eager to explain his position on interpretation to anyone willing to listen. The composer exchanged letters with Frederick Dorian, author of *The History of Music in Performance* (1942), which Stravinsky kept in his library and marked thoroughly. In January 1943, Dorian wrote to ask if he had understood Stravinsky's views on interpretation correctly. A week later he responded:

> It is sufficiently clear—this is why I was astonished that you did not confine yourself to the exactness of my statement concerning Fritz Reiner whom I cite in support of my musical ideology. If I have mentioned in the course of my autobiographical pages other interpreters and performers it was not necessarily always as in support of my ideas, frequently just to the contrary. Also—the fact of one or another specializing in interpretation of music, Russian or any other School does not prove anything conclusively—especially as far as it concerns me. It is also well known that since a long time my work and more than that my musical mind has transcended Russian or any other so called School. I am pointing out this instance as it may somehow confuse those of your readers who are well informed on matters of interpreters of various tendencies.[20]

Any opening to express his hostility toward interpreters was seized. In his copy of a Verdi biography, Stravinsky underlined, "Verdi did something quite unheard of in refusing to allow the singers supplementary arias and rondos; he would not tolerate the slightest alteration in his music, and people had to grit their teeth." Denouncing the endless violations of his works, Stravinsky's rhetoric intensified, as perhaps most stridently stressed by Roland-Manuel in the sixth of the 1939–40 Harvard lectures. The nub of the composer's message (as preserved in his original notes to Roland-Manuel) was, "Being, nothingness, and reality are simultaneous in a musical work." Music could exist only "while it is played and when it is played again. Between these two moments, the music does not exist." From these cryptic thoughts, his remarks swelled into the last of his six lectures, "The Performance of Music," a no-holds-barred sermon dripping with antagonism. An abbreviated English translation of Stravinsky's text (which was originally delivered in French at Cambridge) was distributed to the audience the evening of the lecture. The synopsis was less acerbic than his remarks in the full address, although the message is clear. The synopsis, reprinted here, covered the ten main points of the composer's lecture, followed by a brief epilogue.

I

Music retained by memory or noted on paper has an existence previous to its execution. In this way a musical entity reveals itself in two aspects, because it is conceivable in a potential form before being presented in an active one. To these two states of music—potential and active—correspond two kinds of musicians: the creator and the executant.

II

Two kinds of executants: the mere executant and the interpreter. The former is held only by the obligation to play his part, the latter not only subordinates himself to the necessities of his duty, which is to transmit the music, but must also convey the intentions of the creator. He is the representative of the author; he must be both interpreter and executant; but not vice versa.

III

A musical work seems never to be quite identical with itself. Its presentation depends every time upon the quality of its execution. The executant in the narrow sense of the word is bound only to the literal rendering of his part, whereas the interpreter is expected to give to the work not only a perfect rendering but also a devoted love, even an occult or evident collaboration with the creator.

Dangers of this collaboration. Bad interpretation. Vagaries of the interpreters. Their sins against the spirit of the work. Romanticists, the appointed and natural victims of the vagaries of the interpreter.

IV

A particularly dangerous variety of the type of interpreters: the conductor. His prestige in modern times. His ascendency in music.

V

Duties of the interpreter: infallibility of the execution; submission to the spirit of the work performed which presupposes a technical mastery, a sense of tradition, a perfection of culture.

VI

Music can be "seen." Its plastic rendering unconsciously influences our judgment of it. Necessity for the executant of a harmonious and proper regulation of gestures. This elegant correctness is rather a matter of education than of musical instruction. Importance of that education which is not imparted anywhere.

VII

This lack of education reveals itself in a multitude of ways: for instance in the disproportion between the character of the work and the means employed for its execution. The ostentation of great numbers and of the multiplying of choral and instrumental units. One does not gain power in proportion to the augmentation of the number of executants. To make something thick does not mean to make it strong.

VIII

All creation has a tendency to project itself, to communicate itself. The creator has an unconquerable desire to make other people share in his joy. As a result the listener becomes a partner in the play (le jeu) initiated by the creator. But a participator is not a judge. The audience is not qualified to pronounce an authoritative and final judgment upon the value of a work. Enough that it has been called upon to decide the fate of the composition.

IX

The above mentioned reasons make evident the moral responsibility of the executant. The fate of the work always depends on the quality of its performance, particularly its first one. The public must place its trust in the representatives of the author.

X

How does the listener, the partner of the creator, participate in the musical play? Three different attitudes of the public towards music: active participation uniting the audience to the composer; passive meditation of those who try to follow the development of the composition; indifference of the snobs and the wrong kind of dilettanti. Music imparts a kind of stupidity to those who listen to it without hearing it.

Example of the radio and of the dreadful saturation that it can produce.

EPILOGUE

Recapitulation of the general theses which we have sustained and which are governed by an essential consideration: the pursuit of unity through multiplicity. A constant search for variety brings forth only a vain and ever unsatisfied curiosity. It is natural and healthy to tend rather towards the reality of a limitation than towards the infinite possibilities of multiplicity.

Music is that which unifies. But unity has its reverberations. The accomplished work spreads out in order to make itself known and eventually flows back to its principle. In this way music appears to us as an element of communion with the future—and with the Supreme Being.[21]

Stravinsky's swollen rhetoric could be dismissed as such if it were not that the sentiments expressed were deeply felt. His remarks also clearly betray the fear of relinquishing control to others. And the Norton Professor was not parsimonious with his allegations. Performers and audiences alike were indicted as co-conspirators, as were a host of virtuosi who prospered at the expense of the victimized composer: "These are just so many practices dear to superficial minds forever avid for, and satisfied with, an immediate and facile success that flatters the vanity of the person who obtains it and perverts the taste of those who applaud it. How many remunerative careers have been launched by such practices! How many times have I been the victim of these misdirected attentions from abstractors of quintessences who waste time splitting hairs over a *pianissimo,* without so much as noticing egregious blunders of rendition!"[22]

Egregious indeed, but not without a large measure of truth for one whose exclamations left little latitude for flexibility. No wonder he spent considerable time handpicking conductors and instrumentalists. With careful deliberation, he solicited and engaged performers from all over Europe and the United States, often, as in the near disaster with La Scala, insulting local musicians, irritating contractors, and exasperating lawyers along the way. He reluctantly permitted other pianists to play his Piano Concerto (he had toured with it exclusively for several years), realizing that if he did not release it to others it would not stay in the repertoire. Even so, he told his agent that only certain pianists should be entrusted with its performance—"honest pianists," he remarked—and proceeded to name names.

He was particularly finicky when it came to singers. Elizabeth Schwarzkopf's performance as Donna Elvira with the San Francisco Opera in 1950 prompted him to ask if she would sing in *The Rake's Progress.* He retained the program booklet from her Mozart performance, writing "wunderbar" next to her name; the program remains where he inserted it, in his copy of Leo Melitz's *The Opera Goer's Complete Guide.* In this book, he marked several operas in the table of contents, including Debussy's *Pelléas,* Donizetti's *L'Elisir d'amore* and *Lucia,* Gounod's *Faust,* Massenet's *La Navarraise,* Mussorgsky's *Boris Godunov,* and most of the operas of Mozart, Rossini, Puccini, Verdi, and even Strauss and Wagner. Stravinsky also marked numerous passages in several of these scores, most of which remain in his library—a treasure trove in tracing the composer's operatic models.

In a letter to John Crosby at the Santa Fe Opera in August 1961, Stravinsky urged a careful search for first-rate singers for an *Oedipus* performance since the "last Shepherd in Santa Fe had the vibrato of a roller coaster." Sometimes he was contacted by performers wishing to perform, or who already had performed, a work; and he almost always replied (though often only in the margins of letters received). In a letter of November 1954, a pianist from Rome told the composer how "marvelous" is the Serenata (*Serenade en la*) she had just recorded. She then asked about metronome markings, "are they right?" To which Stravinsky replied in the letter's margin, "Why to ask me *after* the tape recording and not before?"

Stravinsky's learn-as-you-go conducting experience began in the 1920s. It was his name, more than any innate or acquired baton skills, that allowed him immediate access to the finest orchestral ensembles in the world—as it often was for composers wishing to lead their own music. During his 1925 American tour, he conducted the elite orchestras of the nation: New York, Philadelphia, Cleveland, Chicago, Detroit, Cincinnati. By 1928 he could confidently proclaim that he was both comfortable and effective on the podium. Symphony boards and contractors got what they wanted too. Leading his own works "live and in person," the "exotic" composer was a sure draw. Serge Koussevitzky, for one, knew a marketing opportunity when he saw one. Writing to a British booking agency in support of the composer's conducting abilities, Koussevitzky wrote in 1937: "Stravinsky, today, is an outstanding conductor of his own compositions as well as of works by other composers. . . . The appearance of Stravinsky, the great composer of our day, as an outstanding conductor should be an unusual attraction for Australia and a musical event of historic importance."

Stravinsky enjoyed conducting, even though he claimed that he did it mainly as a means of generating revenue and to guarantee that his scores would be played correctly. It was more than that. He surely reveled in the artisan aspect of actually making the music come alive in a way that was quite different from writing it. Conducting provided an immediate, temporal, physical, and even tactile sense of "feeling" his own music as it not only resonated intellectually but also now literally reverberated in his body. He held the fate of his own music in his own hands, retaining control to the final cadence. Some scholars have lamented the fact that Stravinsky spent so much of his energy—and really most of his time—traveling from city to city, country to country, and eventually continent to continent. But the fact is he seems to have taken considerable pleasure in leading orchestras, more than some of his later comments suggest. In interview after interview, especially during his early days as a conductor in the 1920s and '30s, he spoke joyfully of educating musicians through shaping the music directly from the podium.

Some who played for him contend that he buried his head in the score, whereas others speak of a rhythmic energy that was contagious. His own scores, as preserved in Basel, are again instructive. He annotated them heavily as an aid in rehearsing and performing a score. Sometimes he notated the actual concert pitch for transposing instruments, perhaps to save time while rehearsing. He frequently changed the published dynamic markings, sometimes taping over printed measures once he rehearsed and rethought passages. He would circle a passage in red, or mark a specific note, indicating where an emphasis was required. Tempo markings were altered. He corrected notes, time signatures, even misprinted clefs, again confirming how appallingly unreliable many of the published versions of his music remain.

With characteristic acerbity, the composer reacted to critics of his conducting skills. As evident in this October 1957 letter, it became a common theme, intoned whenever comparisons to other conductors were made.

> The other day I read a review of my conducting the premiere of *Agon* in Paris a strange remark . . . "as everybody knows, Stravinsky likes to conduct his own music." What a discovery. . . . By saying so the reviewer does not necessary [*sic*] welcome me in conducting my own music, he merely emphasizes the fact that *instead of leaving it to a regular conductor* I prefer to do it myself. . . . For the reviewer a conductor is nothing else but an animator of orchestral masses, the technical merits of a conductor (if any) are never discussed; a primitive mind always prefers a showman to a technician. And the masses of listeners without any musical culture, tradition, usually without any elementary musical education are left for information about the composition they heard and about its performance to the whims of the described musical judges, unable to read and to judge a score and its performance. Charming civilized world where we are living in today, a world of performers, interpreters and their ignorant laudators.

Boris Schwarz, the amiable violinist and musicologist, served as the concertmaster for the first performance of Stravinsky and Balanchine's 1941 ballet *Balustrade,* set to the music of the composer's 1931 Violin Concerto. Stravinsky conducted. "During the first rehearsal," remembers Schwarz, "the maestro lost a beat during a tricky change of meter in the first movement and found himself waving his hands in the wrong direction, muttering angrily under his breath, *'Mais qu'est ce qu'il y a? Mais qu'est ce qu'ils font?'"* The archives confirm that he was as sensitive to gibes about his conducting as he was to criticism of his music. Often the insults were as censorial as his own assaults on others. In his archives is a copy of *Time* magazine's 1956 review of *Canticum Sacrum* (a work specifically designed for St. Mark's Cathedral in Venice), titled "Murder in the Cathedral." Stravinsky annotated the article copiously. "He loves to conduct, but he can't," said the reviewer, and, "The composer himself appeared looking something like an animated Gothic gargoyle"—a hurtful ad hominem slur to which the composer reacted by underlining the phrase describing his appearance and writing in the margin, "How kind."[23]

Stravinsky's treatment of others, conductors included, could suddenly change. When his old friend Ernest Ansermet rejected his turn to atonal music in the early 1950s as "sterile formalism," the composer lashed out. He made his response not to Ansermet but in a letter in 1958 to the always sympathetic Harold Box, of Voice of America, with whom Stravinsky had worked for years: "Some thirty years ago [Ansermet] was still a faithful performer of my music, but not now any more. Trying to make his own conducting career and also by growing jalousy [sic] he gradually turned his back to me. . . . This actually happened and everybody has to know it. It is wrong to base one's judgment on an old reputation." Stravinsky's published correspondence with Ansermet stops from 1948 to 1966, the point at which they reached a reconciliation, although it was a cool one at best, as the few surviving letters they exchanged thereafter reveal.

Michael Krauz, in "The Tonal and the Foundational: Ansermet on Stravinsky," concluded, "It was because of Ansermet's initial training in mathematics that he was especially equipped to deal with Stravinsky's complicated rhythmic patterns." But this is preposterous, an insult to both Ansermet and mathematicians everywhere. The real reason Ansermet, unlike most other conductors with a maestro complex, "was especially equipped to deal with" Stravinsky was that he submitted to his wishes almost obsequiously—just the kind of fealty the composer expected from friends and interpreters alike. If Ansermet and other conductors of his own generation were fair game for his ridicule, the newer breed of "silver-haired" maestros, as Stravinsky called them, was an even easier target. For Stravinsky, it was nearly axiomatic: The more popular the conductor, the more vitriolic the composer's invective.[24]

Herbert von Karajan ranked high on the composer's blacklist, especially because of the haughty opinion he held of himself. (Stravinsky surely would have enjoyed the often circulated story of a guide pointing out to tourists that Karajan was born in Salzburg, then quickly adding that, incidentally, Mozart was born here too.) When Karajan approached him with an idea for a film about *Le Sacre du printemps,* which would include Stravinsky conducting and discussing sections of the score amid footage shot for the CBS documentary, the composer balked. He was unwilling to participate in any tête-à-tête on camera with Karajan. The composer might be willing to answer some prepared questions before the camera, Craft reported to Stravinsky's publisher on 11

January 1966, but there would be no live interaction between the two. Craft suggested that Karajan prepare a few questions to be shot in an otherwise empty studio, and later the film would be edited so it appeared that the two were together. But when it became clear that Karajan required a personal meeting with Stravinsky, the project was quickly canceled.

Almost a year later, Stravinsky was informed that Karajan would now do a film of himself conducting *Le Sacre* (indeed, the conductor was on a personal mission to film many of the great masterpieces, to preserve both the music and his own legacy). The composer replied in December 1966: "Very glad to hear that Karajan wants to conduct *Sacre* . . . will be extremely happy if [he] will follow as close as possible *my tempo's* [sic] which he will find on my last Columbia Record of the *Sacre.*" There were also several other proposed televised films of the work, but Stravinsky was not interested in entrusting it to other conductors whose affectations might draw attention away from the power of the music itself.

Stravinsky constantly urged conductors to heed his recordings. He also did whatever he could to promote his records commercially. In December 1949, he wrote to RCA's publicity manager, Alan Kayes, "The LA Philharmonic Society will perform my *Orpheus* on January 5 and 6, 1950. I believe you will take all necessary steps to promote our new recordings of this work by advertisements in the program and to make sure that all retail shops here are provided with a sufficient stock of these records." Then, almost immediately, he wrote to Alfred Wallenstein, music director of the Los Angeles Philharmonic, "I believe my recent *Orpheus* RCA Victor records will be able to give you assistance." The conductor replied, "I know of your *Orpheus* recording for Victor, but actually, I felt that you had indicated very clearly in your score exactly what you wanted." In the margin of Wallenstein's letter, Stravinsky scribbled in exasperation, "Hopeless!"

Of all the archival documents dealing with conductors, those addressing Stravinsky's ostensibly warm relations with Leonard Bernstein are the most intriguing. If there was any other contemporary musician whose iconic status caught the public eye as completely as Stravinsky's, it was the debonair young Bernstein. Since their initial meeting in 1944, Bernstein was always attentive to Stravinsky—although those close to Stravinsky claim that it was for the sake of appearance. Still, the archives show that he continually sought both conducting and composing opportunities for the elder composer. He included Stravinsky in one of his *Young People's Concerts,* and he performed *Petrushka* on another broadcast of the popular series. He also championed less popular

Stravinsky with Leonard Bernstein in 1946 (Photograph by Ben Greenhaus; courtesy of the Leonard Bernstein Collection, Music Division, Library of Congress)

works such as *Oedipus* at a time when critics disregarded the work as wooden and obsolete. He televised the opera-oratorio in 1961, adding his signature brand of colorful commentary. Stravinsky seemed to appreciate Bernstein's effort, enthusing in a telegram of 21 February 1961, "Please thank everyone concerned for the exciting presentation. Most of all thanks to yourself for a superb explanation and performance."

But although his correspondence with Bernstein was cordial enough, the archives disclose some hostility in Stravinsky and his circle of friends. Bernstein's *The Age of Anxiety,* Symphony no. 2 of 1949, was inspired by W. H. Auden's book of the same name. Auden was not pleased and quickly distanced himself from any association with the work. He gave Stravinsky a copy of the book in which he wrote on the title page, "Leonard Bernstein is a shit." Stravinsky himself, Craft told me, walked out of a performance of the same symphony and wanted to leave *West Side Story* as well. When Craft played a recording of the *Jeremiah Symphony*, Stravinsky asked him to turn it off. Some of the young American composers who were close to Stravinsky remember that at times he could be terribly indiscreet. David Diamond recalls discussions about Bernstein: "Sometimes I would sit with Craft and Stravinsky and overhear them talking. Stravinsky was rather rude . . . he thought his carrying-on on the podium was pretty terrible and thought his music was awful."[25]

Stravinsky expressed his misgivings with Bernstein's conducting as early as 1944, when the young conductor led a concert at the Hollywood Bowl. Vera Stravinsky reported in her diary on 26 August that Bernstein's performance of *The Firebird* had "disappointed" her husband. In an exchange of letters in late 1946, Diamond wrote to Stravinsky, "Bernstein is making splendid progress and I believe he will be a great conductor one day." But Stravinsky's response attacked Bernstein's recordings of *L'Histoire du soldat* and the *Octet*: "Why not to follow my own tempis [sic] since he knows them from my European Columbia recordings?" Perhaps at the root of his reprobation was an envy of Bernstein's public appeal, as well as an aversion to the charismatic conductor's mission to catechize about music, to convince people "what to feel," as Stravinsky described it. Bernstein had the power of the pulpit and wielded his influence with a fire-and-brimstone zeal that Stravinsky saw as over the top.

His hugely successful television appearances on the Ford Foundation's *Omnibus* series during the 1950s irked Stravinsky, especially the opening telecast in November 1954, of Beethoven's Fifth Symphony (in which the first page of the score was blown up to cover the entire studio floor). Possessing a natural flair that immediately connected with audiences, Bernstein demonstrated how the heroic Beethoven had struggled over countless sketches in an inexorable search, "probing and rejecting in his dedication to perfection, to the principle of *inevitability*. This somehow is the key to the mystery of a great artist." In contrast, Bernstein lectured, things came easily to Stravinsky. He flashed a picture of the finished fair copy of the 1945 Symphony in Three Movements, to show "how neat, how unagonized" it appeared compared with Beethoven's more gut-wrenching sketches—sketches that divulged "the bloody record of a tremendous inner struggle." Of course, the juxtaposition of Stravinsky's fair copy calligraphy with Beethoven's preliminary "feverish scrawls" was a ready-made but totally incommensurable comparison, and Stravinsky justly resented it.

Perhaps Bernstein wished to distinguish two kinds of genius, but Stravinsky would not be manipulated as the object of such superficial comparisons.

It gave Bernstein all the control while marginalizing Stravinsky in a way he would never accept. Bernstein also, though certainly not with malice, had created the unintended impression that Stravinsky's work was facile, even slick—charges that surely stung because they were all too familiar, dating all the way back to the 1920s. According to the young composers close to him, Bernstein really adored Stravinsky, and knew that the public wanted to see the ageless composer as not only a survivor but a genius. To portray him more accurately as a composer who was often adrift, searching for solutions, working hard, making choices, and even struggling to find the exact way he wanted to express an idea was much less romantic in the twentieth century than it was for Beethoven in the nineteenth. But Stravinsky was no different from a Tolstoy, who wrote six or seven drafts of each section of a novel before getting up the nerve to submit it to his publisher, or from a Virginia Woolf or Robert Frost, whose drafts show an endless struggle to finalize even a single sentence. As anyone who has seen the sketchbooks for the *Serenade en la* or *Apollo* or *Agon* can testify, similar battles attended their creation. And while it is true that there are several passages of numerous works that seem to have come easily, there are far more that show a trail of careful thought and constant decision making.

Moreover, and perhaps somewhat out of character, Stravinsky resented being thought of as a genius. It amounted to an abrogation, stripping him of control. The comparison with Beethoven cheated him of the artisanlike effort that went into composing his works, and he interpreted Bernstein's remarks as offensive. When Isherwood once asked if he thought of himself as a genius (as did most of the world), the composer answered, "No, I'm not a genius, but I'm very inventive." The difference may seem trifling, but it was a key one for Stravinsky, who considered himself an inventor who worked hard at finding the right notes. Nor was he alone in such self-deprecation. D. H. Lawrence, whose *Lady Chatterley's Lover* was completed in 1928, the same year as *Apollo*, felt similarly, and the drafts of both the novel and the ballet show a creative kinship in constant revisions of the smallest detail. Lawrence's insistence on such detail was "maddening," his wife Frieda remembered, and people wrongly saw the finesse of his word choices as natural, not earned: "They never called Lawrence a professional writer—always a genius. That made him angry. 'That's my label—a genius—and with that I am dismissed.'"[26]

The many newspaper clippings he saved, especially regarding Bernstein's performances in the late 1950s as he attained the status of a matinee idol, betray Stravinsky's feeling that too much light was shining on the conductor, leaving the music itself in the podium's shadow. Words like "inspired," "dramatic," "virtuosic," "throbbing," and worst of all "emotionally aroused" could only arouse Stravinsky's own emotions—particularly when critics publicly elevated Bernstein's "chorybantics" above his own composing. Bernstein "coped brilliantly with a weak work like *Oedipus,*" one reviewer wrote of the 1961 performance. Such an upside-down perception was so objectionable that, rather than have his works performed by Bernstein, Stravinsky would sometimes opt not to have them played at all. He complained privately that Bernstein "will end up being another Stokowski." As late as December 1963, in a *Houston Post* review of Stravinsky and Craft's newest conversation book, *Dialogues and a Diary,* Stravinsky was pictured with Bernstein; but the composer could not resist writing on the copy in his private file: "What has Bernstein to do with this?"

Commercial record sales were another target of Stravinsky's annoyance. Bernstein was a major competitor for recording royalties, hitting home in a way that Stravinsky could not fail to notice. As John McClure of Columbia Masterworks remembered in an unreleased film clip, Stravinsky never accepted the fact that other conductors, especially dynamic ones like Bernstein, could steal the composer's thunder. Audiences were likely to focus on the performance and the conductor's individual interpretation rather than the composition itself. Stravinsky was particularly annoyed by the reality that recordings by others could garner more royalties than when he himself conducted. McClure further recalls that the composer would often excoriate Columbia for not putting forth more effort in marketing his own recordings. And the plain truth is that Stravinsky's recordings were not nearly as commercially successful as those of Bernstein.

Yet for all his ranting, Stravinsky was hardly the only composer who ever grumbled about his mistreatment at the hands of a conductor. (Schoenberg too, for example, often bitterly criticized such conductors as Bruno Walter and Koussevitzky, as letters to his students show.) Why then the spotlight on Stravinsky's highly publicized scorn for conductors when actually it was anything but unique? Partly, it seems, because Stravinsky made a point of raising the level of his oratory to that of a sideshow. The press devoured it. Shellacking a well-known conductor made for catchy headlines and some good old-fashioned hazing. Whom was the curmudgeonly composer going to sneer at next? What cleverly phrased slap or piquant malapropism would he (and later Craft) come up with this time? How about "the lapdogs of musical life," or "'Great' conductors like 'great' actors soon become unable to play anything but themselves," and what of the mythical "Professor von Schnell," and "Doktor von Langsamer"? Certainly the message behind the humor was serious; but for the enterprising Stravinsky, if a little notoriety might be gained by zinging easy prey with nimble one-liners, then all the better. Witty, sardonic, irreverent—Stravinsky was a masterful satirist. Bashing conductors was just one more way of feathering his own image by drawing attention to himself. And it is the matter of image, and how that image was finessed, that continues to shine as a central issue in his correspondence and other archival materials.

When Robert Craft published his three volumes of Stravinsky's letters in the early 1980s, critics immediately lamented their utterly "unsoulful" content. In a review for *Tempo,* Robin Holloway searched through the correspondence in vain for "the kind of unfolding spiritual testimony and involuntary illumination of the life and work to be found in great creative letter-writers like Keats, Byron, William James, Lawrence, Woolf, Van Gogh." Woolf wrote that an artist's self-consciousness was frequently cleansed through disclosures made in correspondence. Through such confessions we can better understand what Flaubert experienced while writing *Madame Bovary* or follow the struggles that Keats faced in writing poetry "against the coming of death and the indifference of the world." While such letters are capable of capturing those clarion flashes that enkindle mysterious bursts of creativity, they can also quickly remind us of the daily drudgery and burdensome lives that artists often confront. Reading them may swiftly dampen our fantasies.[27]

As with other aspects of Stravinsky's biography, there has been a rush to judgment. We have accepted too many verisimilitudes about the composer's public image, many of which he himself promulgated. Our preconceptions about what we *wanted* Stravinsky to say or do inevitably have led to defeated expectations. The truth is that Stravinsky's correspondence is mostly a clearinghouse for the drab grind of unending business. He publicly professed his weariness over the senseless questions and demands each day's mail brought. But it may be a mistake to assume that the physical act of writing letters was immaterial. Stravinsky was a man of limitless vigor—but a vigor that could not possibly be constantly and intensely focused on producing one masterwork after another. Writing letters provided a spillway, a means of channeling a kind of noncreative energy that nonetheless had to be released. And just as he enjoyed playing solitaire, just as Balanchine insisted on ironing his own clothes, such mindless diversions were functional, permitting ideas to percolate. In retracing his discovery of Fuchsian functions, mathematician Jules-Henri Poincaré wrote in his 1913 essay "Mathematical Creation" of a "sudden illumination" triggered by interludes of rest that were subliminally "filled out with unconscious work." Likewise, in one public declaration after another, Stravin-sky made it clear that thoughts of composition were never far from his con-sciousness. He understood, as did Poincaré, that the mind is never unoccu-pied with the task at hand; rather, the contemplation of ideas took various forms at either the conscious or unconscious levels. Eventually, such ideation manifests itself in notes on the page, sometimes unexpectedly, and in the odd-est of ways. But he also understood that the evolution of the process must pro-ceed at its own pace.

Similarly, in his *Journal of a Novel,* kept as a diary while writing *East of Eden,* Steinbeck endorsed a kind of therapeutic procrastination. He devoted his first day to choosing the pencils he would use: "I will get six more or maybe four more dozens of them for my pencil tray. And that is all I am going to do on this my first day of work." Nor was his second day more productive: "It must be told that my second work day is a bust as far as getting into writing. I suf-fer as always from the fear of putting down the first line. It is amazing the ter-rors, the magic, the prayers, the straightening shyness that assails one." Stravinsky, too, seems to have avoided sitting down and working, and he often spoke of a similar "terror" in facing the blankness of a piece of manuscript pa-per. As Steinbeck was a diary keeper, Stravinsky was an inveterate letter writer. Business had to be handled, and he convinced himself that it had to be han-dled by him alone (or at least proofread by him). Although he spent relatively few hours actually composing, he devoted considerable time to "preparing the soil," as he liked to say. More than transacting business, writing letters may have permitted a period of passive time during which he could—as Steinbeck put it—"moon about" certain problems.[28]

For those looking for a sphinx immune to the vicissitudes of the world around him, the letters are disappointing, "like the empty envelopes from which the contents—the core of the personality, the life, the work—have been extracted, and need to be inferred," as Holloway mourned. But nothing could be more misguided. Stravinsky's letters served as a purgative. Woolf said of Shakespeare, "All desire to protest, to preach, to proclaim an injury, to pay off a score, to make the world the witness of some hardship or grievance was fired out of him and consumed. Therefore his poetry flows from him free and unim-peded." It is true that Stravinsky's correspondence provides few Rosetta stones that might unearth the composer's innermost creative core; but should that have been a realistic expectation? Some may have hoped that Stravinsky's artistic goals were lofty enough to transcend the often tangled nuances of re-lationships, but they simply were not. That we would have discovered solemn contemplations in his correspondence is no more than the kind of wishful thinking that abets the fictionalizing of his image. The letters are what they are, and the sooner we deal with what Stravinsky actually said and did, the better our chances of cutting through the mythology that often misrepresents him.[29]

C·h·a·p·t·e·r ·8·

Boswellizing an Icon:
Stravinsky, Craft, and the
Historian's Dilemma

> I cannot conceive a more perfect mode of writing any man's life, than not
> only relating all the most important events of it in their order, but inter-
> weaving what he privately wrote, and said, and thought; by which
> mankind are enabled as it were to see him live. . . . And he will be seen
> as he really was; for I profess to write, not his panegyric, which must be
> all praise, but his Life; which great and good as it was, must not be sup-
> posed to be entirely perfect. . . . In every picture there should be shade
> as well as light, and when I delineate him without reserve, I do what he
> himself recommended, both by his precept and his example.
> —James Boswell, *Life of Johnson*

In 1791, James Boswell, "the Great Biographer," as history knows
him, published his first edition of one of the most celebrated and controversial biographies in English literature. Two centuries later, the war of the
Boswellians and Johnsonians rages on. The debate finds a contemporary parallel in the musicological commotion surrounding Robert Craft's association
with Stravinsky. Boswell has become a lightning rod, not only sparking heated
disputes among specialists but also posing larger questions about the constitution of historiography. Was Boswell an impartial witness, or was his narrative slanted? Should his elegant prose—which is matched by Craft's own lucid chronicling of Stravinsky's life—be viewed primarily as storytelling that
artfully spins an intricate web of truths, canards, interpretations, and psy-
choanalytic insights? Did Boswell's journal overly dramatize and ultimately
deify Johnson in fabricating a mythical hero who exceeded reality? And is
Boswell's *Life of Samuel Johnson* even a biography at all, as some critics have
asked, or is it more a personal diary that discloses less about Johnson's life than
about Boswell's? Finally, how closely does the correlation really obtain to

Craft's journalizing of Stravinsky—a journalizing that has significantly shaped our understanding of the composer for half a century?

This understanding, as transmitted principally through Craft, has in recent years come under increasingly microscopic scrutiny. A range of historians, including the American scholar Richard Taruskin, the British biographer Stephen Walsh, and the Russian musicologist Victor Varuntz, have compiled critical studies that serve to broaden our understanding of Stravinsky. None of them intend to minimize—and this must be stated categorically—the monumentally indispensable role that Mr. Craft occupied in the composer's life. Still, recent studies such as these frequently begin by challenging what Craft has written, then, quite naturally, move on to detailed corrections of certain inaccuracies and misconceptions that have accrued over the years. As great a debt as the world of Stravinsky scholarship owes to Robert Craft, his axial role in providing so much information about the composer must—as with anyone so closely associated with a historical figure of Stravinsky's importance—be assessed closely.

The image of Boswell walking in Dr. Johnson's shadow on a daily basis, faithfully recording every word, is hardly accurate. Boswell was in Johnson's actual company only about five percent of the almost eight thousand days they knew each other. Still, by the time he released his second edition of the *Life* in 1793, Boswell declared (and apparently with mixed feelings, given what he feared he had wrought) that his work had "Johnsonized" the land. He relied heavily on such reliable authorities as Edmond Malone in "characterizing anecdotes," to use his expression, about Johnson's storied life. By his own admission, too, he knowingly embroidered events that were only vaguely rumored. The poet Anna Seward, "the Swan of Lichfield," as she was known, shared with Boswell verifiable truths about Johnson's early days in Lichfield; but when these tales crossed over into print, Seward immediately rejected Boswell's hyperbole as "false assertions." Where did Boswell draw the line? Was it the same line directors of all those film documentaries about Stravinsky drew in separating the grayness of truth from the power of colorful prose and images to entertain—even if in the process false impressions accrued? Boswell's defenses of Johnson's actions are often concocted, and there are conspicuous gaps and expurgations fueling suspicions. How much "shade as well as light" Boswell really cast leads one to question whether Johnson was "Boswellized," as literary criticism claims—just as contemporary musicology frequently buzzes that Stravinsky's image was intentionally "Crafted."[1]

Boswell was twenty-three when he met Johnson. So too was Craft when he first wrote to Stravinsky in the summer of 1947. More than fifty years later, Craft continues to add to the rich, steady list of writings he has compiled about the composer. He also continues to record the composer's complete works.[2] As Craft and Stravinsky came to know each other, it became evident that theirs was a compatible match. Moreover, Craft surely must have known from the start that his charge would be an important and unique one: that one way or another his journalizing of the composer would have considerable influence on generations to come. As he himself remarked in the preface to his 1994 revised edition of *Stravinsky: Chronicle of a Friendship,* he kept a diary of his association so as to "put a fence around my experience." It is precisely that fence about which historians have become increasingly curious.

From the beginning, it was his ambition to affiliate himself with one of the great figures of modern cultural history, just as Boswell had wished to attach himself to one of the greatest writers of his age. Craft admits that as early as 1936, when he was twelve, his life's goal was to study with Stravinsky. Failing that, he could at least find a way to befriend the composer, and he announced to his Juilliard classmates during the early 1940s, according to Joan Peyser, that "his goal was to become an amanuensis to a great composer."[3] Whatever Craft's motive in wanting to know *Le Sacre*'s creator, history is now faced with rummaging through the particulars of an influential and binding relationship. Moreover, marginalizing Craft as no more than an amanuensis would be a massive blunder. With remarkable speed, Craft progressed from assistant to adviser, defender, collaborator, and—his critics would argue—a resourceful "spin doctor." Stravinsky could be publicly blunt, and Craft's damage control is reminiscent of Boswell's own revisionist portrayal. Johnson knew that Boswell was remaking him, and he didn't like it: "He that recounts the life of another . . . lessens the familiarity of his tale to increase its dignity . . . and endeavours to hide the man that he may produce a hero." Craft was bothered by characterizations linking him with Boswell. He claimed that although Johnson needed a Boswell, Stravinsky did not. Craft's initial function, he remembered in his diary, was to assist Stravinsky with the mechanics of writing letters. But eventually, he added, a "merger" did occur—and a critical one at that, for increasingly he became centrally involved in making executive decisions and offering opinions on creative matters.[4]

Yet Stravinsky needed Craft far more than Johnson did Boswell or Goethe needed Johann Peter Eckermann (whose *Conversations with Goethe in the Last Years of His Life* has a familiar ring to it in light of Craft and Stravinsky's conversation books), or even than Picasso needed Françoise Gilot. Just as

Gilot served as one of the painter's many muses, Craft's youthful intensity and love of music revitalized Stravinsky. He immediately grasped how enormous his role was and how deep Stravinsky's dependency had become. More than a recorder of deeds, Craft became Stravinsky's beacon, shining the way and guiding the composer for a longer period of time than any previous confidant. To music's betterment, Craft was a catalyst energizing Stravinsky's natural vitality. Part of his utility was in promoting the composer's public image; still, to suggest that Stravinsky involuntarily relinquished control to Craft would be specious. It was Stravinsky's nature to be ambitious, and often it was he, not Craft, who continued pushing for tours and publicity when those closest to him advised otherwise. As Isherwood recalled an evening with the composer: "After supper he seemed drowsy and spoke very little. Vera assured Don [Bachardy, Isherwood's companion] once more that it isn't she or Bob who are set on this South American trip, it's Igor himself."[5]

Among what appeared to be qualms of conscience revealed in a disarming series of personal disclosures following Stravinsky's death, Craft offered a list of corrigenda rebutting charges that he controlled the composer's life. But he has also, forthrightly, recused himself as Stravinsky's future biographer, recognizing the uniqueness of his relationship with the composer.[6] Perhaps he wished to protect the often flamboyant Stravinsky from his own well-known impetuosity, or, as some of his detractors have argued, to act as the exclusive gatekeeper to history's assessment of the iconic composer. Whatever the reasons, history has come to see Stravinsky largely through the eyes of a man whose devotion, by his own admission, was sometimes colored, understandably, by his deep affection.

While the litigation snarling the disposition of the composer's estate plodded along during the 1970s, a continuous flow of previously unreleased information about the composer's private life began surfacing. These revelations were almost always filtered through Craft's perspective. By 1979 the *New York Times* could ask, "One might wonder, is there anything left to learn about Igor Stravinsky that Robert Craft has not combed through again and again?" The answer was yes, and soon thereafter Craft unleashed a new barrage of articles, essays, iconographies, diaries, and, perhaps most significant, three volumes of previously unreleased letters, titled *Stravinsky: Selected Correspondence*. In so doing, Craft provided an admirably intended though, some have charged, mixed service, since the letters are sometimes erroneously reprinted or factually misleading. As several reviewers noted, the frequent misdatings, mistranslations, and other apparent changes Craft chose to make raised questions about the reliability of the editing process—the very same questions Boswellian scholars pose. Even more critically, the profusion of ellipses is frequently overwhelming, and they sometimes expunge illuminating discourse.

Moreover, Craft unequivocally asserts that he has quoted Stravinsky's letters exactly as written, without any changes (just as Boswell, in fact, wrote of Johnson's correspondence: "I have been extremely careful as to the exactness of my quotations"). But this is not quite so, and there are several instances in which Craft, in his editorial capacity, determined that the material was unsuitable, and simply expunged it. Yet a growing number of scholars who have compared Craft's edited letters with the originals in Basel have quickly grasped several critical discrepancies. There is, regrettably, no dodging the problem. In a 5 August 1984 review of the second of the three volumes of correspondence, David Hamilton (music critic for *The Nation*) alleged in the *New York Times Book Review* that Craft was "the most obtrusive of editors." He criticized Craft for work that "often falls short of customary scholarly standards of objectivity and consistency." It is a harsh charge, to be sure, but if anything it has only intensified as thousands of unedited letters testing that objectivity continue to surface.

Nowhere have these charges been asked and answered more directly than in the work of Stravinsky's most recent biographer, Stephen Walsh. Although Walsh is quick to recognize the significance of Craft's work, as well as his perceptive commentary and perspicacious writing style, he candidly charges that Craft, despite his unparalleled, encyclopedic grasp of Stravinsky's life and music, displays a questionable "talent for factual or even textual accuracy." Even more sweeping, Walsh questions the wisdom of relying on these sources, once considered dependable (although there was hardly any alternative until recently), arguing that these books are in fact "textually and therefore materially unreliable to the point of being at times positively misleading in their presentation of the facts." Indeed the first volume of Walsh's monumental biography (a second one is forthcoming) largely consists of antidotes intended to rectify much that Craft has argued.[7]

Craft's more than fifteen hundred pages of letters, chronologies, and essays provide only a start. Roughly, less than 5 percent of the letters found in the Sacher collection are represented in Craft's three edited volumes. When I asked why the correspondence published was so selective, Craft forthrightly acknowledged that he had wanted to publish the letters as soon as possible, knowing that legal obstacles resulting from the family split might soon force him to forfeit exclusive access to source materials. He had to act quickly, and the letters released were intended only as a representative sampling. Moreover, many of the errors that have crept into his work are surely attributable to nothing more than haste, rather than any desire to suppress information, let alone mislead the reader. Still, the thirty-seven individual sets of correspondence published prompt several questions.

The letters of the composer Maurice Delage, dating from 1912–23, are a good example. Delage was one of Stravinsky's closest friends around the time of *Le Sacre du printemps*, but by 1923 his criticism of Stravinsky's neoclassicism ruptured their friendship. The correspondence ends, and, presumably, so did their relationship. What we cannot tell from the letters published is that further correspondence, as warm as ever, later resumed following a rapprochement in 1938. Likewise, there is an eleven-year gap from 1918 to 1929 in exchanges between Stravinsky and the British musicologist Edwin Evans. The lapse at least partially stemmed from Evans's published attack on Stravinsky's 1919 Three Pieces for String Quartet. In his copy of the review, Stravinsky boxed the comments he found offensive. Both the Delage and Evans files are symptomatic of his on-again, off-again friendships; the composer was easily affronted and slow to forgive. In the case of his friend and supporter Alfredo Casella, twenty-four letters are published, but another twenty-four are not, though they survive in the archives. Often those omitted would resolve ambiguities raised in the correspondence that is published, but without the earlier, unpublished letters, we are left in the dark.

Such lacunae are largely attributable to Stravinsky's record keeping. There was a Delage file, a Casella file, and so on, but the content of each folder as it arrived in Basel was not complete. Twenty-four Casella letters were published because Stravinsky deposited that many into the Casella folder; but his filing was slipshod. Some letters were dropped into more generic files marked "concert appearances," or "1922 engagements." The twenty-four still unpublished Casella letters (and also eighteen of Evans's) were scattered among the 116 boxes of the archives. Craft didn't intentionally suppress these still unreleased letters; rather, he either chose not to use certain ones or missed them. Whatever the reason, it is crucial to realize that any reliance on what *is* published affords only a partial—and thus potentially distorting—slant.

Textual clarity is also an issue among the letters Craft released. Some errors are nothing more than a translator's slip. Diaghilev is labeled a "fiend" in one letter, a typesetter's misprint for "friend." Elsewhere, Stravinsky claims he is "wary of Chanel," but it should read "I am grateful to Chanel." Mistranslations of several letters in Russian are suspected, particularly in the cases of

Diaghilev and V. V. Derzhanovsky (a Moscow editor with whom Stravinsky had business). In a letter to the composer on 8 March 1915, for example, Diaghilev complains that Prokofiev has misplaced his trust in the popular poet Sergey Gorodyetsky (whose verse Stravinsky had set in an early song). But it is not Gorodyetsky about whom Diaghilev actually wrote: rather, the name should be Nikolay Tcherepnin, Prokofiev's teacher.[8] Other mistakes are more consequential, as in the letters Cocteau and Stravinsky exchanged while jointly drafting *Oedipus Rex*. In one from Cocteau in 1926, Craft attributes important marginalia concerning the scenario to Stravinsky, but the original establishes that Cocteau added these last-minute suggestions to his own letter.[9]

Some of the appendixes should carry a caveat emptor. An essay in the second volume, for instance, addresses the 1939–40 Harvard lectures that resulted in the *Poetics of Music* and upon which Stravinsky's intellectual credentials were largely built. Craft begins the essay, "Roland-Manuel and *La Poétique musicale*," by saying, "The aim of the present investigation is simply to translate and publish Stravinsky's own words, leaving the ideological differences between his annotations and Roland-Manuel's to the reader." In discussing the notes for Stravinsky's second lecture, originally entered under the title "The Musical Work (Elements and Morphology)," Craft includes a listing of the composer's roughly sketched (only about fifteen hundred words), very cryptic thoughts. Topics include "a) the sonorous scale," "b) interval, chord," "c) mode, tonality," "d) melody, theme, motif; phrasing, period, development, *reprise*. Cite examples: sonatas, cantatas, etc. Do not forget *Variations*," "e) harmony," and several other key concepts as well. But as the Basel archives reveal, equally relevant terms that Stravinsky entered in the original manuscript are not, for some reason, included in Craft's summary—such as "polyphony," "cadence," "consonance," and "discourse." Also, without reprinting the original transcript prepared by Roland-Manuel, which was then subsequently rewritten by Stravinsky, we don't know to what extent the composer revised the lectures. Without this critical intermediate document, it is impossible to delineate the "ideological differences" between Stravinsky and Roland-Manuel. How many were there really? Whose voice is it that speaks through these six famous lectures?[10]

In some cases, Craft did not have access to other informative correspondence. Stravinsky and his elder son, Theodore, exchanged hundreds of letters, telegrams, and postcards (most of them written in French between 1923 and 1969). In a 1945 letter, Stravinsky divulged his private criticisms about various versions of *The Firebird*. He now welcomed the restaging of the ballet, because, he complained, he had been forced to write too much music "expressly for useless pantomime" in the original Diaghilev and Fokine production of 1910. He also related that Marc Chagall's more recent scenery was a grand success but that Adolph Bolm's choreography was "très quelconque," completely crushing the "Shagal," as he spelled it. He disapproved of the current production's orchestra and especially the conductor, adding that "I have come to see the opinion that Balanchine had of Lucia Chase and the Ballet Theatre's production."

Craft chose to withhold numerous letters sent directly to him. Often the authors of this correspondence wanted to sidestep the composer and quietly enlist Craft's help. But these exchanges also establish just how important Craft was as a mediator, as well as how highly he was regarded as a musician in his own right. The Stiftung's "Craft Collection" contains hundreds of letters from prominent musicians, including Milton Babbitt, Luciano Berio, Nadia Boulanger, Aaron Copland, Elliott Carter, Henry Cowell, Luigi Dallapiccola, Glenn Gould, Igor Markevich, Darius Milhaud, Andrés Segovia, Rudolf Serkin, Roger Sessions, Edgard Varèse, and others. Many of their letters deal with performances and recordings in which Craft was involved, but frequently he is asked to lobby the mercurial Stravinsky, testing the waters before even his friends dared to approach him with ideas and requests. For those who have unfairly associated Craft with Stravinsky's music exclusively, these letters provide a measure of redress. Lillian Libman, for example, declares that upon Stravinsky's death, "the whole reason for [Robert's] existence had been taken away." Naturally Craft was terribly shaken by Stravinsky's death—how could he not be?—but Libman's overstatement ignores his success in maintaining as much musical independence as he could under the circumstances. Moreover, it seems to have been an independence that Stravinsky himself unselfishly fostered, even when it involved his perceived "enemies."[11]

Glenn Gould's letters speak to Craft's championing of Schoenberg's music, and while the association of Craft and Stravinsky is an immediate one, history often underestimates how much he did to bring Schoenberg to the attention of American audiences. In several letters, Craft and Gould planned a recording of Schoenberg's Piano Concerto in late 1958, and the pianist later praised the conductor for his part in producing the recording. Gould clearly was very pleased with his collaboration with Craft—not a compliment paid lightly, given Gould's often pugnacious disposition. He offered sincere congratulations on the conductor's musicianship and insight. This was not music to be undertaken by those with faint heart. Not only were the scores themselves difficult to learn, but audiences had precious little interest in hearing the few performances that were given. In this sense, Craft was a courageous and knowledgeable pioneer. Other letters dating from the same period indicate that Gould considered learning Stravinsky's *Movements* (the composer had been unhappy with the pianist who premiered the intricately constructed work at New York's Town Hall in January 1960). And later still, in 1963, Gould once more wrote to Craft, praising his conducting and interpretation of Schoenberg's music—music with which Gould was most often associated as one of the leading interpreters of his day.

This, however, was his last letter to Craft, and their friendship apparently deteriorated after Gould made his scathing remarks about Stravinsky in his lecture on Soviet music at the University of Toronto in 1964. That Gould's name never appeared again in any of Stravinsky's or Craft's writing while the composer was alive was surely not coincidental. Craft may have resented Gould's attack, and he chose to end their once productive musical partnership, not only for his own sake but perhaps more as a gesture of loyalty to Stravinsky. Craft makes no mention of their letters in the original 1972 version of his *Chronicle*, but in the 1994 edition a few passages of Gould's letters openly commending Craft's musicianship are added, as well they should be.

Gould's perception of Craft's musical sensitivity in approaching Schoenberg is important, especially in the context of Craft's introducing Stravinsky to the vocabulary of serialism. His grasp of dodecaphonic principles was far deeper than Stravinsky's, although from the 1964 *Variations* on, it was apparently Claudio Spies who, at Craft's request, carefully proofed Stravinsky's scores. Stravinsky was not so interested in the avalanche of serial exegeses then in vogue among academicians. Just as he once received requests from would-be composers wishing to study with him, now the mail brought doctoral dissertations and master's theses analyzing his own serial works. In one such study from 1961, numerous corrections of graphs and insightful alternative analyses are entered throughout the dissertation's margins; but, as the handwriting confirms, the annotations are Craft's, not Stravinsky's. Stravinsky's characteristically cursory comments were limited to correcting the student's citing of performance dates, publishers, and other nonanalytical matters, for his interest simply went no further.

There are several exchanges during the 1950s between Craft and Ernst Krenek, but with hardly a mention of Stravinsky's name. What is rather remarkable is the degree of reliance, even dependency, that Krenek himself demonstrated in constantly soliciting Craft's advice on musical matters.

Among the holdings of Stravinsky's library preserved in Basel, Krenek's 1953 monograph *Johannes Ockeghem* is thoroughly marked. But once more the markings are not by Stravinsky but by Craft, who studied the book carefully, underlining fundamental musical concepts such as "tempus," "prolatio," "modus." Krenek alludes to history's ignorance of Ockeghem's life: "Was he a happy man? How did he spend his days and nights? Was he melancholy, solitary, gray, gregarious? Did he have a family?" Craft's response, written in the margin (where, as we have seen, Stravinsky often recorded his own reactions), dismisses these questions as irrelevant. Yet the exchanges between Craft and Krenek should not suggest that Stravinsky was uninterested in Krenek's pedagogical writings. The composer himself wrote to the publishing house of Alexander Broude on 20 February 1959: "May I ask you to send me KRENEK, E. 'Tonal Counterpoint in the style of the 18th Century.'"

Many of the letters dealt with Craft's conducting performances of compositions by Krenek, and there are several scores for this music in Stravinsky's extant library. Some of Stravinsky's closest friends at the time indicated that many of his ideas about transposition, rotation, and other serial devices are traceable to his study of Krenek's music. Even Edgard Varèse, whom Stravinsky knew fairly well and whose music (some of it, at least) he admired, exchanged letters with Craft on completely non-Stravinskyan matters, again no doubt because of Craft's recording of some of the composer's works. Varèse was quite complimentary in thanking Craft for producing and conducting a Webern album that would help call attention to that composer's music, as it surely did. What emerges in reading so many of these unpublished letters is that Craft was faced with gingerly balancing his conducting and recording of other composers' music while still serving as Stravinsky's assistant and spokesperson.

Such letters invite a reassessment of Craft's "other" life—a life marked by his affinity for the music of Schoenberg and his followers. Given Stravinsky's and Schoenberg's recognition of the immutable divisiveness with which history had saddled these two Hollywood neighbors, what was Craft to do? How resourcefully could the youngish Craft bridge one of the twentieth century's most unbridgeable gulfs—one that was established long before he entered the picture? It was almost as if Stravinsky and Schoenberg had learned to play scripted roles as the leading protagonists in the century's great drama of opposing musical worlds. As Roger Sessions once observed, the two composers ineluctably became "two contradictory, even irreconcilable poles of contemporary music," and the composer and intimate of Stravinsky Arthur Lourié once characterized Schoenberg as the "Thesis" and Stravinsky as the "Antithesis." But whatever the analogy, there was a geopolitical ring to it all from the very start, particularly at a time when countries were eagerly extolling both their political and cultural sovereignty. "You avenge many things for us," wrote the French author and editor Jacques Rivière to Stravinsky in 1918, "notably that irritating, sentimental rhetoric in which Germany would like to submerge us." Craft, unenviably, had to avoid the potential land mines of both camps while the story continued to unfold. During the late 1940s and early 1950s, he was not only viewed suspiciously by some in Stravinsky's own family as an intruder and a surrogate son (moving into Soulima's house and taking over his role in many ways), but he also had to mollify what became a potentially explosive "demilitarized zone" between Schoenberg and Stravinsky.[12]

T. W. Adorno's transparent attacks on Stravinsky as early as the 1920s were vicious. By 1949, Adorno's *Philosophie der neuen Musik* (used by Thomas Mann as a resource in writing *Doctor Faustus*) ruthlessly denounced Stravinsky as a directionless, regressive composer—one who refused to confront "the crisis of modernism" and resorted to an "unrelenting cheerfulness" responding "to the need for luxury goods of a new bourgeoisie no longer served by 'inwardness.'" Further, Adorno labeled Stravinsky an "inhumane" composer who had done music a horrible disservice with his "machine-inspired dehumanization." Schoenberg, conversely, was characterized as a "dialectical composer" whose "incomprehensible music" proved its "essence and significance."[13] The treatise not only disturbed Stravinsky, it angered Schoenberg as well, for he (and earlier, his student Alban Berg) thought Adorno's calumny embarrassing and "disgusting," as he told his biographer H. H. Stuckenschmidt in 1949. Nonetheless, Stravinsky could not have dismissed Adorno's opprobrium lightly, and Craft, probably more than anyone, was sensitive to an always about-to-detonate state of peril, knowing that Schoenberg's was not a name to be whispered in Stravinsky's home.

Schoenberg was recognized as a leader of a compositional school whose exponents knew that the general public could never grasp their musical ideas, deeply expressive though they were. To the intelligentsia, exclusivity was a desideratum. Always aware of images, Stravinsky may have reasoned that there was something to be said for artistic obscurity. He found heroism in it. It gave Schoenberg (as it did Mahler in Mann's *Death in Venice*) an aura of valor, like many of the misunderstood, victimized Greek characters with whom Stravinsky had always identified. The fact is, Stravinsky wanted it both ways. He wanted to be important enough to be invited to the White House by the

Kennedys, but also important enough *not* to be considered a composer who could be easily understood by the masses. An unpublished document reveals that, in 1952, Stravinsky was invited to the International Contemporary Music Festival as one of "the six composers of this century who ranked highest in significance in [a] poll conducted by an international jury of 87 musicians and musicologists." The six included Arthur Honegger and Roy Harris (hardly the composers with whom Stravinsky wanted to be compared) but noticeably shunned Schoenberg and Webern. Stravinsky declined the invitation.

With Craft now around as a constant reminder, Stravinsky witnessed the powerful impact Schoenberg was having on the younger generation of composers (as well as Olivier Messiaen's influence in Paris), and it worried him. But Stravinsky himself really had no desire to teach (and he claimed he had no gift for it). His position on the perils of teaching was well known. As with much of what he said, he stamped his view with an unbendable insistence that troubled many American composers—composers who often resorted to teaching at the university level to sustain their careers. Many of them (some who knew Stravinsky quite well) responded by attempting to soften the interpretation of the composer's stance. Surely, they reasoned, he really did not mean what he said. His position here as elsewhere was only one more jab in a series of inflated, purposely quizzical views. A set of twenty-three essays responding to some of the composer's statements regarding teaching appeared in an article titled "The Composer in Academia: Reflections on a Theme of Stravinsky." The responses varied from transparent defensiveness to accusatory dismissals—"the old man whose music I love but who has never learned to mind his own business"—to the convenient conclusion that "one need not take it seriously." Others danced around the issue, some called him ignorant, and still others agreed with him.[14]

Whatever his true feelings about pedagogy, Stravinsky assumed that the compositional strength of his works would prevail, thus assuring his legacy. Then, too, Boulanger, as we have seen, served as Stravinsky's personal conservatory, molding countless students who migrated to Paris and Fontainebleau to study his music with her. Schoenberg, on the other hand, was a teacher from his earliest days, though not initially enthralled with the prospect of teaching as a career. In turning down a position in Vienna in 1912 (the other finalist for the post was the important music theorist Heinrich Schenker), Schoenberg explained: "The position . . . would mean spending my whole life, up to my 64th year, droning over harmony and counterpoint. And that I cannot do." But his labors as an instructor quickly reaped rewards beyond the merely monetary by constantly establishing a network of acolytes eager to spread the teachings of their master. He knew that through his students his impact would be felt throughout Europe and America. His vision was also broad enough that he could recognize the grassroots importance of public school orchestras, realizing that education and the formation of taste began there. "This," he argued, "is where the fight against this infamous conservatism must begin." Such a concern was of absolutely no interest to Stravinsky.[15]

While Adorno was attacking Stravinsky during the 1920s, others rose to his defense. George Antheil was one, although his remarks irritated Stravinsky (as they often did) with their pointless and gratuitous comparison.

> Let me come to the point right away. Stravinsky is the greatest living composer. He has absolutely no competition; all of the various cults centered about other composers, and to whom we give importance today, cannot hold a candle to his tremendous innovations; in the light of a severe investigation they all pale into either false-noting Mendelssohns (instance the group in Germany and Austria about Schoenberg) or they become faded-out Debussy imitators. The chief of these composers is Arnold Schoenberg who has been heralded as the greatest innovator of the time. . . . It is a shame and significant of the muddy critical atmosphere of the age to throw Stravinsky in the same boat with Schoenberg, and let them go floating about upon the sea of public opinion without effort to distinguish master from craftsman, genius from talent. . . . In reality Schoenberg is a bore, and recognized as a bore by really intelligent critics.[16]

Where does one go from there in striking a truce? Stravinsky and Schoenberg were genuinely but cautiously curious about each other. Programmed to remain adversaries, they never spoke during their Hollywood years. Besides, as Leonard Stein once asked, what would they have discussed? "What kept them apart was more a matter of cultural background, one that divided the [Hollywood] community along national lines—the German-speaking Central Europeans on one side, the French and Russians on the other." Perhaps, but for Stravinsky, at least, crossing such lines with Mann and Viertel, as well as British and American authors and actors, seemed natural. Nonetheless, this "great divide" became "a parlour game," as Stravinsky and Craft termed what many saw as the differences separating the two composers. They even compiled an inventory of "not very waterproof generalities" side by side in *Dialogues*: Stravinsky saw himself as the fox, Schoenberg as a hedgehog; Stravinsky was a composer of ballets, Schoenberg had no interest in this nonmusical form; Stravinsky considered himself a student, never a teacher, Schoenberg was characterized as an "autodidact" but also always a teacher; Stravinsky's music was metronomically regulated and rejected expression marks, Schoenberg's music made use of *rubato* and was very *espressivo*—and so the list continued.[17]

In many ways, Stravinsky's and Schoenberg's insecurities, their self-values, their defense systems were similar. They both possessed what Maritain once called the "sacred egoism of the creative spirit." Schoenberg's teleological vision guaranteed the continuing musical supremacy of the Germanic tradition (he boldly and publicly promised in the early 1920s), but privately he feared that history would pass him by. As early as 1911, Schoenberg dreaded the "inevitable moment" when he would lose whatever influence he had ("I wish I could be a powerful man soon, so as to carry out that which I consider good . . . in the service of moral ends," he wrote to his student Alban Berg). Schoenberg was envious of the popularity Stravinsky enjoyed—a popularity achieved not only through the relative accessibility of his music but also through what Schoenberg decried as his archrival's contemptible shenanigans. Still, he compared himself to Stravinsky as a measure of his success: "I am universally esteemed here," he wrote to Berg from Hollywood in 1934, "as one of the most important modern composers; along with Stravinsky . . . Gershwin, Copland, etc." Similarly, Stravinsky complained to his friends in unpublished letters that history had mistreated him, and he was not quick to forget an injustice. Stephen Spender wrote a diary entry in May 1962 on a dinner with Stravinsky, Boulez, Simone Signoret, and Craft: "I sat far away from Stravinsky. When the party broke up Stravinsky was still very lively, violently denouncing to the Head of French Radio the attitudes of French writers to him in 1922."[18]

Schoenberg, an avid tennis player (sometimes the partner of George Gershwin), felt compelled to run to the net after each missed shot, offering lengthy explanations for miscues, blaming the wind, the racquet, anything that could be used to deflect his own shortcomings. Stravinsky, rather than confronting criticism, preferred publicly to cast it off as a worthless endeavor; but privately he responded to it, as seen in the margins of his private papers and in annotations found in the many books he studied. In his copy of Howard Hartog's *European Music in the Twentieth Century*, probably brought into the Stravinsky library by Craft, the composer recorded his reaction to statements contrasting his compositional methodology with Schoenberg's. One of the book's chapters, by Eric Walter White, related that Stravinsky had told Antheil in 1922: "I write my music now on sheets of music paper glued together, so that the staves are continuous and then I paste this continuous sheet around the four walls of my study. I start on the right-hand side of the doorway and keep on composing, going as intensely as I can until I reach the other side, or the left-hand side of the doorway. When this happens, the composition is finished. In this way I am enabled to make my music 'continuous' that is to say, into large broad lines instead of tiny breathless chunks, as, for instance, Schoenberg does." Because Stravinsky understood little of atonal music in 1922, it seems unlikely that he would have presumed to make such a statement, and the brackets and question marks with which he marked the passage surely indicate his disavowal of Antheil's recollection.

White also reported that Schoenberg's student Egon Wellesz recalled—and rather incredibly if it is true—that Stravinsky "had a copy of Schoenberg's *Three Pieces for Piano, Opus 11* with him when he started to compose *The Rite of Spring.*" It is an astounding claim, one that Stravinsky underlined and denied (with his customary "???" signaling his disbelief). The chapter on Schoenberg, by Walter and Alexander Goehr, "Arnold Schoenberg's Development Towards the Twelve-Note System," is heavily annotated. Responding to Schoenberg's statement that "dissonances are equal to heightened consonances," Stravinsky added in the margin, "No, there is comparative dissonance in *Erwartung & G.H. [Die glückliche Hand].*" He also underlined several references in the same chapter to Simon Sechter, Joseph Schillinger, Messiaen, Hugo Wolf, and Schenker. He bracketed the statement "At the turn of the century, the discovery by Freud of the existence of free associations and the consequent feeling for less logically and more subjectively connected associations in art have the greatest significance for the development of Expressionism." And later, when the authors claimed that Schoenberg's "variants and free associations are well moulded into an overall shape," Stravinsky circled and bracketed the passage, again indicating how curious he was about such assertions—assertions he would not have considered for a moment while Schoenberg was alive. Certainly he would not have allowed Schoenberg's tenets to infiltrate his life, creating the ultimate hypocrisy (as some would in fact eventually charge), had Craft not been prescient enough to see that such models might stimulate Stravinsky's thinking.

When Schoenberg died in the summer of 1951 (and sad to say, the deaths of composers whom Stravinsky viewed as competitors sometimes stirred relief rather than compassion, as his unpublished comments reveal), the problem resolved itself. Following the tepid reception of *The Rake's Progress*, premiered only a few months after his rival's death, he could no longer delude himself. More and more, the younger generation of American composers considered him a dinosaur. His newer works caused little more than a ripple. In *Music Since the First War*, Arnold Whittal claimed that, following the opera, "We have no real idea of how Stravinsky saw his own future at the time." Maybe not, but certainly he understood that it would be a bleak future unless he shifted course.

In early 1952, Stravinsky apparently felt that his life as a productive composer had reached a dead end. Craft reports that the sixty-three-year-old composer "broke down and actually wept." But this nadir soon passed, immediately leading to an opportunity to begin anew. The turnaround was largely due to Craft's crucial intercession. It came in the form of an awakened interest in serialism, especially in Webern ("the first architecnologist of our time . . . a real hero," as Stravinsky praised him). Webern's music began being performed regularly around 1948 in Los Angeles, and it certainly was making its presence known more than Stravinsky's was. Craft knew the music well, and his intercession at this critical juncture in Stravinsky's life was one that other composers would have welcomed. As Copland remarked to his friend Verna Fine, "I don't feel comfortable with the twelve-tone system . . . and remember, Verna, I don't have a Robert Craft. Stravinsky was lucky that he had a young guy around showing him Webern, bringing him music with which he wasn't familiar. I don't have anybody coming to me all the time to show me the new things."[19]

Stravinsky's initial adoption of dodecaphonic techniques in the 1950s was tentative. Still, dipping even one toe into the waters of serialism constituted an apostasy. In the world of classical music, Stravinsky "going serial" was the equivalent of Bob Dylan "going electric" a decade later—it just wasn't right. Such betrayals shook the foundations of deep musical beliefs. Notwithstanding the wall history erected between him and Schoenberg, Stravinsky's natural curiosity led him to wonder about the disciplined, ordered procedures of twelve-tone composition. But even more than the myriad ordering possibilities of serialism, his interest was aroused by its basic utility as just one more technique to help achieve compositional coherence.

Yet there is no reason to believe that such an interest was to any significant degree tied to a taste for academic serial theory, then all the rage at many American universities. As with so many other facets of this complex man, painting Stravinsky as a one-sided creator would be specious. His close friend Suvchinsky also justifiably contended that Stravinsky was hardly a "theoretician," but rather a composer who quite naturally combined intuition and rea-

Robert Craft with Aaron Copland, *center,* and Lukas Foss, *right* (The Fred and Rose Plaut Archives, courtesy of the Yale University Music Library)

son in perfect balance. The preponderance of evidence in the Sacher archives confirms that Suvchinsky was quite right. Stravinsky never delved into the arcane ratiocinations that often went hand in hand with serialist thinking. His library in Basel includes dozens of scores by Babbitt, Berg, Carter, Dallapiccola, Henze, Krenek, Schoenberg, and Stockhausen, but it was always Craft who acquired this "new music." How closely Stravinsky studied these scores is not clear, although it appears from his notations that he took only what was needed to set his mind in motion. His own serial works, beautifully conceived as they are, rarely approached the sophisticated architectonics exemplified in Webern's music.

Several primary sources establish the kind of rudimentary compositional operations Stravinsky employed. A 1958 Christmas greeting from Milton Babbitt included very elementary numerical rotations, which could easily be applied to ordering pitches. Stravinsky found such "magic squares" magical indeed. No doubt he took great delight in these little acrostics, as he learned the craft of serialism step by step in the same way he assimilated new ideas all his

life. For those capable of getting beyond what Stravinsky *should* have continued to write, there is an excitement in watching the wonderful transformation
unfold, one composition at a time, through the 1950s and 1960s.

He also relished all the renewed fuss about his music. He must have chuck-
led at eager young scholars rushing to propound some convoluted exegesis or
to unshroud compositional intent where none existed. Stravinsky thought little of such cerebrations as a portal to musical meaning: "I wish people would
let me have the privilege of being at least a little bit unconscious. It is so nice
sometimes to go blind, just with the *feeling* for the right thing," he once told
Dahl. In his often cited article "Remarks on the Recent Stravinsky," Babbitt
alluded to Stravinsky's mistrust of theorists, although he then proceeded to
marvel at the labyrinthine web of compositional procedures evident in Stravinsky's recent serial works: hexachordal rotations, combinatorial sets, in-
variant trichords, and so on. Paul Horgan remembered that Babbitt's famous
1962 Santa Fe lecture—described as "a highly technical exposition of Stravinsky's musical fabric"—left the composer "spellbound." It was the "only one
possible way to discuss music," he told Babbitt. Yet in looking over the sketches
for Stravinsky's 1959 *Movements,* Babbitt apparently pointed out a particularly intriguing hexachord, to which Stravinsky replied, "Oh yes, I like it *very*
much!" How thoroughly Stravinsky understood the hexachordal properties of
certain sets would not have deterred his welcoming the intuitive powers others ascribed to him. Why not go along with it, as Cocteau would have encouraged: "Since these mysteries are beyond me, let's pretend that I arranged
them all the time."[20]

His library included numerous scholarly articles and books, many of them
richly annotated. Whenever journals such as *Melos* or *The Score* featured one
of his works, the composer immediately ordered additional copies. He wanted
to know what scholars were saying about his latest music, even as he regularly
proclaimed his distaste for analysis. Here again, however, his marginalia
demonstrate that his corrections seldom went beyond printing errors or biographical inaccuracies. As late as his eighty-fifth birthday, he corrected an article in the British journal *Tempo,* in which the author mistakenly claimed that
Stravinsky had recently become a Roman Catholic; the composer circled the
statement and wrote, "No, No, I still am orthodox!"[21] In Humphrey Searle's
article "Webern's Last Works," Stravinsky marked in red and circled an incorrect printing of rests in one musical example from the *Opus 30 Variations.* Curiously, Searle's article appeared in the *Monthly Musical Record* of December
1946—several years before Stravinsky's turn to serialism. Yet it seems safe to

assume that it was Craft who later introduced the article to the composer as a way of encouraging him to familiarize himself with Webern.

In fact, the Webern score specifically grabbed Stravinsky's attention. In his own copy, and on separately enclosed sheets, Stravinsky marked segments of the series Webern used. Likewise, in his score of Boulez's *Structures,* Stravinsky began to mark the original ("O") and inversional ("I") forms of the row, but by the second page he abandoned tracing the series. Generally, the analytical remarks Stravinsky offered, as noted in his library copies, were quite superficial, sometimes only describing his pre-1950s music as being in a certain major or minor key, or mode.

When Jerome Robbins proposed a staging of *Les Noces (The Wedding)* for La Scala in early 1954, he wrote to Stravinsky in November 1953 seeking advice. He included a copy of Victor Belaiev's famous analysis in *Igor Stravinsky's "Les Noces": An Outline* (1928), explaining: "There are so many things I do want to ask you concerning the essential spirit of certain episodes and in general terms the particular qualities and purpose that you as composer were attempting to portray. So what follows are some of the questions that loom most large on the horizon. . . . The last [Tableau] really has me worried. This is where I need most advice as to its approach. I am sending to you Balaiev's [*sic*] analysis of the exterior form of the whole work. If possible I should like your comment."

Stravinsky respected Robbins, and he took the time to enter corrections on the copy the choreographer sent. He marked on the score changes in key centers from major to minor, tonalities to modalities, and other elementary alterations more descriptive than analytic. Craft includes a few of Robbins's very specific questions in *Stravinsky in Pictures and Documents*—questions reflecting the choreographer's intimate knowledge of the score. Missing, however, are other important inquiries posed by Robbins: "I would be curious to know for instance which way you would like to see it done at No. 2 in your score: would you want the accents to come on the sixteenth notes, or to have a steady eighth beat running through the whole section with the music making the accents against the pattern. . . . To what degree to you see this work in colloquial peasant times. I know it is a rite and that this is a ritualization of the happy and sorrowful events of the wedding preparations and ceremonies."[22]

Stravinsky's interest in pre-tonal music (also engendered largely after Craft moved into the Stravinsky house) is well documented. It was Craft again who read in far greater detail the many scholarly writings on Renaissance models—models upon which Stravinsky frequently patterned his early serial music. In a 21 December 1952 interview with Jay Harrison of the *New York Herald-Tribune*, Stravinsky stated that the late-fifteenth-century Flemish composer Heinrich Isaak was currently his favorite. "He is my hobby, my daily bread. I love him. I study him constantly. And between his musical thinking and writing and my own there is a very close connection. . . . Here is the newly published volume of his 'Choralis Constantinus,' Book III: A great work. Not a home should be without it."

Still, in the many early-music books in his library, Stravinsky's only notations are corrections of pitch errors. There is nothing suggesting that he wrestled with deeper musicological or analytic problems. In addition to Krenek's monograph on Johannes Ockeghem, Stravinsky owned Edward Lowinsky's much discussed (because of the new theories it advanced) *Secret Chromatic Art in the Netherlands Motet* (1946). His correspondence with Lowinsky gives the impression that he had studied the book carefully. Perhaps, but it is Craft's unmistakable highlighting of passages on nearly every page, and his marking of several footnotes for future reading, that collectively demonstrate his familiarity with the material's concepts. There are no annotations by Stravinsky, who normally annotated everything he read. One must therefore consider the distinct possibility that here again Craft was the knowledgeable guide—and by Stravinsky's own admission, this was "Bob's music."[23]

Stravinsky seemed heartened that broadly informed scholars continued to take the time to pore over his music. He needed the kind of intellectualized "babbittry" (as Glenn Gould once mocked it) that filled the pages of scholarly journals. It furnished a much needed imprimatur, reassuring him that he was still in the vanguard of new music at a time when the public's sympathy for what he was doing had dwindled. In his mind, such ivy-covered esoterica nullified a growing chorus of doubters, including *Saturday Review*'s Irving Kolodin, who spoke almost pitiably of the aging composer's new works as no more than a "mere trickle from the old fountainhead." It was a time of academic tribalism. Babbitt's famous 1958 manifesto, "Who Cares If You Listen?" trumpeted an apocalypse: unless enlightened audiences woke up and came on board, "music will cease to evolve, and, in that very important sense, will cease to live." Thus it became entirely incumbent upon listeners to develop their "perceptual and conceptual abilities," something Stravinsky had been futilely preaching for forty-five years. Of course the benefits of such an alliance cut both ways. As Babbitt honestly admitted in another important article, "Remarks on the Recent Stravinsky": "There is little point in denying that there were attendant and peripheral satisfactions and gratifications experienced by some of us when Stravinsky asserted: 'Those younger colleagues who already regard "serial" as an indecent word . . . [are] I think, greatly in error.'"[24]

Craft's important association with Schoenberg is one that often becomes lost in the glare of "Stravinskyana." The young conductor exhibited genuine interest in Schoenberg's music, prompting the Viennese composer to jot a note to himself, "encourage Craft." He also wrote to Craft in 1950, thanking him for performing *Pierrot Lunaire* and other works—a letter Craft has published in his revised *Chronicle*. Stravinsky, of course, knew of his assistant's affection for his neighbor. Craft would walk around the corner to Schoenberg's home, but apparently he would do it quietly, so as not to antagonize Stravinsky. So did others. Balanchine, probably out of a mixture of fear and deference for his old friend Stravinsky (and even two years after Schoenberg's death), visited with Mrs. Schoenberg in Craft's presence (but obviously not Stravinsky's) to discuss choreographing one of her husband's works.

In addition to his close association with Schoenberg and younger serialists, Craft exchanged correspondence with Stravinsky's closest literary friends: Sir Isaiah Berlin, Aldous Huxley, Christopher Isherwood, Lincoln Kirstein, and Stephen Spender. These distinguished writers regarded Craft's own prose highly: "You are truly a novelist who has no need to write what's usually called a novel," wrote Isherwood in 1975, praising Craft's review of an article addressing the working relationship of Auden and Stravinsky on *The Rake* twenty-five years earlier. Just a month after the composer's death in April 1971, Stephen Spender warmly praised Craft in a letter as both a caring individual and an outstanding writer. Nor should Craft's influence in nudging Stravinsky toward reading these contemporary authors' writings be underestimated. Even though Stravinsky knew all these thinkers years before Craft came on board, it was only after his arrival that many of the works of Auden, Isherwood, Huxley, and others found their way into his home.

The Craft Collection in Basel includes pertinent missing compositional sketch materials essential in completing chronologies for works such as *The Flood*. Some scholars who have already offered opinions about certain works may have formed a misleading picture, based on study of the Stravinsky archives while briefly held at the New York Public Library around 1984 or on sketches and other primary sources at the Sacher Stiftung before the Craft materials began arriving in the 1990s. It is only with a study of the Craft Collection that certain puzzles become solvable. Additionally, even in those materials that Craft has published, chronologies are sometimes jumbled, especially those retracing the compositional evolution of works—many of which appear in *Stravinsky in Pictures and Documents,* where Craft chronicles a day-by-day unfolding. Analysts, in the business of deriving "B" from "A," must be cautious when relying solely upon Craft's summaries. The compositional histories of *Apollo, Jeu des cartes, Orpheus,* and *Agon,* to mention several important ballets, are sometimes erroneously recounted. Stravinsky often began by sketching materials that were used at some intermediary point in a composition, then later returned (sometimes much later) to work out the opening of a piece. In effect, it is often the opening compositional material that is actually "derived"—a useful way of better assuring the work's overall structural coherence.[25]

Stravinsky seems not to have objected to the buffer zone Craft provided. In fact, he needed a shield, even from friends and relatives who constantly approached him about matters ranging from serious musical questions to financial favors. His exterior may have seemed impervious, but those who were close to him indicate a certain vulnerability that he was unwilling to expose to the public. Those who knew him well also intimate that the composer did not at all mind others speaking and writing for him, even if what was promulgated was not necessarily completely true. It endowed him with the kind of detachment the public often assumed was perfectly natural for "great men." He deserved the shelter provided by ghostwriters and speakers. Craft often acted, with Stravinsky's blessing, on his behalf. When Minna Lederman wanted to convert a series of articles originally written in 1948 for *Dance Index* into her book *Stravinsky in the Theatre* (1949), she asked for Stravinsky's help, but he declined. "Never before was I as busy as now and must it be just now I receive letters and requests as yours." The solution was to engage Craft, who, Stravinsky wrote, "knows everything about me and can be very helpful to you." Craft's responsibilities multiplied rapidly, frequently including solicited advice.

Sometimes he acted assertively. In an unpublished letter dated 30 March 1953, John Thatcher, director of Dumbarton Oaks, offered Stravinsky a fifteen-hundred-dollar commission for a work to be titled the *Dumbarton Oaks Septet.* In his handwritten marginalia on the original letter, Craft suggested to Stravinsky that the fee was too low and that his financial expectations for future commissions should be higher. He also questioned the wisdom of accepting Thatcher's suggestion for the title, since the work could be confused with the composer's earlier concerto of the same name. Responding to Thatcher a few days later, Stravinsky adopted each of Craft's suggestions, point for point. Nor should Craft's counsel be misconstrued: he was merely safeguarding the composer's best interests and performing one of the duties expected of him. Shortly after the work, ultimately titled *Septet*, was composed, Craft also offered his view on some important performance considerations in an unpublished letter (apparently written while Craft was on tour in March 1954). He made several very specific suggestions to the composer about articulating certain notes, and he provided a convincing rationale for his ideas. Here again, those who thought Craft little more than a "factotum," as he once described himself, undervalued his importance both in influencing commissions and in shaping the actual performance of certain scores.[26]

Screening commissions became part of Craft's job. Helping to decide which project the composer should next undertake placed Craft in both an influential and a tenuous position. Ten years after the composer's death, in a 1982 issue of the *Atlantic Monthly*, Craft openly declared that he had set the course for Stravinsky's choice of compositional projects beginning in 1953. He had "directed and controlled" Stravinsky, to use Craft's own description, in suggesting one commission over another; and, beginning with the composer's *Three Songs from William Shakespeare*, Craft added, each work came about as a result of "discussions between us." The compositional choices Stravinsky faced ranged from easy rejections to those requiring considerable finesse. David M. Keiser, for example, president of the New York Philharmonic Society, invited him to write and conduct a work for the opening of Lincoln Center. Leonard Bernstein sent a telegram encouraging him to consider the commission, but in February 1960 Stravinsky declined, largely because he was already committed to completing *The Flood*.[27]

A few years later, in 1964, Lincoln Kirstein envisaged another work involving Lincoln Center—this time the opening of the New York State Theater. He approached Craft, however, not Stravinsky, informing him that the new theater was to open on 23 April with two of the composer's most important Balanchine ballets, *Agon* and *Movements*. He asked Craft if he thought Stravinsky might compose a short fanfare. It could be as short as fifteen seconds and perhaps played by silver trumpets, Kirstein added, and he suggested that this herald call could be sounded from the balcony of the new theater as a way of calling people's attention to the opening of the evening's performance. Kirstein offered one thousand dollars, adding that this would be his gift to George Balanchine, who had worked for so many years in designing the marvelous new theater (which still functions as the home of the New York City Ballet).

The letter debunks several public explanations offered by both Kirstein and Craft. Publicly Kirstein wrote, "We had commissioned no novelty to serve as an appropriate launching of the occasion, but Stravinsky sent us a delight-ful surprise—a twelve-tone fractured fanfare with trumpets sounding from the top balcony."[28] Given his magnanimous support of both Balanchine and Stravinsky, it is admirable that Kirstein chose to remain the behind-the-scenes angel here, and the fiction of a "delightful surprise" is harmless. But in a film clip cut from Palmer's documentary, Craft, leafing through one of Stravinsky's sketchbooks, points out the actual sketches for what eventually became the "Fanfare for a New Theatre," adding that the brief work was composed in a single afternoon. But he also states for the camera that Stravinsky originally refused Kirstein. Here his memory eludes him, for on the original unpublished Kirstein letter of 5 March 1964, retained in the Sacher archives, Craft wrote in the margin to Stravinsky that he should decline Kirstein's offer. He even suggested the specific wording of a note that the composer should send to Kirstein, making appropriate excuses about being too busy, he wishes he would have been asked earlier, he is preparing to leave for a tour, and so on. Once again Craft surely was concerned with Stravinsky's limited time and no doubt was acting in his best interest. But the fact remains, the composer didn't turn down the commission, and on the afternoon of 23 March he drafted the short work, methodically working out, as the unpublished sketches show, the various serial forms of the twelve-tone row he employed. Sometimes Stravin-sky took Craft's advice, sometimes he didn't.

Several attempts were made by the BBC to film Stravinsky in 1965. In one, producer Christopher Burstall asked him to contribute to an Auden docu-mentary, to which the composer agreed on the condition that the shooting take place in his Hollywood home. Auden would formulate a question, which the composer would then answer on tape (to be included in the film later); it was not Auden, however, who composed the question, but Burstall. The issue of Craft's reliability in publishing chronologies and editing text again comes into question in the first volume of *Stravinsky: Selected Correspondence*, where he confuses the filming dates, reporting that Stravinsky viewed his filmed re-sponse in October. The composer did not actually tape his response until a month later: it was the CBS documentary that he saw in October. Further-more, Stravinsky did not read his original response to Burstall's question but rather one that Craft had edited, mainly to improve the language. Stravinsky then marked and underlined words he wanted to emphasize, as he commonly did with all his English scripts. He originally typed the response himself; then, as the archival typescript demonstrates, Craft added his corrections in red, and Stravinsky accepted them, as he nearly always did.

The response is notably different from what is presented in *Memories and Commentaries* (1960), and later *Themes and Conclusions* (1966), which were at a minimum largely shaped by Craft himself (both dealing with the evolution of *The Rake*'s libretto). Craft's editing of Stravinsky's original response consists mostly in rewording of sentences, adding more descriptive adjectives, and creating a smoother textual flow. There are a few embellishments that do not significantly change the points being made but still seem calculated to improve Stravinsky's unadorned, directly stated thoughts. In some cases Craft chose not only to reword what the composer had written but also to add new sentences. Although such emendations do not substantively alter Stravinsky's intent, one is left wondering why the text was changed at all. Why create the impression that Stravinsky was more fluent in the language than he really was? Stravinsky evidently welcomed such sprucing, obviously wanting his image to appear as it did, not only in the BBC film but in other films and written texts as well.

Yet there are those who contend that the language ascribed to Stravinsky was entirely his own. In a January 1972 issue of the *New Yorker,* Winthrop Sergeant charged that the composer's writings "were the work of his amanuensis, Robert Craft," and that Craft added language of his own. But Stravinsky's friend Paul Horgan immediately countered, noting that the composer's English was richly "pungent [and] grammatically correct, precise (often devastatingly so) in vocabulary, and original in style." Certainly Horgan is right on the mark in terms of the composer's disarmingly quick wit in tossing off the sharpest of rejoinders—as evinced, for example, in some of the extant film footage. Still, one wonders about the language employed in 1965 to answer questions about Webern, as posed by a University of Washington interviewer—a synthetic dialect that came to be associated with the composer in his later years: "The fact that Webern is suffering from the latter at present is simply the result of an oversupply of simulacrums produced by cheap, or rather—since Foundation wages are generous—superficial labor. No doubt even the thought of such a position accorded him (above Schoenberg!) by, for example the *Domaine musical* with its anti-Brahms deaf spot (and, hence, the Brahmsian heredity in Schoenberg) would have given him a mortal shock. Nothing was more absurd in those appraisers of a decade ago than the Schoenberg-Webern syzygy."[29]

From the start, Craft sensed that Stravinsky was interested in his opinion, not because of any assumed musical maturity or wisdom but because he could offer a fresh, new, American voice: "In fact Stravinsky was seeking my opinion precisely because of my age, my lack of position, and my non-alignment with any academic or other organization. I was slow to understand this, and that my elders had axes of their own to grind: careers as composers, conductors, and performers. If I had been his near contemporary, as was Arthur Lourié, his amanuensis in the 1920s, Stravinsky would probably not have exposed himself in this way. . . . What must be admitted is that Stravinsky *wanted* to be influenced."[30]

Perhaps more to Craft's astonishment than anyone else's, an unhesitant Stravinsky placed his trust in the young man he hardly knew, even rallying to his defense as early as 1949. When Ralph Hawkes chided Stravinsky for permitting Craft to conduct a "free performance" of his works at Town Hall, the composer scolded Hawkes in a letter on 5 May for his "stupid and mean behavior." He admonished Hawkes for a "way of thinking" that was not like that of other "top publishers" with whom he had worked, and he praised Craft as "a most excellent, reliable and devoted interpreter of my music." He even offered to cover the performance expenses if Hawkes insisted, declaring, "rather than let Bob Craft dig into his poor earning, I would rather pay myself."[31]

Who could blame Craft for tempering, wisely in fact, Stravinsky's candor while the composer was alive, thus probably salvaging commissions, collaborations, and performances that might otherwise have evaporated? But how far he went after Stravinsky's death in condoning the composer's sometimes inexpiable behavior is a more complex matter that some scholars are now questioning. In the preface to volume 1 of *Stravinsky: Selected Correspondence*, Craft notes that following the composer's passing, he came upon several letters seemingly at odds with the man he had come to know—yet a man capable of penning ignominious statements while living in France after 1920 or so. Unpublished correspondence in the Sacher archives confirms the reason for Craft's surprise. Ultimately, Craft told me, he concurred with some of Stravinsky's closest friends that it served no useful purpose to publish some of the more egregious epithetic remarks the composer had written.

Craft could easily have opted to destroy several repugnant letters, as Stravinsky no doubt would have done (and just as many "great men" regularly did, including Dr. Johnson and his American contemporary Thomas Jefferson), thus protecting not only the composer but himself as well. Craft was surely conscious of the detoxified picture he felt obligated to bequeath, but he may also have realized that eventually his role in editing several letters would be discovered, and that ultimately it would be up to history to judge his actions. I believe he did what he felt he had to do, sometimes with the advice and consent of Stravinsky's friends, and for the sake of the man he served. Whatever one may make of all this, it is clear that the Stravinsky pictured in his published letters does not always yield a complete portrait.

The composer was invigorated by the interest that people showed in his every pronouncement. Like the wise old soothsayers in *Le Sacre* half a century earlier, Stravinsky himself now became the augur. From his feelings about Wagner's prose to his jaunty quips on rock music, spouting wisdoms and reconstructing faded memories became part of his public image. Nowhere is that image more deliberately framed than in the six famous conversation books that began appearing in the late 1950s. As the Sacher archives reveal, Columbia Records was eager to have the composer record excerpts from some of his earlier writings. Although the marketing strategy seemed a sure thing, Stravinsky did not seem especially interested. If there was one consistency in the composer's life, it was his recognition that his career as an artist was a work in progress. He did not wish to be held to statements he had made years earlier in a context that might be narrowly construed and thus misinterpreted, to say nothing of the possibility that he had simply changed his mind about one issue or another. Several attempts to have him revise his autobiography were floated, but the unclear text itself had always posed difficulties. "The Stravinsky autobiography represents a big problem," wrote one interested editor in 1957 to the composer's friend Goddard Lieberson. "Human values practically don't exist in it. . . . He established some kind of record for getting that many human experiences into so few words, but he leaves the reader wondering whether he's human."

For another publisher, the idea of capitalizing on his fame by updating his "musical philosophy, which we think Stravinsky might like to revise now that it is twenty-two years later," was appealing. In early 1957, the seventy-five-year-old composer provided a set of "Answers to Thirty-Six Questions" posed by Craft. These question-and-answer exchanges proved popular and were widely reproduced elsewhere.[32] From there the dialogue format mushroomed, continuing into the late 1960s and eventually including the six conversation books. For many Stravinsky scholars, the perennial question persists: how much of what Stravinsky purportedly said in these most readable coffee-table books is Stravinsky, and how much was either written or at least "massaged" by Craft? Essentially, Craft merely improved Stravinsky's still very rough English. As pages of unpublished typescripts in the Sacher archives show, the composer first jotted down his ideas in Russian, then attempted his own translation, which Craft then edited.

A word-by-word comparison of the composer's original responses with the version of answers eventually published in all six conversation books would offer the clearest examples. But without permission to reprint the unpublished original drafts, a summary of changes will suffice. The differences between the composer's original drafts and the published versions sometimes amount to more than simple copyediting. Craft would ornament the composer's straightforward answers, thereby reinforcing the more engaging notion of Stravinsky as a quick-witted cynic (which in fact he already was). To a question about his days as a university student in *Conversations with Igor Stravinsky*, Stravinsky responded simply that attending lectures was optional, but the published version is framed more sardonically, with additional language that Stravinsky did not originally use. At times nostalgic references are interposed, again making the language more evocative. In *Memories and Commentaries*, for example, Stravinsky mentions that he shared a room with his brother Gury, commenting simply that they spent a great deal of time there together. But the published sentence reads, "Our room was like *Petrouchka*'s cell, and most of my time was spent there"—a much more picturesque image indeed. Numerous other examples abound—new sentences are added, clearer and more poignant language is interpolated, and generally a more appealing interpretation of the original is substituted.

Many pages of the original typescripts exhibit Stravinsky's corrections and deletions, suggesting that he studied his responses and refined them after Craft had transcribed his remarks. Yet there are just as many instances demonstrating that, rather than reproducing Stravinsky's own thoughts verbatim, the original responses were initially Craft's. It seems that Craft sometimes answered his own questions, then later Stravinsky was asked to revise them. It is the evidence of small factual changes that leaves a trail. The original typescript states that Stravinsky's father studied engineering, but Stravinsky corrects the statement: his father was a law student. Originally a response indicates that a stove in Stravinsky's school was white, but the composer amends this answer, stating that it was blue. The typescript records that Stravinsky's father knew Petipa well, but Stravinsky corrects this, stating that he was a "contemporary" of the choreographer, but not an "intimate." These are small changes, to be sure, but they suggest that Stravinsky was a respondent to language that had been presented to him, and sometimes took it upon himself to correct inaccurate statements.

There are substantive corrections as well: the original typescript for a section in *Memories and Commentaries* dealing with the ballet *Apollo* states that it was originally choreographed by Lifar and Balanchine, but then Stravinsky deleted Lifar's name. Would he really have written both names initially and later changed his mind on such an important matter only when doing the last-minute proofing of his own answers? And regarding the passage dealing with *Apollo* published in another of the conversation books, *Dialogues,* the archives show that Stravinsky simply tossed off some very rough thoughts. The original transcription, however, shows that Craft had prepared the first full draft (not unlike Roland-Manuel drafting statements from Stravinsky's cryptic notes), and later Stravinsky corrected and approved it. The original typescript included some discussion of Diaghilev's and Ansermet's very negative feelings about Stravinsky's ballet *Apollo.* The suggestion is made that it was their distaste for the ballet that occasioned the infamous cut of the Polyhymnia variation, known to ballet historians everywhere. Stravinsky ostensibly also remarked that Ansermet particularly hated the variation, but none of these statements survive in the published version.

Several statements were deleted altogether, presumably for the sake of propriety, with which Craft was evidently very concerned. He acted with prudence, here as elsewhere taking on the role of ombudsman in protecting the composer from his own indiscretions. Allusions are made to Nijinsky's sexual history, for example, but the remarks are cut, perhaps out of fear of the litigation that was actually threatened by the dancer's family. The original typescript establishes that Stravinsky initially dictated some particularly harsh sentences about Nijinsky's syphilitic condition, but Craft wisely intercedes, advising the composer that these sentiments will need to be "expunged." The same is true of Stravinsky's memory of Ravel, eventually published in *Memories and Commentaries.* The original typescript included an entire paragraph about that composer's problems with sexual impotence, but this passage too was struck. In another first draft, Stravinsky's mother was treated much more callously than ever before. What survives in *Memories and Commentaries* amounts to a more sanitized version of the composer's feelings about his mother. Had Stravinsky gone forward with his original thoughts, those feelings would have disclosed a deeply encrusted bitterness for a woman who constantly made him feel shameful and unwanted. She preferred the music of Scriabin, Stravinsky also bemoaned in the original typescript, adding that until the day she died she referred to *Sacre* as a hideous piece of music. Indeed the composer's deeply embedded anxiety about his relationship with his mother spills over much more intensely in his original remarks; but none of these comments survive.

Unsurprisingly, Craft faced charges of scripting Stravinsky. In examining the archive's original typescripts (some of which were also given by Craft to the Sacher Stiftung), it appears that the charges are frequently unsubstantiated or exaggerated, yet in other places justified. Aware of such fabrications and embellishments, Stravinsky made it clear that he was uncomfortable. His copy of *Conversations with Igor Stravinsky* includes questions about Craft's garnishing of simple responses, for instance in a floridly descriptive phrase, "kaleidoscopic montages for contortuplicate personalities." Stravinsky underlined the passage and expressed his surprise with an exclamation mark in the margin. Had he approved such tumescent language in earlier galleys, or did he really not see it, as his marginalia suggests, until in its published form? Whatever the truth and the allegations about these conversation books, they have generally not deterred anyone from employing them a little too frequently as an irrefragable representation of Stravinsky's beliefs.

Even Craft has made no secret of the fact that Stravinsky was concerned about the alterations. In a letter to Deborah Ishlon in 1958, Stravinsky insisted that Craft be credited as the author, because he "did write the book, it is his language, his presentation, his imagination, and his memory, and I am only protecting myself in not wanting it to appear as though I write or talk in that way. It is not a question of simple ghostwriting, but of somebody who is to a large extent creating me." (Craft published this letter in *Stravinsky in Pictures and Documents*, along with a page in Stravinsky's hand. But an examination of the complete archival materials reveals that of the hundreds of manuscript pages surviving, less than 5 percent are initially in Stravinsky's own hand.) A week after the first letter to Ishlon, a still anxious Stravinsky wrote to thank her for including a retainer from the publisher, but requested that she hold the check until he was sure that Craft would be credited fully for his participation; otherwise, he indicated, it would weigh heavily on his mind. Another week later, Stravinsky wrote to T. S. Eliot (the publisher of *Conversations* for Faber and Faber), insisting that Craft had to appear either as the primary author, without further qualification, or at least as the person who helped write the book for him.

In the revised edition of his *Chronicle*, Craft admits that the interviews that made up the majority of the later conversation books were of little interest to Stravinsky; but the interviews, even if completely staged, were encouraged by his attorney to justify Stravinsky's continuing activity as a musician, since by 1967 he was seldom engaged in conducting or composing. For the purpose of meeting IRS requirements for tax deductions, the interviews were printed under his name as an indication of his ongoing work as a musician.[33]

In an unreleased film trim, Alexei Haieff remarked, "I think Mr. Craft and his . . . conversations make Stravinsky much more an erudite man than he actually was. He was a typical man of intuition through his genius." But, as we have seen, it was Stravinsky himself who always felt compelled to project the image of a cognoscente. How much of this Craft personally endorsed, only he can answer, but there is little doubt that he felt obligated not only to guide the composer but to act in what he thought were Stravinsky's best interests. As with all mythmaking, those interests seem to have included boosting the impression that Stravinsky was more than he really was.

In *Journal of a Tour to the Hebrides,* the diary of his travels with Johnson, Boswell observed, "A page of my Journal is like a cake of potable soup. A little may be diffused into a considerable portion." The tapestry of facts, commentaries, conclusions, and assumptions that Craft has provided over the years has likewise given us much to think about, and at times it has led us to inferences that may need to be rethought. Some have argued that Craft's judgments became clouded, just as Boswell's critics have pronounced his efforts unwarranted and intrusive. Still, while Craft is frequently castigated for suppressing or misstating information, such charges must be viewed in the context of his complicated and fateful conjunction with Stravinsky—an alliance that finds no clear parallel in music history. Never has he claimed to be a biographer, a musicologist, or an impartial scholar, although these are the grounds on which he is regularly judged. He has, however, become the principal "vessel," to use Stravinsky's old analogy from *Le Sacre,* through which our image of the composer flows. Craft was ethically bound to protect Stravinsky. What else could one expect of an impressionable young musician whose lot was cast in 1948 and whose devotion deepened thereafter? We must allow that Craft's vested perspective, one of unapologetic advocacy, was a distinctive one. Craft knew with whom he was dealing. He understood, perhaps more than anyone else could, that he was living in the presence of a man who had already attained the status of an icon—a creative giant whose stamp on the century was undeniable. Through his writings and his remembrances, it is clear that even though he became the composer's associate and friend, he remained awestruck.

Igor and Vera Stravinsky
(The Goddard Lieberson Papers, courtesy of the Yale University Music Library)

Such openhearted adulation—even worship, as Stephen Spender once characterized Craft's devotion—could only lead hopelessly to a noose that Stravinsky himself tightened through his often impolitic statements, actions, and demands. It remained for Craft to unravel, or at least attenuate, as best he could, its potential repercussions. It fell to him not only to interpret Stravinsky for the world outside but to ensure his status as a twentieth-century hero. In the years following the composer's death, Craft conceded that he was unsure what to make of his relationship with the great man. His investment was substantial and very personal, and he was in the worst imaginable position to speak or act dispassionately. By his own description, he felt "paralyzed" in trying to make sense of the star-crossed forces that placed Stravinsky in his life and him in Stravinsky's. His role in the composer's life must be considered only one part of the puzzle, albeit a central one. Craft more than anyone is fully aware that scholars will inevitably have to consider his custodial role; for it was he more than any other individual who controlled access to Stravinsky's documents, writings, compositional sketches, and, in some respects at least, the story of his later life. Nor was Craft unaware that charges would be made, especially once the doors to the archive were opened. Ultimately, however, neither an indictment nor an exoneration of Craft is useful. We must simply go about the business of screening, evaluating, balancing, restoring, and assembling as accurately as we can a complete profile of Stravinsky. Only then will a fuller understanding of one of the century's most fascinating and complex cultural figures begin to emerge.

Epilogue

The notion that some day people will try to probe into the private world
of my thoughts and feelings is very sad and unpleasant.
—Peter Ilich Tchaikovsky, letter of 10 August 1880

Stravinsky died in New York early on the morning of 6 April 1971.
Although the news was mentioned on several morning broadcasts, I first heard
of it from Walter Cronkite later in the afternoon. The CBS network, in a "we
interrupt our regular programming" bulletin, reported the death of the great
"Russian-American" composer with the same momentous tone that it used for
any dramatic news event. Cronkite's announcement was not only sad for musicians everywhere, more broadly, it was sobering historically. An epoch had
ended.

I never knew, met, or even saw Stravinsky. But from my first acquaintance
with his music, I immediately understood that he was an extraordinary composer—a composer whose concept of musical ideas intrigued me in ways that
I could not then articulate. I'm still not sure that I can. In that sense, his music is, of course, enough to consume one without any deeper probing. My out-
look changed, however, when I began to study with his son, close to the time
of his father's death. Whether I wanted to or not, I began to think about
Stravinsky as a person—a human being not only capable of breathtaking at-
tainments but also susceptible to the missteps and blemishes that mark the
flux of one's life. Soulima's presence provided a reification of what until then
had been only a vaguely envisioned notion of his father. Suddenly I recognized
Stravinsky's existence, not simply as a composer, but as a person who composed. It bothered me that the creator of so many transcendent works was not
himself transcendent. He was not the disembodied, mythological Apollo I

once assumed. Just as naïveté can be reassuring, myths too are comforting. "I wonder if we could contrive some magnificent myth," Plato wrote, "that would in itself carry conviction to our whole community." A seductive notion, to be sure; but Stravinsky was real, and initially that reality both disturbed and disappointed me.

As I worked with Soulima during those final few years of his father's life, I was troubled that one of the great cultural figures of our age would soon be gone. I'm still struck by a memory that Stephen Spender related. Toward the end of the composer's life, the two listened to the late Beethoven String Quartets: "Some we played so often you could only hear the needle in the groove," remembered Spender. It was difficult to picture the vital, kinetic Stravinsky now sitting and listening, rather than personally reaching into the firmament and once again yanking out another masterwork. And if I needed further proof of Stravinsky's impermanence, it came one terrible, jarring day in Basel while I was examining the composer's personally marked copy of Bach's *Well-Tempered Clavier*—his "daily bread," as he called it, for he regularly used the music as a stimulant in getting his own "creative juices" flowing. It was the same music, Craft recalled, that Stravinsky had been playing only a few days before his death. The familiar red and blue notations the composer had inserted in the score were weak and tremulous, the words he wrote difficult to decipher, the suggestions he made not particularly cogent, although the powerful drive to keep "making" was painfully evident. I felt not only humbled, but also embarrassed to witness the extinguishing of the once indomitable spirit that now faded in the manuscript before me.

Thinking in such emotional, human terms is unsettling. It begs consideration of the convoluted social and cultural context that engulfs and shapes us all. It demands a confrontation with the conflicts one inevitably encounters in a demythologized world. Stravinsky was more than real: he was the consummate realist, and for many, that verity proves deflating since it robs us of our fantasies. There was a sense of purpose to nearly everything that he did. The fact that he often was adrift in self-reflection, while his music remained thoroughly confident, is in no sense incongruent. In one of his last essays, William James addressed competing "tender-minded and tough-minded" dualities—dualities that were only reconcilable through the lens of pragmatism as a mediating philosophy. One could be both a rationalist and an empiricist, both an idealist and materialist, religious and irreligious, "intellectualistic and sensationalistic," to use James's words. In Stravinsky's case, the gamut is run. Moreover, his individuality is largely attributable to an alluring elusiveness, a communal elusiveness shared by many of the great creative artists and thinkers of any age. He wanted, perhaps even needed, to outfox those who might question the inconsistencies of his humanness, transparent though they often were. As a result, we are left with the need to reconcile the glitzy image of a master showman with the interior struggle of a solemn artist who thought soberly about his role in the world around him.

Stravinsky's resistance to authority would not permit him to acquiesce to the preconceptions of others. The need to challenge conformity at every turn originated deeply and earnestly within him. It clearly distinguishes him, and consequently distinguishes his music as an extension of his most profound beliefs. The confluence of so many clashing cultural worlds in which he lived, blended with his own mixture of idealism, pragmatism, and just plain unpredictable behavior, contributes to the intangibility of his character. Such dichotomies are not particularly uncommon among creative people; nor is it unusual for them to disguise, or even cull from history's record, the foibles of their lives. In writing about Mozart, Wolfgang Hildesheimer suggests that the Viennese composer's private documents, more than his music, illuminate his interior being. Yet a host of devoted biographers—as well as Mozart himself— willingly and systematically concealed such documents. "This is the sorry nature of trite biographies: they find easy explanations for everything, within a range of probability we can comprehend," Hildesheimer writes. "The primary source and the motivation are the same: wishful thinking."[1]

What might Stravinsky have thought of the biographical voyeurism that constantly stalked him? In a 1948 article titled "From Billy Rose to God," Lawrence Morton wrote, "I wonder if, sometimes [Stravinsky] is not . . . disturbed by the adoration of disciples and admirers, the kind of adoration usually reserved for the dead." Stravinsky, though, was anything but disturbed by the attention. His archives reveal that he expected, even demanded adulation while publicly feigning indifference. When Morton approached Stravinsky about writing his biography, he admitted being "unnerved" by the composer's reaction: "If you are really writing a book about me, say what you have to say— but be kind."[2]

As the archives demonstrate, Stravinsky accumulated a repository of files documenting virtually every particle of autobiographical minutiae. Each footstep the composer left behind suggests what he surely saw as an inexorable march toward historical enthronement. Yes, he destroyed papers and directed that several packets of his correspondence be extracted upon his death. But such protective instincts shouldn't be misconstrued; he merely wanted to control his image. Indeed, control was the engine that drove his every action. Unquestionably Stravinsky knew that he would eventually occupy a central position in the history of the twentieth century, yet he consistently denied having any interest in thinking about, let alone shaping his legacy. But as politically judicious as this response was, his archives disclose that he was utterly incapable of standing aside and entrusting his fate to others. Not only did he worry that he might be forgotten, but like so many of history's icons, he desperately wanted to be judged as one of its major players. Nor did he demonstrate any compunction in steering history toward reaching a favorable verdict. Stravinsky didn't mind being the subject of biography: he minded being its defenseless object.

His search for identity was a twisting and intriguing journey. Was it "one single and long sentence without caesura," as the composer's old friend St. John Perse described the evolution of his own works, or was it a series of "discontinuities," as some music analysts have described his music? Has the time come to abandon the myopia of theories splitting the man and his music into divisible but ultimately fabricated categorizations? With the archives now bidding a broader context for consideration, history must formulate different views based on different sources—untainted sources impelling us to have a fresh look. In reevaluating, we must admit forthrightly that, as disquieting as it sometimes may become, it is impossible to separate public and private persona. We must recognize the complexity of a man whose robustly lived life consisted of a layered psychology best understood by the broadest of analyses.

We are on the cusp of a new Stravinsky scholarship. Positivists will continue contributing to our understanding of the music itself through their informative specialized studies. But we live in an era that increasingly recognizes the need to question issues in a more expansive, more humanistic context. Only by rethinking what we have been told about Stravinsky will a more sharply defined portrait unifying the mythological exterior with the inner man emerge, even if in the cold light of such a synthesis, a sharper focus might mean a cloudier one, and occasionally even an unflattering one. There is no doubt that Stravinsky's imaginative, vigorous music will endure, filling us with an admiration we eagerly confer upon societal icons—who, once their fictional images have been stripped away, often prove disconcertingly and perhaps a little too recognizably human. In the end, our image of Stravinsky may tell us as much about ourselves as it does about the composer. Tchaikovsky should not have been made to worry over history's judgment of the private world of his thoughts; but alas, the urge for the deification of heroes seems innate, and our praise and admiration too often come with a set of conditions. For all of our invasiveness, it is not our icons' untouchable accomplishments that run the risk of being irreparably stained; rather, it is our need to accept and even rejoice in the realization that the human condition is fraught with frailties. That such creative giants as Stravinsky rise above themselves to enrich us with their memorable, hard-won artistic triumphs should provide us with hope, not disappointment.

Notes

Abbreviations

SPD   Vera Stravinsky and Robert Craft, *Stravinsky in Pictures and Documents* (New York: Simon and Schuster, 1978).

SSC I, II, III   Robert Craft, editor, *Stravinsky: Selected Correspondence* (New York: Alfred A. Knopf, vol. 1, 1982; vol. 2, 1984; vol. 3, 1985).

Chapter 1: Truths and Illusions

1. Howard Gardner, *Creating Minds* (New York: Basic Books, 1993), 119; Stephen Spender, *Journals, 1939–1983,* ed. John Goldsmith (New York: Random House, 1986), 227–28.

2. Malcolm Cowley, introduction to *Anna Karenina,* by Leo Tolstoy (New York: Bantam Books, 1960), v–xii.

3. Harold N. Box to Stravinsky, 6 August 1947, the Paul Sacher Stiftung, Basel, Switzerland. Stravinsky responded the same day. The composer knew Box through their exchanges in conjunction with several Voice of America interviews. Stravinsky was no doubt further angered by White's article "Stravinsky—Latter-Day Symphonist," published in the November 1947 issue of *Horizon.* White reported that Edith Sitwell had said of Stravinsky, "The brown bear rambles in his chain," a clear reference to the fact that no matter what Stravinsky did, he could not abandon his "Slavonic birthright." White argued that even the composer's newer American works could not rid themselves "of the animal [and] if it were encouraged and became too friendly, its embrace might easily prove fatal."

4. Eric Walter White, *Stravinsky: A Critical Survey* (London: John Lehmann, 1947).

5. Some of White's unpublished drafts indicate that Stravinsky (and sometimes Craft) did take the time to enter corrections. Just how sensitive White was to the composer's wariness is apparent in a 13 March 1950 letter: "I know that in the past you have expressed the opinion that my book is in no case the best written about you." And in a subsequent letter the biographer said Craft had suggested that White write a new version of what had by that point become the standard Stravinsky biography. White

again demurely says he "doubts he can excel" Roman Vlad's biography, which Vlad's publisher claimed Stravinsky had declared "the best study of my music which has yet appeared in any country of the world." But Stravinsky then used White's letter as an opening to denigrate Vlad's work as well: "Nothing disturbs me so much . . . as the blurb on Signor Vlad's book since I never said any such thing and, indeed, have not even read the book"—although of course he had.

In the early 1970s, while I was completing a doctoral dissertation on the piano music of Stravinsky, Mr. White wrote to me: "I thought you would be interested to know that I have edited two 'new' piano works of [Stravinsky] for publication in the near future." He also dispatched to me prepublication proofs of the works (both of which survived in libraries in the Soviet Union) along with his own comments. Our correspondence, which continued for several years, all evinced a much kinder man than Stravinsky portrays.

6. Just as Stravinsky did nothing to dissuade the frequent employment of the "world's greatest living composer" cognomen, Beethoven raised no objection to having his name published as Ludwig "von" Beethoven, rather than the much less aristocratic "van." As Alessandra Comini writes, "The assumption that Beethoven was of noble birth was widely circulated. . . . This was a presumption Beethoven did nothing to correct. . . . Thus one of the earliest Beethoven 'myths'—that he was of nobility—was encouraged by Beethoven himself in an attempt to force reality into paralleling what he felt he needed to believe about himself" (Alessandra Comini, *The Changing Image of Beethoven* [New York: Rizzoli, 1987], 13–21).

7. Francis Steegmuller was in fact authorized by Stravinsky to write his definitive biography, although nothing came of this. The composer retained several of Steegmuller's books, including his translation of *The Selected Letters of Gustave Flaubert* (New York: Farrar, Straus, and Young, 1953), which he gave to the composer in 1966. Steegmuller said of Flaubert that the "objective novelist . . . spent hours seeking a phrase, or a week revising a page. . . . [He] was capable of letting himself go in lengthy, almost unblotted letters to friends . . . he analyzes himself, discusses the social forces that shaped his period, and expounds his ideas on art and the creative process." Steegmuller wisely judged that the letters "may serve also to test the validity of certain deductions and conclusions concerning Flaubert and his art commonly offered in more or less good faith by his admirers and detractors." And, further, "The writer of the letters is often, at first sight, highly contradictory, and yet in each case the letters supply also the solution to the apparent contradiction." Finally, he spoke of Flaubert's "famous realism, his dogged determinism to render the slightest detail correctly. . . . By nailing down reality in words . . . he is enabled to 'rub the noses of the bourgeois in their own turpitudes'" (xvii).

8. Edward T. Cone, ed., *Roger Sessions on Music: Collected Essays* (Princeton: Princeton University Press, 1979), 380; Suzi Gablik, *Has Modernism Failed?* (New York: Thames and Hudson, 1984), 23, 74.

9. Balanchine was in fact kind enough to have *Requiem Canticles* videotaped for Stravinsky because the composer was too ill to attend. Vera Stravinsky remembers that her husband approved of the performance. Moreover, Stravinsky and Balanchine actually discussed the choreography, as demonstrated by the wonderful set of photographs included in Arnold Newman's *Bravo Stravinsky* (1967). Nor was this the first time that Stravinsky—privately, at least—insinuated that he had not approved of a Balanchine project. In a clipping from the 13 November 1960 *New York Herald-Tribune,*

a photograph of Stravinsky and Balanchine is included along with a caption reading: "Igor Stravinsky and George Balanchine discuss a detail in the composer's score entitled *Monumentum Pro Gesualdo.* The work serves as the basis for Mr. Balanchine's latest ballet *Monumentum* which will be given its world premiere by the NYCB on Wednesday at the City Center." But Stravinsky wrote in the clipping's margin, "I never 'discussed' this score with Balanchine and it was a surprise to me that he staged this music."

10. This unpublished letter is part of the Goddard Lieberson Collection in Yale University's School of Music Library. I wish to thank Brigitta Lieberson for allowing me to reprint sections of her husband's letters.

11. Carl Sagan et al., *Murmurs of Earth: The Voyager Interstellar Record* (New York: Random House, 1978), 187; the description is Timothy Ferris's, from his essay "Voyager's Music." The Stravinsky music is one of twenty-seven excerpts included on the *Voyager* spacecraft. The only other Western art music represented is by Bach, Mozart, and Beethoven. Several American popular pieces are included, as are examples of non-Western classical and folk repertoire.

12. The political environment enveloping Stravinsky's music in Germany during the late 1920s and the 1930s is explored by Professor Joan Evans in "Die Rezeption der Musik Igor Strawinskys in Hitlerdeutschland," *Archiv für Musikwissenschaft* 55/2 (1998): 91–109. As Evans concludes, Stravinsky was eventually viewed by the Third Reich "as an 'Aryan' composer with acceptable political beliefs, whose tonally-based music exhibited an appropriately 'national' orientation. As such, Stravinsky was pronounced suitable for inclusion in the cultural life of the new Germany" (109). Craft reports that in 1956 Pierre Suvchinsky spoke openly to him about Stravinsky's sympathetic feelings for Italy. Not only was the composer welcomed by Mussolini, Suvchinsky reported, but he even presented a signed copy of his autobiography to the Fascist dictator. (Robert Craft, *Stravinsky: Chronicle of a Friendship,* revised and expanded edition [Nashville: Vanderbilt University Press, 1994], 154.)

13. By Stalin's direct order, Shostakovich had been dispatched to what was billed as the "First World Peace Congress" in New York. More than nineteen thousand people attended his performance of a piano reduction of his popular Fifth Symphony. Stravinsky's dismissal of the event, in which he declared that he could not join in welcoming Shostakovich, was, naturally, attacked by the Soviet press. Stravinsky himself was quickly dismissed as "a traitor and enemy of our fatherland." (Elizabeth Wilson, *Shostakovich: A Life Remembered* [Princeton: Princeton University Press, 1994], 238–39.) The Cultural and Scientific Conference received considerable press. Thomas Mann, Albert Einstein, Frank Lloyd Wright, Judy Holliday, and a number of musicians including Aaron Copland and Leonard Bernstein were involved. Copland testified before Joseph McCarthy's committee, and because of a congressional objection his *Lincoln Portrait* was withdrawn from Eisenhower's inaugural concert. Meryle Secrest reports in her 1994 biography of Bernstein that he permitted his photograph to be published by *Life* magazine with the near libelous headline "Dupes and Fellow Travelers Dress Up Communist Fronts" (Meryle Secrest, *Leonard Bernstein: A Life* [New York: Vintage Books, 1994], 172). Stravinsky thought himself also "duped" by efforts a few years earlier to use his name in conjunction with a concert supporting a fellow film musician (Hanns Eisler) who was accused of concealing his membership in the Communist Party. Several young American composers participated, including Copland, Roger Sessions, Roy Harris, and others. Many other luminaries supported

the concert, among them John Houseman, Thomas Mann, and Olivia de Havilland. But Stravinsky felt betrayed, not realizing that a propagandistic pamphlet would be distributed with the concert programs. Thereafter, he was advised by his lawyer to avoid becoming involved in any such matters, especially Shostakovich's visit.

14. André Gide, *The Journals of André Gide*, vol. 3, ed. Justin O'Brien (New York: Alfred A. Knopf, 1949), 8.

15. Stravinsky did, however, demonstrate enthusiasm for some of the writings of Albert Camus; indeed, a letter to him from Camus in 1952 (reprinted in *SSC III*, 197) shows a mutual affection, as well as an attempt to interest Stravinsky in writing music for a ballet conceived by the poet René Char, although nothing came of this.

16. Léonie Rosenstiel, *Nadia Boulanger: A Life in Music* (New York: W. W. Norton, 1982), 313.

17. Igor Stravinsky, *Poetics of Music*, trans. Arthur Knodel and Ingolf Dahl (Cambridge: Harvard University Press, 1975; orig. pub. 1947), 30. Other occupants of the Norton poetry chair included Stravinsky's friend T. S. Eliot, e. e. cummings, and, in 1973, Leonard Bernstein. Like Stravinsky, Bernstein relied heavily on the ideas of a close friend, in his case Thomas Cothran, who apparently guided Bernstein's initial thoughts, helping to make sense of them for public presentation. And just as Stravinsky used the Harvard post as a platform to attack everything from the evils of interpretation to the "avatars" of Soviet realism, so too did Bernstein anger many contemporary serial composers with his defense of tonality as a divinely given musical order.

18. Poincaré's 1913 essay was familiar to many musicians seeking a reconciliation between art and science. In *The Value of Science* (1907), Poincaré wrote, "It is only through science and art that civilization is of value." Thomas Levinson also writes of a natural juxtaposition between the mathematician and Stravinsky, observing that while Poincaré at least hinted at "a construction of an aesthetic order out of the entire realm of imagination," it was left for Stravinsky to grapple with the problem that Poincaré had articulated. This was especially so in a momentous work such as *Le Sacre du printemps*, where as Levinson sees it "the warring impulses of choice and fate" had no choice but to collide (Thomas Levinson, *Measure for Measure* [New York: Touchstone, 1994], 233–40).

19. Paul Henry Lang, "The Position of Igor Stravinsky," *New York Herald-Tribune*, 18 March 1956. As early as 1942, Theodore Chanler reviewed Harvard's original publication in French of the *Poétique musicale*. He stressed the composer's link with Jacques Maritain, his thoughts on Suvchinsky and ontological time, and his ideas about the creative process—all expressed, said Chanler, with an "almost boyish outspokenness," a good description indeed for many of Stravinsky's famous utterances (Theodore Chanler, "Stravinsky's Apologia," *Modern Music* 20 [November–December 1942]: 17–22).

20. Aldous Huxley, *The Doors of Perception, and Heaven and Hell* (London: Grafton, 1956), 61.

21. Unpublished letter of 30 December 1949 to Armitage, whose collection of essays about Stravinsky in 1936 was the first to appear in English. Armitage released a second collection of commentaries in 1949, the same year he received Stravinsky's letter. Stravinsky used the same Schopenhauer quotation in his 1957 documentary for NBC, as part of the network's *Wisdom* series (discussed in Chapter 6).

22. Unpublished response of April 1951. Stravinsky's list of "no-thank-you" refusals of honorary doctorates later included offers from the University of Oxford

(1953), Colgate (1959), University of California at Berkeley (1959), University of New Mexico (1962), University of Illinois (1962), Washington University in St. Louis (1962), and Bard College (1967). Stravinsky felt tricked into accepting a doctorate at the University of Rochester (Eastman School) in 1966 when he traveled there only to conduct. While he was adamantly opposed to such academic recognitions, his list of honors, prizes, and society memberships was extensive. A partial listing includes a diploma from the Accademico Onorario di Santa Cecilia (1916); Membre étranger, Académie tchécoslovaque des Sciences et des Arts (1932); Academico Honorario, Academia de Bellas Artes de San Fernando, San Sebastian (1938); Honorary Member, the Musicians Club of Pittsburgh (1941); Honor Roll, Association of Music for the Wounded, Los Angeles (1946); Member, National Institute of Arts and Letters (1949); Star of the Italian Solidarity, first class diploma (1953); Honorary Member, Royal Academy of Music, London (1959); Knight of Mark Twain (1962); "World Life President" of the Martin Buber Society; Kentucky Colonel, Commonwealth of Kentucky (1962); Knight Commander with Star of Sylvester, presented by Pope John XXIII (1963); Prix Roland-Manuel (recording prize, 1963); and the Sibelius Prize (1963, for the second time). Stravinsky would sometimes use his medallions as payment for services rendered, for example, to physicians who cared for him.

23. David King Dunaway, *Huxley in Hollywood* (New York: Harper and Row, 1989), 430. For Huxley's complete letter (in which not only Bernstein but Rodgers and Hammerstein were mentioned as possible collaborators, see Grover Smith, ed., *Letters of Aldous Huxley* (New York: Harper and Row, 1968), 820–21.

24. Stravinsky, *Poetics of Music*, 27.

25. Vernon Duke, "The Deification of Stravinsky," *Listen: A Music Monthly*, May–June 1964 and September–October 1964. Duke's two-part essay understandably infuriated Stravinsky. His insinuation that Stravinsky was another "Liberace" on his way to the bank headed a long list of contemptible charges. He pronounced the composer a spent artist who "leads no longer" and whose public now runs "faster in the opposite direction." He claimed that Stravinsky had produced a string of "successive failures" that only his claque of "idolaters" admired—and so the litany continued. So angry was the composer that a response appeared in the magazine's September–October issue titled "A Cure for V. D." In it, Stravinsky responded in kind, remarking, "I cannot reply to such a spew—a hose or a refuse-removal department are the proper tools for that," and added, "The spectacle of a bad composer going sour is not new . . . and there is little new in the sourness of the very bad composer V. D."

26. Claudio Spies, "Notes in His Memory," commemorative issue of *Perspectives of New Music* 9 (1971): 155–57. In this important issue, many of Stravinsky's friends offered short eulogies.

27. Lincoln Kirstein, *Mosaic Memoirs* (New York: Farrar, Straus & Giroux, 1994), 213.

28. Tim Page, ed., *The Glenn Gould Reader* (New York: Vintage Books, 1984), 181. Most of the lecture is reprinted here, at 166–84.

Chapter 2: Rediscovering the American *Apollon Musagète*

1. For more on Stravinsky's early acquaintance with American popular music, see Barbara B. Heyman, "Stravinsky and Ragtime," *Musical Quarterly* 68 (1982): 543–62.

2. Diaghilev's portrayal of America as a "barbaric country" would have strongly in-

fluenced Stravinsky, especially before he had made his first voyage. As Vera Stravinsky often mentioned, he was susceptible to believing most anything Diaghilev said when it came to cultural tastes. Diaghilev's quoted comments were originally reported by Tamara Geva in *Split Seconds: A Remembrance* (New York: Harper and Row, 1972), 349. Massine's impressions were recorded in Léonide Massine, *My Life in Ballet,* ed. Phyllis Hartnoll and Robert Rubens (London: Macmillan, 1968), 80.

3. Pitts Sanborn's article, "Honors of the Season," originally appeared in the June 1924 issue of the newspaper. The review is reprinted in *Stravinsky in Modern Music,* compiled and introduced by Carol J. Oja (New York: Da Capo, 1982), 5–8. For a more detailed recounting of Stravinsky's encounter with Gershwin, see Edward Jablonski, *Gershwin* (New York: Doubleday, 1987), 93–94.

4. See the chapters on *Apollo* in my forthcoming book on Stravinsky and Balanchine, to be published by Yale University Press in 2002. There is little question that Stravinsky studied the works of Maritain intently. For example, several works of the theologian are counted among the small portion of the composer's library that survives as part of the Sacher Stiftung, including *La Pensée de Saint Paul, Reflections on America,* and *Raissa Maritain: Les grandes amitiés.* But surely Stravinsky was familiar with a far greater range of Maritain's writings. The Stiftung also retains a file of correspondence exchanged between Stravinsky and Maritain.

5. On those few occasions when the Washington premiere of *Apollo* is mentioned in passing, its reporting is often inaccurate. When the work was first performed in Baltimore in 1949, a press release from Boosey & Hawkes stated that the actual ballet was originally produced by Diaghilev in Paris, and that only the concert version (that is, the undanced orchestral score) of *Apollo* was given in Washington in 1928. Even more recently, Pieter van den Toorn implies that Balanchine was the choreographer for the American commissioned work, but this too is incorrect (Pieter van den Toorn, *The Music of Igor Stravinsky* [New Haven: Yale University Press, 1983], 485). Even in such recently updated and standard biographies of Balanchine, such as Bernard Taper's, the Washington connection is not even mentioned, though Balanchine, as we shall see, was clearly aware of and influenced by the American commission.

6. American composers had been commissioned to write ballets before, but not composers from the Old World, and certainly none with the status of Stravinsky. On Stravinsky's "first completed American commission," to be accurate, the composer was approached during his American tour by the Brunswick gramophone firm about recording some of his piano music. This gave him the idea of composing the *Serenade en la.* Whether or not this constituted a true commission, the work was not recorded by Brunswick but rather by French Columbia almost a decade later.

7. Los Angeles Philharmonic Orchestra program notes of February 1935, by Bruno Ussher, retained in Stravinsky's private papers in Basel. It is quite unusual not to find reviews of almost any performance in the archives inasmuch as the composer clipped and marked virtually any critical press review. Yet there is nothing from the reviews (discussed later in this chapter) of the Washington performance found in the archives.

8. Igor Stravinsky, *An Autobiography* (New York: W. W. Norton, 1962), 141. The English translation of *Chroniques de ma vie* was first published in 1936 by Simon and Schuster.

9. Virgil Thomson, "The Official Stravinsky" (review of Stravinsky's *Chroniques de ma vie* of 1935), *Modern Music* 12 (May–June 1936): 57–58.

10. Igor Stravinsky and Robert Craft, *Dialogues* (Berkeley: University of California Press, 1982; rev. ed. of *Dialogues and a Diary,* Garden City, N.Y.: Doubleday, 1963), 32.

11. Correspondence between Stravinsky and Gavril Grigorievich Païchadze (who often acted as the composer's business representative) is held in the Sacher archives. A brief portion of this 1928 letter appears in *SPD,* 200.

12. Coolidge's association with the chamber music genre arose from her own sense of pragmatism—something Stravinsky would have appreciated. As Coolidge scholar Cyrilla Barr notes, Coolidge's "reasons for devoting herself so exclusively to this intimate medium stem partly from her eagerness to participate in the music making herself, and partly from a desire to retain a degree of control that would not be realistic in the case of opera or symphonic music" (Cyrilla Barr, "A Style of Her Own: Reflections on the Patronage of Elizabeth Sprague Coolidge," in *Cultivating Music in America,* ed. Cyrilla Barr and Ralph Locke [Berkeley: University of California Press, 1997]). For the most authoritative discussion of Coolidge's life, see Cyrilla Barr, *Elizabeth Sprague Coolidge: American Patron of Music,* with a foreword by Gunther Schuller (New York: Schirmer Books, 1998), published in cooperation with the music division of the Library of Congress. I wish to thank Professor Barr for her generous help in sharing many of the unpublished comments reprinted here.

13. Constitution Hall, with a seating capacity well over three thousand, was originally intended by the Daughters of the American Revolution as a convention center and was made available for concerts only in 1930. Nine years later, the famous occasion of Marian Anderson singing on the steps of the Lincoln Memorial because she was not permitted to appear in Constitution Hall is remembered as one of several early and wildly successful (the concert drew thousands) protests against racial segregation. The event is now beautifully captured by Mitchell Jameson's famous mural gracing the Department of the Interior.

14. As early as 1916 Coolidge established the Berkshire String Quartet (originally known as the Kortschak Quartet, consisting of members of the Chicago Symphony Orchestra), and within a year she began plans for a series of concerts to be given at South Mountain in the Berkshires of Massachusetts, near her Pittsfield summer home. She funded the building of the "Temple of Music," literally a shrine to chamber music, and in 1918 the first Berkshire Festival of Chamber Music was held. The festival grew in importance over the next several years, encouraging Coolidge to expand her scope by establishing her foundation at the Library of Congress. Coolidge was committed to musicological scholarship as well. She procured numerous important holographs for the Library that still serve the scholarly community interested in retracing the composer's creative process. Many of the holdings in Washington far surpass the status of fair copies. Sketches, revisions, commentaries, corrections by publishers, and even a few unpublished materials are available. Stravinsky himself "donated" (clearly for tax purposes, since the gifts were regularly made in December of various years) more than forty important manuscripts ranging from some early pianola transcriptions for *Petrushka* to proofs of the 1964 Huxley *Variations.* Quite naturally, the holograph for *Apollon Musagètes,* signed and dated "Nice le 20 janvier 1928," is included in the collection. For a complete listing of Stravinsky's works held in Washington, see Charles M. Joseph, "Stravinsky Manuscripts in the Library of Congress and the Pierpont Morgan Library," *Journal of Musicology* 1 (July 1982): 327–37.

15. The letter to Engel is dated September 1926 and is reproduced in Cyrilla Barr's

"The 'Faerie Queene' and the 'Archangel': The Correspondence of Elizabeth Sprague Coolidge and Carl Engel," *American Music* 15/2 (summer 1997): 159–82.

16. These documents are found in various uncataloged files marked "Stravinsky Old Correspondence," "Bolm Old Correspondence," and simply the "Coolidge Collection." I wish to express my gratitude to Gillian Anderson of the Library of Congress for directing me to these important source materials.

17. In his classic article "Music in the Ballet," Arthur Berger unknowingly reinforced Stravinsky's claim that Coolidge had permitted the composer "to write in any form he chose" and that he had independently "settled on a ballet" (Arthur Berger, "Music in the Ballet," in *Stravinsky in the Theatre*, ed. Minna Lederman [New York: Da Capo, 1975], 44). This misconception is frequently repeated, most recently in Paul Griffiths, *Stravinsky* (New York: Schirmer Books, 1992), 96, which states, "*Apollo* need not have been a ballet at all, since Elizabeth Sprague Coolidge had merely commissioned a half-hour instrumental score." The fact is, Stravinsky was free to choose the subject of the ballet, but a ballet it had to be.

18. Stravinsky and Falla were friends too. Nowhere in their correspondence, at least, is there any indication that Stravinsky was ever aware that Falla had been asked first, nor does Falla seem to have told Stravinsky of Coolidge's earlier invitation. Engel's May 1927 letter to Coolidge is reprinted in Barr, "The 'Faerie Queene' and the 'Archangel,'" 182.

19. *SPD*, 275. The excerpt is taken from a 2 December 1927 interview in *L'Intransigeant*.

20. Lincoln Kirstein, *Dance* (Princeton, N.J.: Dance Horizons Princeton Book Company, 1987), 317.

21. Stravinsky, *An Autobiography*, 142.

22. Ibid.

23. See Suzanne Carbonneau, "Adolph Bolm in America," in *The Ballets Russes and Its World*, ed. Nancy Van Norman Baer and Lynn Garafola (New Haven: Yale University Press, 1999).

24. Bolm's letter is dated 8 July 1940: "To Whom It May Concern: [Stravinsky's] admission to the United States of America as a permanent resident would be a just tribute to his genius and to this country it would mean a most valuable addition to its cultural and educational development."

25. The letter is reproduced in *SPD*, 273.

26. Cyrilla Barr shared this letter with me.

27. Lincoln Kirstein mistakenly claims that four Muses were employed (see Kirstein, *Dance*, 317). Actually, given the prominence of Apollo's lyre in the scenario, it seems at least plausible that Stravinsky might have considered including Melpomene, the Muse of lyre-playing, though there is no corroboration in any extant document as to whom the fourth muse might have been. Bolm claimed that his staging of *Apollo* was precisely what Stravinsky had in mind, although there is not a shred of proof to signal any Stravinskyan approval or disapproval of a single aspect of the Coolidge premiere.

28. Kindler and his wife Alice were on familiar terms with "Elizabeth," as they cordially referred to Coolidge. One gets the impression from reading much of their unpublished correspondence that the production of *Apollo* and the other ballets was very much an internal, family affair with Stravinsky being "acquired" for his international fame. The piano reduction was not really a reduction at all but rather an accurate pro-

jection of how Stravinsky envisioned the music from the start, including the first indications of curtains and other stage directions. Virtually everything that initially appeared in the materials sent to Washington was retained for the Diaghilev production in Paris. As for Kindler's editing, see Charles Rosen, "The Frontiers of Nonsense," in *The Frontiers of Meaning* (New York: Hill and Wang, 1994), 12–13.

29. The Mayoral interview, taken from "Le Veu de Catalunya," is translated by Malcolm Macdonald and reprinted in *Igor and Vera Stravinsky: A Photograph Album, 1921–1971* (New York: Thames and Hudson, 1982), 17–18. Frederick Jacobi, "The New Apollo," *Modern Music* 5/4 (May–June 1928), 11; Lawrence Gilman, untitled review in the *New York Tribune*, 30 April 1928.

30. Oscar Thompson, "Stravinsky Goes Astray Again," *New York Sun*, 28 April 1928.

31. Page had commissioned and danced to Balanchine's choreography of some Scriabin music two years earlier in Monte Carlo, when she was briefly affiliated with Diaghilev's company. She also danced with Bolm and his Chicago company, including in 1922 a performance of Saint-Saëns's "Danse macabre," preserved in a film held in the Dance Collection in the New York Public Library for the Performing Arts at Lincoln Center.

32. Stravinsky and Coolidge did finally meet during the spring of 1940 at a dinner party she gave in his honor following a New York concert organized to raise funds for the French War Relief effort (*SSC II*, 393). Ever on the lookout for sponsorship, Stravinsky apparently raised the idea of her commissioning what would become his Symphony in C for the Chicago Symphony, a composition that was written on both sides of the Atlantic, the first two movements in Paris and the final two in the United States. Certainly Stravinsky was aware of the Chicago connection with Coolidge; but perhaps with the composer's indifference toward the Washington *Apollo* still fresh in her mind, Coolidge chose not to commission the work (it was commissioned by Mrs. Robert Woods Bliss, commemorating the fiftieth anniversary of the orchestra).

33. Remisoff also was a friend and associate of Bolm, having worked with him as recently as 1926 in providing scenery for Bolm's productions. Coolidge's association with Chicago, especially through her philanthropic support of the Chicago Symphony Orchestra, naturally added to the "Chicago connection" with the Washington production.

34. John Martin, "The Dance—4 Ballets in a Season Review," *New York Times*, 6 May 1928, 7. Martin had joined the paper as its first full-time dance critic only a year earlier.

Chapter 3: Fathers and Sons

1. Stephen Walsh, *Stravinsky: A Creative Spring* (New York: Alfred A. Knopf, 1999), 55. Walsh's source, as cited on p. 563, n. 24, is Victor Varuntz, ed., *I. F. Stravinsky: Perepiska s russkimi korrespondentami. Materialï k biographi*, volume 1 (Moscow: Kompozitor, 1997), 39.

2. Igor Stravinsky and Robert Craft, *Memories and Commentaries* (Berkeley: University of California Press, 1981; orig. pub. Garden City, N.Y.: Doubleday, 1960), 19–20.

3. Janet Flanner reported in the *New Yorker* for 5 January 1935 that Igor Stravinsky's legal name was Igor Fyodorovich Soulima-Stravinsky, with the "Soulima" trace-

able to the Polish counts of Soulima from which his father had descended. But an examination of the composer's birth and baptismal certificates now held in the Sacher Stiftung do not corroborate this. I wish to thank Victor Varuntz of the Moscow Conservatory for sharing this examination of the documents with me. Soulima's full name was Sviatoslav-Soulima Igorievich Stravinsky.

4. Walsh, *Stravinsky: A Creative Spring,* 531.

5. Interview with Soulima Stravinsky by Marvin Weisbord, "The Way to the Future," *Etude,* July 1954. *Etude* was a popular magazine for pianists.

6. Interview with Soulima Stravinsky by Gunnar Asklung, "What Makes a Composer Great," *Etude,* September 1949.

7. "Memoirs of the Late Princesse Edmond de Polignac," *Horizon* 12 (August 1945): 134–35.

8. Stravinsky seems to have had several affairs during the early 1920s, not only with Sudeikina, but also with Gabrielle Chanel, Zhenia Nikitina, and others. His most embarrassing tryst was with Dagmar Godowsky (in the late 1930s), the one-time silver-screen love interest of Rudolph Valentino. Godowsky (daughter of Leopold, the famous pianist) later knew Stravinsky in Hollywood.

9. Arlene Croce concludes that Vera was Stravinsky's "only Muse?"—or, as Boris Kochno apparently referred to Vera, the "Muse of Muses" (Arlene Croce, "Is the Muse Dead?" *New Yorker* [26 February–4 March 1996]: 164). Croce's description of Catherine as no more than Stravinsky's "first cousin and closest woman friend," who "raised a family" for him, is coldly dismissive. Until the end of his life, Stravinsky (often in expurgated letters and film clips) looked nostalgically back to his happy early years with his first wife, to whom, as late as 1925, he dedicated *"a ma femme"* his *Serenade en la.* He continued to preview for her each new composition.

Croce quotes from Vera's checklist, "Duties of an Artist's Wife" (found in John E. Bowlt's sumptuously illustrated *The Salon Album of Vera Sudeikin-Stravinsky* [Princeton: Princeton University Press, 1995], xv), written during the early years of her marriage to Serge Sudeikin. These obligations included everything from "forcing the artist to work" to keeping herself "physically perfect, and, therefore, his model forever." Bowlt's album includes on page 98 a wonderful ink-on-paper sketch of poetry and a line of music written for Vera by Stravinsky and Kochno in September 1921, just a few days before Diaghilev invited Vera to play the Queen in his new staging of *The Sleeping Princess* (and by which time Stravinsky was already in love with her). The sketch is also reproduced in *Igor and Vera Stravinsky: A Photograph Album, 1921–1971* (New York: Thames and Hudson, 1982), but Bowlt's insightful comments throughout his album are worth consulting.

10. Letter of 18 August 1921 (*SSC III,* 62).

11. Louis Andriessen and Elmer Schönberger, *The Apollonian Clockwork: On Stravinsky,* trans. Jeff Hamburg (New York: Oxford University Press, 1989), 127.

12. Interview with Soulima Stravinsky, "The Way to the Future."

13. The Concerto for Piano and Winds serves as an illustration. Richard Taruskin traces Stravinsky's writing to certain "violinistic *bariolage* effects," seen so often in Bach, as models for some of his piano writing (Richard Taruskin, *Text and Act* [New York: Oxford University Press, 1995], 117–29). To go further, the precise "figural" differences between the Piano Concerto and the Bach keyboard concertos that Taruskin cites arise directly from Stravinsky's unidiomatic pianism. Just as much as the rhythmic and metric features that Taruskin rightly labels Stravinskyan, the idiosyncratic pi-

anistic passagework could not possibly have been employed by any other composer. Literally, Stravinsky's "hand" is present as a distinguishing stylistic trait, and this should not be overlooked in understanding how the composition was put together. Even in matters as refined as pitch selection (discussed so often by music theorists), he willingly broke free from abstract, precompositional pitch collections if, in fact, certain "vagrant" notes more comfortably fit his hand—an important consideration in balancing Stravinsky's "intellectual" and instinctive sides (discussed in Chapters 7 and 8).

14. Lillian Libman, *And Music at the Close: Stravinsky's Last Years* (New York: W. W. Norton, 1972), 237.

15. The father began using Soulima as his substitute in concerts where the public wanted to see the more famous Stravinsky. In a letter to Willy Strecker dated 1 February 1936, Stravinsky complained that he really would prefer not to have to play his *Capriccio* in a concert Strecker was arranging, since he hadn't performed it in a while and it would take too much time to relearn. This much of the letter is reprinted in Craft's edited version of Stravinsky's correspondence (SSC III, 240). What is not included (there is an ellipsis) is Stravinsky's suggestion that Soulima "play either the *Capriccio* or *Piano Concerto*. This would be infinitely more agreeable to me." It was agreeable to Strecker as well, who responded that the most important issue was that the elder Stravinsky participate in the concert in some way. One must be particularly careful in reading Craft's edited correspondence involving any favorable mention of Soulima. Generally, as Walsh also notes in his biography, positive "remarks about Stravinsky's children are omitted from SSC" (Walsh, *Stravinsky: A Creative Spring*, 656n.35).

16. Pound's August 1934 review is reprinted in R. Murray Schafer, ed., *Ezra Pound and Music* (New York: New Directions, 1977), 371–72.

17. Still, several letters in the Sacher Stiftung reveal that Stravinsky continued to send money to his children to cover various domestic expenses. He did so even into the 1960s, cursing his children privately to his friends, but feeling the obligation to support them (and by his own words, as a means of living with his conscience as a father).

18. "What Makes a Composer Great," *Etude,* 17.

19. Robert Craft, *Present Perspectives* (New York: Alfred A. Knopf, 1984), 313–85. Moreover, one of Stravinsky's attorneys, interviewed by Palmer (although the lawyer's remarks were entirely cut), claimed that the composer never even mentioned his children after 1947, mainly because Stravinsky felt they were conspiring against him to obtain his manuscripts. But the fact is, as late as 1966 in a public forum held at the Eastman School of Music in Rochester, New York, Stravinsky spoke openly and fondly of his son Soulima. Regrettable as the escalating rhetoric between attorneys and clients became, it was indicative of the nearly complete breakdown in formal relations between father and children. In yet another deleted section of Palmer's film, Soulima says his father wanted to stay in California to the end, adding, "and I know that he suffered from going back to New York when they took him to New York despite his desire to stay and not be bothered." Madeleine Milhaud, composer Darius Milhaud's wife, concurred, saying (in still one more Palmer trim) that "going away from Hollywood at that moment was a tragedy for him [at the end of 1969] since he missed Milene."

20. *Daily Telegraph* (London), 2 December 1994, 29. Pierre Suvchinsky accused Soulima of being a "Nazi collaborator" in comments recorded by Craft in 1956 and reprinted in Robert Craft, *Stravinsky: Chronicle of a Friendship,* revised and expanded

edition (Nashville: Vanderbilt University Press, 1994), 152–53. Suvchinsky claimed that Soulima wrote music for Nazi propaganda films and requested that Willy Strecker arrange concerts for him in Germany during the war; but Suvchinsky's feelings about Soulima and the other Stravinsky children by the 1960s are not surprising. And, as mentioned earlier, there is ample archival evidence to suggest that it was Igor who quietly but actively sought acceptance by Hitler's regime through Strecker, at a time when Soulima was still very much under his father's wing.

21. Letter from Ivan Turgenev to A. A. Fet, 18 April 1862, reprinted in A. V. Knowles, ed., *Turgenev's Letters* (New York: Scribner's, 1983), 103.

Chapter 4: The Would-Be Hollywood Composer

1. Christopher Isherwood, *Diaries,* vol. 1 (1939–1960), ed. Katherine Bucknell (London: HarperCollins, 1996), xii. By the time Isherwood began writing *Prater Violet,* he had worked on the Paramount lot, assisting in Somerset Maugham's *The Hour Before Dawn,* one of several Maugham scripts Isherwood rewrote for the screen.

2. Ibid., 53.

3. Christopher Isherwood, "Los Angeles," *Horizon,* October 1947, 144.

4. The exchange survives among the correspondence of Stravinsky and Cendrars preserved in the Sacher Stiftung. Cendrars had known Stravinsky since around 1917 and was interested in publishing Stravinsky's compositions at Editions de la Sirène, a publishing house he was directing. Picasso, Matisse, Apollinaire, Cocteau, and other luminaries were among the artists he wished to represent. Cendrars published the famous Picasso drawing (depicting two musicians) as the cover for the composer's 1919 *Ragtime*—one of Stravinsky's early instrumental attempts in the jazz idiom.

5. Bolm bumptiously added that a "crowd of 18 to 20 thousand people acclaimed *Usine* [one of his ballets] in the famous Amphytheatre!" He outlined the prospect of forming his own company, apprising Stravinsky of his intention to engage forty to fifty dancers and choreographers "who will assist me in mounting ballets and dancing some of the principal roles. We will prepare new works, as well as the great standards." Bolm was eager to have Stravinsky compose something for the fledgling company, but the composer surely leaped over his friend's invitation, sensing the potential for his own personal advancement by tapping the same Hollywood cache underwriting Bolm's venture.

6. Aldous Huxley, *The Doors of Perception, and Heaven and Hell* (London: Grafton, 1956), 130; P. G. Wodehouse, *Laughing Gas* (London: Penguin, 1957), 26.

7. Lillian Libman, *And Music at the Close: Stravinsky's Last Years* (New York: W. W. Norton, 1972), 328.

8. George Antheil, "Composer in Movieland," *Modern Music,* (January–February 1935): 62–68.

9. SSC III, 263. Strecker's response cautioned Stravinsky in negotiating with Disney. As early as 1932, Warner Brothers had approached the composer about incorporating sections of the popular ballet into various films. Indeed a film did appear in America about this time using Stravinsky's music. The composer sued, but to no avail, winning a judgment in France, where he still resided, for the token sum of one franc. Nor was *Firebird* the only well-known score finding its way into commercial release. More than twenty years later, excerpts from *Petrushka* were used for an animated tele-

vision cartoon, in the mid-1950s. Stravinsky describes in some detail those portions of the score used for the synchronized soundtrack in a 27 February 1956 letter to Boulanger held by the Sacher Stiftung (a translation of which appears in *SSC I*, 397).

10. The original contract is retained at the Sacher Institute in Stravinsky's unpublished Disney file. Disney's memory was also faulty. The contract confirms that he never offered Stravinsky ten thousand dollars, as he asserted. Stravinsky's claim that he received only five thousand dollars and distributed it to a "dozen" intermediaries is also erroneous. He received six thousand dollars and shared a small part of the stipend not with a dozen but with two other parties.

Disney's license to use *Le Sacre du printemps* as part of *Fantasia* was again recently disputed. The Walt Disney Company and Buena Vista Home Video were taken to court by Stravinsky's assignee, Boosey & Hawkes, for the distribution in foreign countries of the videocassette and laser disc version of the movie. The United States Court of Appeals for the Second Circuit vacated the initial judgment and in April 1998 decided that Disney's distribution was permissible. Stravinsky's 1939 contract with Disney is reprinted and analyzed by the court in its rendering. Details of the original agreement, as well as a summary of the more recent case, are available on the Internet at http://law.touro.edu/2ndCircuit/April98.

11. Dorothy Thompson, review of *Fantasia* in the *Cincinnati Enquirer*, 25 November 1940. Thompson seemed especially eager to lambaste Disney's work generally: "Snow White was not the dream child of innocence; she was a step removed from a little Hollywood floozy with Max Factor makeup." One shudders to think what the reviewer would have thought of Mae West's quip (as remembered by Joseph Weintraub in *The Wit and Wisdom of Mae West*): "The only picture that made money recently was *Snow White and the Seven Dwarfs*, and that would have made twice as much if they had let me play Snow White."

The specter of *Fantasia* still haunted Stravinsky thirty years after Disney had appropriated his music. Unpublished letters in the Sacher archives dating from 1969 indicate that Disney once again approached the composer about using his music, this time for an audio recording based on the original soundtrack for *Fantasia*. Given the composer's earlier acrimonious dealings with Disney, one might reasonably assume that Stravinsky would have rejected the idea outright, but he didn't. Inexplicably, a new agreement with Disney for further film productions was signed, based on—of all things—even more Russian folk compositions: *Firebird, Fireworks,* and *Renard.* This time, however, an ironclad contract was prepared, ensuring that Stravinsky would maintain the rights to approve cuts, supervise the reshuffling of segments, and in general be consulted about all production matters.

Even as the new millennium began, the Stravinsky-Disney film connection continued. The well over $100 million production of *Fantasia 2000* opened at IMAX theaters throughout the world on 1 January 2000. It was, as Disney's producer and nephew Roy Disney proclaimed, an update of the original, just as his uncle had always planned (indeed, a sequel had been planned immediately after the 1940 original, but it proved a financial nightmare). Now it is James Levine conducting the Chicago Symphony, rather than Stokowski and Philadelphia. And except for the retention of Mickey Mouse's bewitching performance as the Sorcerer's Apprentice, all the sequences and music are new. Among the "updated" composers are Elgar, Gershwin, Respighi, Saint-Saëns, Shostakovich, and, yes, Stravinsky. It is not the volcanic *Rite of Spring* that chronicles the birth of Planet Earth, however, as it did in the original, but rather another Stravinsky ballet, The Firebird—at least the closing moments of the ever popular work (used here to depict the rebirth of nature).

12. Norman Lebrecht, The Maestro Myth (New York: Citadel Press, 1995), 140.

13. Igor Stravinsky, An Autobiography (New York: W. W. Norton, 1962), 72–73. The composer's remarks were offered in the context of explaining his rationale in writing the theatrically conceived L'Histoire du soldat.

14. Hanns Eisler, Composing for the Films (New York: Oxford University Press, 1947), 8–9.

15. Igor Stravinsky and Robert Craft, Memories and Commentaries (Berkeley: University of California Press, 1981; orig. pub. Garden City, N.Y.: Doubleday, 1960), 109.

16. Charles Chaplin, My Autobiography (New York: Penguin, 1992), 390–91. Stravinsky's correspondence with Sam Dushkin in late 1937 and early 1938 reveals how eager the composer was to collaborate with Chaplin. In several letters, he begged Dushkin's intercession in determining whether Chaplin (who seems not to have answered Stravinsky's inquiries) is still interested in a joint project. Chaplin was also friends with Arnold Schoenberg, whose music he seems also to have admired.

17. George Antheil, "On the Hollywood Front," Modern Music 14 (November–December 1936): 46–47. In fact it was Isherwood who was to write the screenplay of a Chopin movie, not for Columbia but for MGM, where he signed a contract in 1940. He studied the correspondence of Chopin and George Sand, hoping to dramatize their "secret" relationship in the movie, although the project was later abandoned. Antheil constantly wished to attach himself to Stravinsky, often writing letters that the composer found "idiotic," just as he looked unfavorably on Antheil's comments in his intentionally provocative 1945 book, Bad Boy of Music.

18. The unpublished letter is quoted in Aaron Copland and Vivian Perlis, Copland: 1900 Through 1942 (New York: St. Martin's/Marek, 1984), 271. Materials in the Sacher Stiftung demonstrate that Stravinsky and Morros discussed several projects, including a proposed film titled The Knights of St. David, though as usual nothing came of the idea.

19. Aaron Copland, "Second Thoughts on Hollywood," Modern Music 17 (March–April, 1940): 141–42.

20. Stravinsky's adaptation of folk songs in Scherzo à la russe is discussed in Richard Taruskin, Stravinsky and the Russian Traditions, vol. 2 (Berkeley: University of California Press, 1996), 1624–32. Taruskin claims that the compositional sketches are "unusual among the pencil drafts . . . [since] they are written not on staves of his own ruling, but on standard-format music paper issued by the film studio" (1626). In fact, sketches for many works of this period were written on commercial manuscript paper, including the 1945 Ebony Concerto, for Woody Herman's band (in those sketches, several harmonic progressions were provided as models by someone familiar with the jazz idiom, and written on the lined manuscript paper Stravinsky used for his sketching).

As for The North Star, Copland never mentioned Stravinsky's original involvement. The picture was a multimillion-dollar project for Samuel Goldwyn and was enthusiastically endorsed by the U.S. Office of War Information. The film included such celebrities as Anne Baxter, Dana Andrews, Walter Huston, and Walter Brennan. Copland wrote to Boulanger in 1943: "The film I am doing calls for a great variety of music—songs, choruses, orchestral interludes, etc. It is like having a new toy to play with. But in Hollywood, one never can foretell the result. In my case I am learning a lot—

excellent preparation for operatic writing!" For a detailed account of Copland's involvement, see "The War Years, 1943–1945," in Aaron Copland and Vivian Perlis, *Copland: Since 1943* (New York: St. Martin's Press, 1989), 13–23.

21. Robert Craft, ed. *Dearest Bubushkin: The Correspondence of Vera and Igor Stravinsky, 1921–1954,* trans. Lucia Davidova (New York: Thames and Hudson, 1985), 125.

22. Edward Jablonski, *Gershwin* (New York: Doubleday, 1987), 168. Though Stravinsky denied that the conversation ever took place (suggesting instead that Gershwin approached Ravel, not him), Jablonski adds that Richard Hammond, a friend of the composer's, was present and confirmed the exchange.

23. Robert R. Faulkner, *Music on Demand: Composers and Careers in the Hollywood Film Industry* (New Brunswick, N.J.: Transaction Books, 1983), 2. Faulkner further reports that Newman would often help his fellow film composers when they were unable to come up with a "suitable melody in a particularly troublesome score." Newman would "dash off a few bars on sketch paper, and hand the tune over to the composer." One cannot conceive of Stravinsky participating in such an act of cooperation—on either the giving or the receiving end.

24. Igor Stravinsky and Robert Craft, *Dialogues* (Berkeley: University of California Press, 1982; rev. ed. of *Dialogues and a Diary,* Garden City, N.Y.: Doubleday, 1963), 51. A fuller description of Stravinsky's remembrances of the sources that inspired this film music appears at 50–52.

25. The film score for *Jane Eyre* was eventually completed by Bernard Herrmann. Stravinsky attended the film in 1944, and he remained on friendly terms with the film composer during this period, rating his talents "very highly," according to Vera Stravinsky's diary. Herrmann, who also composed the score for *Citizen Kane,* was one of the leading Hollywood composers of the time and a friend of Copland from their days together in Tanglewood. Herrmann's association with Alfred Hitchcock (whom Stravinsky also knew and liked very much) was a long one, producing many well-known film scores for such movies as *The Wrong Man* and *North by Northwest.* Perhaps most memorable is Herrmann's score for Hitchcock's *Psycho* (1960), especially the screeching strings used to accompany the famous blood-drenched shower scene with Janet Leigh.

26. For excellent summaries of Huxley's career as a music critic, see Basil Hogarth, "Aldous Huxley as Music Critic," *Musical Times* 76/1103 (December 1935): 1079–82, and John Alpin, "Aldous Huxley and Music in the 1920s," *Music and Letters* 64/1–2 (January–April 1983): 25–36. Huxley was not the only member of the "Bloomsburys" who attended concerts of Stravinsky's music and published reviews. Writing in the *Nation & Athenaeum* of 17 November 1928, Virginia Woolf reviewed a staged performance of *The Tale of a Soldier.* "Like all highly original work, it begins by destroying one's conceptions, and only by degrees builds them up again," she wrote, adding that the performance was a welcome chance to hear music that was too seldom performed.

27. David King Dunaway, *Huxley in Hollywood* (New York: Harper, 1989), 67. The letters from Maria Huxley to Jeanne Neveux are dated August 1937 and October 1938.

28. Ibid., 242.

29. Interview with Isherwood by David King Dunaway, 2 June 1985 (Dunaway, *Huxley in Hollywood,* 178).

30. "Igor Stravinsky on Film Music," *Musical Digest* 28/1 (September 1946): 35. If Stravinsky's mordancy about "mass culture" seems harsh, it is nothing compared

with his friend Huxley's, who wrote that moviegoers are "more than likely plain, have an insufficient or unromantic sex life; are married and wish they weren't, or unmarried and wish they were; are too old or too young; in a word, are themselves and not somebody else. Hence those Don Juans, those melting beauties, those innocent young kittens, those beautifully brutal boys, those luscious adventuresses. Hence Hollywood." Quoted in Dunaway, *Huxley in Hollywood,* 87; originally from Huxley's *The Olive Tree and Other Essays.*

31. David Raksin, "Hollywood Strikes Back," *Musical Digest* 30/1 (January 1948): 5–7. Raksin first came to Hollywood in 1935 to work with Charlie Chaplin on the film score for *Modern Times.* A versatile musician, he wrote music for more than a hundred films and three hundred television shows. He is probably best remembered for his score to the horror movie *Carrie,* and earlier for his memorable music to Otto Preminger's film noir, *Laura* (1944). Preminger originally had planned to use Duke Ellington's "Sophisticated Lady" as the musical theme, but Raksin refused and composed the singable "Laura" tune over a weekend. He also prepared numerous arrangements for radio broadcasts, including the imaginative version of Gershwin's "I've Got Rhythm" performed by Oscar Levant.

Ironically, Raksin was once employed by Stravinsky to prepare the band arrangement for *Circus Polka,* and it was that arrangement that Barnum and Bailey used in the production of a Balanchine ballet for which Stravinsky wrote the farcical music. Mr. Raksin told me that Stravinsky had first approached Robert Russell Bennett about preparing the instrumentation for the ballet. When the always busy Bennett (one of the most sought-after orchestrators in Hollywood) declined, Raksin was contacted. He and Stravinsky met often and struck up a warm relationship. Indeed, over half a century after their very public dispute, Raksin remembers with great fondness his friendship with Stravinsky as they worked together between vodka toasts and frequent Russian meals. "His mind was like an attic," Raksin remembered. "Everywhere you looked there were precious ideas to be rediscovered or explored." But Raksin also recalled that Stravinsky knew little about writing for band. There were frequent discussions about how woodwinds could be used effectively, about the balance of instruments, and even about the possibility of using a Hammond organ as a circus-like instrument for the band arrangement. Raksin also claimed that Stravinsky endorsed the descriptive program notes that Dahl had written for the Symphony in Three Movements. Although Stravinsky always adamantly denied this, in fact Raksin's memory is accurate.

32. Unpublished letters of Roth and Powell, 5 and 12 January 1953. Stravinsky did respond, expressing interest and stipulating conditions, but the deal was never made.

33. Christopher Isherwood, *Prater Violet* (London: Minerva, 1946), 77. Other film prospects continued to arise even into the 1960s, and the composer continued to consider them.

Chapter 5: Television and *The Flood*

1. William Boddy, "The Beginnings of American Television," in *Television: An International History,* ed. Anthony Smith (New York: Oxford University Press, 1995), 40. The decade preceding the 1962 broadcast of *The Flood* was an especially eventful one in television's growth, and it shaped the environment into which Stravinsky's new work would be born: in 1952 alone, NBC's *Today Show* was first broadcast; Richard Nixon's infamous "Checkers the dog" speech was aired; television's first soap opera, *The Guid-*

ing Light on CBS, was premiered; and the first nationally televised complete coverage of both the Democratic and Republican party conventions was broadcast. Other important milestones included Edward R. Murrow's confrontation with Joseph McCarthy in a 1954 *See It Now* broadcast; videotape was first used in 1956 (and in fact was employed for the one and only broadcast of *The Flood* six years later, although viewers were led to believe that the performance was live); television cameras followed Dwight D. Eisenhower's deployment of troops to Little Rock in 1957 to assure school integration, the same year that *American Bandstand* began broadcasting daily from Philadelphia. And by 1960, seventy million people watched the Nixon-Kennedy debates. It was into this powerful medium that Stravinsky was about to enter.

2. Richard Franko Goldman, "Current Chronicle," *Musical Quarterly* 48 (October 1962): 514–17.

3. Jack Gould, "The Future of OMNIBUS," *New York Times,* 24 February 1957, sec. 2, p. 11. Gould later observed, in reviewing a television production of *Romeo and Juliet,* that there simply was no chance of Shakespeare competing with Lucille Ball and George Burns.

4. The first interview, with Robert Lewis Shayon, was given in *Saturday Review,* 16 June 1962. The second was published two weeks later in the 30 June 1962 issue.

5. Christopher Isherwood, *Diaries,* vol. 1 (1939–1960), ed. Katherine Bucknell (London: HarperCollins, 1996), 866.

6. Ibid., 847.

7. Igor Stravinsky and Robert Craft, *Dialogues* (Berkeley: University of California Press, 1982; rev. ed. of *Dialogues and a Diary,* Garden City, N.Y.: Doubleday, 1963), 79.

8. Interview with Balanchine by Bernard Taper, "Television and Ballet," included in *The Eighth Art,* by Eugene Burdick (New York: Holt, Rinehart, Winston, 1962), 118. See also Edward Villella with Larry Kaplan, *Prodigal Son* (New York: Simon and Schuster, 1992), in which one of television's most popular classical male dancers in those early days speaks often of his interactions with the medium. In a 1979 interview with Balanchine, Don McDonagh remembers that the choreographer often turned down opportunities to present his company on *The Ed Sullivan Hour* and other nationally known programs. "He didn't like the way that the camera made the dancers' noses and feet long and their legs short," wrote McDonagh in his biography *George Balanchine* (Boston: Twayne Publishers, 1983), 118.

9. Arthur Todd, "What Went Wrong," *Dance Magazine* 36 (August 1962). Balanchine's comments were offered during the CBS taping of the choreography. As Todd reported, "Quite naturally [Balanchine] has envisaged the movement only to enhance and enliven the score, but never to illustrate it." Todd, who was a keen witness to the process as it unfolded, spoke of Balanchine always having the camera in mind, and by extension, of course, his concern for the viewer. Todd's excellent article includes Martha Swope's photographs of the taping—photographs not easily found in any other source. Stravinsky was not present at the taping. Todd sent his article along with the above-cited letter to Stravinsky on 20 August. In an unpublished letter to the composer, Todd reported on the taping: "Through the kindness of Mr. Balanchine, I spent some 17 hours in the CBS Studio watching the taping of *The Flood* sections, and it was indeed a memorable experience to watch Mr. Balanchine creating at first-hand." Some of Balanchine's choreographing was shown as part of the original broadcast. Despite Balanchine's enthusiasm, and regardless of his personal efforts to supervise the

dance segments, in the end he was just as dismayed as he had always been with television's inability to transmit the artistic message he envisaged. He told McDonagh that the taping of the choreographic sections was constantly under pressure from the director, and often flawed takes were used in the final film. McDonagh adds, "Balanchine had ideas for ways to use the new medium innovatively as well, but was overruled at almost every turn. In a way it was a repeat of his frustration in Hollywood thirty years previously" (McDonagh, *George Balanchine*, 118).

10. Lincoln Kirstein, *Thirty Years of the New York City Ballet* (New York: Alfred A. Knopf, 1978), 277, remarks made in June 1976. Kirstein also refers to Edward Mendelson's "surgical analysis of the conditions of television," as originally published in the *Times Literary Supplement* of the same month. Mendelson referred to the "drumbeat of the market message," the need to sell "more gas, beer, soap, or cars," always at the expense of the artistic message—an expense especially high for dance since its "three-dimensional plasticity is always deformed through the lens," and the built-in limitations of such a small screen. Finally, for a view from abroad, see A. H. Franks, "Television Ballet," *Ballet Annual* 14 (1960): 59–64, in which the author says of BBC productions: "Although it is understandable that people prefer to sit at home and look at rubbish rather than go out and pay money to look at rubbish in the cinema, general standards have gone down yet further in this transformation of our habits, for if we were to be faced in the cinema with an image of the same poor quality which we accept from the cathode tube, we should rise in a body and attack the manager."

11. Craft reprints this letter in *SPD*, 540–41.

12. Stravinsky and Craft, *Dialogues*, 72–80. None of these visions was successfully executed in the original broadcast. Paul Horgan, referring to the non-televised concert premiere in August 1962, felt that the concert performance of the work was actually "much more interesting than the version with visual effects seen over a television network early in the year [where] the work fulfilled its remarkable vision of man's primal earthly salvation entirely in the realm of sound, spoken, sung, played" (Paul Horgan, *Encounters with Stravinsky* [New York: Farrar, Straus & Giroux, 1972], 219). Perhaps the strangest visual realization of *The Flood* came in a bizarre studio adaptation in 1985, designed and directed by Jaap Drupsteen and produced by NOS-TV and the Stiftung Muzt, Amsterdam (now commercially distributed as a videotape through NVC Arts International). This Dutch production, with a psychedelic, computer-generated light show animating the work in the most vivid graphic images, actually employs the original 1962 "sound track" of the Columbia Symphony Orchestra and Chorus as conducted by Craft.

13. Robert Craft, *Present Perspectives* (New York: Alfred A. Knopf, 1984), 260. Indeed that manuscript, as well as others cited herein, are in the Craft Collection of the Sacher archives.

14. Igor Stravinsky and Robert Craft, *Expositions and Developments* (Berkeley: University of California Press, 1981; orig. pub. Garden City, N.Y.: Doubleday, 1962), 123–27.

15. The complete typescript, held by the Sacher Stiftung, is labeled "Meeting with Mr. Robert Graff," and is dated 4–6 May 1960. The content of this approximately one-thousand-word document provides many of the "missing" details for musicians who have long wondered how Stravinsky went about planning the flow of the composition. It is an invaluable source in understanding the genesis and the form of the work.

16. The article, dated November 1961, is reprinted in *SPD*, 465.

17. The detailed scenario is also held by the Sacher Stiftung as part of the Craft Collection. Once again it is an indispensable document for musicians studying the work's history.

18. Part of the letter is summarized in *SPD,* but the specifics, as detailed in a letter found in the Sacher archives, have gone unpublished.

19. Unpublished letters from Stravinsky to Graff, 21 February 1962, and Stravinsky to Liebermann, 22 March 1962. The Arutunian sketches are in the Sacher Stiftung. As it happens, Stravinsky's concern about the narrator was well founded, since problems often seemed to beset the part of the narrator in several subsequent performances.

20. Walter Terry's 15 June 1962 review of *The Flood* for the *Herald-Tribune* is reprinted in Mark Wentink, ed., *I Was There* (New York: Marcel Dekker, 1978), 417–18. Also see Arlene Croce's review of the 1972 restaging by the New York City Ballet, which was based on some of the original CBS videotapes, reprinted in Arlene Croce, *Sight Lines* (New York: Alfred A. Knopf, 1987), 60.

21. Benjamin Boretz served as music critic for *The Nation* during the 1960s, often writing about Stravinsky's music. His review of *The Flood* originally appeared in the 28 July 1962 issue and was reprinted as "Stravinsky: A Flood of Genius" in the January 1963 issue of *London Magazine.*

22. Jack Gould, "Noah Submerged—Program Shows a Lack of Cooperation Between TV and Leaders in Arts" (review of *The Flood*), *New York Times,* 24 June 1962.

23. Goldman, "Current Chronicle," 516.

24. One of the more perceptive reviews of the performance appeared in *Time,* 22 June 1962: "The production—which resembles an oratorio in form—ran into trouble only because its diverse elements—orchestral music, song, narration, mime and dance—never quite had a chance to demonstrate their virtues in a massive production crammed into 21 minutes." The review was cut out, marked, and saved by Stravinsky.

Chapter 6: Film Documentaries

1. Quoted in A. William Bluem, *Documentary in American Television* (New York: Hastings House, 1965), 13.

2. A complete catalog of the composer's filmed appearances is impossible to compile. The task is complicated by the fact that many admirers made amateur films that were never released. Leonard Bernstein, as one notable cameraman, filmed Stravinsky frequently, and British filmmaker Tony Palmer attests that Bernstein showed him five different films, although none have been made available.

3. Stravinsky eventually accepted an advance of $3,500, a certain amount for television reruns, and a hefty 50 percent of all profits should the film become popular enough to be shown in movie theaters.

4. Craft reprints some of this outline in *Present Perspectives* (New York: Alfred A. Knopf, 1984), 271–72, although Stravinsky's responses as given there don't quite match the original typescript held by the Sacher Stiftung.

5. The CBC made several films on Stravinsky during the 1960s, and the Canadian National Film Board was one of the most active producers of documentaries worldwide during this period. John Grierson helped to establish the board during the late 1930s, later becoming its director.

6. Stephen Spender reports, in a 1962 conversation with Balanchine regarding

the tempi of sections in the ballet *Agon,* that the composer's conducting was difficult to follow because he was aging. "It's a matter of his arm," Balanchine says. "He begins quite right. The mind knows. But the muscles do not quite function. So he begins to get slow. It is a question of sickness, the muscles of the right side. But if one understands one can adjust oneself" (Stephen Spender, *Journals, 1939–1983,* ed. John Goldsmith [New York: Random House, 1986], 238). This conversation unfolded during a celebration for Stravinsky's eightieth birthday in Hamburg (while *The Flood* was being broadcast in the United States). Spender asked Craft if Stravinsky was tired: "'Not tired, just drunk.' Bob Craft said later . . . 'The last time he was sober was in Paris on March 17th.'"

7. See Suzanne Farrell, *Holding On to the Air* (New York: Summit Books, 1990), for her account of her relationship with Balanchine.

8. Most of the CBS film cans are preserved at the Sacher Stiftung. They were originally procured by Tony Palmer for his own Stravinsky documentary, and he reports that the cans were just "laying around" at CBS and that nobody seems to have known about them until a secretary found a discarded box containing the outtakes.

9. See, for example, Craft's "Sufferings and Humiliations of Catherine Stravinsky," which first appeared in *SSC I.* For a more recent and informative discussion of Stravinsky's relationship with his wife, based on previously unavailable documents, see Stephen Walsh, *Stravinsky: A Creative Spring* (New York: Alfred A. Knopf, 1999).

10. In one sequence of film, the musicians are asked to stay an extra half hour for an extended rehearsal. All agree, except for a young Doc Severinsen of *Tonight Show* fame, who raises an objection. The musicians are also instructed to wear the same clothes for all rehearsals so that CBS can create the illusion that the recording was accomplished in one sitting.

11. The final version of the documentary shows Stravinsky in the wings at the Chicago premiere. With score in hand, he listens, then comes on stage to take his bows. There are post-performance interviews in the concert hall lobby, in which people speak with excitement about this new "space age" music. In fact, the recording that is used in the film is not from the Chicago performance, but rather a recording by the Warsaw Philharmonic Orchestra with Craft conducting, as mentioned in the film credits.

12. Farrell, *Holding On to the Air,* 152.

13. Robert Craft, *Stravinsky: Chronicle of a Friendship,* revised and expanded edition (Nashville: Vanderbilt University Press, 1994), 31 May 1965, 421.

14. For the CBC documentary *The Life and Times of Igor Stravinsky,* many valuable interviews with such friends as Isherwood, Nicolas Nabokov, Vera Zorina, Balanchine, and others were conducted, but not all were incorporated into the final print of the thirteen one-hour programs.

15. The Educational Media Associates of America (Berkeley, California) programs consisted of ten segments released not on film but on fifteen stereo recordings. See *SPD,* 564, for a complete listing of the interviewees. Frédéric Mitterand has compiled the most recent documentary of the composer's life for French television, entitled *Les Grands amants du siècle.* The footage—some of which, according to Craft, is not to be found in any other film—is described in considerable detail in Robert Craft, *The Moment of Existence: Music, Literature, and the Arts, 1990–1995* (Nashville: Vanderbilt University, 1996), 265–71. Overall, his review of this French television film is mixed.

16. Charles Rosen is listed as the principal consultant for the production. A copy

of the audiotape is among the holdings of the Stravinsky/Diaghilev Foundation archive, held by the Harvard Theatre Collection.

17. I wish to thank Mr. Palmer for his cooperation in sharing many of the unpublished, behind-the-scenes details of the enormous undertaking of *Aspects of Stravinsky.* Palmer kindly met with me on 18 December 1991 in Zurich. He has directed several films on composers and performing artists, including Benjamin Britten, William Walton, Maria Callas, and more recently Yehudi Menuhin. He was especially pleased with his Stravinsky film because many of Stravinsky's friends are recorded here in what were to be some of their last interviews, including Lifar, Balanchine, Geva, Theodore Stravinsky, and Marie Rambert.

Palmer interviewed (or consulted previously filmed interviews with) around fifty individuals, including many family members, friends, and associates of the composer, as well as Stravinsky scholars. For various reasons, not all of the interviews were included. The following list includes those whose interviews are preserved on film now held by the Sacher Stiftung (names appearing in italics represent people who were interviewed but excluded from the released version of the film): *W. H. Auden,* Georges Auric, George Balanchine, Nadia Boulanger, *Elliott Carter,* Jean Cocteau, *Aaron Copland,* Robert Craft, Alexandra Danilova, Lucia Davidova, *Louise Dushkin, Sam Dushkin,* Kyron Fitzlyon, *Lukas Foss,* Tamara Geva, Alexei Haieff, *Christopher Isherwood,* Boris Kochno, Serge Lifar, *Elisabeth Lutyens, Igor Markevich,* Alicia Markova, John McClure, *Madeleine Milhaud, Pierre Monteux, Lawrence Morton,* Kyra Nijinsky, *Yevgenia Petrovna,* Marie Rambert, *Vittorio Rieti,* Tatiana Rimsky-Korsakov, *Kyriena Siloti, Claudio Spies,* Milene Stravinsky, Soulima Stravinsky, Theodore Stravinsky, Vera Stravinsky, *Virgil Thomson, Krassovskaya Vershinina,* Arnold Weissberger, Jean Wiener, *Charles Wuorinen, Alexander Yakolev,* and Vera Zorina.

The first American screening of the film took place at the International Stravinsky Symposium in San Diego, California, in September 1982. The film has now been commercially released by Kultur Films on two videotapes. The Sacher Stiftung acquired all of Palmer's original film (well over sixty hours' worth) as well as many of the CBS film cans that Palmer had previously obtained. In addition to the actual films, the Stiftung prepared transcripts of most (but not all) of the interviews included and excluded in Palmer's final film version. Conversely, some written transcripts were preserved for films that have not survived. Only a combined examination of both the actual films and the transcripts provides an accurate and as complete as possible account of Stravinsky's film history.

Originally, according to Palmer, Craft said he would not appear if the Stravinsky children did, and the children responded in kind. Eventually Theodore Stravinsky, the composer's elder son, convinced his brother Soulima and sister Milene to appear on the condition that they be allowed to approve the film so as to ensure its integrity. Arnold Weissberger, Stravinsky's longtime lawyer, interceded for Palmer with Craft and Vera Stravinsky, who also eventually agreed to participate with the proviso that Craft be involved to a certain extent in constructing the film. Palmer told me that Craft did participate and was both extremely cooperative and also quite helpful in facilitating the filmmaking through his contacts with so many of Stravinsky's associates. Craft also accompanied Palmer to Russia, where he helped in identifying and filming several of the churches, fairs, and activities eventually included in the documentary. The three Stravinsky children were sent cassettes of the rushes, and they all approved the film as released. Palmer stated that no restrictions were placed on him and that he, in the end, retained all cutting rights. He invited all participants interviewed to review the portions of the film in which they appeared, agreeing not to use any section that a participant found unacceptable.

18. Craft, *Present Perspectives,* 410–15.

19. The distinct possibility of such an intriguing Stravinsky-Kochno collaboration is confirmed by others, including Richard Buckle: "Stravinsky wanted to write a modern *Barbiere di Siviglia*: it was referred to as *Sevilsky Bradobrei.* This opera would be scored mainly for guitar and castanets; and there was to be a bullfight. In the end both Stravinsky and Diaghilev thought the *flamenco* music so perfect in itself that the idea was abandoned." Richard Buckle, *Diaghilev* (New York: Atheneum, 1979), 378.

20. Lifar is not always the most objective witness to events unfolding in the Diaghilev world. Kochno, in his own cut remarks from the film, tells Palmer that most any comment made about Diaghilev, especially by Lifar, was patently false: "They are all liars," he charges. In fairness, it must be said that Lifar's inclination to ramble, straying from the topic frequently, surely must have contributed to the exclusion of much of his interview from the film. For a fuller discussion of Lifar's comments, as well as those of other Diaghilev dancers cut from the Palmer film, see Charles M. Joseph, "Diaghilev and Stravinsky," in *The Ballets Russes and Its World,* ed. Nancy Van Norman Baer and Lynn Garafola (New Haven: Yale University Press, 1999).

21. Spender, *Journals,* 420–21.

Chapter 7: Letters, Books, Private Thoughts

1. Paul Sacher was not the first of Stravinsky's old Swiss friends interested in acquiring the composer's archives. As early as 1948, an unreleased letter from Werner Reinhart (the composer's friend during his World War I Swiss exile and the dedicatee of the 1918 *L'Histoire du soldat*) speaks of "an active interest in the foundation of an Archive of your manuscripts in Switzerland." Twenty years thereafter, in October 1968, another unpublished document discloses that Stravinsky was planning the compilation of his archives, as attested in a formal contract with another old friend, Pierre Suvchinsky, who lays out the details of their agreement. Signed by the composer on 11 October 1968 in Paris, Suvchinsky was to receive an annual payment over five years to collect, prepare, and publish Stravinsky's correspondence and other archival materials, as well as to assemble additional correspondence that the composer considered relevant. The publication of these documents was subject to the approval of Stravinsky and his wife. The agreement was eventually voided.

2. See *SPD,* 407, for one part of this 1951 letter. Other first performance possibilities in America were considered, especially at the University of Southern California, but also Juilliard, and even Broadway (Stravinsky approached Billy Rose about doing the opera as a "show"). See also Paul Griffiths, *The Rake's Progress* (Cambridge: Cambridge University Press, 1982), for a more complete history of the production.

3. There were several attempts by Roth to dissuade Stravinsky from pursuing his private arrangement with Venice. As Roth continued to argue in another unpublished portion of a letter from 27 January (Craft reprints selected passages in *SPD*), if he could not convince Stravinsky on the grounds of a legally binding contract, then perhaps he could appeal to his well-known position on a reliable interpretation of the music: "I have been there [Venice] since the war repeatedly and have always been surprised that

in the end the curtain could rise at all. I only need to tell you what happened with your *Orpheus* when Markevitch came from Switzerland to Venice and the choreographer (Aurel Miloss) with his Ballet from Rome, it turned out that the dancers had studied everything at a much quicker tempo than permissible. The introduction of the right tempo put the whole choreography out of gear, there were wild excesses at the rehearsals and Mr. Miloss left the theatre in the middle of the dress rehearsal."

4. See *SSC III*, 347, for Craft's summary of this debacle.

5. A copy of Balanchine's reply is held in the George Balanchine Archive as part of the Harvard Theatre Collection. Another letter from the same collection, dated 9 August 1952, confirms that Rudolf Bing, general manager of the Metropolitan Opera, also corresponded with Balanchine about other production matters. For example, Balanchine had requested that Barbara Karinska, whom he trusted implicitly, prepare the costumes. But the request came "much too late," Bing responded, for he had already contracted someone else.

6. In the appendix to Jann Pasler, ed., *Confronting Stravinsky: Man, Musician, and Modernist* (Berkeley: University of California Press, 1986), Craft includes an abbreviated catalog of some of the items in Stravinsky's extant library—specifically ones that were "Inscribed to and/or Autographed and Annotated" by the composer. The Widor book is included, but Craft's remarks are not always quite accurate. Regarding the treatise, Craft suggests that the composer purchased the book perhaps as early as 1910, that is, around the same time he had just completed *The Firebird*. Of the notations Craft mentions, the most interesting are those dealing with Stravinsky's experimentation regarding multiple string stops. The composer took the time to write out various possibilities in chart form, apparently as a guide for his own use.

7. The letter is dated 23 January 1963. Schloezer's biography of Stravinsky, presented to the composer in 1929, also did not meet with his approval. He entered in it many protesting remarks about *Les Noces, Renard, Ragtime,* and other works of that period.

8. The original poem was sent by Robert Brent Goodsell on 24 April 1961, and Stravinsky responded on 2 May.

9. Several unpublished letters demonstrate Hawkes's direct involvement. As early as 1949, he planned for the premiere of *The Rake's Progress* in London, discussing the size of the hall, the choice of conductor, production costs, and so on. Even earlier, in 1948, Hawkes pressed Stravinsky for a ballet production of *Le Sacre* at Covent Garden, thinking it would be good advance publicity for *The Rake,* which he assumed would be first presented there.

10. The letter is dated 18 June 1951. Stravinsky's attorney had written to Roth a month earlier, saying that Stravinsky wanted to do a recording immediately and that Decca would produce and sell fifty thousand copies at one dollar each: "Even 300 performances . . . would [produce] far less than Stravinsky is likely to receive from the direct recording sales," he explained. Almost predictably, Roth responded a few weeks later, "Your news about negotiations with Decca for the recording of *The Rake's Progress* has come to me as a surprise, similar to the one I had when Mr. Stravinsky concluded his contract with Venice."

11. Nor was the only occasion that Stravinsky crossed swords with Leeds over the ballet, as letters in the Sacher Stiftung establish. Clearly the composer was thus predisposed to monitor the publisher's actions carefully. He became upset, understandably, in October 1945 when Leeds delivered the wrong orchestral parts of his newly re-

vised *Firebird Suite* to Lucia Chase's ballet company (originally Ballet Theatre, now American Ballet Theatre). Stravinsky complained that "the conductor before starting orchestra rehearsals had to devote additional time to straighten out all parts in order to be able to procede [sic] with his rehearsals. . . . This unexpected occurance [sic] horrifies me especially, and in view of my concert tour this season when I programmed this *Firebird Suite* [for] a total of 12 performances." He further informs Leeds that given their "failure," he would "prefer to withdraw it from my programs." Moreover the outraged composer advises the publisher that he will now have to cancel a planned recording session scheduled for January 1946 in which he was to conduct the New York Philharmonic Orchestra. Finally, he asks that the score "on which I personally annotated in long hand the various changes and from which you made a copy" be returned to him immediately. "This is most urgent."

12. The Lili Boulanger Memorial Fund was founded by Lili's sister Nadia in 1939. In her biography of Nadia, Léonie Rosenstiel admits that Boulanger "ratified" all decisions, but it was more than that (Léonie Rosenstiel, *Nadia Boulanger: A Life in Music* [New York: W. W. Norton, 1982], 328). In addition to Boulanger and Stravinsky, the judges included Haieff, Walter Piston, and Aaron Copland. Winners included Wallace Berry, Claudio Spies, and Charles Wuorinen. The archives demonstrate that, understandably, the judges often disagreed, but as Boulanger's secretary, Winifred Johnstone, pointed out, "We who know Nadia realize that she must be left with the major powers of decision—and it was this point that Copland brought out" (letter of 18 March 1958). In 1961, Johnstone wrote to Stravinsky: "This year the Trustees sent Nadia a score of . . . a young composer, born in New York. . . . Piston and Nadia (who [were] very much struck by his ability and work) are voting for him, and Copland and Haieff, to whom the score has just been sent, are certain to follow suit. I am enclosing a vote for you to sign, and would appreciate your returning it at your earliest convenience."

13. John Steinbeck, *Journal of a Novel* (London: Mandarin, 1991; orig. pub. New York: Viking, 1969), 106.

14. The lecture is reprinted in Pierre Boulez, *Orientations: Collected Writings by Pierre Boulez,* ed. Jean-Jacques Nattiez, trans. Martin Cooper (Cambridge: Harvard University Press, 1986), 87. Boulez's comments on "coding" refer to one part of a "circuit" that ties the composer, interpreter, and audience together.

15. Unpublished letter of 8 April 1946 from the composer to Greta Rauch of Columbia Records. In the same letter, Stravinsky addressed several other business matters. He informed Rauch that he had already consented "to conduct the CBS (Invitation to Music) December 18th and January date to be setteled [sic]"; that he wished to record the *Symphony of Psalms* "at the time of my New York sejourn [sic]. Don't tell me that it is already too late"; and finally that he must know "the exact time when Woody Herman with his Orchestra will be in Los Angeles, as planed [sic], this summer [because] they have asked me to conduct my EBONY CONCERTO for your recordings." In a subsequent letter a month later, the composer informed Columbia that he had already made the recording with Szigeti, as well as recording a few other violin and piano arrangements—Szigeti's name being an audience draw: "Please notice . . . this would be of particular interest for the Szigeti's fans [sic] which is *practical* [Stravinsky's emphasis], hence advantageous."

Although Stravinsky wrote in his letter to Columbia Records of his "great disappointment" in losing Milstein as his recording collaborator in 1946, that disappointment would have been appreciably lessened had he lived to read the violinist's 1990 autobiography. In the chapter "Stravinsky and His Interpreters," Milstein refers to his old friend as "a tragic figure," a composer "who did not understand the violin as an instrument very well." He declares that Stravinsky was "afraid that a major artist with a strong personality would interfere in the composition, make suggestions, insist on changes," and it was principally on that basis that he chose his performing partners (Nathan Milstein and Solomon Volkov, *From Russia to the West: The Musical Memoirs and Reminiscences of Nathan Milstein,* trans. Antonina W. Bouis [New York: Henry Holt, 1990], 126, 134).

16. Joseph Szigeti, *With Strings Attached,* 2d ed. (New York: Alfred A. Knopf, 1967), 125–26. Stravinsky and Szigeti's performance is preserved on the Sony Classical CD *Chamber Music and Historical Recordings,* SM2K 46297.

17. Increasingly, the composer disparaged the recording process. Still, for those interested in his written "interpretive" notations, the Sacher Stiftung holds hundreds of published scores from which Stravinsky conducted (scores that include his own markings); music of other composers that he studied and marked; and audiotapes of performances of his own works as well as his conducting of Tchaikovsky and Mussorgsky scores. Examples include his copy of Verdi's *La Forza del destino,* in which Stravinsky drew a diagram of a stage at the top of the first page of Act I, positioning Leonora and other characters in the opera; indeed there are many stage directions marked throughout the score. Sometimes the notations are in Russian, at other times in English. Cherubini's *Anacreon Overture* is also heavily annotated by Stravinsky, and it is clearly the score from which he conducted in 1937 in Naples. Haydn's *Die Jahreszeiten* shows copious markings in which Stravinsky commented about instrumentation or added such remarks as "here Haydn (*erzielt*) an especially deep *Wirkung.*" Stravinsky's copy of Tchaikovsky's Third Symphony reveals many cuts marked in the first movement— as many as sixty measures at one point. He studied Falla's harpsichord concerto—a piece he also conducted—carefully, pointing out imitations and circling certain measures to alert him to metric shifts.

18. Craft conducted the recording of the *Capriccio* and was credited. Beginning with recordings in the late 1940s, Craft's role as a listener was highly valued. For details of the Stravinsky-Craft recordings, as well as a comprehensive look at the composer and the recording studio, see Philip Stuart, *Igor Stravinsky: The Composer in the Recording Studio* (Westport, Conn.: Greenwood Press, 1991).

19. Ben Johnston, "An Interview with Soulima Stravinsky," *Perspectives of New Music* 10/1 (1971): 17.

20. The letter is dated 22 January 1943. Stravinsky's marginalia are especially harsh regarding Serge Koussevitzky.

21. The English translations of the synopses for all six lectures are held in the Charles Eliot Norton Lectures collection, as part of the Harvard Archives (5614.39, Box 39), Cambridge, Massachusetts. I wish to thank Harvard University for permitting me to reprint the original synopsis.

22. Igor Stravinsky, *Poetics of Music,* trans. Arthur Knodel and Ingolf Dahl (Cambridge: Harvard University Press, 1970; orig. pub. Cambridge: Harvard University Press, 1947), 124.

23. Boris Schwarz, "Stravinsky, Dushkin, and the Violin," in *Confronting Stravinsky,* ed. Pasler, 306. "Murder in the Cathedral," *Time,* 24 September 1956; Craft reprints part of the article in *SPD,* 434, but without Stravinsky's response.

24. Michael Krauz, "The Tonal and the Foundational: Ansermet on Stravinsky," *Journal of Aesthetics and Art Criticism* 42 (1984): 383–86.

25. William Westbrook Burton, *Conversations About Bernstein* (New York: Oxford University Press, 1995), 19.

26. Frieda Lawrence, foreword to *The First Lady Chatterley,* by D. H. Lawrence (New York: Penguin Books, 1994), 14.

27. Robin Holloway, review of *SSC I* in *Tempo,* March 1984, 40; Virginia Woolf, *A Room of One's Own* (New York: Harcourt Brace Jovanovich, 1929), 53. Woolf's remarks were made in a discussion of models and creativity.

28. Steinbeck, *Journal of a Novel,* 10, 45.

29. Robin Holloway, review of *SSC III* in *Tempo,* March 1986, 42.

Chapter 8: Boswellizing an Icon

1. For three excellent studies on the Boswell-Johnson question, see Marlies K. Danziger and Frank Brady, eds., *Boswell: The Great Biographer* (New York: McGraw-Hill, 1989), which draws on the Boswell collection at Yale University; John A. Vance, ed., *Boswell's Life of Johnson: New Questions, New Answers* (Athens: University of Georgia Press, 1985); and Peter Martin, *A Life of James Boswell* (New Haven: Yale University Press, 2000), now generally considered the most complete biography available.

2. In recent years Craft has undertaken to record all of Stravinsky's works on compact disc for MusicMasters. For an appraisal of this important project and remarks on Craft's interpretation of the composer's music for this series, see Allen Shawn, "Craft's Stravinsky," *Atlantic Monthly,* August 1998, 97–100. There is, of course, an abundance of Stravinsky recordings, beginning with those the composer himself conducted or supervised. In the centennial year 1982, a set of thirty-one recordings was released representing the whole of Stravinsky's work (CBS Masterworks—"The Recorded Legacy," produced by John McClure with "musical preparation by Vera Zorina"). In 1991 Sony released a set of twenty-two compact discs as a remake, although it should be noted that this is not an exact replication of everything represented on the earlier CBS release.

3. Joan Peyser, "Stravinsky-Craft, Inc.," *American Scholar* 52 (fall 1983): 513–18.

4. Robert Craft, *Stravinsky: Chronicle of a Friendship,* revised and expanded edition (Nashville: Vanderbilt University Press, 1994), 510. The comparisons with Boswell were inevitable. Just so, in a review of Craft's *Chronicle* (originally published in 1972) in the *New York Times Book Review* (2 July 1972), Simon Karlinsky wrote, "The part Craft played in Stravinsky's life has been described as anything from Boswell (a view that Craft himself emphatically rejects) to Svengali." Karlinsky goes on to echo Craft's own comments, describing him as Stravinsky's "equal partner in all of his musical and literary activities."

5. Isherwood's diary entry of 18 June 1960, Christopher Isherwood, *Diaries,* vol. 1 (1939–1960), ed. Katherine Bucknell (London: HarperCollins, 1996), 866.

6. Robert Craft, *Present Perspectives* (New York: Alfred A. Knopf, 1984), 228.

7. Stephen Walsh, *Stravinsky: A Creative Spring* (New York: Alfred A. Knopf, 1999). Especially see Walsh's introductory comments, ix–xiv. Nor is Walsh the only reputable Stravinsky scholar who has, without malice and in the interest of objectively citing the facts, felt compelled to set the record straight. See, for example, Richard

Taruskin's introduction in *Stravinsky and the Russian Traditions* (Berkeley: University of California Press, 1996), 1–19, wherein the author raises questions about the reliability of the so-called conversation books, to be discussed later in this chapter.

8. The letter appears in *SSC II*, 19. I wish to thank Professor Victor Varuntz for pointing this out to me. Varuntz contends that several letters are incorrectly translated and that many linguistic nuances, especially in the letters of Diaghilev, have been missed. For a more complete collection of several of Stravinsky's heretofore unpublished Russian letters, see Victor Varuntz, ed., *I. F. Stravinsky. Sbornik statey* (Moscow: Moscow State Conservatory, 1997). In 1992, Mr. Varuntz was kind enough to share some of these unpublished letters with me—letters that correct many of our impressions of Stravinsky's youthful days in Russia.

9. *SSC I*, 96–99, letter of 6 March 1926.

10. *SSC II*, 511–17. As noted in Chapter 1, others, especially Paul Valéry and Pierre Suvchinsky, had a hand in guiding Stravinsky's thinking about the Norton lectures at Harvard. Maritain, Henri Bergson, and Arthur Lourié should be added to the wellspring from which Stravinsky drew. Stravinsky's concept of *chronos*, for example, a topic he stressed in his second lecture, "The Phenomenon of Music," is directly traceable to Suvchinsky's notion of *chronometrics*, which Suvchinsky had discussed in "La Notion de temps et la musique" (*Le Revue musicale*, March 1939). For reactions to the lectures and comments from some of the Harvard students with whom Stravinsky worked during weekly composition classes, see *SPD*, 349–53. The six lectures themselves were as much a social occasion as an intellectual stimulus—"a series of brilliant social events," reported Frederick Jacobi, Jr. (then in his first year at Harvard) in the October–November 1939 issue of *Modern Music*. Jacobi spoke of an audience arriving in "sleek limousines [beginning] to drive up with Beacon Hill dowagers radiating white hair, evening dresses, diamonds and dignity." Stravinsky himself was disappointed in the audience, and Vera Stravinsky's diary entry for 13 March 1940 recorded that for the fourth lecture "not many people are there and Igor was not pleased" (Robert Craft, ed., *Dearest Bubushkin: The Correspondence of Vera and Igor Stravinsky, 1921–1954*, trans. Lucia Davidova [New York: Thames and Hudson, 1985], 112.

11. Lillian Libman, *And Music at the Close: Stravinsky's Last Years* (New York: W. W. Norton, 1972), 26.

12. Despite whatever encampment existed, Stravinsky's works were often included in Schoenberg's "Verein für Musikalische Privataufführungen in Wien," from 1918–1921. For example, pianists Rudolf Serkin and Edward Steuermann played the four-hand version of *Petrushka* in the autumn of 1920. Rivière's letter of 29 June 1918 is reprinted in *SSC II*, 179. The entire letter is xenophobic, touting Stravinsky's role as the musical monarch of the French camp. Rivière was editor of *La Nouvelle revue française*.

13. See Max Paddison, *Adorno's Aesthetics of Music* (Cambridge: Cambridge University Press, 1993), 45, for a fuller description of Adorno's charges against not only Stravinsky but other neoclassic and folkloristic composers, including Bartók and Hindemith. In *The Story of a Novel*, Mann spoke of Adorno's "rigorous manner of veneration, the tragically cerebral relentlessness of his criticism of the contemporary situation," which Mann used as the encompassing motive of *Doctor Faustus*—"the closeness of sterility, the innate despair that prepares the ground for a pact with the devil."

14. The essays appeared in *CMS Symposium* 10 (Fall 1970): 58–98, and included

contributions by Jon Appleton, Howard Boatwright, Milton Babbitt, Elliott Carter, Ingolf Dahl, Paul Creston, George Rochberg, Charles Wuorinen, and others.

15. In an October 1946 article by J. Douglas Cook for *Opera* magazine, "Visits to the Homes of Famous Composers," Stravinsky claimed that he didn't teach simply because he didn't know how. "A composer brought me a Symphony of 200 pages and wanted me to give him lessons. I know nothing about teaching so I spent two years rewriting his Symphony and I learned a great deal while doing it." The pupil was Ernest Anderson, and Vera Stravinsky's diary entries indicate frequent meetings (sometimes more than one a day) between her husband and the would-be composer during the early 1940s. In response to questions posed at the aforementioned 8 March 1966 convocation at the Eastman School of Music, Stravinsky, even at eighty-three, remembered his only pupil. Anderson was an aged Swedish man, he recalled, whose principal occupation was the invention of gadgets. He showed Stravinsky some "idiotic music," as he further remembered. So poor was the music, but so great Stravinsky's need for remuneration, that he remembered having no choice but to offer as the one reasonable solution: "We will compose a Symphony together—meaning I compose it!"

Stravinsky's five-day residence at Eastman was to be one of his final campus appearances (which included the conferring of an honorary doctorate) while he was still in relatively good health. It came amidst a busy winter and spring that found him conducting concerts across the country and Europe while continuing to compose his last large work, *Requiem Canticles*. Both Stravinsky and Craft conducted several performances during the Eastman festival—performances that included the early 1908 *Fireworks* (conducted by the composer) and even sections of *The Flood* (conducted by Craft). During the convocation, Stravinsky was still as sharp as a tack, responding to questions from students and faculty, transmitted by Walter Hendl, the school's director. The composer urged that contemporary music be taught to students in public schools—the younger the child the better. Asked if musicians should take an active role in political affairs, he retorted, "Depends on the affair." When one student asked about the *Ebony Concerto* written for Woody Herman, Stravinsky described Herman as a kind and cooperative man, but not a particularly good clarinet player. He expressed his reservations about recordings, now taking the position that since he as a person changed every five years, so did his interpretation of his own music. But he continued to complain about the liberties taken by orchestral conductors, especially with his tempi.

Fully cognizant of his high-profile image as an "elder," he admitted that more people were now interested in his name than in what he was writing. He brushed aside a question about the value of electronic music by confessing that he could not tell the difference between good and bad music written in that medium. He concluded his remarks with a remembrance of his teacher, Rimsky-Korsakov (who had been like a father to him, he said), and unusually high praise for the operas of Alban Berg, which Stravinsky now considered masterpieces. Throughout the thirty-minute session he held sway, peppering his responses with humor while answering most of the questions with an informative directness. An archival recording of the session is held in the Sound Recording Archive of Eastman's Sibley Music Library. I wish to thank Ms. Esther Gillie for calling this to my attention, and also the Eastman School of Music for permission to include Stravinsky's comments.

16. George Antheil, *Chicago Tribune Sunday Magazine*, 17 February 1924.

17. See Leonard Stein, "Schoenberg and 'Kleine Modernsky,'" in *Confronting*

Stravinsky: Man, Musician, and Modernist, ed. Jann Pasler (Berkeley: University of California Press, 1986), for a fuller discussion of the Schoenberg-Stravinsky relationship. Igor Stravinsky and Robert Craft, *Dialogues* (Berkeley: University of California Press, 1982; rev. ed. of *Dialogues and a Diary,* Garden City, N.Y.: Doubleday, 1963), 107–8, contains the complete list of contrasts, as well as the "parallelisms," of Stravinsky and Schoenberg that Craft included—their "common belief in Divine Authority," for example, or their "common exile to the same alien culture, in which we wrote some of our best works."

18. Stephen Spender, *Journals, 1939–1983,* ed. John Goldsmith (New York: Random House, 1986), 227. Berg's and Schoenberg's letters are reprinted in Juliane Brand, Christopher Hailey, and Donald Harris, eds., *The Berg–Schoenberg Correspondence: Selected Letters* (New York: W. W. Norton, 1987). In many letters to Berg, Schoenberg speaks of the frequency with which Stravinsky's works are played in America, "but not a single note of mine."

19. Craft's memory of Stravinsky's "crisis" is reported in Craft, *Present Perspectives,* 253; he also describes this turning point (in slightly different words) in Craft, *Stravinsky: Chronicle of a Friendship,* 72–73. Copland's statement appears in Aaron Copland and Vivian Perlis, *Copland: Since 1943* (New York: St. Martin's Press, 1989), 137. Verna Fine was the wife of the composer Irving Fine, a friend of Stravinsky's.

20. Ingolf Dahl, "Stravinsky in 1946," *Modern Music* 23/3 (summer 1946): 65; Milton Babbitt, "Remarks on the Recent Stravinsky," *Perspectives of New Music* 2 (1964): 35–55; Paul Horgan, *Encounters with Stravinsky* (New York: Farrar, Straus & Giroux, 1972), 216. As might be expected, the explanations offered for Stravinsky's turn to serialism are as diverse as every other speculation about his actions. For one of the more well known suggestions offered for Stravinsky's late-in-life rejection of "play" in favor of "idea," see Boulez's "Stravinsky: Style or Idea?" reprinted in Pierre Boulez, *Orientations: Collected Writings by Pierre Boulez,* ed. Jean-Jacques Nattiez, trans. Martin Cooper (Cambridge: Harvard University Press, 1986), 349–59. As Boulez remarks, "Stravinsky's profound self-confrontation during the last years of his life [and] his reconsideration of all his basic concepts, clearly shook him profoundly."

21. The article, "Stravinsky's Choral Music," by Stephen Walsh, appeared in *Tempo*'s 1967 summer issue (pp. 41–51) celebrating the composer's eighty-fifth birthday. Walsh quoted Eric Walter White's discussion of the *Canticum Sacrum,* whereupon the composer circled White's name and wrote in the margin, "Why to mention him? E. W. White, as everybody knows, is an incompetent writer of my music, which he discovered very recently."

22. Robbins flew to California to discuss *Les Noces* with Stravinsky, although the Milan performance fell through. He later staged the work in 1965 for Lucia Chase's Ballet Theatre, in what Bernstein called the best ballet performance since the 1957 premiere of *Agon.* In an unpublished 24 March 1965 letter, Robbins wrote to Stravinsky, "It's ten years since I visited you on the coast to go over the score of *Les Noces.* Now I have finally choreographed it and it opens on Tuesday." Robbins invited the composer to attend (which he did) and welcomed his opinion of the performance. In all his correspondence with Stravinsky (remembering birthdays, sending congratulations), Robbins always displays respect and genuine affection for the composer. Stravinsky's admiration for Robbins as a choreographer has for whatever reason never come out. But several projects were discussed, almost always with enthusiasm on Stravinsky's part.

23. Stravinsky also wrote a foreword for Lowinsky's later book *Tonality and Atonal-*

ity in Sixteenth-Century Music (Berkeley: University of California Press, 1961). This three-page endorsement concludes with an informative précis of the composer's own views: "The subject matter of Professor Lowinsky's study is for me perhaps the most exciting in the history of music, his method is the only kind of 'writing about music' that I value."

24. Milton Babbitt, "Who Cares If You Listen?" *High Fidelity Magazine,* February 1958; Babbitt, "Remarks on the Recent Stravinsky," 46. Apparently the hostile-sounding title "Who Cares If You Listen?" was not Babbitt's but was imposed by an editor without his knowledge or permission. I wish to thank Professor Claudio Spies for calling this to my attention.

25. A discussion of Stravinsky's compositional process—as with any creative process—is both complex and often speculative. Beyond *SPD,* Craft has written or spoken on several occasions about Stravinsky's sketches, sometimes charting the evolution of a work with very illuminating examples. See for instance several essays in the appendixes to all three volumes of *SSC.* More recently, and still as only two of many recent publications, see Craft's essays "Discoveries in Stravinsky's Sketches," and "On *Apollo* and *Orpheus,*" in *The Moment of Existence: Music, Literature, and the Arts, 1990–1995* (Nashville: Vanderbilt University Press, 1996).

In 1991 a Dutch documentary titled *The Final Choral,* originally telecast in Amsterdam, included commentary by Craft. The film, directed by Frank Scheffer with performances by members of the Netherlands Wind Ensemble conducted by Reinbert de Leeuw, was rereleased on videotape in 1999 by Films for the Humanities and Sciences (#BVL8754). Unlike the documentaries discussed in Chapter 6, this fifty-minute production follows the course of a single work, the important *Symphonies of Winds* from 1920. It stresses the fact that the work was in effect composed backward, beginning with an independently constructed choral drafted at the piano, from which Stravinsky then assembled the entire piece. While it does rely heavily on previously used footage of Stravinsky from CBS and elsewhere, it is particularly useful for a general audience interested in seeing and hearing some of the work's sketches performed as the piece, ostensibly, unfolded in the composer's mind. Sketches that seem to have been initially conceived for strings rather than winds, for example, are performed as such.

Craft provides a useful context for the brief work, discussing how shocking it first appeared to audiences, and what a milestone it marks in the composer's evolution. (Moreover, this was the work that first brought Craft and Stravinsky together through their correspondence in 1947.) Still, beyond the useful historical backdrop that Craft provides, one must be cautious. He speaks, for example, about the germinal chord for the piece, an oddly spaced construction that while first drafted at the piano is anything but pianistic, he contends, because it does not "sustain." But for Stravinsky, the chord is anything but unpianistic, and hardly unprecedented. Indeed, for the composer's exceptionally large hands, it is one of his most preferred pianistic sonorities. Not only is it found in earlier works such as the 1912 Russian cantata *Zvezdoliki,* or the 1930 *Symphony of Psalms* (in both of these orchestral-choral works the chord serves a central function), but it is used repeatedly in many of the composer's most familiar piano works, including the Piano Concerto (1924), the *Serenade en la* (1925), the *Capriccio* (1929), and throughout the piano obbligato of the Symphony in Three Movements (1945)—to name but a few instances where the chord is texturally central. For those interested in a more detailed compositional analysis of the *Symphonies of Winds,* see Craft's "'Hymns of Praise' for Debussy: Stravinsky's *Symphonies of Winds,*" in *Stravin-*

sky: Glimpses of a Life (New York: St. Martin's Press, 1992), 370–81; André Baltensperger and Felix Meyer, *Igor Stravinsky: Symphonies d'Instruments à Vent* (Winterthur: Amadeus-Verlag, 1991), which includes a richly illustrated examination of the sketches held by the Paul Sacher Stiftung in Basel; and Stephen Walsh, "Stravinsky's Symphonies: Accident or Design?" in *Analytical Strategies and Musical Interpretation: Essays on Nineteenth- and Twentieth-Century Music,* ed. Craig Ayrery and Mark Everist (Cambridge: Cambridge University Press, 1996), 35–71.

26. The unpublished letter was handwritten on Vera Stravinsky's stationery while Craft was on tour and dated 2 March 1954.

27. For the Lincoln Center inaugural, Bernstein programmed the "Gloria" from Beethoven's *Missa Solemnis,* for he wanted a religious tone to mark the opening of this new temple of music. What Stravinsky would have written in keeping with this spirit is difficult to imagine, but he must have feared whatever music he wrote being "upstaged" by "America's most powerful musical figure," as one Bernstein biographer has labeled him. The concert was as much a social event as an artistic milestone, with many dignitaries, including Jacqueline Kennedy, in attendance. Among other proposed commissions Stravinsky received around this time, in September 1959 the Harpsichord Music Society, directed by Sylvia Marlowe, offered five thousand dollars if he would write a work "for the Harpsichord with either a chamber orchestra or for any other combination of instruments." The soloist was to be Marlowe herself, but Stravinsky declined.

28. Lincoln Kirstein, *Thirty Years of the New York City Ballet* (New York: Alfred A. Knopf, 1978), 184.

29. Horgan's comments were made in an editorial response to Sergeant and sent to the *New Yorker.* The full letter appears in Horgan's *Encounters with Stravinsky* (New York: Farrar, Straus & Giroux, 1972), 285–86. For the full interview of Stravinsky, see "Introduction: A Decade Later," in *Anton Webern: Perspectives,* compiled by Hans Noldenhauer and edited by Demar Irvine (Seattle: University of Washington Press, 1965), xix–xxvii.

30. Craft, *Present Perspectives,* 259.

31. Most of the letter is published in *SSC I,* 362. Much of what Hawkes had calmly attempted to explain to Stravinsky had to do with contractual problems, ASCAP matters, and the loss of income, about which the composer constantly complained. As late as 1967, Stravinsky was still willing to support Craft financially. An unpublished letter to John McClure dated 11 November 1967 reveals that Stravinsky was quite willing to help cover the cost of Craft's then new (and by now legendary) CBS recording of Schoenberg's music. The composer went so far as to volunteer the attachment of his own recording royalties over a six-month period against the debt of the Schoenberg project—an unusual act of generosity given his legendary parsimony. More important, it was a sign of both support and confidence in Craft's broader abilities as a musician. Stravinsky was also sincerely interested in the recording, especially because he now wanted to hear the music, and few conductors other than Craft had the interest or ability to conduct Schoenberg's demanding scores.

32. Stravinsky remained eager to disseminate his "answers" widely. In a 2 February 1958 letter to Deborah Ishlon, who sometimes acted as his agent, the composer directed Ishlon to send the manuscript of *Conversations with Igor Stravinsky* to the editor of *The Observer,* who had asked for an interview. Stravinsky thought it more convenient to comply with the editor's request this way. Besides, he insisted to Ishlon, he

had read the magazine's ongoing series of interviews with Picasso, Cocteau, and others, and his conversations with Craft were better. Therefore, he advised, Ishlon should find out what Picasso and Cocteau had been paid, then "ask a little bit more."

For Craft's account of how the conversation books evolved, see the chapter "Conversations with Stravinsky" in Craft, *Present Perspectives,* 265–75. In tracing this history, several unpublished letters from Ken McCormick of Doubleday and Herbert Weinstock of Knopf are useful. As early as 1950, Weinstock asked if Stravinsky would like to update his 1935 *Autobiography.* Stravinsky quickly responded that he was too busy with *The Rake,* but still wanted to provide such an update a little later when he had more time. In 1952 a determined Weinstock suggested that Stravinsky's son Theodore write a new autobiography for the composer and that Stravinsky edit it; the 10 October 1952 unpublished response from Stravinsky agreed that this might be a possibility and hoped they could reach agreement on an appropriate format. By 1957 Weinstock was still trying (for "the fifth or sixth time," he mentioned in a letter), but by then Stravinsky had committed to the conversation format.

Craft has added that Knopf wanted to publish the first of the six books as early as 1957 but "did not meet Stravinsky's financial terms" (Craft, *Present Perspectives,* 266n.4). In an unpublished letter of 15 January 1958, Stravinsky demanded 15 percent and rejected the 10 percent offered for the first of the conversation books. He claimed he had received 20 percent on his *Autobiography* twenty years earlier, "and in the meantime the value of the dollar has depreciated, not my reputation." But he was perhaps purposely forgetful here, for the royalties from his *Autobiography* were only 10 percent, and his ghostwriter Walter Nouvel received a third of that for his collaboration. Craft admitted, "it must be said that [Stravinsky] was not indifferent to the pecuniary potential" (Craft, *Present Perspectives,* 265). The correspondence concerning this aspect of the publications is nearly as long as the dialogues themselves.

33. Craft, *Stravinsky: Chronicle of a Friendship,* 474. On 24 February 1967, Stravinsky did conduct "an orchestra of leading local musicians in his *Firebird* score, excerpts from *Petrouchka,* and his version of *The Star Spangled Banner,*" according to an article in the *Miami Herald* by Doris Reno. He also met with the local press, whom he told, "My newest compositions are too hard to play even for good orchestras, without lots of rehearsals, so I don't program them in this country." So frail was his health that a special railing was built around the podium to support him while he conducted. I wish to thank my colleague Professor Isabelle Williams for calling this to my attention.

Equally sensitive is the matter of recordings made in the 1960s. Stravinsky was uncomfortable with the issuing of records that listed him as conductor when in fact Craft had held the baton. He made his uneasiness clear to Goddard Lieberson of Columbia Records in an unpublished letter of 1 November 1967, but he still left a little maneuvering room. He admitted that he was "guilty" (to use his description) of some "misleading," as in the recording of *The Flood,* for which he had conducted only a few short passages. But he hastened to add that he had full confidence in Craft, who could now "represent my wishes, and more faithfully than I am able to do myself, at my age." He also attached a listing of nine recordings that Craft had conducted, saying that he realized this "blemishes" the marketing concept of "Stravinsky conducting Stravinsky" and adding cryptically that "a true picture with blemishes is better than a fake." Mrs. Brigitta Lieberson, perhaps better known to the worlds of dance, Broadway, and Hollywood as Vera Zorina, had a highly successful career as a ballerina and stage and screen actress and was close friends with Stravinsky, often performing as the narrator in his melodrama *Perséphone*. She told me that her husband's awarding of a "lifetime contract" to Stravinsky for all future recordings was indeed exceptional and indicative of Lieberson's commitment to the composer (even though the sales for Stravinsky's recordings were not particularly large).

Epilogue

1. Wolfgang Hildesheimer, *Mozart,* trans. Marion Faber (New York: Noonday Press, Farrar, Straus & Giroux, 1982), 7.

2. Lawrence Morton, "Stravinsky at Home," in *Confronting Stravinsky: Man, Musician, and Modernist,* ed. Jann Pasler (Berkeley: University of California Press, 1986), 333.

Index